GLOBE FEARON

LITERATURE

Silver Level

Upper Saddle River, New Jersey
www.globefearon.com

PROGRAM REVIEWERS

Kathy Babigian, Coordinator, Tioga Literacy Center, Fresno, California

Pat Bartholomew, M.A., Reading Specialist, Milton, Ohio

Jennifer Dilks-Mundt, English Teacher, Brant Rock, Massachusetts

Ann Fitzgerald, M.A., Education Director, Southshire Community School,
North Bennington, Vermont

Pat Miller, M.A., Reading/English/Language Arts Supervisor, Prince Georges County
Public Schools, Maryland

Artie P. Norton, English Teacher, Suffern, New York

Timothy Rasinski, Professor of Curriculum and Instruction, Kent State University, Kent, Ohio

Cynthia Saska, M.A., Professor of English, University of Texas, San Antonio, Texas

Margaret-Mary Sulentic, Ph.D., Assistant Professor of Literacy, Department of Curriculum
and Instruction, University of Southern Mississippi, Hattiesburg, Mississippi

Dr. Helen W. Taylor, Director of Programs K-12 Curriculum and Instruction, Portsmouth City
Public Schools, Virginia

CONSULTANTS

Dr. Virginia Bryg; Josephine Gemake, Ph.D.; Alfred Schifini, Ph.D.; Deborah Walker; Robert
Wandberg, Ph.D.

Supervising Editor/Team Leader: Karen McCollum
Editors: Ayanna Taylor, Amy Greenberg, Theresa McCarthy
Editorial Developer: Pearson Education Development Group
Marketing Assistant: Kate Krimsky
Production Editor: Travis Bailey
Associate Production Editors: Amy Benefiel, Alia Lesser
Senior Designer: Angel Weyant
Manufacturing Buyer: Mark Cirillo
Cover and Interior Design/Production: Pearson Education Development Group
Photo Research: Pearson Education Development Group

ABOUT THE COVER

3rd and Rhode Island, LeDetroit Park, Hilda Wilkinson Brown. From the Hilda Wilkinson Brown
Collection. Courtesy of Lillian Thomas Burwell. This oil painting shows a simple scene of a street in
Detroit. This is a reflection of Brown's ideals. She was described as a "traditional woman, an
idealist in manner and mores of the then womanhood." How is Brown's painting a representation
of traditional American values?

ISBN 0-130-23578-4

Printed in the United States of America
1 2 3 4 5 6 7 8 9 10   04 03 02 01 00

Globe
Fearon

1-800-848-9500
www.globefearon.com

Preview

UNIT 1 *Voices of Colonial America*

Writing • Vocabulary • Grammar, Usage, and Mechanics

Speaking and Listening • Critical Thinking • Effective Studying

• Test Preparation

UNIT 2 *Writers in a Growing Nation*

UNIT 3 *New England Speaks*

UNIT 4 *A Nation Expresses Itself*

Writing • Vocabulary • Grammar, Usage, and Mechanics
Speaking and Listening • Critical Thinking • Effective Studying
• Test Preparation

UNIT 5 *The Modern View*

UNIT 6 *The Contemporary Perspective*

References

HOW TO USE THIS BOOK

Welcome to *Globe Fearon Literature*. As you read this textbook, you will learn about many new worlds. By reading literature you can experience the past and the future, and you can learn about people—how they feel and how they think.

To get the most out of this book, you will need to become an active reader. Active readers think about reading materials before they begin, during, and after they read.

TIPS FOR IMPROVING YOUR READING

Before You Read
- Think about the title of the selection. What does it tell you about the topic? What do you already know about the topic?
- Determine the genre of the selection. For example—if the selection is a poem, ask yourself, "How will this be different from reading an essay or short story?"
- Set a purpose for reading. What do you think you will learn by reading this selection?

As You Read
- Predict what you think will happen next. Then pause occasionally and ask yourself if your predictions were correct.
- Form questions about what you are reading. For example, ask yourself, "What idea is the author trying to convey?"
- When you encounter a word you are unfamiliar with, use the help that Globe Fearon Literature gives you. Difficult words are defined at the bottom of the page they appear on.

After You Read
Consider the following questions:
- Did the selection end the way you anticipated?
- What did you learn from reading this selection?
- How does this selection relate to others you have read?

THE BOOK IS ORGANIZED TO HELP YOU

Your literature book has been organized into units. Each unit is introduced with a piece of fine art and a quote. Look at these pages. What do you think this unit will be about?

The next two pages of the unit give you a preview of what to expect. These two pages will help you set the stage for reading and understanding the selections. You may want to refer back to these pages as you read through the unit.

The "Focus On" feature gives you some tips to help you understand specific genres of literature, such as fiction or poetry You will notice that each Model selection has blue notes in the margin. These are study hints to help you read actively. The notes relate back to the "Focus On" feature. The notes will help you identify key elements of the genre. Later, you can look for similar elements in other selections as you read independently.

Before each selection, you will be introduced to a reading skill, a literary skill, and a writing activity. The reading skill will help you understand what you are reading. The literary skill will call your attention to elements of literature. The writing activity will help you relate the literature to your own life.

There are review questions at the end of each selection. These questions help you think about what you have just read. They will also help you relate this selection to others that you may have read.

Globe Fearon Literature was created for you. Reading literature can be one of the most rewarding experiences you can ever have. There are new worlds to explore and exciting people to meet. It's all here. So, let's begin. . .

Voices of Colonial America

In this our western world
Be Freedom's flag unfurl'd
Through all its shores!
May no destructive blast
Our heaven of joy o'ercast,
May Freedom's fabric last
While time endures.
                                        —Philip Freneau

The Landing of the Pilgrims, 1620. 19th century, Anonymous.
The Granger Collection

1650 Anne Bradstreet publishes the first poetry written in colonies.

1683 *The New England Primer* is Colonies' first textbook.

1704 *The Boston News-Letter* is first successful newspaper.

1732 Franklin's *Almanack* is read by 10,000 people.

| 1650 | 1660 | 1670 | 1680 | 1690 | 1700 | 1710 | 1720 | 1730 | 1740 |

1683 First free public library system founded in South Carolina.

1692 Salem Witch Trials begin in Massachusetts.

HISTORICAL HIGHLIGHTS

Voices of Colonial America

This country has gone through many drastic changes in the past two centuries. The population has grown tremendously, and modern technology has given us jet planes, automobiles, and many other advances.

In colonial America people depended on horses and on ships for transportation. The colonists built their settlements near the harbors where their ships had landed. Here they were able to receive shipments of goods they needed from Europe. Ships were the best way to move goods.

The Native Americans, who had been in America for hundreds of years before the colonists, generally did not live in the settlements. Instead they lived in the great wilderness that made up most of colonial America. Here they survived by farming, hunting, and fishing.

■ NONFICTION IN COLONIAL LITERATURE

The colonists most likely enjoyed reading for many reasons. They were probably most interested in reading in order to get information. Remember, people could not get the news on television or radio in colonial times.

Most colonial literature is nonfiction—writing that deals with facts or ideas. Like us, the colonists published newspapers. They also wrote almanacs—publications that contain a variety of practical information. In this unit, you will read a selection from *Poor Richard's Almanack*, written by Benjamin Franklin.

Since there were no telephones, colonists kept in touch by writing letters, which were delivered by men on horseback or carried by packet ships that sailed along the coast. You will read a letter from a famous letter writer, Abigail Adams.

1771 Franklin begins his *Autobiography*.

1776 Thomas Paine's *Common Sense* sells 100,000 copies.

1800 Library of Congress is founded.

1828 Webster publishes *American Dictionary of the American Language*.

| 1750 | 1760 | 1770 | 1780 | 1790 | 1800 | 1810 | 1820 | 1830 | 1840 |

1754 French and Indian Wars begin.

1774 First Continental Congress meets in Philadelphia.

1775 Battles at Lexington and Concord begin Revolutionary War.

1783 Treaty of Paris ends Revolutionary War.

1821 First public high school opens in Boston.

■ TOPICS IN COLONIAL LITERATURE

The colonists were passionately interested in politics—after all, they witnessed the American Revolution and the founding of the United States. They liked to discuss citizens' rights. Patrick Henry's "Speech in the Virginia Convention" and George Washington's "Farewell Address" are typical of this kind of writing.

Colonists also wondered what it meant to be an American. Jean de Crèvecoeur tried to answer that question in a short essay you will read called "What Is an American?"

Biography fascinated the colonists. They enjoyed reading about people who overcame obstacles. They also believed in the importance of moral values. Benjamin Franklin's *Autobiography* deals with these subjects.

Poetry is the genre, or literary form, that the colonists often used to write about love. You will read one love poem, "To My Dear and Loving Husband," in this unit.

The colonists also enjoyed writing that offered humor through exaggeration. "Sunrise in His Pocket" is an example of a tall tale, a story that uses wild exaggeration to make people laugh.

This unit includes selections from Native American literature. "Song Concerning a Dream of the Thunderbirds" is a poem. "Godasiyo, the Woman Chief," is a legend written down by the 20th century author, Dee Brown.

As you read the selections, imagine what life was like for these colonial Americans. Ask yourself what reading might have meant to you if you had lived in colonial times.

Learn About

The Boating Party, Mary Cassatt. National Gallery of Art, Washington, DC/Index/Bridgeman Art Library

READING FOCUS

Identify Cause and Effect A cause is what makes something happen. An effect is what happens as a result of an event. Each event can have many causes, and a cause can have many effects.

A writer who explores the questions "What happened?" and "Why did it happen?" must use cause and effect in his or her text. As you read Bradstreet's poem, think about the events and emotions she describes. What has caused her to feel the way she does? What are the effects of her feelings?

TONE

When you speak, your voice carries a meaning beyond the words you use. For example, if you say to someone, "I'm going shopping," your tone of voice will reflect whether you feel hope, dread, excitement, or boredom. It is not just the words you speak, but your tone of voice that reveals your feelings about the shopping trip.

Beneath the surface of their words, writers show their feelings and attitudes, too. **Tone** is the literary term used to describe a writer's feeling and attitude toward the subject matter and toward the reader. Is the writer's tone playful or serious, respectful or rude, personal or impersonal, loving or angry, light or grim—or any of many other possible attitudes?

As you read "To My Dear and Loving Husband," ask yourself:

1. What is the writer's tone?
2. How early in the poem do you recognize the tone?

WRITING CONNECTION

Write a paragraph describing your favorite movie. Write a second paragraph describing a movie you did not like. Read your paragraphs and pay close attention to the tone of each one. How do the tones of your paragraphs differ?

To My Dear and Loving Husband

by Anne Bradstreet

Portrait of Mr. and Mrs. Thomas Mifflin (Sarah Morris), John S. Copley. Philadelphia Museum of Art

If ever two were one, then surely we;
If ever man were loved by wife, then thee;
If ever wife was happy in a man,
Compare with me, ye women, if you can.
5 I prize thy love more than whole mines of gold,
Or all the riches that the East doth hold.
My love is such that rivers cannot quench,
Nor ought but love from thee give recompense.
Thy love is such I can no way repay,
10 The heavens reward thee manifold, I pray.
Then while we live in love let's so persever
That when we live no more we may live ever.

---

quench (KWENCH) satisfy thirst or other need
ought (AWT) anything (variation of *aught*)
recompense (REHK um pens) repayment
manifold (MAN uh fohld) in many ways
persever (pur SEV ur) continue to uphold; keep on trying
   (Today the word is spelled *persevere* and pronounced *pur suh VEER*.)

Review the Selection

UNDERSTAND THE SELECTION

Recall

1. To whom is Anne Bradstreet writing?

2. Above what does she prize her husband's love?

3. What does she pray rewards her husband?

Infer

4. How does Anne Bradstreet feel about her husband?

5. How does Bradstreet's love compare with the love of other wives?

6. How does she think her husband feels about her?

7. How long does Bradstreet want their love to last?

Apply

8. How do you think Anne Bradstreet's husband felt when he read her poem?

9. How might her husband have responded to the poem?

10. Bradstreet chose poetry to communicate her feelings. What would you write to communicate love?

Respond to Literature

Anne Bradstreet was a Puritan. Why is it surprising that this poem was written by a Puritan?

WRITE ABOUT THE SELECTION

In this selection, Anne Bradstreet chose poetry to express her feelings to her husband. He understood how she felt from the tone of her poem. Do you think she expressed herself clearly? Why or why not? What do you think his reaction was? How did he feel about her? Assume you are her husband and have decided to respond to her poem—not in poetry, but in prose.

Prewriting Compile a list of things you might say to Anne Bradstreet. Let your mind roam freely over possible responses you might make. Jot them down without thinking of how important or unimportant they may be. When you have a sizable list, consider which ones you want to use in your response. Organize your notes in the order you want to discuss them.

Writing Use your informal list to write a paragraph in the first-person ("I") point of view. Remember that you are supposed to be the husband. Make clear how you feel. Remember to keep the tone consistent.

Revising When you revise your paragraph, add details that maintain the same tone.

Proofreading Read over your paragraph. Be sure that all your sentences end with a period, question mark, or exclamation point.

THINK ABOUT TONE

Tone is the literary term used to describe the writer's attitude toward his or her readers, toward his or her characters, and toward the subject matter of the piece. Tone contributes greatly to the effectiveness of a work. If the reader misunderstands a writer's tone, he or she will miss much of the meaning of the work.

1. Does this poem sound like a casual conversation? Explain your answer.

2. Why do you think the writer chose poetry as the genre rather than a letter?

3. What do the comparisons used in lines 5 through 10 tell the reader about the depth of the writer's emotion?

4. How does the tone contribute to the mood of the poem?

5. What effect would a touch of humor have had on the poem?

READING FOCUS

Identify Cause and Effect You have paid attention to what caused the writer to feel the way she does and the effects of those causes. Name at least one cause and one effect in this poem.

DEVELOP YOUR VOCABULARY

You cannot understand the meaning of a literary work unless you understand the meanings of the words the author uses. Sometimes the **context**—the words surrounding the unfamiliar term—will suggest a meaning. When it does, you should confirm your guess by looking up the word in a dictionary.

Another place to check for the meaning of unfamiliar words is in the book itself. Sometimes, as in this book, you can find the meaning of unfamiliar words in footnotes at the bottom of the page. They also may be given at the end of a selection or in a special glossary at the end of the book.

Review the meanings of the following words from "To My Dear and Loving Husband." Write an original sentence using each word.

1. quench
2. ought
3. recompense
4. manifold
5. persevere

Learn About

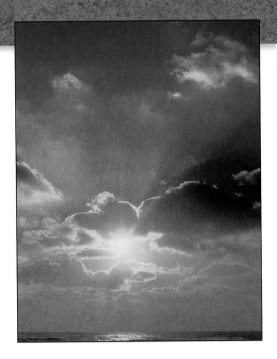

RHYTHM

Rhythm is the repetition of a pattern of sounds. It occurs in natural speech; rhythm is the "swing," or sense of movement, that the ear hears when successive syllables are stressed or unstressed.

Most poetry has very strong rhythm because the poet writes into a poem a pattern of strongly stressed syllables alternating with a pattern of unstressed syllables. Such a pattern is called **meter**. Not all poems have meter, but that does not mean that they lack rhythm. In non-metrical poetry, rhythm is irregular and comes from the natural rise and fall of syllables. The effect is sometimes enhanced by the repetition of words or word patterns.

As you read this selection, ask yourself:
1. How does the poet use rising and falling sounds to create rhythm?
2. What two phrases does the author repeat three times? How do they affect the reader?

READING FOCUS

Understand the Speaker's Purpose
People speak and write to communicate their ideas to others. They may want to describe, to entertain, to inform, or to persuade.

Diction and tone are two elements of a text that can help you determine the speaker's purpose. Look at the speaker's diction, or word choice. Ask yourself what it tells you about the speaker's tone, or attitude, toward both the subject and the audience.

WRITING CONNECTION

Write down the lyrics of your favorite song. Then explain how the songwriter used rhythm to create an effect.

Song Concerning a Dream of the Thunderbirds

by the Teton Sioux

Friends, behold!
Sacred I have been made.
Friends, behold!
In a sacred manner
I have been influenced
At the gathering of the clouds.
Sacred I have been made.
Friends, behold!
Sacred I have been made.

Red Thing That Touches In Marching, 1832. George Catlin.
The Granger Collection

---

thunderbird (THUN dur burd) in the mythology of certain North American tribes, an enormous
bird supposed to produce thunder, lightning, and rain

Review the Selection

UNDERSTAND THE SELECTION

Recall

1. To whom is the writer speaking?

2. What change did the writer undergo during the dream?

3. Where was the writer when the change took place?

Infer

4. When do you think the Sioux might sing this song?

5. Who was present at the gathering of the clouds?

6. What do you think the Sioux believe caused thunder, lightning, and rain? Why?

7. Why do you think the Sioux visualized a thunderbird as a large bird?

Apply

8. Assume you are a Sioux living in the 18th century. When might you have asked a thunderbird for help?

9. Predict what might happen after the Sioux sang this song.

10. Do you think the Sioux still tell the legend of the thunderbird? Why?

Respond to Literature

How do you think "Song Concerning a Dream of the Thunderbirds" is representative of the literature of Native Americans?

WRITE ABOUT THE SELECTION

When you read a story, you form a specific image of each character in your mind. Sometimes the writer gives a detailed description of each character. At other times, you are required to visualize the characters' appearance from context clues or information learned from another source.

In this selection, you learned that the mythical creature, the thunderbird, is huge and is supposed to cause rain and storms. This you discovered in the vocabulary definition. Still, you can envision more. For example, do you envision a large head? What is the shape of the bird's eyes, wings, claws? Describe in detail how you picture the thunderbird.

Prewriting Begin by listing at least four characteristics of your vision of the thunderbird. Include several details for each characteristic. Try to use precise and vivid words. Be sure to include some interesting adverbs to help describe how the bird moves. Describe the kind of sound it makes.

Writing Use your list to write a paragraph describing the thunderbird's appearance. In it, briefly explain the setting that surrounds the bird.

Revising Add specific details that allow others to visualize your impressions of this creature.

Proofreading Be sure each sentence begins with a capital letter.

THINK ABOUT RHYTHM

Rhythm is the repetition of a pattern of sounds. Even natural speech has a rhythm of stressed and unstressed syllables. A two-syllable word with the stress on the second syllable will create a rising sound. A two-syllable word with the stress on the first syllable will create a falling sound. Words with a mixed pattern will create a rising and falling rhythm.

1. Describe the use of repetition in this poem.

2. Why do you think the song begins and ends with the same two lines?

3. What two-syllable, six-letter word accented on the second syllable does the writer repeat?

4. What two-syllable, six-letter word accented on the first syllable does the writer repeat?

5. What kind of rhythm do these accented words create?

READING FOCUS

Understand the Speaker's Purpose You have studied this song to determine the speaker's purpose, or reason for the song. What is the purpose of the line "Friends, Behold!"? What is the purpose of the repetition of the word *sacred*?

DEVELOP YOUR VOCABULARY

Synonyms are words that mean the same or nearly the same. For example, you might use either *strange* or *weird* to describe something odd. Writers try to use synonyms to make their writing more interesting. Paragraphs that use the same words over and over make dull reading.

Following is a list of words you might use in writing about the meaning of the poem, "Song Concerning a Dream of the Thunderbirds." For each, write a synonym.

1. holy
2. interesting
3. invitation
4. metaphor
5. big
6. influenced

Write a short description of the poem in which you use some of your synonyms for the words in the list.

Patrick Henry, after Alonzo Chappel. Archive Photos

READING FOCUS

Recognize Fact and Opinion Statements of fact can be proven true or false. Opinions are statements of belief. They cannot be proven true or false.

Patrick Henry tries to persuade his listeners of something. Therefore, he must give them reasons to believe what he says. As you read, look for statements of fact that his listeners can prove or disprove. Look for statements of opinion that his listeners will have to consider.

THEME AND THESIS

Theme is the main or central idea in a literary work. It is usually a broad, abstract idea, expressed directly or indirectly.

Theme in drama, poetry, and fiction is usually expressed indirectly. It may not be apparent until after the reader has finished reading the work and thought about it. Then readers draw their own conclusions about the meaning of the work.

In nonfiction, on the other hand, theme is usually expressed directly. The reader knows it immediately because theme and the subject matter of the work are usually identical.

Writers of nonfiction not only announce their theme, they often make a statement that tells just what position they will try to prove or support. This statement is called the **thesis statement**.

As you read Patrick Henry's speech, ask yourself:

1. What is the theme, or central idea, of Henry's speech?
2. Does he make a thesis statement? If so, what is it?

WRITING CONNECTION

Choose a newspaper editorial. Write down its theme, or central idea. Then look for the thesis statement and write it down.

Speech in the Virginia Convention

ADAPTED

by Patrick Henry

Mr. President: No man thinks more highly than I do of the patriotism and intelligence of the worthy gentlemen who have just addressed the house. But reasonable men sometimes disagree. I intend no disrespect toward the other speakers. Still, entertaining, as I do, opinions of a character very opposite to theirs [*disagreeing with their viewpoint*], I shall speak my thoughts freely and without reserve [*openly and honestly*]. This is no time for ceremony [*empty courtesy*]. The question before the house is one of grave importance to this country. For my own part, I consider it nothing less than a question of freedom and slavery. The issue is that significant. The debate must be uncompromising. It is only in this way that we can hope to arrive at the truth and fulfill the responsibility we owe to God and our country. If I held back my opinions at such a time, for fear of giving offense [*insulting someone*], I would consider myself guilty of treason toward my country. I would be lying before God.

Mr. President: It is only natural to hope for the best in any situation. In times of peril, though, hope may be a dangerous illusion. Hope may mean that we are shutting our eyes to avoid seeing a painful truth. Hope may mean that we are listening to a siren's song until she turns us into beasts [*ignoring reality and hearing only what we want to hear*]. Is this the role that wise men should play when they are engaged in a great and difficult struggle for liberty? Do wise men pretend that all is well when their eyes and ears tell them different? For my part, whatever anguish of spirit it may cost [*no matter how painful it is to me*], I am willing to hear the whole truth: to know the worst that can happen and make plans to avert it.

I have but one lamp by which my feet are guided [*know only one way to find my path in the dark*]. That is the lamp of experience. I know only one way to predict the future. That is by the experience of the past. Judging by the past, I would like to know what the British have done to make us believe there is hope for peace. The last time we asked them to consider our rights as royal subjects, they smiled. Trust not that smile, sir, it will prove a snare to your feet [*will turn out to be a trap*].

---

grave (GRAYV) of a threatening nature; indicating great danger
significant (sig NIF uh kunt) important; momentous
siren (SY run) in Greek and Roman mythology, a sea nymph represented as part bird and part woman who lured sailors to their death by singing

Do not allow yourself to be betrayed by a kiss [*deceived by a false show of friendship*]. Compare their words with their actions. Why do warlike preparations cover our waters and darken our land? Are fleets and armies necessary if peace is the British intention? Have we appeared so committed to rebellion that they must use force to win back our loyalty? Let us not deceive ourselves, sir. Fleets and armies are the implements of war and enslavement. When threats have failed, fleets and armies are the arguments to which kings resort.

I ask you, gentlemen, I ask you, sir, what means this martial array [*what is the purpose of this military buildup*]? They mean to force us into submission. Can gentlemen think of another possible motive for their actions? Has Great Britain any threatening enemy in this part of the world? No sir, she has none. These armies and navies are meant for us. They can be meant for no other. They are sent over the sea to bind and rivet those chains which the British ministry has been forging for so long.

How can we oppose them? Shall we try logic? Sir, we have been trying that for the last ten years. Have we anything new to say upon the subject? Nothing. We have discussed the subject from every possible viewpoint. Shall we resort to entreaty and supplication [*pleading and begging*]? What can we say that has not been said before? Let us not, I beseech you sir, deceive ourselves any longer.

Sir, we have done everything that could be done to avert the coming storm. We have petitioned; we have protested; we have pleaded. We have knelt before the king and asked for his justice. Our petitions have been slighted. Our protests have led to additional violence and insult. Our pleas have been ignored; and we have been spurned with contempt by the king.

Do we wish to be free? Do we mean to preserve unbroken those precious rights for which we have so long fought? Do we plan on continuing this noble struggle? Will we keep our pledge not to abandon the struggle until our liberty is won? Then we must fight! I repeat it, sir, we must fight. An appeal to arms and God Almighty is all that is left us [*our only hope*].

They tell us, sir, that we are weak. They say we cannot cope with so formidable an adversary [*so strong a foe*]. But when shall we be stronger? Will it be next week, next year? Will it be when we are completely disarmed, and when a British guard is stationed in every house? Shall we grow strong through indecision and delay? Shall we acquire the means of effective resistance lying on our backs, hugging the delusive phantom of hope [*clinging to a false hope*] until our enemies have bound us hand and foot?

---

array (uh RAY) an orderly arrangement of troops
petitioned (puh TISH und) made a formal request of someone in authority
adversary (AD vur ser ee) opponent; enemy
delusive (dih LOO siv) misleading; unreal
phantom (FAN tum) something that seems real but does not exist

Patrick Henry Speaking Against the Stamp Act in the Virginia House of Burgesses in 1765, 19th century.
The Granger Collection

Sir, we are not weak if we make a proper use of the means at our disposal. We number three million. Three million people, armed in the holy cause of liberty, in such a country as this, can defeat any force our enemy sends against us. Besides, sir, we shall not fight alone. There is a just God who presides over the destinies of nations [*rules the universe*]. He will raise up friends to fight alongside us. The battle, sir, is not won by strength alone. Battles are won by the vigilant, by the active, by the brave. Besides, we have no choice. If we were dishonorable enough to desire peace at any price, it is not too late to retire from the contest [*surrender*]. We could retreat and accept submission and slavery. The British have already forged the chains of our bondage. Their rattling can be heard on the plains of Boston. The war is inevitable. Let it come. I repeat, sir, let it come.

There is no need to extenuate the matter [*no need for further discussion*]. Gentlemen may cry "Peace, peace"—but there is no peace. The war is actually begun! The next gale that sweeps [*strong wind that blows*] from the north will bring to our ears the clash of resounding arms [*the sounds of battle*]! Our brethren are already in the field. Why stand we here idle? What is it that gentlemen wish? What would they choose? Is life so precious, or peace so sweet, as to be purchased at the price of chains and slavery? Forbid it, Almighty God! I know not what course others may take; but as for me, give me liberty or give me death!

---

inevitable (in EV ih tuh bul) certain to happen
extenuate (ik STEN yoo ayt) to lessen the seriousness of
resounding (rih ZOUND ing) loud, echoing, or prolonged sound
brethren (BRETH run) brothers; fellow members of a group

Review the Selection

UNDERSTAND THE SELECTION

Recall

1. On what does Patrick Henry depend in order to predict the future?

2. Whom does Henry think the British plan to attack?

3. What does Henry say are his only alternatives?

4. What was the population of the colonies at this time?

Infer

5. What position had those who spoke before Patrick Henry taken?

6. Does Henry trust the British? Explain.

7. With what does Henry equate defeat in the coming revolution?

Apply

8. If you had been a delegate to the Virginia Convention, would you have supported Henry? Explain.

9. Do you think Patrick Henry's speech changed the minds of some delegates? Why or why not?

10. Would Henry's argument have been more effective as a letter? Explain.

Respond to Literature

Why do you think this speech was of interest to people in other colonies?

WRITE ABOUT THE SELECTION

Imagine that Patrick Henry is delivering his speech today. You are a television reporter covering the Virginia Convention. It is important that you report the main points of his speech.

Prewriting   List the main points of his speech. What was the main idea of Henry's speech? What were the most important elements? Include details by quoting one or two of his lines. Add other details about the reaction that members of the Virginia Convention had.

Writing   Use your list to write one or two paragraphs that will allow the viewer to understand the main ideas of Henry's speech. Always keep your audience in mind. Be sure to use words and ideas to which they can relate. In your report, use the quotations accurately to illustrate the main points. Add the details of how the audience reacted.

Revising   When you revise your paragraph(s), be sure to add specific details that clarify his point of view. Try to make your report more vivid by using precise details. Check to be sure your report does not contain informal words or phrases. If you find you have used informal language, substitute more appropriate terms.

Proofreading   Read over your paragraphs. Be sure you have placed quotation marks at the beginning and the end of any direct quotations you have included.

THINK ABOUT THEME AND THESIS

Theme is the main or central idea in a literary work. It is a comment on life or on a situation in life. Nonfiction writers state their theme directly; it is the subject matter of the work. They may also make a **thesis statement**—an announcement of the position that will be proved or supported in the work.

1. What is the theme of Patrick Henry's speech?

2. Summarize Henry's thesis statement.

3. List three arguments that Henry makes in support of his thesis, or position.

4. How do you think his listeners would have reacted if he had started his speech with the paragraph beginning: "Gentlemen may cry peace, but there is no peace!"

5. What action does Henry recommend as the inevitable result of Britain's refusal to listen to the colonists' pleas and petitions?

READING FOCUS

Recognize Fact and Opinion You looked carefully at Henry's speech to distinguish between fact and opinion. Name three opinions and the facts that Henry used to support each opinion.

DEVELOP YOUR VOCABULARY

Rhetoric is the art or science of using words effectively in speaking or writing. A rhetorical question is a question that does not require an answer from the listener. It is a technique used by speakers and writers in order to make a point. The author is actually making a statement. It is phrased as a question only for dramatic effect.

Patrick Henry uses this technique extensively. For example he asks, "Do wise men pretend that all is well when their eyes and ears tell them it is not?" This is a rhetorical question. The answer is so obvious that Patrick Henry does not answer it. However, he answers in detail the rhetorical question, ". . . what is the purpose of this military array?" He presents his answer as arguments to support his position.

Find three other rhetorical questions in this selection. Review the meanings of the vocabulary words from this selection. Then answer each of the three rhetorical questions in original sentences that make use of a word from the vocabulary list.

Focus ON NONFICTION

What is nonfiction? **Nonfiction** is the branch of literature that communicates information and ideas. It presents factual information. Nonfiction often offers an interpretation of the facts it presents. It can also propose opinions and theories. Nonfiction is written in prose, or ordinary language.

Forms of Nonfiction   Nonfiction can be broken down into four categories, or forms. The four forms are exposition, persuasion (or argumentation), description, and narration.

Exposition is writing that explains. There are a number of writing methods used in exposition. One is definition, writing that explains the meaning of a term, such as *democracy*. Another is classification, writing that groups things or ideas according to their similarities or differences. Breaking down nonfiction into four forms involves classification. Still another method of exposition is comparison and contrast. This is writing that explains how one thing is like or unlike another thing. Writing that shows the similarities and differences between baseball and stickball is an example of comparison and contrast. A fourth type of exposition is analysis. Analysis is writing that examines the different parts of something and tells how they fit together to form a whole. Explaining the parts of a steam engine and how they work together is an example of analysis.

Persuasion (or argumentation) is writing that attempts to convince a reader or listener by showing that a statement is either true or false. While expository writing aims merely to explain, persuasion seeks to influence the reader or listener. An editorial in the newspaper urging people to vote in the next election is an example of persuasion.

Description is writing that paints word pictures of the details, qualities, or appearances of something. Specific details make the word picture come alive. The details are the result of careful observation, with attention to shapes, sizes, colors, tastes, sounds, and textures.

Narration is writing in which an event or a series of events is told. While description is concerned with how things look, narration is concerned with what happens when events occur.

Rarely will only one element of nonfiction be used in a single piece of writing. Most writing makes use of two or more.

Organization of Nonfiction Most nonfiction follows a three-part organization. There is an introduction, a body, and a conclusion.

The **introduction** may state a problem or give background or examples. In expository and persuasive writing, the author may make a **thesis statement**. This is an announcement of what is to be proved or supported in the writing. The central idea, or general topic of discussion, in exposition and persuasion is the *theme*. Writers of description use details to create a *dominant impression*. The **body** of the work is used to develop or discuss the ideas of the work. Narration is organized chronologically; that is, in the order in which events have occurred. Other kinds of writing are organized in some kind of logical order. The **conclusion** rounds out the work. It may do so by restating the thesis, by summarizing the main ideas in the body, by answering a question that was raised, or by urging the reader to future action.

Types of Nonfiction Many different kinds of literature fall into the category of nonfiction. Biography, autobiography, diaries, memoirs, journals, and letters tell about people's lives. Reports, articles, news stories, and essays deal with facts, theories, and ideas. There are many different kinds of essays. Orations, like those made by Patrick Henry and George Washington, are essays that are spoken rather than written.

Farewell Address

ADAPTED

by George Washington

FOCUS ON
NONFICTION
STUDY HINTS

The author introduces
his speech and states
the background.

The author gives
a personal reason
for speaking.

The author explains
his personal reason.

The author tells what
he intends to do in the
speech. This is his thesis
statement.

The author begins the
body of the speech.

Friends and Fellow Citizens: My second term as President of the United States will soon expire. The time for another presidential election is drawing near. Your thoughts should be turning in that direction. It is in the public interest, therefore, that I disclose a decision I have reached. I will not be a candidate for reelection. I will not seek a third term as president.

For some time now, I have wished to retire from public life, but the affairs of state were unsettled. A sense of duty compelled me to stay on. I am happy to say my services are no longer needed. The Foreign and Domestic affairs of our country are now in order. I can pursue my inclination with a clear conscience.

Here, perhaps, I should stop. But my concern for your welfare will not end with my term in office. My affection for you will only end with my death. Therefore, I will offer for your consideration some advice. These sentiments are the result of many years of experience and much observation of human nature. They are the thoughts of a parting friend, uncolored by personal or political motive.

Love of liberty is woven through every fiber of your hearts. You need no counsel from me to strengthen that attachment.

Remember, though, that the one nation you forged from thirteen colonies is the pillar on which that liberty stands. It is that

---

inclination (in kluh NAY shun) a particular disposition or bent of mind
uncolored (un KUL urd) not influenced by
counsel (KOUN sul) advice

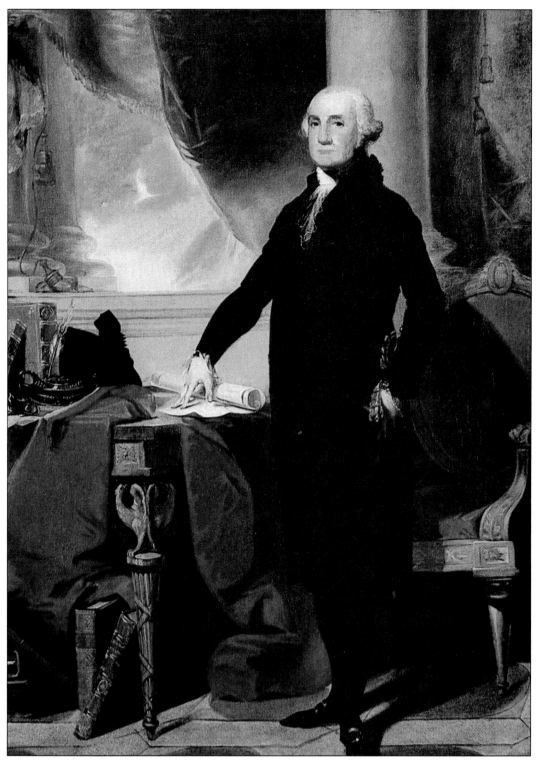

George Washington, after Gilbert Stuart. The Granger Collection unity of government which is the source of your real independence. The union makes possible your tranquility at home and peace abroad. Your prosperity and your liberty depend on the strength of that union.

You are all Americans. It is to America that you owe your first allegiance, not the region of your birth. That name, *America*, embraces all the common bonds you share: your manners, customs, and political beliefs. You have fought and triumphed together in a common cause. The independence and liberty you now possess result from those joint efforts and shared suffering.

Regional loyalties are a threat to your liberty. More dangerous yet is party allegiance. Party spirit is rooted in human nature. Political parties exist to some extent under all forms of government. But it is in a democracy that they are seen in their most dangerous form.

Parties win some elections and lose others. A party newly come to power may be tempted to take revenge for earlier defeats. You have seen how party rivalry in France has led to the execution of leaders who lost public favor. Such wickedness leads to chaos.

The public, alarmed at the threat of lawlessness, becomes inclined to place absolute power in the hands of one strong leader who can restore order. Sooner or later, this leader raises himself above the law and becomes a tyrant. Liberty is left in ruins. Such a calamity need not happen. A wise people can prevent it by discouraging and restraining party loyalty.

The framers of the Constitution wisely gave no one branch of government absolute power. The president, the congress, and the courts have separate spheres of influence. No one of the three branches can be permitted to encroach upon the powers of the others. Consolidation of power in any one branch leads to tyranny.

The need for Constitutional change may arise. Consolidation of power may seem a convenient means of effecting change. But it is the customary weapon by which free governments are destroyed. The permanent evil it sets loose outweighs the temporary

---

tranquility (tran KWIL uh tee) calmness; peacefulness
encroach (en KROHCH) to intrude upon the rights of others
consolidation (kun sol uh DAY shun) strengthening

benefit that results. If change is needed, let it come through a Constitutional amendment ratified by the people.

Public morality and an educated citizenry are indispensable to the preservation of liberty. Life, reputation, and property are only safe in a land which values virtue. Only an informed public can make wise choices. Encourage, therefore, public education and the growth of educational institutions.

Be honest and generous in dealings with other nations. Strive to be at peace with all peoples but maintain a strong defense. A strong defense is the surest guarantee of peace.

The author states his third point; he warns against foreign entanglements.

Do not be drawn into European affairs. Expand trade relations but avoid permanent political alliances. The nations of Europe have warred upon each other for centuries and will continue to do so. Honor those temporary treaties signed in a time of emergency but do not extend them.

The author supports his third point with a reminder of the nation's obligations.

European quarrels are not our quarrels. We are separated by an ocean. Our destiny lies in the future. Do not be drawn into Europe's past. And in both public and private affairs, remember the maxim, "Honesty is the best policy."

I offer these thoughts as an old and true friend. I realize my words alone are no safeguard against an uncertain future. It is enough if now and then the nation remembers a friend's counsel: Discourage and restrain party allegiance. Guard against those who would use patriotism to conceal selfish interests. Avoid entanglement in European intrigues.

The author begins his conclusion. He restates his thesis and summarizes his main points.

As president, I committed no intentional errors, but I am aware of my own human frailties. Whatever mistakes I have made, I ask God to correct in the course of time. I hope my countrymen will forgive my failings, realize my good intentions, and remember my zeal to serve this land to the best of my ability.

---

ratified (RAT uh fyd) approved or confirmed

Review the Selection

UNDERSTAND THE SELECTION

Recall

1. What decision did Washington disclose to his audience?

2. What did he say was more dangerous to liberty than regional loyalties?

3. What two things did he say were indispensable to liberty?

Infer

4. Why did Washington choose this time to make the remarks he did?

5. Did he owe his first loyalty to Virginia or America?

6. Why did he believe education was indispensable?

7. Why did he believe we should avoid permanent alliances with Europe?

Apply

8. Which of Washington's warnings do you think is most effectively stated?

9. What opinion do you think he held of the framers of the Constitution?

10. Do you think Washington would have approved of today's voting system?

Respond to Literature

List Washington's warnings about dangers to democracy. How do his themes reflect Washington's time?

WRITE ABOUT THE SELECTION

You have been studying the elements of nonfiction in this unit. Now it is time for you to apply that knowledge. Suppose that you are George Washington and that you are President today. You have decided not to run again and to retire to your estate at Mount Vernon. You make another "Farewell Address." What would you warn the people about today? Would any of the concerns in the original address be meaningful today?

Prewriting   Decide what you will talk about in the body of your speech. Which issues will you discuss? Jot down the points that you will make in your speech. Then decide how you will introduce your speech and with what conclusions you will end.

Writing   Use the information collected during the prewriting exercise to compose your speech. Some authors write the body first and then the introduction and conclusion. Write an opening and closing paragraph and at least one paragraph on an issue. If you write about two or more issues, write a brief paragraph on each.

Revising   When you revise, think about adding detail. You want to have enough evidence to support your conclusion.

Proofreading   Read over your essay. Be sure all your subjects and verbs agree. If the subject is singular, be sure your verb is singular. If the subject is plural, make sure your verb is plural.

THINK ABOUT NONFICTION

An **oration** is a speech that is intended to inspire listeners to action. In Washington's day, oratory was a highly regarded and eagerly enjoyed mode of communication. It was especially prevalent in courtrooms, on the political stump, and at religious gatherings.

1. How many parts did George Washington's address have? Name the parts.

2. What action did George Washington hope his listeners would take?

3. Does Washington make a thesis statement in his speech? If so, what is it?

4. Summarize the three main points about which Washington cautioned his listeners.

5. Patrick Henry made a very emotional speech in defense of liberty. How would you characterize the tone of Washington's "Farewell Address"?

DEVELOP YOUR VOCABULARY

A word can sometimes be used as either a noun or a verb. For example, in the title of this selection, "Farewell Address," the word *address* is a noun meaning "speech." However, in the sentence "I will address this package to Jim J. Johnson," the word *address* is a verb meaning "to write the destination on." The meanings are clearly not the same.

The following words are also found in this selection. Each word can be used either as a noun or as a verb. If you are not certain of the meanings of each of the words, check the definitions in a dictionary.

Write a sentence using each word as a noun. Then write a sentence using each as a verb.

1. triumph	6. offer
2. result	7. defeat
3. form	8. change
4. favor	9. benefit
5. counsel	10. quarrel

Abigail Adams, 1766, Benjamin Blyth.
The Granger Collection

READING FOCUS

Make Inferences Many times you figure out how a person feels about something without being told directly. You make inferences, or use the information given to understand something not stated. As you read this selection, you will be able to make inferences about how Abigail Adams feels about living in the White House. Look for the descriptions that help you make the inferences.

DESCRIPTION

Description is one of the four main forms of writing. Writers use it when they want to paint a picture in words or help the reader know what something looks, sounds, tastes, or feels like.

Details make a description come alive. Writers carefully choose the details they use in order to create a main focus for the description. This focus is called the dominant impression. The dominant impression contributes to the mood of the description and helps the reader to experience a scene or a sensation as the writer wishes. The description becomes real to the reader.

To understand a writer's dominant impression, notice not only the details selected but also the choice of words. Description is especially effective when it makes precise use of words and phrases.

As you read the selection, ask yourself:

1. On what details does Abigail Adams focus?
2. What is the dominant impression in her letter?

WRITING CONNECTION

Look at the artwork in this unit. Describe one person pictured. Create a dominant impression for your description.

Letter to Her Daughter from the New White House

by Abigail Adams

Washington, 21 November, 1800

My Dear Child:

I arrived here on Sunday last, and without meeting with any accident worth noticing, except losing ourselves when we left Baltimore and going eight or nine miles on the Frederick road, by which means we were obliged to go the other eight through woods, where we wandered two hours without finding a guide or the path. Fortunately, a straggling black came up with us, and we engaged him as a guide to extricate us out of our difficulty; but woods are all you see from Baltimore until you reach the *city*, which is only so in name. Here and there is a small cot, without a glass window, interspersed among the forests, through which you travel miles without seeing any human being. In the city there are buildings enough, if they were compact and finished, to accommodate Congress and those attached to it; but as they are, and scattered as they are, I see no great comfort for them. The river, which runs up to Alexandria[1], is in full view of my window, and I see the vessels as they pass and repass. The house is upon a grand and superb scale, requiring about thirty servants to attend and keep the apartments in proper order, and perform the ordinary business of the house and stables; an establishment very well proportioned to the President's salary. The lighting of the apartments, from the kitchen to parlors and chambers, is a tax indeed; and the fires we are obliged to keep to secure us from daily

---

extricate (EK strih kayt) to set free; release; disentangle
cot (KOT) cottage or small house
interspersed (in tur SPURST) scattered among other things
[1]**Alexandria:** A city in northeastern Virginia

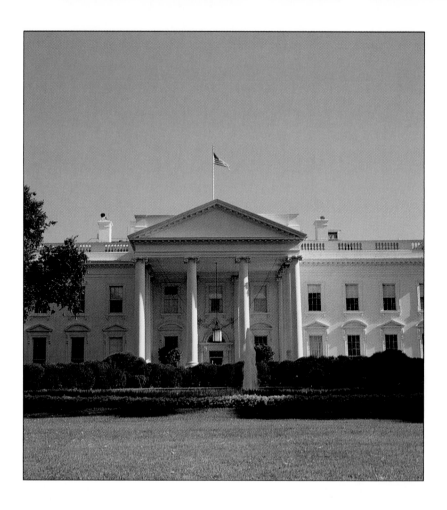

agues is another very cheering comfort. To assist us in this great castle, and render less attendance necessary, bells are wholly wanting, not one single one being hung through the whole house, and promises are all you can obtain. This is so great an inconvenience, that I know not what to do, or how to do. The ladies from Georgetown[2] and in the city have many of them visited me. Yesterday I returned fifteen visits—but such a place as Georgetown appears—why, our Milton is beautiful. But no comparisons—if they will put me up some bells and let me have wood enough to keep fires, I design to be pleased. I could content myself almost anywhere three months; but, surrounded with forests, can you believe that wood is not to be had because people

---

ague (AY gyoo) violent fever
[2]**Georgetown:** A section of Washington, DC

cannot be found to cut and cart it? Briesler entered into a contract with a man to supply him with wood. A small part, a few cords only, has he been able to get. Most of that was expended to dry the walls of the house before we came in, and yesterday the man told him it was impossible for him to procure it to be cut and carted. He has had recourse to coals; but we cannot get grates made and set. We have, indeed, come into a *new country*.

You must keep all this to yourself, and, when asked how I like it, say that I write you the situation is beautiful, which is true. The house is made habitable, but there is not a single apartment finished, and all withinside, except the plastering, had been done since Briesler came. We have not the least fence, yard, or other convenience, without, and the great unfinished audience room I make a drying-room of, to hang up the clothes in. The principal stairs are not up, and will not be this winter. Six chambers are made comfortable; two are occupied by the President and Mr. Shaw; two lower rooms, one for a common parlor, and one for a levee room. Upstairs there is the oval room, which is designed for the drawing room, and has the crimson furniture in it. It is a very handsome room now; but, when completed, it will be beautiful. If the twelve years, in which this place has been considered as the future seat of government, had been improved, as they would have been if in New England, very many of the present inconveniences would have been removed. It is a beautiful spot, capable of every improvement, and, the more I view it, the more I am delighted with it.

Since I sat down to write, I have been called down to a servant from Mount Vernon,[3] with a billet from Major Custis, and a haunch of venison, and a kind, congratulatory letter from Mrs. Lewis, upon my arrival in the city, with Mrs. Washington's love, inviting me to Mount Vernon, where, health permitting, I will go before I leave this place. . . .

Affectionately, your mother,
Abigail Adams

---

procure (proh KYUUR) to obtain or secure
recourse (REE kawrs) a turning back for aid, safety, etc.
habitable (HAB it uh bul) fit to be lived in
levee (LEV ee) a morning reception held by a person of high rank
billet (BIL it) a brief letter
[3]**Mount Vernon:** Home of George Washington, located in northern Virginia

Review the Selection

Recall

1. From what city was Abigail Adams writing?

2. What surrounded the White House?

3. What home did Mrs. Washington invite Abigail Adams to visit?

Infer

4. What elected position did Abigail Adams's husband hold?

5. How was the White House heated at that time?

6. Why did Adams ask her daughter to keep the negative comments about the White House a secret?

7. In what year did Americans begin to consider building the White House?

Apply

8. List three personal qualities you think apply to Mrs. Adams.

9. If you were in Mrs. Adams's situation, how would you spend your time?

10. How would Mrs. Adams's description of the White House differ today?

Respond to Literature

How does this selection illustrate the characteristics of colonial literature?

WRITE ABOUT THE SELECTION

In this letter, Abigail Adams described her impressions of the White House to her daughter. She painted a vivid picture of both the interior and the exterior of this famous building. As a reader, you feel as though you are being given a personal tour. If you could design your "dream house," what would it look like? Describe the appearance and the setting in which you would build it. Write about the house so that a person who has never seen it could picture it from your description.

Prewriting   List the characteristics you would choose for your dream house. Include details of the interior as well as exterior features of the building. Organize your details according to room sizes, layout, placement of items, location of exterior features, building materials used, and so on.

Writing   Use this list to write at least one paragraph describing the best features of your house. Select words that paint a vivid picture.

Revising   When you revise your description, be sure to add specific details that illustrate the appearance of the house and its setting.

Proofreading   Read over your selection. Be sure all the words are spelled correctly. If you are unsure of the spelling of a particular word, look it up in the dictionary.

THINK ABOUT DESCRIPTION

Writers use description to paint a picture for the reader. Effective writers do not list every feature of the object being described. They select those that will support their sense of what is important.

1. List five features of the White House that Mrs. Adams selected for her description.

2. What are some reactions that Mrs. Adams had to the house?

3. What was the dominant impression created in your mind by her description of these features?

4. If Mrs. Adams were describing the White House for a newspaper article, what dominant impression do you think she would try to create? Why would her description to a newspaper be different from the description written to her daughter?

5. If she were describing the White House today, how do you think her description would differ?

READING FOCUS

Make Inferences How does Abigail Adams feel about being in the White House? Find three descriptions that helped you make inferences about her feelings.

DEVELOP YOUR VOCABULARY

Language is always changing. People invent new words, and others drop from current usage. New words form as the need for them arises. Sometimes old words acquire new meanings. These new meanings become part of common usage along with the original meanings of the words. At other times, the commonly used meaning of a word changes entirely. The original meaning may become lost, or **archaic**. The word may remain in the language but assume an entirely new meaning.

Using a dictionary, look for the meaning of each of the following words as they were used in Mrs. Adams's letter. Remember, these may be unusual or archaic meanings today. Then compare that meaning with the usual, or common, meaning of the words today. Write an original sentence using each word in its older meaning. Then, write an original sentence using its contemporary meaning.

1. expended
2. attend
3. design
4. audience
5. tax

NARRATION

Narration is one of the four main forms of composition. It is the primary form of novels, short stories, and narrative poems, as well as of biography, autobiography, and news reports. In short, narration is the form used in fiction and nonfiction storytelling.

Stories, whether true or fictional, are about events—the birth of a new island in the Pacific, the rescue of a lost child, the appearance of Peter Rabbit in Mr. MacGregor's garden, your first birthday party. To make a good narrative, the events should have a beginning, a middle, and an end. This is part of the normal development of the plot.

The unique feature of narration is chronology. Events happen in time, and every story is told in some kind of time order. The most common time order is straightforward—from beginning to end.

As you read the next selections, ask yourself:

1. What kind of narrative writing is Franklin presenting?
2. In what order is he telling his stories?

WRITING CONNECTION

Write a paragraph in which you tell of an important event in your life. Give your paragraph a beginning, a middle, and an end.

READING FOCUS

Make Generalizations As you read, you often make generalizations, or use the information given to understand a broader idea. What generalizations can you make from Franklin's writings about his personality and about the values of the time?

from
The Autobiography

ADAPTED   *by Benjamin Franklin*

[*This excerpt reveals events from Franklin's teen-age years.*]

When I was about 16 years old, I happened to read a book written by a man named Tryon. He recommended a vegetable diet. I decided to try it. My brother, a bachelor, did not own a home. He and his apprentices boarded in another family's house. My refusal to eat meat or fish was an inconvenience, and I was frequently chided for it.

I learned Tryon's ways of preparing some dishes, such as boiling potatoes, or rice, making hasty pudding, and a few others. Then, I made my brother a proposition. If, each week, he would give me half the money he paid for my board, I would buy my own food. He agreed instantly.

I soon discovered that I could save half what he paid me. This gave me extra money to buy books. There was another advantage to this situation. My brother and the others went from the printing house to their meals. I remained there alone.

My meals were light. Often, I ate only a biscuit, or a slice of bread, a handful of raisins or a tart from the bakery. A glass of water was my beverage. After eating, I had the rest of the time until they returned to study. I learned quickly since my mind was clear from practicing moderation in eating and drinking.

On my first voyage from Boston, the ship was becalmed off Block Island.[1] The people aboard started fishing. They hauled up

---

excerpt (ehk SURPT) a passage taken from a book; quotation
boarded (BAWRD id) had rooms and meals provided regularly for pay
chided (CHYD id) scolded
hasty pudding (HAYS tee PUUD ing) cornmeal mush
tart (TAHRT) small, filled pastry; small pie
moderation (mod uh RAY shun) avoidance of excess
becalmed (bih KAHLMD) to make motionless from lack of wind
[1]**Block Island:** an island off the coast of Rhode Island

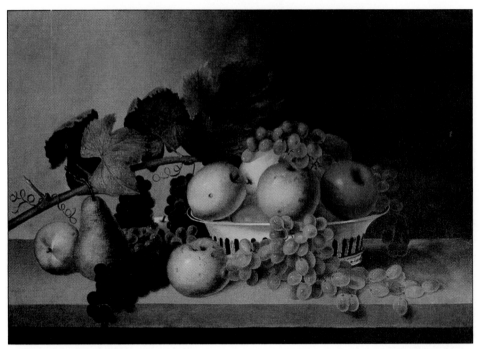

Still Life, 1857, Rubens Peale

a great many cod. Until then, I had stuck to my resolution. I had not eaten animal food. At this time, I considered catching any fish as a kind of unprovoked murder. None of them had, or ever could, do us any injury that might justify the slaughter. All of this seemed to make sense to me.

Still, I had once been a great lover of fish. Every cod that came hot from the frying pan smelled delicious. For some time, I could not decide between principle and inclination. Then I remembered something. When the fish were cut open, I had seen smaller fish taken out of their stomachs. I thought to myself, "If you eat one another, I don't see why I should not eat you." So I eagerly ate the cod, and have continued to eat with other people. Only now and then do I return to a vegetable diet. It is a convenient thing to be a reasonable creature. It enables us to find or make a reason for everything we want to do.

---

resolution (rez uh LOO shun) decision as to future action
unprovoked (un pruh VOHKT) not to stir up an action
slaughter (SLAWT ur) the killing of animals for food
principle (PRIN suh pul) a fundamental truth or rule of conduct
inclination (in kluh NAY shun) a liking or preference

[This excerpt deals with Franklin's early career.]

My brother began to print a newspaper, the *New England Courant*, in the year 1720 or '21. It was only the second paper to be published in America. Some of his friends tried to dissuade him, saying one newspaper was enough for America. In hindsight, their judgment seems questionable. Today, in 1771, there are at least twenty-five newspapers. No matter, my brother was determined. He composed the type[1] and printed his first edition. I was employed as the paper boy.

Some of his friends amused themselves by writing short pieces for his paper. When these gentlemen visited, I would hear them tell about the public compliments they received for their work. I decided to try my own hand.

I was still a boy and suspected that my brother would not agree to print my work. So, I disguised my handwriting and slipped an anonymous work under the printing house door. He found it in the morning. When his friends dropped by, he discussed the mysterious article with them. I listened in secret delight as they discussed its merits. Imagine my pleasure as each tried to guess the author's identity, naming only men known for their learning and imagination. Looking back, I suppose I was lucky. Being a boy, I think I overestimated their ability to judge literary merit.

At the time though I was encouraged. I submitted several more anonymous articles. Each was approved and printed. I kept my secret until I ran out of ideas. Then I revealed my identity.

---

anonymous (uh NON uh mus) written by a person whose name is withheld
[1]**composed the type:** set a piece of writing into type

Young Franklin as an Apprentice in James' Printshop. Corbis Bettmann

My brother's friends were impressed, but he was not pleased. He thought, probably with good reason, that I was becoming vain. This may have been one of the reasons we began to quarrel at this time.

He was my brother, but he considered himself my master. I was his apprentice in the printing trade. He expected the same services from me that he would from any other apprentice. I thought some of my assigned chores were demeaning. I expected better treatment from a brother. It did not help that my father generally took my side. My brother had a temper and often beat me. This did not improve my attitude. I longed for some means of shortening my apprenticeship. The opportunity arose in an unexpected way.

---

apprentice (uh PREN tis) a person under legal agreement to work for a specified time under a master craftsperson in return for instruction and, formerly, support

demeaning (dih MEEN ing) lowering in status or character; degrading

The members of the governing assembly took offense at an article which appeared in our paper. I have forgotten what it was about. My brother refused to identify the author. He was imprisoned for a month. I was questioned but let go with a warning. I suppose they thought it was the duty of an apprentice to keep his master's secrets.

Despite our differences, I resented my brother's confinement. I managed the paper in his absence and, on occasion, poked fun at the assembly. My brother approved of this. Others saw me in a different light. They saw me as a young genius flawed by a liking for satire and libel.

My brother was released from prison. The Assembly ordered "that James Franklin should no longer print the paper called the *New England Courant*." My brother and his friends tried to find a way around the order. Some suggested he change the name of the paper. James didn't like that idea. Someone suggested that the paper be printed under the name of Benjamin Franklin. James would still be held accountable if his apprentice was the publisher. So I was released from my apprenticeship. It was a very flimsy scheme. Still, we printed the paper under my name for several months.

Soon my brother and I had another disagreement. Since he had released me from my apprenticeship, I began looking for a new job. Under the circumstances, I suppose I was taking unfair advantage. My guilt was assuaged though when he beat me.

When he realized I was serious, James had me blackballed. No other printing house in Boston would hire me. Leaving town did not seem a bad idea at the time. I was afraid that my association with the paper would soon bring trouble. I did not want to end up in jail as James had. I decided to see New York.

My father joined my brother in opposing my plans. I secretly booked passage on a boat bound for New York and left without saying goodbye. Three days later I landed there. I was a boy of

satire (SA tyr) a literary work in which vices, stupidities, etc. are held up to ridicule and contempt
libel (LY bul) any written statement, not made in the public interest, tending to expose a person to public ridicule
accountable (uh KOUNT uh bul) responsible for
assuaged (uh SWAYJD) calmed
blackballed (BLAK bawld) to exclude from social life, work, etc.

seventeen, with a great deal of optimism and very little money.

I sought a job with old Mr. William Bradford. He had been the first printer in Pennsylvania but now published in New York. He had no openings in his firm. He suggested that I go on to Philadelphia. His son who operated a printing house there had recently lost an apprentice through death. So I set out by boat for Philadelphia.

The boat encountered foul weather, and we tried to land at Long Island. A raging surf made that impossible. So we dropped anchor and swung round towards the shore. Some curious spectators watched from the beach. We shouted to them for assistance, and they called back. But the wind was so high and the surf so loud that we could not understand each other. There were some canoes on the shore. We signaled that they should use them to bring us ashore. They either did not understand or else they thought it was a foolish idea. Soon after, they left.

Night was coming on. We had no choice but to lie at anchor until the wind died. We lay down to get some sleep. That was almost impossible. The spray from the surf washed over the boat and down upon us. We lay soaking wet all night and got very little rest.

The next day was calm and dry. We set out for Amboy. We reached port by nightfall. We had been on the water thirty hours without food.

Once on land, I realized I had a fever. I had read somewhere that cold water was a remedy for that condition. I drank large quantities of it and went to bed early. By morning the fever had left me. I set out on the next leg of my journey by foot. It was a fifty-mile walk to Burlington, New Jersey. In Burlington, I could find boats that would take me to Philadelphia.

As luck would have it, it rained hard all that day. By noon, I was thoroughly soaked and very tired. I stopped at a run down inn where I stayed the night. At this point, I began to wish I had never left home. I was a sad sight. People, seeing my condition, began to question. I could tell from their tone that they thought I was a runaway servant. I feared arrest on that suspicion.

I proceeded on my way the next morning. By evening of that day, I had gotten within eight to ten miles of Burlington. I stopped at an inn owned by a Dr. Brown. He began a conversation with me as I ate. Finding I was well read, he became very sociable and friendly. It was a chance meeting, but we struck up a friendship that lasted until the day he died.

I stayed that night in his inn. The next morning, I reached Burlington. To my dismay, the regularly scheduled boats had just left. The next scheduled departure was Tuesday. This was only Saturday.

I bought some gingerbread from an old woman and asked her advice. She invited me to stay at her house until I could get passage by water. I was sick of traveling by foot and accepted the invitation. Learning I was a printer, she suggested I stay there and start a business. I explained that I did not have the money needed to open my own shop. She was a very good hostess, and I thought I would have a pleasant stay until Tuesday, but it was not to be.

In the evening I took a walk by the river. A boat came by bound for Philadelphia. They agreed to take me on board, and I instantly agreed. As there was no wind, we rowed all the way. By midnight, some of the passengers began to argue that we must have passed the city in the dark. They would row no further. None of us knew where we were. We decided to go ashore. We rowed up a creek and landed near an old fence. It was a cold October night. We used the fence rails to build a fire and stayed where we were until daybreak.

By the light of day, one of the crew recognized the place. We were at Cooper's Creek a little north of Philadelphia. We rowed on and soon saw the outline of the city. We arrived about eight or nine o'clock Sunday morning and landed at the Market Street Wharf.

I have described my journey in some detail. I will do the same when telling of my arrival at that city. You may see the contrast between such unlikely beginnings and my current situation. I was wearing work clothes. My good clothes were being shipped from Boston. I was dirty from the trip. I had no suitcase. Dirty clothes hung from my pockets. I knew no one and nothing about the city. I was exhausted from the rowing and lack of sleep. I was very hungry.

I had only a Dutch dollar and a few coins to my name. The coins I gave to the boatman for my passage. They were reluctant

---

sociable (SOH shuh bul) enjoy the company of others

Benjamin Franklin, after J.S. Duplessis. The Granger Collection to take money since I had rowed. I insisted, not wanting them to think I was poor.

I set out up the street, looking about as I went. Near the markethouse, I stopped at a bakery. Being from Boston, I asked for a biscuit. I was told they were not made in Philadelphia. I then asked for a threepenny loaf and got the same response. I asked for threepenny worth of any bread. The baker gave me three large puffy rolls. I was shocked at their size.

Having no room in my pockets, I set off down the street with a roll under each arm and eating the third. I went up Market Street as far as Fourth. I did not know it at the time, but I passed the home of Mr. Read, whose daughter would become my wife. I made a circle and found myself again at the Market Street Wharf near where I had landed. Being full, I gave two of the rolls to a woman and a child standing waiting for a boat.

I took a drink of water from the river. Thus refreshed, I walked again up the street. There were now many well-dressed people walking about. I followed them into a large meetinghouse and sat down. The room was quiet. Being drowsy, I fell fast asleep. Someone was kind enough to wake me when the meeting broke up. This meetinghouse, then, was the first house I entered or slept in, in Philadelphia.

[*The following excerpt relates events that occurred several years later.*]

About this time, I set a personal goal. I would attain moral perfection. I wished to be without fault. I would conquer temptation. I knew or thought I knew right from wrong. It seemed easy enough to do one and avoid the other. I soon learned such a task was easier said than done.

While concentrating on avoiding one fault, I slipped into another. Habit took over. Desire was stronger than my will. I concluded that good intentions were not enough to prevent slipping.

Bad habits must be broken. Good habits must be acquired and practiced. That was the way to reach perfection. I conceived a plan.

In books about virtue, no two writers seemed to agree on definition. Temperance, for example, some defined as moderation in eating and drinking. Others thought temperance meant moderation in every pleasure and passion. I decided to write my own definitions. I chose thirteen words that identified all the virtues I thought necessary or desirable. I defined each in an aphorism.

The thirteen virtues were: Temperance, Silence, Order, Resolution, Frugality, Industry, Sincerity, Justice, Moderation, Cleanliness, Tranquility, Chastity and Humility. A few examples of the aphorisms are:

Silence: Speak only when you have something to say that may benefit yourself or others.

Industry: Waste no time; always be employed in doing something useful.

Moderation: Avoid extremes; forgive and forget insults.

Cleanliness: Tolerate no uncleanliness in body, clothes, or home.

I wanted to practice all these virtues. I thought the best way to go about it was to master one at a time. I believed that acquiring some would help me in mastering the others. I began with Temperance since a clear head makes it easier to guard against bad habits. I was anxious to gain knowledge while acquiring virtue. We learn from what we hear, not what we say. Therefore, silence would be next. I went on thus, arriving at the order shown above.

I decided to keep a record of my progress. I took a book and allotted one page to each virtue. I drew seven columns on each page, one column for every day of the week. Whenever I fell into a bad habit, I would place a black spot in the appropriate column.

I decided to practice each virtue for one week. Thus, in the first week, I practiced avoiding the least offense against Temperance. I took my chances with the others. If at the end of the week, there were no black spots in the book, I would consider Temperance to be acquired. I would then move on. I hoped that by seeing progress in my record book, I would be encouraged to continue my efforts.

I began my self improvement plan immediately. Surprisingly, I found I had more faults than I had realized. Still, I had the

---

aphorism (AF uh riz um) a short, pointed sentence expressing a truth or precept
frugality (froo GAL uh tee) careful economy; thrift
tranquility (tran KWIL uh tee) calmness, peacefulness
chastity (CHAS tuh tee) decency; modesty
humility (hyoo MIL uh tee) humbleness; the absence of pride

satisfaction of seeing myself improve. I soon needed a new record book. At first I kept diligent records. As the years went by, I became lax in my record keeping. I was too busy to take the time. Eventually, I stopped keeping records altogether. Still, I always carried my little book with me.

Order gave me the most trouble. When I was a journeyman printer, I had time to concentrate on Order. As I rose in the world, I found it became necessary to meet with business associates at their convenience. This necessity made it impossible for me to follow a preplanned schedule. I thought of giving up the attempt to acquire Order. I could live with myself if lack of Order was my only fault. This attitude was similar to that of the fox in the fable. Unable to reach some grapes, he quit trying and comforted himself with the thought that they were probably sour anyway.

The thought occurred to me that I was going to extremes by trying to be perfect. My attempts might really be a form of conceit, which is the opposite of Humility. If others found out, I might look ridiculous. Furthermore, people often hate and envy perfection in others. I convinced myself that a kind person should allow himself a few faults, if only to avoid making his own friends embarrassed by their own failings.

Now that I am old and my memory is bad, I wish I had mastered the virtue of Order. On the whole, though I never came close to achieving perfection, I think I am a better and happier man for the effort.

My descendants should know that I owe my happiness in this my seventy-ninth year to that effort. Temperance has kept me healthy. Through Industry and Frugality, I became knowledgeable and wealthy. Sincerity and Justice have gained me the respect of my countrymen. Lastly, even the imperfect practice of virtue has won me friends. I hope, therefore, that some of my descendants follow my example and reap the benefit.

---

diligent (DIL uh junt) hardworking; done with careful, steady effort
lax (LAKS) not strict or exact; careless; loose
journeyman (JUR nee mun) a worker who had satisfied his apprenticeship
    and thus qualified himself to work at his trade

Poor Richard, 1733.

AN
Almanack

For the Year of Chrift

1733,

Being the Firft after LEAP YEAR:

	Years
And makes fince the Creation	
By the Account of the Eaftern *Greeks*	7241
By the Latih Church, when ☉ ent. ♈	6932
By the Computation of *W. W.*	5742
By the *Roman* Chronology	5682
By the *Jewifh* Rabbies	5494

Wherein is contained

The Lunations, Eclipfes, Judgment of the Weather, Spring Tides, Planets Motions & mutual Afpects, Sun and Moon's Rifing and Setting, Length of Days, Time of High Water, Fairs, Courts, and obfervable Days.

Fitted to the Latitude of Forty Degrees, and a Meridian of Five Hours Weft from *London*, but may without fenfible Error, ferve all the adjacent Places, even from *Newfoundland* to *South-Carolina*.

By *RICHARD SAUNDERS*, Philom.

PHILADELPHIA:
Printed and fold by *B. FRANKLIN*, at the New Printing-Office near the Market.

Poor Richard's Almanack, Title Page, First Edition, 1733. Benjamin Franklin.
The Granger Collection

from
Poor Richard's
Almanack

ADAPTED   *by Benjamin Franklin*

[*The following aphorisms appeared in Franklin's almanac, which he began publishing in 1733.*]

1. The things which hurt, instruct.

2. Early to bed and early to rise, makes a man healthy, wealthy, and wise.

3. The sleeping fox catches no poultry.

4. Beware of little expenses; a small leak will sink a great ship.

5. Fish and visitors stink after three days.

6. A country man between two lawyers is like a fish between two cats.

7. The worst wheel of the cart makes the most noise.

8. Be slow in choosing a friend, slower in changing.

9. At the *working* man's house, hunger looks in, but dares not enter.

10. Sally laughs at everything you say. Why? Because she has fine teeth.

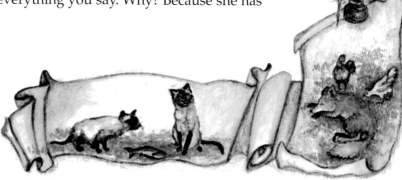

Review the Selection

UNDERSTAND THE SELECTION

Recall

1. Which foods did Franklin not eat?

2. Where did he finally settle after leaving Boston?

3. "Early to bed and early to rise makes a man" what?

Infer

4. In the first excerpt, why did Franklin have extra money to buy books?

5. Why did Franklin seek employment outside of Boston?

6. Why did Franklin leave New York City so quickly?

7. Why do you think ". . . visitors stink after three days"?

Apply

8. How difficult would it be for you to stay on a vegetable diet? Why?

9. Predict what might have happened if Franklin had stayed in Boston.

10. If you were making the trip from Boston to Philadelphia today, how would you travel?

Respond to Literature

How do you think Franklin's works reflect the lifestyle of the colonists?

WRITE ABOUT THE SELECTION

At the conclusion of the first excerpt, Franklin succumbs to the tempting aroma of fish. Suppose he had traveled by land instead of water, and that he stopped at an inn where the cook was roasting a side of fresh beef. Rewrite the conclusion to the selection. Describe in detail how the beef would tempt Franklin and cause him to go off his vegetable diet.

Prewriting   Jot down your ideas of the inn, describing the activity in the kitchen and Franklin's reaction to the aroma of roasting meat. Give several reasons for Franklin's decision to eat meat. (Remember cows do not eat other cows, as fish eat other fish. Thus, you will have to invent another justification for Franklin's decision.) Put your ideas into an informal outline, showing the sequence in which you will write your paper.

Writing   Use your informal outline to write a paragraph or two that will serve as a new conclusion to the selection.

Revising   When you revise your paragraph, be sure the tone is consistent and similar to Franklin's tone. Check to see if you can duplicate Franklin's tongue-in-cheek ending. Try to use humor in your paragraph, as Franklin does, to make the piece more enjoyable for the reader.

Proofreading   Read over your selection. Add quotation marks if you quote your own thoughts as Franklin did.

THINK ABOUT NARRATION

Narration is writing in which events are related in chronological order. It is used in fiction (novels and short stories), poetry (narrative poems), and nonfiction (biography, autobiography, and news stories).

1. What type of nonfiction are Franklin's stories?

2. Do you think a serious sermon on the subject of excusing one's own actions would have been more effective than the humorous ending of "A Vegetable Diet"? Explain your answer.

3. Do you think Franklin's account of his struggle with self-improvement would have been more or less effective if he had been writing of someone else's struggle? Explain your answer.

4. Explain the difference between a short story and an autobiography.

5. Why would a story in Franklin's newspaper be called a narrative?

READING FOCUS

Make Generalizations Write two generalizations about the values of Franklin's time. Then write two generalizations about Franklin's personality. Be sure to support your generalizations with details from the selection.

DEVELOP YOUR VOCABULARY

A **root** is a word or word part that is used to form other words. The addition of various prefixes or suffixes to the root word usually yields a variety of words. The root usually carries the central meaning of the word. For example, the root word *temper* is used to form the word *temperance*. *Temper* means "to regulate or mix properly." *Temperance* means "to regulate or have self-restraint in conduct, expression, or appetite." Many times you can use the root word to help you understand the meaning of a larger word. This is especially true if you know the meanings of various prefixes and suffixes.

Find the root in each of the following words. Use the root to figure out the meaning of each word. Check each meaning in a dictionary. Then write an original sentence for each word.

1. resolution
2. becalmed
3. unprovoked
4. tranquility
5. inclination
6. accountable
7. frugality
8. moderation

POINT OF VIEW

Essayists and storytellers choose a point of view from which to write. **Point of view** is the position from which an author writes.

In nonfiction, three points of view are used. If writers make themselves the speaker, they have used the first-person point of view. You can recognize first person by a writer's use of *I* and *me*.

If the writer addresses the reader directly, the choice is the second-person point of view. You can recognize second person by the use of the pronoun *you*.

If writers position themselves outside the material altogether, they have used the third-person point of view. You can recognize third person by a writer's use of the pronouns *he, she* or *it*.

As you read "What Is an American?" ask yourself:

1. Which point of view did Crèvecoeur use?
2. Would his essay have been as effective if he had chosen a different point of view?

READING FOCUS

Compare and Contrast To compare two things, you look at what they have in common. To contrast two things, you look at ways in which they differ.

You have your own opinions about what it means to be an American. As you read, think about your own views. Compare and contrast them with those of Crèvecoeur.

WRITING CONNECTION

Write three sentences, using first-person point of view, about your participation in an after-school activity. Rewrite the sentences, using third-person point of view.

What Is an American?

ADAPTED   *by Jean de Crèvecoeur*

What is an American, this new man? He is a person from Europe, or the descendant of a person from Europe. I could show you a man descended from an English father and a Dutch mother. This man married a French woman. His four sons married wives from four different nations.

He is an American. He does not share the prejudices and customs of his ancestors. In America, individuals of all nations intermarry and form a new nationality. Their labors and heritage will one day cause great changes in the world. Americans are the western pilgrims. They are carrying with them the arts, sciences, vigor, and industry of all their ancestors.

People with the American spirit were scattered about in the different European countries. Here they are all part of one of the finest systems which has ever appeared.

The American, therefore, should love his country much better than the land in which either he or his ancestors were born. In America, hard work will be quickly rewarded. If he lived in Europe, his children would be hungry. In America, they are well-fed and healthy. They gladly help their father clear those fields where crops will grow. No cruel prince, rich abbot, or mighty lord will demand to share their riches.

The American is a new man. He acts from a belief in new principles. He must therefore listen to new ideas with an open mind and form new opinions. He has left behind him in Europe idleness, dependence, poverty and useless labor. In America, he will be richly rewarded for hard work. This is an American.

---

descendant (dih SEN dunt) a person who is the offspring of a certain ancestor, family, group, etc.

prejudice (PREJ uh dis) a judgment or opinion formed before the facts are known; intolerance or hatred of other races, creeds, etc.

heritage (HER ih tij) something handed down from one's ancestors, such as a characteristic, culture, or tradition

abbot (AB ut) a man who is head of a monastery

Review the Selection

UNDERSTAND THE SELECTION

Recall

1. Where were the colonists from?

2. What will Americans' labors bring?

3. In America, what is quickly rewarded?

Infer

4. What is one European prejudice Americans did not share?

5. Which nations affected our arts and sciences?

6. What was the advantage of being gathered together in one country?

7. Why would the American love this new country so much?

Apply

8. If you lived in the 18th century, which arts and sciences would you have valued most?

9. Predict what would have happened to people with the "American spirit" if they had stayed in Europe.

10. Which new ideas would have appealed to you if you had lived at that time?

Respond to Literature

Do you think Crèvecoeur would have supported the American Revolution? Why or why not?

WRITE ABOUT THE SELECTION

At the time that Crèvecoeur wrote this selection, Americans were primarily of western European descent. Is this still true today? He discusses the opportunities these early immigrants had and indicates that they did not share the prejudices of their ancestors. Has this changed in any way? What are your views on what an American is today? How has the situation changed?

Prewriting Jot down all the details you can think of describing what you think an American is today. Formulate some opinions that you will want to use as main ideas. For each main idea, include details to back up the opinion it expresses. It might help you to refer to the selection for ideas.

Writing Use your notes to write two or three paragraphs that express your opinions of what an American is today. In your paper, explain your views of various nationalities and opportunities and tell whether you think prejudice plays a role in either. You might want to compare or contrast today's situation with the situation that existed in Crèvecoeur's time.

Revising When you revise your paragraph, select specific details or personal experiences that support your ideas.

Proofreading Read over your selection. Be sure you have written complete sentences that include at least one subject and verb.

THINK ABOUT POINT OF VIEW

Point of view is the position writers take in relation to their subject matter. Because their subject matter is often factual, or theoretical, essay writers frequently choose the third person. Some topics, however, lend themselves to the use of the first or second person.

1. Is Crèvecoeur's point of view first, second, or third person?

2. The author never states that he is an American. Would the reader be more or less likely to accept Crèvecoeur's opinions as fact if the essay began, "I am an American..."? Explain your answer.

3. Do you think Crèvecoeur is accurate in his opinions about Americans and Europeans? Explain your answer.

4. At one point in the essay, the author makes a statement about living conditions in Europe. What is Crèvecoeur's opinion of life in Europe?

5. Select one of the author's opinions. Explain why you think it is true or not true today.

READING FOCUS

Compare and Contrast You have explored your own ideas about what it means to be an American and read about Crèvecoeur's ideas. Now write a paragraph in which you compare and contrast your views with those of Crèvecoeur.

DEVELOP YOUR VOCABULARY

Etymology is the study of word origins. Every word has a history. This includes the names of the town, city, and state in which you live. Place names may reflect the ancestry of the original settlers. Dutch colonists named one of their settlements New Amsterdam after the capital of their native country, the Netherlands. When the English drove them out, the name was changed to New York. York is a city in England. This is why there are so many place names in America that include the word "new." How many can you think of?

Use a dictionary or encyclopedia to find the origin of the following place names. List each on a sheet of paper. Write your answer in an original sentence beside the name.

1. New Hampshire   3. Newark
2. Maine   4. Boston

Places may also be named for people, events, geographical features, or other characteristics. Using local sources (if necessary), find the origin of the name of your town or city and the state in which you live.

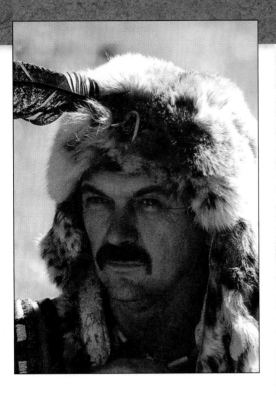

FOLKLORE

People who have no written tradition pass their beliefs on from generation to generation as **folklore**. The materials passed on consist of myths, stories, riddles, proverbs, superstitions, ballads, songs, and customs. Among the stories told are legends and tall tales.

A **legend** is a story of the past. It often tells of an extraordinary happening. The people who tell the legend believe it. The main character may be heroic, with superhuman powers and excellent character. Legends often try to explain some mystery of human life.

A **tall tale** is a form of humor popular in early American history. It is usually set in the narrator's lifetime. For its humor, it relies on exaggeration. Its plot is deliberately outrageous and unbelievable.

As you read the next two selections, ask yourself:
1. Which selection is a legend?
2. Which selection is a tall tale?

Look up the word *hero* in a dictionary. Choose a popular athlete or entertainer. Describe this person in heroic terms. Write your description so that it has the characteristics of either a tall tale or a legend.

READING FOCUS

Recognize Main Idea and Supporting Details The main idea of a story is the most important point—the statement or concept that the writer or storyteller wants you to remember. The writer provides details—descriptions, reasons, and examples—that support that main idea.

As you read "Sunrise in His Pocket" and "Godasiyo, the Woman Chief," think about the main idea of each. How can you summarize each in one sentence? What are some details that support the main idea?

Sunrise in His Pocket

by Davy Crockett

I'm that same Davy Crockett that is fresh from the backwoods. I'm half horse, half alligator—and part snapping turtle, too. I can wade the Mississippi River and leap over the Ohio River. I can ride upon a streak of lightning. Thorns wouldn't dare to scratch me. I can whip my weight in wildcats—and if anyone pleases—I'll wrestle a panther, or hug a bear too close for comfort. Here is what I did on the day the sun froze.

One January morning, it was so cold the trees were too stiff to shake. The very daybreak froze solid just as it was trying to dawn. The tinder-box I used to light my fire wouldn't spark. It would no more catch fire than a raft sunk to the bottom of the sea.

Well, I decided the only way I was going to get some fire was to make it myself. I brought my knuckles together like two thunderclouds, but the sparks froze before I could collect them. So out I walked whistling "Fire in the Mountains!" as I went along in double quick time. Well, after I had walked about twenty miles I came to Daybreak Hill and discovered what was the matter.

The earth had actually frozen fast on her axis. She couldn't turn round. The sun had gotten jammed between cakes of ice under the wheels. The sun had been shining and working to get loose until he froze in his cold sweat.

---

tinderbox (TIN dur BAHKS) formerly, a metal box for holding flint for starting a fire

"C-r-e-a-t-i-o-n!" thought I. "This is the toughest form of suspension. It mustn't be endured. Something must be done or human creation is done for!"

It was so cold that my teeth and tongue were all collapsed together as tight as an oyster. But I took a fresh bear from my back. (I had picked it up along the road.) I beat the animal against the ice until the hot oil began to pour out of it on all sides. I then held the bear over the earth's axis. I squeezed the hot bear oil until I'd thawed the earth loose. Then, I poured about a ton of the hot bear oil over the sun's face.

I gave the earth's cogwheel one kick backward until I got the sun loose. I whistled, "Push along; keep moving!" In about fifteen seconds the earth gave a grunt and began to move.

The sun walked back up into the sky. It saluted me with such gratitude that it made me sneeze. Then I shouldered my bear and saluted back. As I walked home, I introduced people to the fresh daylight with a piece of sunrise in my pocket.

---

suspension (suh SPEN shun) temporary stoppage
cogwheel (KAHG hweel) a wheel with a rim notched into teeth, which
    mesh with those of another wheel to transmit or receive motion

GODASIYO, the Woman Chief

a Seneca legend retold by Dee Brown

At the beginning of time when America was new, a woman chief named Godasiyo ruled over an Indian village beside a large river in the East. In those days all the tribes spoke one language and lived in harmony and peace. Because Godasiyo was a wise and progressive chief, many people came from faraway places to live in her village, and they had no difficulty understanding one another.

At last the village grew so large that half the people lived on the north side of the river and half on the south side. They spent much time canoeing back and forth to visit, attend dances, and exchange gifts of venison, hides, furs, and dried fruits and berries. The tribal council house was on the south side, which made it necessary for those who lived on the north bank to make frequent canoe trips to consult with their chief. Some complained about this, and to make it easier for everybody to cross the rapid stream, Godasiyo ordered a bridge to be built of saplings and tree limbs carefully fastened together. This bridge brought the tribe close together again and the people praised Godasiyo for her wisdom.

Not long after this, a white dog appeared in the village, and Godasiyo claimed it for her own. Everywhere the chief went the dog followed her, and the people on the north side of the river became jealous of the animal. They spread stories that the dog was possessed by an evil spirit that would bring harm to the tribe. One day a delegation from the north bank crossed the bridge to the council house and demanded that Godasiyo kill the white dog. When she refused to do so, the delegates returned to their side of the river, and that night they destroyed the bridge.

L. Knabel

From that time on people on the north bank and those on the south bank began to distrust each other. The tribe divided into two factions, one renouncing Godasiyo as their chief, the other supporting her. Bad feelings between them grew so deep that Godasiyo foresaw that the next step would surely lead to fighting and war. Hoping to avoid bloodshed, she called all members of the tribe who supported her to a meeting in the council house.

"Our people," she said, "are divided by more than a river. No longer is their goodwill and contentment among us. Not wishing to see brother fight against brother, I propose that those who recognize me as their chief follow me westward up the great river to build a new village."

Almost everyone who attended the council meeting agreed to follow Godasiyo westward. In preparation for the migration, they built many canoes of birch bark. Two young men who had been friendly rivals in canoe races volunteered to construct a special watercraft for their chief. With strong poles they fastened two large canoes together and then built a platform which extended over the canoes and the space between them. Upon this platform was a seat for Godasiyo and places to store her clothing, extra leggings, belts, robes, moccasins, mantles, caps, awls, needles, and adornments.

At last everything was ready. Godasiyo took her seat on the platform with the white dog beside her, and the two young men who had built the craft began paddling the double canoes beneath. Behind them the chief's followers and defenders launched their own canoes, which contained all their belongings. This flotilla of canoes covered the shining waters as far as anyone could see up and down the river.

After they had paddled a long distance, they came to a fork in the river. Godasiyo ordered the two young canoeists to stop in the middle of the river until the others caught up with them. In a few minutes the flotilla was divided, half of the canoes on her left, the others on her right.

The chief and the people on each side of her began to discuss the advantages and disadvantages of the two forks in the river. Some wanted to go one way, some preferred the other way. The arguments grew heated with anger. Godasiyo said that she would

---

flotilla (floh TIL uh) a fleet of boats or small ships

take whichever fork her people chose, but they could agree on neither. Finally those on the right turned the prows of their canoes up the right channel, while those on the left began paddling up the left channel. And so the tribe began to separate.

When this movement started, the two young men paddling the two canoes carrying Godasiyo's float disagreed as to which fork they should take, and they fell into a violent quarrel. The canoeist on the right thrust his paddle into the water and started toward the right, and at the same time the one on the left swung his canoe toward the left. Suddenly, Godasiyo's platform slipped off its supports and collapsed into the river, carrying her with it.

Hearing the loud splash, the people on both sides turned their canoes around and tried to rescue their beloved chief. But she and the white dog, the platform, and all her belongings had sunk to the bottom, and the people could see nothing but fish swimming in the clear waters.

Dismayed by this tragic happening, the people of the two divisions began to try to talk to each other, but even though they shouted words back and forth, those on the right could not understand the people on the left, and those on the left could not understand the people on the right. When Godasiyo drowned in the great river her people's language had become changed. This was how it was that the Indians were divided into many tribes spreading across America, each of them speaking a different language.

Dee Brown (1908–)

Dee Brown has spent a lifetime writing about the American West. His popular histories are authentic, and provide a great deal of wisdom regarding human nature.

In the area of nonfiction, he is well known for his book *Bury My Heart at Wounded Knee*. In the book, Brown uses the words of such famous Native Americans as Crazy Horse and Sitting Bull to tell the history of Native Americans between 1860 and 1890. Brown has been one of the few writers to treat westward expansion from the viewpoint of its victims—the Native American tribes.

In his most popular fictional work, *Creek Mary's Blood*, Brown tells the story of five generations of Native Americans. He wrote this story after he found an item about Creek Mary in an old book. She stormed Savannah, Georgia, with a group of male warriors to drive out the British during the Revolutionary War.

Among Brown's other works is a book about trail-driving days and the woman's role in the Old West. His first book, written in 1941, was about Davy Crockett.

Brown was born in a lumber camp in Louisiana. He grew up in Arkansas, where he first became interested in Native American history and the West.

He went to college in Arkansas and later did graduate work at George Washington University in Washington, D.C. Upon graduation, he went to work for the Department of Agriculture as a librarian. In 1948, he became a librarian at the University of Illinois. Being at the university allowed him to do extensive research on his favorite subject—the American West. Because of Brown's many years of careful research and sensitive writing, people are better able to understand the devastating effect westward expansion had on Native Americans.

Review the Selection

UNDERSTAND THE SELECTION

Recall

1. In "Sunrise in His Pocket," what did Crockett use to thaw the earth?

2. How many languages did all the tribes speak during Godasiyo's rule?

3. Why did the tribe on the north bank want Godasiyo to kill the white dog?

Infer

4. Why did Godasiyo refuse to kill the white dog?

5. Why did Godasiyo want to move her supporters?

6. What did the legend of Godasiyo attempt to explain?

7. How did Crockett portray his character in "Sunrise in His Pocket"?

Apply

8. Predict what would happen if the sun actually did freeze.

9. Imagine Davy Crockett telling his story to a live audience. How do you think the audience would react?

10. Predict what would have happened if Godasiyo had killed the white dog.

Respond to Literature

How do heroes in tall tales reflect the spirit of their time?

WRITE ABOUT THE SELECTION

In the tale, "Sunrise in His Pocket," Davy Crockett used his imagination to exaggerate an event that did not and—realistically—could not happen. His audience loved the humor. Assume you are asked to tell a story about "The Day I Met a Creature from Outer Space." Use your imagination to exaggerate and make this experience humorous.

Prewriting Write an informal outline indicating the creature's appearance, how you met, and what occurred. Include any conversation you might have had. You might want to also include information about why the creature came to earth and whether it is friendly or dangerous.

Writing Use your informal outline to write your tall tale. In it, exaggerate various features of the creature and the events that happened during your time together. Try to make the story exciting. If possible, work in some humor.

Revising When you revise, make certain you have what appears to be a logical beginning and ending to your tale. Even though your story is not of a realistic type, it should still develop in a clear, well-organized manner.

Proofreading Read over your story. Be sure you have spelled all the words correctly. Remember, if your creature has a name, it should begin with a capital letter. The same is true for the name of the creature's home planet.

THINK ABOUT FOLKLORE

Folk stories tell about many wonderful characters—talking animals, tricksters, magical beasts, supernatural helpers, ogres, numskulls, and heroes. The legend and the tall tale both tell of heroic persons. All the tales have one thing in common; they come from an oral tradition.

1. Is "Sunrise in His Pocket" a legend or a tall tale? What characteristics in the story tell you which it is?

2. Is "Godasiyo, the Woman Chief" a legend or a tall tale? What characteristics in the story tell you which it is?

3. Compare the heroic qualities of Crockett and Godasiyo.

4. The legend writer is trying to teach a history lesson. How would the use of exaggeration interfere with the writer's purpose?

5. If exaggeration were eliminated from Crockett's story, would it become believable? Why or why not?

READING FOCUS

Recognize Main Idea and Supporting Details Summarize the main idea of each story in one sentence. Then provide at least three details from each story that support the main idea.

DEVELOP YOUR VOCABULARY

There are many ways of using language for humorous effect. In "Sunrise in His Pocket," Davy Crockett used exaggeration as his main tool for humor. The use of exaggeration for literary effect is called **hyperbole**. Some everyday examples of hyperbole, not necessarily humorous, are "as old as the hills" or "my feet are killing me." Neither of these expressions is meant literally, but the pictures they bring to mind are vivid. Think about what people really mean when they use these expressions.

Writers who use hyperbole for humorous effect must make it clear that they do not expect the reader to believe the exaggerations. If they do not make it clear, the statements would be taken seriously and the humor would be lost.

Look through "Sunrise in His Pocket" and choose three examples of hyperbole. List each of your choices and explain what each would mean if taken literally. Then tell why the example succeeds in being funny.

UNIT 1 Review

Write About the Literary Period

Most of the authors in this unit lived during the time of the Revolutionary War. Select one author. Think of the experiences that author may have had during the Revolution. Describe those experiences in a nonfiction literary work—in a speech, letter, or autobiography.

Prewriting Before you begin to write, review your author's selection, noting its tone, theme, and point of view. Freewrite your ideas. As a way to begin, ask yourself what seemed most important to that author. This may help you to determine your theme. Ask what attitude the author might have toward the war. This may help you to determine your tone. Then ask whether you want your author to be a participant or an observer. This will determine your point of view.

Writing Use your freewriting as a basis for your composition. As you begin your writing, remember to make a thesis statement. Develop the arguments for points you wish to make. If you draw a conclusion, be certain it is consistent with your thesis statement.

Revising As you revise, be sure to eliminate anything that interferes with clarity of theme, consistency of tone, or consistency of point of view.

Proofreading Make a final check of your composition. Use a dictionary to check your spelling, if necessary.

Write About Genre

You have studied the organization and types of nonfiction works. You can use your knowledge to analyze one of the nonfiction selections you have read. Choose a nonfiction work that you liked particularly well. You will analyze the work to show the impact it had on you as a reader.

Prewriting Review Focus on Nonfiction on pages 18–19. Then make notes about the beginning, body, and conclusion of the work. Name the theme of the work and look for a thesis statement. If the piece is descriptive, determine its dominant impression. If it is a narrative, try to determine its sense of movement and its meaning. Organize your notes in the way you think they should be presented.

Writing When you write, summarize the points, arguments, or events the author used to support the thesis statement, dominant impression, or sense of movement in the selection. In your conclusion, state whether you think the supporting details were adequate and what the work meant to you.

Revising Check to see if you have put your ideas in a sensible order. Transpose sentences or phrases to a better place if necessary.

Proofreading Check to see if you have used commas correctly.

Vocabulary

A **compound word** is made up of two or more smaller words that are used as a single word. They are written in three different ways. Many compound words are combined and written together as single words. Such words are called **closed compounds**. Examples are *newspaper* and *sunrise*. Other compound verbs are written as separate words, although they have a single meaning. Such words are called **open compounds**. Examples are *hasty pudding* and *frying pan*.

A third way of writing compounds is with a hyphen between the two parts. Such words are called **hyphenated compounds**. Examples are *make-believe* and *flare-up*.

Most of the following words were used in the selections you have just read, but some of them have been written incorrectly here. Look up each compound word in a dictionary. Then write an original sentence, using the correct form of the word in your sentence.

1. back-woods
2. snappingturtle
3. thunder clouds
4. journeyman
5. meeting-house
6. know how
7. watercraft
8. day-break
9. cross-reference
10. wild cat

Grammar, Usage, and Mechanics

Abbreviations may be used for titles such as Dr., Mr., or Ms. when they are used before proper names. Notice that these abbreviations begin with a capital letter and end with a period. Abbreviations should not be used in most writing for the names of cities, states, and countries or for the months and days of the week.

Example **(incorrect):** It was a fifty-mile walk to Burlington, NJ.

Example **(correct):** It was a fifty-mile walk to Burlington, New Jersey.

Copy the following sentences. Correct unacceptable abbreviations. If abbreviations have been used correctly, write "acceptable" after the sentence.

1. His countrymen referred to him as Dr. Franklin to show their respect.

2. Abigail Adams dated her letter November 21, 1800.

3. Mr. President, I would like to address the VA Convention.

4. From Boston, Ben Franklin traveled to NY and Phila.

5. Mrs. Bradstreet wrote poetry on Saturday and attended church on Sun.

SPEAKING AND LISTENING

Someone once said that if you want a good speech, you should make it simple and short. If you want a great speech, you should make it even simpler and shorter! Here's the secret to preparing a successful speech:

- Tell them what you're going to tell them.
- Tell them.
- Tell them what you've told them.

That sounds easy enough. The following suggestions provide specifics on how to deliver an effective speech.

1. The hardest part of any speech is the introduction. If you don't interest your audience in the first few seconds, your speech will probably fail. So, come up with a good introduction. Tell an anecdote about yourself, use a quotation, give a real-life example, or use a comparison. Make it interesting and tantalizing.

2. Don't try to say everything in the body, or main part, of your speech. Stick to one big topic. Focus your topic and organize your material. If you are giving an oral book report, tell the audience about the plot in its natural time sequence.

3. Once you've given the body of your speech, start to wrap it up. Don't drag on with extra ideas or thoughts that you don't have time to develop. Provide an interesting ending that your audience will remember. You could end with a quotation from the selection you're talking about, or simply end with a statement that gives your audience something to think about.

4. To prepare to give your speech, you'll want to follow a few simple procedures.

   - Recite the speech aloud to yourself. Use notes to help you stay on the topic.
   - Deliver the speech in front of a mirror. Notice your gestures.
   - Deliver the speech to a friend. Ask for constructive criticism and practice eye contact.
   - Practice before a small group of friends to help you get over being nervous.

Now, choose a story from this unit and give an oral report on it. Since the stories are relatively short, keep your speech to approximately three minutes. You should need only a little explanation to prepare your audience. Before you give your speech, follow the guidelines above to help you organize what you are going to say.

CRITICAL THINKING

Make Observations   Observation means more than just casually looking at something. It means giving close attention to the details of whatever is under scrutiny.

An observation consists merely of sensory impressions until these impressions are put into words. The observer must note the unique qualities of whatever is being observed. An object, for example, has shape, size, color, and texture. A food also has flavor. A musical instrument makes a sound. Burning leaves create an odor. Close observation makes use of all the five senses—sight, hearing, taste, smell, and touch.

Writers are keen observers. They make readers see a scene, an object, a person, or an event as though the reader were present. They note tiny details and write them so that the images come alive. Several selections in this unit provide good examples of closely observed scenes. Choose one selection that has vivid observations and answer the following questions:

1. Consider the details in the selection. Are they specific? Why do you think the writer included them? To which of the five senses do they appeal?

2. Are any important details missing? What details would you need to get a clearer picture of the event, person, object, or scene?

EFFECTIVE STUDYING

Note Taking   To study well, you must do more than just read. You will remember more if you take notes as you read and study.

Taking notes will help you to distinguish between important and unimportant ideas. Your notes will help you to remember what you read, too, because you will have to think about what to write down. Here is a guide for taking notes effectively.

1. Before reading, look at the headings in the material to be studied. They will give you clues to the organization and purpose of the material.

2. If the material you study is difficult, take notes on one section at a time.

3. In reading, separate important ideas from minor ones. Look for key words and topic sentences in specific paragraphs or passages.

4. Use your own words to record your notes except when exact quotations are needed. If you quote, use quotation marks.

5. Be brief, but avoid abbreviations that might be confusing later.

Test Preparation
You can use your notes to prepare for a test. Your notes will be a handy way to review what you have studied.

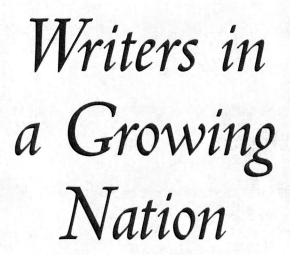

Writers in a Growing Nation

There's a better day a'coming,
Will you go along with me?
There's a better day a'coming,
Go sound the jubilee!
       —Pre-Civil War Spiritual

Allegory of Freedom, c. 1863, Anonymous. The Granger Collection

1820 Washington Irving publishes *Rip Van Winkle*.

1814 Francis Scott Key writes "The Star-Spangled Banner."

1823 James Fenimore Cooper introduces Natty Bumppo in the "Leatherstocking Tales."

1800	1805	1810	1815	1820	1825	1830	1835

1803 Louisiana Purchase doubles the size of U.S.

1801 Thomas Jefferson becomes the third president.

1812 U.S. declares war on England.

1836 Texas secures independence from Mexico.

HISTORICAL HIGHLIGHTS

Writers in a Growing Nation

Have you ever done something so wonderful that you felt you just had to boast about it? That is the way many Americans felt after the Revolutionary War. They had established a new nation, and they wanted to tell each other—and the rest of the world—about it.

Writers in the early 19th century liked to write about the beauties of the American scenery. They wrote optimistically about America's future.

As the Civil War approached, the mood changed. American writers became more concerned with social issues, such as slavery.

■ CHARACTERISTICS OF THE LITERATURE

In the early 19th century, many American writers turned to fiction to express their ideas.

Washington Irving wrote stories about New York's Hudson Valley. In this unit, you will read "The Legend of Sleepy Hollow," a radio adaptation of one of his most famous stories.

America's first important nature poet, William Cullen Bryant, liked to write poems about the countryside. You will enjoy the precise descriptive details and musical quality as you read his lyric poem "To a Waterfowl."

Just as American politicians were trying a new form of government, American writers were experimenting with new forms of literature. Edgar Allan Poe was highly original. If he were writing today, he would be called a horror writer. Many people give Poe credit for inventing the modern short story. In this unit, you will read his suspenseful work "The Tell-Tale Heart." You will also read "Annabel Lee," one of his poems.

James Fenimore Cooper, the first great American novelist, was as good at describing the wilderness as he was at creating characters. His greatest character is Natty Bumppo, a fictional frontiersman, whose

1845 Edgar Allan Poe writes *"The Raven."*

1852 Harriet Beecher Stowe's *Uncle Tom's Cabin* appears in installments.

1868 Louisa May Alcott wins acclaim with *Little Women.*

| 40 | 1845 | 1850 | 1855 | 1860 | 1865 | 1870 | 1875 |

1848 Mexico cedes present-day Arizona, California, Utah, and New Mexico to United States.

1861 Civil War begins at Fort Sumter.

1865 Civil War is officially ended.

1877 Chief Joseph leads the Nez Percé on freedom march.

life and deeds are told in five novels known as the "Leatherstocking Tales." You will meet this adventurer at the end of his life in an excerpt from *The Prairie*, the last of the tales.

■ AFRICAN AMERICAN LITERATURE

In 19th century America, the evil of slavery shamed the land. You will read selections by two freed African American slaves. In *My Bondage and My Freedom*, Frederick Douglass eloquently condemns slavery. Sojourner Truth's defiant work "Ain't I a Woman?" tells what it was like to be a woman and an enslaved person.

Growing opposition to slavery in the mid-19th century was one cause of the Civil War. In "A Night," Louisa May Alcott describes the horrors of the war as she experienced them while working in Union Army hospitals. The selection you will read is taken from her book, *Hospital Sketches*.

■ NATIVE AMERICAN LITERATURE

After the Civil War, America resumed its westward expansion. Treaties guaranteeing Native Americans rights to their land were broken. Many times Native Americans were forcibly relocated to reservations on poor lands.

Chief Joseph of the Nez Percé tribe expresses the Native Americans' point of view in "No More Forever."

In this unit, you will sample the literature of a young and growing America. As you read, ask yourself how the literature reflects the changing times.

Learn About

AUTOBIOGRAPHY

An **autobiography** is the true story of a person's life told by that person. Since autobiography consists of facts about a person's life, it is nonfiction.

A person's life is a story—a true story, of course. Thus, it is told in **narrative** form. That is, it tells about events as they happened, usually in chronological order. Autobiographies are usually long; most make up a whole book. Besides the facts of a person's life, the author usually writes of his or her thoughts, ideas, and inner struggles.

The point of view in an autobiography is the first person. It is the natural point of view of someone telling a personal story.

As you read this selection, ask yourself:
1. What part of his life was Douglass writing about?
2. How would his story have sounded if he had used the third-person point of view? In what way might it have been more effective? In what way might it have been less effective?

Make a list of some events or ideas that you would include in your autobiography. What point of view would you use? Would you write in chronological order?

READING FOCUS

Make Inferences An inference is an understanding based on ideas or things already known. In an autobiography, you can make inferences by thinking about the significance, or importance, of events in the author's life that the author has decided to include. You may also make inferences about the author's character and values. As you read, make inferences based on the actions of the people and the events described in the autobiography.

from

My Bondage and My Freedom

ADAPTED

by Frederick Douglass

For seven years, I lived in Baltimore with Master Hugh's family. During this time my condition was, as weather forecasters like to say, "variable." On a positive note, I learned to read and write. On a negative note, I had to use deceit to attain this knowledge. Privately, this was humiliating to me.

My mistress, out of kindness, had begun teaching me. Her husband, Master Hugh, learned of this, forbade it. Following the letter and spirit of his orders, she stopped teaching me herself and tried to prevent my learning by other means.

In fairness to her, she did not take these steps immediately. She may have thought it unnecessary. Perhaps, she could not bring herself to shut me up in mental darkness. She needed time to harden herself to the role of slaveholder. She had to learn to ignore my humanity, to treat me as property that had no moral or intellectual worth. As I have said, my mistress, Mrs. Auld, was a kind and tender-hearted woman. When I first went to live with her, she tried her best to treat me as one human being ought to treat another.

It is easy to see that some experience is helpful in carrying out a slaveholder's duties. Nature has done almost nothing to prepare men or women to be slave or master. Only rigid training can make a person one or the other. It is hard to forget the love of freedom. It is no easier to lose respect for another's love of freedom. To her credit, Mrs. Auld was ill prepared to play the part of slaveholder. It is an unnatural position. She was more unequal to its demands than anyone I have ever met.

When she looked at me, she did not see chattel. She saw the curly-haired boy who stood by her side or sat on her lap.

---

variable (VAIR ee ih bul) likely to change
humiliating (hyoo MIL ee ayt ing) lowering of pride or dignity
tender-hearted (TEN dur hahrt id) easily moved to pity; sympathetic
chattel (CHAT ul) a movable article of personal property; owned property

View of Baltimore, Maryland, 1839. The Granger Collection

She saw her son Tommy's friend. I was more than property. She knew it in her heart.

I could talk and sing. I could laugh and weep. I could remember, and I could reason. I could love and hate. I was human. She, dear lady, in her mind and her heart, knew all this. How could she bring herself to treat me as a brute? Her every inclination opposed it.

The will and power of her husband said she must. He won the battle. Her noble intentions were defeated, but he did not escape the consequences.

When I entered their house, it was a happy home. She was a model of affection and concern. She was pious and upright. It was impossible to meet her without thinking, "This woman is a Christian." The sight of the least sorrow or suffering brought a tear to her eye. Innocent joy brought an immediate smile to her face. She gave bread to the hungry and clothes to the naked. She comforted every mourner within her reach.

Slavery stole those qualities from her. Domestic happiness left with them. Conscience is like a foundation. When the foundation is damaged, the building cannot be repaired. The house may collapse

---

inclination (in kluh NAY shun) a bent of mind; tendency

on the slave Monday. It will fall about master's head on Tuesday. Conscience must stand entire, or it does not stand at all. If I suffered, the family suffered.

Master Hugh had begun a chain of events. He had violated nature and conscience. He had arrested the kindness that would have enlightened my young mind. When she stopped teaching me, she had to justify her actions to herself. Having taken his side in the debate, she had to reject all her former kindness.

One needs very little knowledge of moral philosophy to see what happened. She became more violently opposed to my learning to read than her husband was. It was not enough to follow his orders. She resolved to go one step further. She became infuriated at the sight of me reading a book or a newspaper. She would rush at me in a rage and snatch the book or paper from my hands. She acted like a traitor might, if caught in the company of a dangerous spy.

Mrs. Auld was an intelligent woman. Her husband's advice and her own experience soon demonstrated to her satisfaction that education and slavery are incompatible with each other. Having convinced herself of this, she watched my every move. If I remained in a room by myself for any length of time, I was suspected of reading a book. I was at once called upon to explain my absence.

All this was entirely too late. The damage had been done. In teaching me the alphabet, in treating me with the kindness accorded another human, she had given me the inch. Nothing could prevent me from taking the yard.

I had determined that I would learn to read at any cost. I found the ways to achieve that end. The strategy I hit upon, and it was a very successful one, was to use my young white playmates as teachers.

I carried constantly a copy of Webster's spelling book in my pocket. On errands or at play, I would take my young friends aside for a lesson. I generally paid my tuition with bread which I always carried in my pocket. For a single biscuit, any of my hungry little comrades would give me a lesson more valuable than bread.

Not everyone demanded payment. There were those who took pleasure in teaching me whenever the opportunity arose. I am strongly tempted to give the names of two or three of those boys to show my affection and gratitude to them. Prudence tells me that is not a good idea. It cannot harm me, but it might embarrass them. I remember what happened to my mistress. It is an unpardonable offense to do anything, directly or indirectly to promote a slave's freedom in a slave state. It is enough to say that my warm-hearted playmates lived on Philpot Street near Durgin & Bailey's Shipyard.

---

enlightened (en LYT und) to have given the light of knowledge to
moral philosophy (MAWR ul fuh LOS uh fee) ethics; standards of
  conduct and moral judgment
incompatible (in kum PAT uh bul) not in agreement
prudence (PROOD uns) the quality of being cautious or discreet in conduct
warm-hearted (WAWRM hahrt id) kind, sympathetic

Slavery was a delicate subject in Maryland. Grownups talked about it cautiously. Nevertheless, I talked about it freely with the white boys. Sitting on a curbstone or a cellar door, I would say, "I wish I could be free, as you will be when you are men. You will be free, you know, when you are twenty-one. You can go where you like, but I am a slave for life. Have I not as good a right as you to be free?"

Words like this always troubled them. It was very satisfying to me when, occasionally, the boys would bitterly condemn slavery. I could tell this was their true feeling, not the message society had taught them. Conscience is purest when it has not been compromised by the daily struggle for survival. While I was in slavery, I never met a boy who approved of the slave system. Often they would console me, wishing that somehow I would be freed. Over and over, they would say that they believed I had as much right as they did to be free. They would say that God never made anyone to be a slave. The reader can easily see that these conversations did nothing to weaken my love of liberty. They only increased my discontent at being a slave.

I read as much as I could, especially anything about the free states. By the time I was thirteen, the thought that I would be a slave for life had become intolerable. I saw no end to my bondage. I cannot tell you how much the terrible reality of my condition depressed me.

For better or worse, I had by this time made enough money to buy what was then a very popular schoolbook, the "Columbian Orator." I bought this book from Mr. Knight, on Thames Street, Fels Point, Baltimore. It cost me fifty cents. I first learned of this book from hearing some white boys discuss it. They were learning selections from it to recite at the Exhibition. The book was, indeed, fascinating. For a time, I spent every spare minute reading it.

There were many speeches about the principles of liberty in the book. Their content poured floods of light on the evil nature and character of slavery. As I read, I suddenly understood why Master Hugh was so intensely opposed to my education. I was no longer the light-hearted, happy-go-lucky boy who had arrived in Baltimore. Knowledge had opened my eyes. Before me, I saw a horrible pit and a frightful dragon waiting to pounce upon me. I saw no way to escape.

In those days, I often wished that I was a beast or a bird—anything but a slave. I cannot begin to describe my gloom and despair. I was too thoughtful to be happy. This constant thinking distressed and tormented me, but I could not get the thoughts out of my mind. Every waking moment brought a reminder.

---

curbstone (KURB stohn) stone or concrete edging of a sidewalk
compromised (KOM pruh myzd) to give up one's ideals for short-term convenient reasons
intolerable (in TOL ur uh bul) unbearable
light-hearted (LYT hahrt id) free from care

A House Slave and His Mistress at Baltimore, 1861.
The Granger Collection

understand my problem, and I was afraid to tell her. If I could have told her the reason for my depression, it might have been better for both of us. Her abuse was useless. Blows only made the wish for liberty stronger. Nature had made us friends; slavery had made us enemies.

My interests were in direct opposition to hers, and we both had our private thoughts and plans. Her goal was to keep me ignorant. I was determined to learn despite the fact that the more I learned the more unhappy I became.

My feelings would have been the same if I had been treated kindly. I could no longer accept being a slave under any conditions. It was slavery—not its incidental abuses that I hated.

I had been cheated out of my birthright. Feeding and clothing me well could not atone for stealing my liberty from me. The smiles of my mistress could not remove the sorrow in my heart. In time, they only came to deepen my sorrow. She had changed. The reader can see that I had changed too.

She, the mistress, and I, the slave, were both victims of the same overshadowing evil—slavery. I will not censure her harshly. She cannot censure me because she knows I speak the truth. I have acted from opposition to slavery. She herself would have done the same if our circumstances had been reversed.

There was no turning back. Liberty was the birthright of every man. Every object I saw and every sound reminded me of this. I was constantly tormented by the realization of my condition. The more beautiful my surroundings, the more desolate my condition seemed. I did not exaggerate when I say that reminders looked down from every star, smiled at me from every ray of sunlight, breathed in every wind and moved in every storm.

It may be that my changed attitude was in part responsible for the change in my mistress. I can easily believe that my downcast, discontented look was very offensive to her. Poor lady! She did not

---

birthright (BURTH ryt) the rights that a person has because he/she was born
   in a certain family, nation, etc.
downcast (DOUN kast) sad
incidental (in suh DENT ul) casual; secondary
overshadowing (oh vur SHAD oh ing) hanging or looming over
censure (SEN shur) blame

Review the Selection

UNDERSTAND THE SELECTION

Recall

1. Who began teaching Douglass?

2. Where was Douglass enslaved as a young child?

3. In what book did Douglass find writings about the principles of freedom?

Infer

4. Why did Douglass say that Mrs. Auld was ill-prepared to be a slaveholder?

5. Why did Douglass never meet a boy who approved of the slave system?

6. Why was Master Hugh so opposed to Douglass's education?

7. Why were Douglass and Mrs. Auld both victims of slavery?

Apply

8. Why did Mrs. Auld teach Douglass to read?

9. In what way did Master Hugh pay for his victory over his wife's natural kindness?

10. If Douglass had not learned to read, predict what might have happened.

Respond to Literature

What does the popularity of Douglass's writings reveal about the changing attitude toward slavery at the time?

WRITE ABOUT THE SELECTION

Frederick Douglass wrote *My Bondage and My Freedom* after he had run away and escaped slavery. In this selection, you can relate to his situation and suppose how you might have felt if you were a slave. He indicated that had the roles been reversed, Mrs. Auld would have run away from slavery, too.

Assume that Mrs. Auld, the slaveholder, has just learned of Douglass's escape. Keep in mind the type of person he has indicated that she once was and how she had changed. Does she react violently or does she secretly rejoice that he has escaped? What measures, if any, does she take to have him returned? Write a paragraph describing how you think Mrs. Auld would have reacted.

Prewriting   Write an informal outline of what Mrs. Auld might have thought, said, or done. Freewrite comments she might have made.

Writing   Use your informal outline to write a paragraph explaining Mrs. Auld's actions upon her discovery that Douglass was gone. In it, describe whom she might have contacted and what she might have said.

Revising   When you revise your paragraph, add details that illustrate how she felt.

Proofreading   Read over your selection. Be sure all your sentences end with a period, question mark, or exclamation point.

THINK ABOUT AUTOBIOGRAPHY

An **autobiography** is the history of a person's life, written by him- or herself. It is a narrative. A well-written biography tells of the inner struggles of the author, interprets the events in the light of history, and draws thoughtful conclusions about life in general.

1. Why is an autobiography written in narrative form?

2. Do you think Douglass's characterization of Mrs. Auld was accurate? Why or why not?

3. Douglass could not read Mrs. Auld's mind. On what could he judge what she might be thinking?

4. Do you agree that first-person point of view is appropriate for an autobiography? Why or why not?

5. Why do you think learning to read was so important to Douglass?

READING FOCUS

Make Inferences As you read the excerpt from *My Bondage and My Freedom*, you were asked to make inferences about different aspects of the narrative. What inference did you make about how Douglass felt about Mrs. Auld? Tell which details from the autobiography helped you to make this inference.

DEVELOP YOUR VOCABULARY

Nouns can be classified in various ways. One useful distinction is between concrete and abstract nouns. **Concrete nouns** name things that exist in the physical world. The things they name can be felt, seen, heard, smelled, or tasted. Examples are *wind*, *mountain*, *horn*, *perfume*, *soup*. **Abstract nouns** name ideas, qualities, or characteristics that do not exist physically and cannot be recognized by the senses. Examples are *liberty*, *beauty*, *kindness*.

Frederick Douglass used many abstract nouns in his autobiography. List the following words from the Douglass selection. Beside each word write whether it is *concrete* or *abstract*.

1. slaveholder
2. humanity
3. freedom
4. conscience
5. newspaper
6. playmate
7. prudence
8. schoolbook
9. slavery
10. joy

Sojourner Truth, 1864. The Granger Collection

READING FOCUS

Understand Persuasive Techniques
Writers sometimes try to persuade readers to agree with their opinions by appealing to the readers' emotions. Persuasive techniques, such as appealing to the readers' emotions, can be very effective. Think about the emotions the author is appealing to as you read.

PERSUASION

Have you ever tried to persuade your parents that you need new, more expensive tennis shoes? Have you ever tried to convince a teacher that you deserve a higher grade? Did you use supporting statements or arguments to back up your appeal? Then you have used a form of discourse called **persuasion**.

The purpose of persuasion is to convince readers or listeners of the truth or falsity of a proposition. A **proposition** is a statement of what is supported or upheld. In your persuasive appeals, the propositions would have been something like: "I need new shoes" or "I should get a better grade." Then you would have given some arguments that your statements were true.

As you read this selection, ask yourself:

1. What proposition is Sojourner Truth trying to uphold?
2. Why do you think she repeats the question in the title so often? What is the purpose of repetition?

WRITING CONNECTION

Assume that you are running for the office of class president. Write a paragraph showing that you are the best person for the job. Include facts to support your propositions.

AIN'T I A WOMAN?

ADAPTED   *by Sojourner Truth*

Well, Children, where there is so much racket there must be something out of kilter. I think that between the Negroes of the South and the women at the North, all talking about rights, the white men will be in a fix pretty soon. But what's all this here talking about?

That man over there says that women need to be helped into carriages, and lifted over ditches, and to have the best place everywhere. Nobody ever helps me into carriages, or over mud puddles, or gives me any best place! And ain't I a woman? Look at me! Look at my arm! I have ploughed and planted. I have gathered into barns, and no man could head me! And ain't I a woman? I could work as much and eat as much as a man—when I could get it—and bear the lash as well! And ain't I a woman? I have borne 13 children, and seen them most all sold off into slavery. When I cried out with a mother's grief, none but Jesus heard! And ain't I a woman?

Then they talk about this thing in the head; what's this they call it? ["Intellect," someone whispers.] That's it, honey. What's that got to do with women's rights or Negro's rights? If my cup won't hold but a pint, and yours holds a quart, wouldn't you be mean not to let me have my little half-measure full?

Then that little man in black there, he says women can't have as much rights as men, 'cause Christ wasn't a woman! Where did your Christ come from? Where did your Christ come from? From God and a woman! Man had nothing to do with Him.

If the first woman God ever made was strong enough to turn the world upside down all alone, these women together ought to be able to turn it back, and get it right side up again! And now they is asking to do it, the men better let them.

Obliged to you for hearing me, and now old Sojourner ain't got nothing more to say.

---

kilter (KIL tur) good condition; proper order
plough (PLOU) plow; to make furrows in the earth
lash (LASH) whip

Review the Selection

UNDERSTAND THE SELECTION

Recall

1. How many children did Sojourner Truth have?

2. What happened to her children?

3. Who does Truth believe can straighten out the world?

Infer

4. Who is Sojourner Truth?

5. What do you think Truth really means when she asks, "Ain't I a woman?"

6. What group of women does Truth represent in expressing her feelings?

7. Why does she believe she should have as many rights as men?

Apply

8. Assume a loved one is sold into slavery. How would you react?

9. Suppose you live in the nineteenth century. You hear Truth give her speech. How does the audience react?

10. Do you think Truth presented a persuasive argument? Explain.

Respond to Literature

In what way does this selection illustrate the sentiments toward African Americans and women during the nineteenth century?

WRITE ABOUT THE SELECTION

In this selection, Sojourner Truth presents a persuasive argument of human rights for African American women as well as equal rights for all women. Remember that persuasive writing presents personal viewpoints. Write an editorial to Sojourner's oration as if you were a member of the audience when she gave the speech. Which points were most important? How did she impact your own thoughts as a 19th century person?

Prewriting   Decide whether you, as a 19th century person, will agree or disagree with Sojourner Truth. Jot down ideas supporting your position. Include details of why you feel this way.

Writing   Use your notes to write a paragraph in the first-person point of view. Remember that you are supposed to be a person from the 19th century. In your paragraph, make certain that your opinion is clear.

Revising   When you revise your paragraph, be sure to add specific points that support your opinion.

Proofreading   Read over your paragraph and check your punctuation.

THINK ABOUT PERSUASION

Like Patrick Henry's and George Washington's speeches in Unit 1, Sojourner Truth's "Ain't I a Woman?" was originally an oration. An **oration** is a speech that is meant to inspire listeners to take some action. The orator appeals to the listener's intelligence but also to the listener's emotions.

1. What does Sojourner Truth accomplish by the constant repetition of her title question?

2. A rhetorical question is asked for its effect on the audience; it does not require an answer. Find at least one rhetorical question, other than the title question, in Truth's speech.

3. Does Truth's use of *ain't* and other colloquial words and phrases add to or detract from the effect of her speech? Explain your answer.

4. Which argument do you think is Truth's most effective one? Why?

5. Which aspect of Truth's speech made the stronger impression on you—her reasons or her emotional appeal? Explain your answer.

READING FOCUS

Understand Persuasive Techniques
Sojourner Truth made several powerful points to appeal to the audience's emotions. Choose the point you found most compelling and explain why it made an impact on you.

DEVELOP YOUR VOCABULARY

Many words have more than one meaning. When you read these words, it is always important to understand which meaning the author intends. For example, the word *racket* can have several different meanings. In this selection, *racket* means loud, confused talk. What other meanings can it have? If a word appears to be familiar, but the meaning does not make sense in a sentence, look in a dictionary for another meaning that does make sense. By paying close attention to context clues, you will be able to figure out the correct meaning.

Following are common words that have more than one meaning. Read the list, then think of two meanings for each word. Check your meanings in a dictionary. Then, write an original sentence for each meaning of each word. Be sure that your sentences make it clear which of its meanings the word is carrying.

1. racket
2. ball
3. board
4. foot
5. band
6. ring
7. fork
8. address
9. kind
10. strike

The Legend of Sleepy Hollow, Anonymous.
Corbis Bettmann

READING FOCUS

Identify Hyperbole Hyperbole is an exaggerated statement often used to suggest that something is greater than it really is. An example is: "better than Mom's apple pie." Hyperbole is often found in figures of speech that compare two things, such as "my love burns brighter than the stars above."

As you read, look for instances where the author is comparing two things. Then decide if it is an exaggeration, or hyperbole. Ask yourself: Does the exaggeration make the situation humorous? Does it heighten the suspense about what will happen next?

PLOT

Plot is the series of events that make up the story line of a literary work. Conflict and climax are two main elements of plot.

Conflict is a clash between two opposing forces. The clash provides the dramatic action. The opposing forces may be two people—the protagonist, or main character, and an antagonist, or rival character. Sometimes the opposing forces are the main character and nature, or the main character and different impulses in his or her own mind.

The main character's attempts to resolve the conflict advance the plot toward the climax. The **climax** is the decisive turning point in the action. It is the moment when the character begins to resolve the conflict. The climax is followed by the **dénouement**, the final resolution, or outcome.

The next selection, a radio drama, is meant to be heard, not read or seen by the audience. As you read it, ask yourself:

1. Who is the protagonist in the play?
2. Why is a narrator used in the play?

WRITING CONNECTION

Summarize the plot of a movie you have seen recently. Name the protagonist, and explain the conflict and its resolution.

THE LEGEND OF
Sleepy Hollow

a radio play based on the story
by Washington Irving

CHARACTERS

ANNOUNCER
ICHABOD CRANE, *village schoolteacher*
MASTER YOST VAN HUTEN, *pupil*
KATRINA VAN TASSEL, *daughter of a wealthy Dutch farmer*
FROW VAN TASSEL, *Katrina's mother*
MYNHEER VAN TASSEL, *Katrina's father*
BROM VAN BRUNT, *young man*
HANS VAN RIPPER, *farmer*
FROW VAN RIPPER, *his wife*
FARMER VAN TIL, *neighbor*
Two Men, a Woman, several Children, a Minister

MUSIC: *"Memories." Fade in, then out slowly under voice.*
ANNOUNCER: Washington Irving's famous "Legend of Sleepy Hollow" was first read by a delighted public more than 160 years ago. But the church mentioned in the story still stands today as Irving described it, and automobiles rattle over the Headless Horseman's Bridge near Tarrytown, New York.
MUSIC: *An old tune takes us back in time.*
ANNOUNCER (*with lowered voice*): Long ago the valley called Sleepy Hollow was a place bewitched.
SOUND: *Indian war whoops. Fade and hold.*
ANNOUNCER: Some say that the old Indian chiefs held their meetings there, long before the explorer Henry Hudson discovered the spot.

---

fade in (FAYD IN) in radio, to become more distinct

SOUND: *War whoops up briefly and out.*

ANNOUNCER: Some say it was a meeting place of witches . . .

SOUND: *Odd shrieks and laughter. Fade and hold.*

ANNOUNCER: . . . after they were driven out of New England . . . and you can still hear their voices in the air . . . high above the treetops.

SOUND: *Shrieks and laughter up briefly, then fade out.*

VOICES: Graymalkin! Brimstone! Meet me in the forest!

ANNOUNCER: But everyone in Sleepy Hollow agreed on one thing . . . and that was the headless ghost of a Hessian[1] soldier on horseback.

SOUND: *Wind and horse's hoofs. Fade and hold.*

ANNOUNCER: His head had been shot off by a cannonball, and he roamed the valley on windy nights.

SOUND: *Wind and hoofs up briefly. Fade slowly under and out.*

ANNOUNCER: Many worthy citizens had heard the headless horseman, and not a few of them had actually seen him with their own eyes. Of all the legends that hung about—this was the favorite legend of Sleepy Hollow.

MUSIC: *Simple country tune. Up, under, and out.*

ANNOUNCER: The schoolhouse in Sleepy Hollow was ruled over by a man named Ichabod Crane. He was tall and thin, with hands that dangled a mile out of his sleeves, and feet that might have served for shovels. He had huge ears, large glassy-green eyes, and a long nose like a bird's beak. When he walked along on a windy day, one might have taken him for a scarecrow escaped from some cornfield. But inside his own schoolroom, inside the four log walls, he ruled supreme.

SOUND: *Voices of children, up and under. Up briefly between next three speeches.*

VOICE: Sixty seconds make a minute. Sixty minutes make an hour. Twenty-four hours make a day. . . .

VOICE: The state of Connecticut is south of Massachusetts, west of Rhode Island. . . .

VOICE: The fat cat ate the rat. Run, cat, run.

SOUND: *Noise of ruler hitting desk. Children's voices fade out quickly.*

---

fade out (FAYD OUT) in radio, to become less distinct
[1]**Hessians:** German soldiers who fought for the British during the
   Revolutionary War

ICHABOD (*a loud comedy voice that seems to come half through the nose*): Silence, children. I observe that Master Yost Van Huten is more than usually busy with his chalk and writing board. Come forward, Master Yost, and let us all admire your work.

YOST (*unhappily*): Please, teacher, I don't wanna.

ICHABOD: You will bring me your writing board at once, Master Yost. Thank You. . . . Hmmm. . . . What have we here?

SOUND: *Children laughing behind their hands.*

ICHABOD (*with sound of ruler on desk*): You would draw a funny picture of your teacher, would you, Master Yost? Read aloud what you have written.

YOST (*unhappily*): Teacher's mad and I am glad,
              And I know what'll please him . . .

ICHABOD: Go on.

YOST: A bottle of wine to make him shine,
       And Katrina Van Tassel to tease him.

SOUND: *Laughter.*

ICHABOD: I have always carried in mind that wonderful rule: "Spare the rod and spoil the child:" I would not for any reason have Master Yost Van Huten spoiled. You will hold out your hand, Master Yost.

YOST: Aw, I don't wanna!

SOUND: *Ruler on child's hand and child crying out. The ruler fades, but the child continues to cry.*

ICHABOD: I am only doing my duty by your good parents, Master Yost! There! It may hurt now, my gifted young poet, but you will remember it and thank me for it in the longest day you have to live.

MUSIC: *Up to close scene, then under and out.*

ANNOUNCER: Despite his rule in the classroom and his peculiar appearance, Ichabod Crane was thought of as a man of great learning. He would quote whole pages of Cotton Mather's history of witchcraft in New England. He was the singing teacher of Sleepy Hollow, and he led the singing in church every Sunday morning.

These accomplishments put Ichabod ahead of the local country boys in winning the favors of the blooming Katrina Van Tassel, daughter of the wealthiest Dutch farmer in the neighborhood. On afternoons, when his work at the school house was over, he would walk to the Van Tassel farmhouse

(*Fading*) on the bank of the Hudson River in a green and . . .

ICHABOD: And how are you, Miss Katrina? Hmmmm! Always busy spinning, weaving, or baking your delicious little cakes, ahem—such delicious cakes!

KATRINA: It's nice of you to praise 'em, Master Crane. Won't you try some of today's baking? This honey loaf and these doughnuts. And a bit of the new cheese and a glass of father's cider.

ICHABOD (*with mouth too full, smacking lips*): Mmm! Just a bit! Just a little bit! Just a little, little bit! I'm a light eater, Miss Katrina. I take only enough to keep body and soul together!

KATRINA: But you must do more than just taste my honey loaf, Master Crane. And the coffee cake. Here, let me refill your glass, too.

ICHABOD (*speaking with difficulty through a full mouth*): Miss Katrina, your charms have made a deep impression on my heart!

KATRINA (*giggling*): Oh, Master Crane, how do you talk!

ICHABOD: (*mouth full*) Katrina, there is something I must tell you. . . . I'll thank you to pass the peach jam. . . . Something I have long been hoping. . . . Well, just a drop more cider if you insist. . . . Katrina, I love you!

KATRINA: Hist! Here comes Mother! I'll be singing!

ICHABOD: Here's my tuning fork!

SOUND: *Tuning fork sounds "A."*

KATRINA: Do-re- mi. . . . (*Sings scale. Breaks off.*)

MOTHER: (*Fade in*) Good day to you, Master Crane! I see you're giving my girl a lesson.

ICHABOD: Yes, indeed, Frow Van Tassel. Now give me an "A," Miss Katrina.

SOUND: *Tuning fork strikes "A."*

KATRINA: Ahhhh!

ICHABOD (*like a sheep*): Ahhh!

KATRINA (*up one tone*): Ohhh.

ICHABOD (*through his nose*): Ohhh! And now for the hymn for next Sunday.

BOTH: By the still stream we sat and wept,
    While memory still to . . .

MOTHER (*interrupting*): Very nice, I'm sure. . . . Well, I must run along to my farm duties. Geese and ducks are foolish things, but girls can look after themselves. . . . (*Fading*) Do a good lesson, Katrina.

ICHABOD: Miss Katrina, as I was saying . . . (*Singing scale*) do-re-me-fa-sol-la-I Love you-u-u.

KATRINA (*singing scale*): Do-re-mi-fa-sol-la. This is so sudden, Master Crane!

ICHABOD: Your place forever is in my heart. . . . Just how large is this farm, Miss Katrina?

KATRINA: Three hundred acres. Ahhh!

ICHABOD (*proudly*): Three hundred acres! Miss Katrina, I adore you! Tell me you'll be Missus Ichabod Crane!

KATRINA (*shyly*): You must give me time to think it over. I'll give you your answer—

ICHABOD: When?

KATRINA: Next Friday week—at our. . . at my parents' big party! Do—re—mi—fa—sol—la—a—a.

MUSIC: *Up fast, then fade slowly under and out.*

ANNOUNCER: Next Friday week. . . . The days passed slowly for our impatient lover. Already, in his own mind, Ichabod saw himself master of the rich fields, the great barns, fat pigs, snowy geese, whole armies of turkeys! He knew, however, that there was someone else who wanted Katrina's hand in marriage. This was Brom Van Brunt, a husky young farmer who won all the neighborhood races and was the leader of a gang of mischief makers. Brom had bragged that he would "double the schoolteacher up and lay him on a shelf in his own schoolhouse," but Ichabod did not take his words very seriously.

To pass the time until the Van Tassels' party, Ichabod reread Cotton Mather's book on witchcraft from cover to cover. He remained at his desk in the log schoolhouse one evening so late that it was pitch-dark when he at last started homeward. As he walked along through the hollow, his teeth began to chatter, and the ordinary sounds of the night took on ghostly terrors.

MUSIC: *Notes of worry.*

SOUND: *Footsteps on gravel. Crickets. Hold under.*

ICHABOD (*to self*): Ooo . . . what a spooky night. . . . J-j-just the night for the h-h-headless horseman to ride. W-w-what if I should m-m-meet him?

SOUND: *Hoot of owl.*

ICHABOD: It sounds like an owl . . . but it might be a witch. There was old Nance Dinwiddie of Salem and Bess o'Bedlam . . . she that makes cows' milk go sour and puts tar in the baby's hair. O-o-o-h.

SOUND: *Hoot of owl*

ICHABOD: Mercy on us! What a dreadful sound! Some poor homeless ghost, I make no doubt. (*Pleading*) Get back to your grave, do, that's a good ghost!

SOUND: *Hoot of owl at distance.*

ICHABOD: What a black night! Not a single star. Oooooooh! There goes one now . . . shooting across the sky. A falling star means death. Then there was that black cat I met yesterday—that's a sure sign of trouble.

SOUND: *Bullfrogs croaking.*

ICHABOD: Ahhh! Is that a bullfrog or a ghost?

SOUND: *Fade footsteps and crickets.*

MUSIC: *Up over fading sounds.*

ANNOUNCER: Finally came the evening of the big party at Mynheer Van Tassel's. Ichabod wanted to arrive in style at the home of his lady love, so he borrowed an old plow horse called Gunpowder from Hans Van Ripper, the farmer in whose home he was then staying. On this animal he made a curious sight indeed. His legs were so long that his bony knees came up to the top of the saddle, and the motion of his arms was like the flapping of great black wings. Such was the figure that arrived at Mynheer Van Tassel's farmhouse (*Fading*) to find the merrymaking in full swing.

MUSIC: *Fade in dance tune of the period.*

SOUND: *Fade in sounds of country dance and small crowd noise. Sounds and music fade down and hold.*

ICHABOD: Ah, Mynheer Van Tassel, (*Through his nose*) this is a happy event indeed!

VAN TASSEL: Evenin', Ichabod, evenin'! Fall to and help yourself to the food!

ICHABOD: What a feast! What a delightful feast! Apple and pumpkin pies . . . broiled fish and roasted chickens . . . jams made of plums and peaches from *my* own trees . . . ah, I should say *your* own trees, Mynheer Van Tassel!

MUSIC: *Dance tune ending.*

Ichabod Crane and Katrina Van Tassel, George Henry Boughton.
New York Historical Society, New York

VOICES (*calling*): Ichabod, Ichabod Crane! Show us how you dance
   the shakedown!

ICHABOD (*proudly*): If Miss Katrina will be my partner.

KATRINA: Yes, here I am.

MUSIC: *Fast music up, down, and hold.*

SOUND: *Clapping hands and stamping feet to time of music.*

VOICES (*together*): Go to it, Ichabod! Hooray! See the schoolmaster!
   etc.

SOUND: *All sound and music fade to distance.*

ANNOUNCER: But Brom Van Brunt, who also wanted to marry
   Katrina, did not feel so gay as the rest of the party.

SOUND: *All sound and music up again.*

VAN BRUNT (*Over voices, viciously*): You'd think it was Master Grasshopper himself clattering round the floor. He's put together so loose he'll fall apart if he don't watch out!

MAN'S VOICE (*laughing*): Aha, Brom Van Brunt, they make a pretty pair dancing together, eh?

WOMAN'S VOICE (*laughing*): They say the schoolmaster is counting his chickens before they're hatched.

ANOTHER'S MANS VOICE: Look at the schoolmaster eyeing her!

VAN BRUNT (*between teeth*): You wait and see. I'll fix him! I'll fix him!

MUSIC: *Dance ending.*

SOUND: *Clapping and stamping out with music. Hold sound of crowd low.*

VOICES (*together*): Great, Ichabod! Wonderful, Master Crane! *etc.*

VAN TASSEL (*shouting*): Bring in the hot cider. Fall to, neighbors. You've got a cold ride home.

SOUND: *Glasses rattle.*

MAN (*smacking lips*): Ahhhh! This is the stuff to put heart into a man! Eh, Van Til?

VAN TIL: Give me a few mugs of friend Van Tassel's hot cider, and I'll laugh at the headless horseman himself!

ICHABOD (*through his nose, unsteadily*): The headless horseman! (*Lowering voice*) Has he been seen of late?

MAN: Yes, just t'other night old Brower met the horseman. "I hear you don't believe in me," says the ghost. "That I don't," says old Brower. "I think you're a lot of—" But just then the ghost caught him for such a ride as never was. Then with a clap of thunder he turned into a skeleton and flung Brower into the brook. "That'll teach you not to believe in honest ghosts," says he as he disappeared.

VOICES (*together*): I hadn't heard that ! Do you mean . . . *etc.*

ICHABOD (*chattering of teeth*): W-w-what a thing to happen to a body!

VAN BRUNT: Ah, that's nothing! I met the headless horseman myself t'other night coming from Tarrytown. . . .

MAN (*laughing*): Coming back from the Flowing Bowl Tavern you'd see anything!

VAN BRUNT: No, I hadn't been in any tavern. I offered to race the ghost to the inn for a bowl of punch. And I'd have won the race, too, but just as we got to the bridge by the churchyard (*Pause*) he vanished into a ball of fire!

ICHABOD (*low*): A ball of fire! The Sleepy Hollow bridge, you say! And tonight I have to cross it!

VAN BRUNT (*teasing him*): If you get by Major André's[2] hanging tree alive, you mean, Schoolmaster. They say the goings-on around that tree, the moanings and the groanings, are terrible these nights.

VAN TIL: Well, ghosts or no ghosts, I've got to be getting home! I've got a barn full of cows to milk at daybreak.

ALL (*together*): That's right. Me, too. Good-by, neighbor Van Tassel! (*Fade*) Thank you. A fine party, neighbor, *etc.*

VAN TASSEL: Good-by, friends!

FROW VAN TASSEL: And thank you all for coming!

SOUND: *Crowd noises fade out under.*

ICHABOD: I want to speak a word to your lovely daughter before I depart, Van Tassel. You—ah—give in pretty much to her wishes, I take it?

VAN TASSEL (*laughing*): I love that girl even better than my pipe, Schoolmaster, and I've had just one rule bringing her up: Let her have her own way!

ICHABOD: Good! Ah! (*Calling*) Miss Katrina! Miss Katrina! May I speak with you alone?

KATRINA: (*Fade in*) Have you brought your tuning fork, Master Crane? I don't know as we would be able to talk without that! (*Giggles . . . fade out*)

MUSIC: *Up, then under and out.*

ANNOUNCER: What was said at this interview, I wouldn't pretend to say. But something must have gone very wrong, for Ichabod came forth after a while looking like a very sad scarecrow. He went into the barn, kicked poor Gunpowder awake, and set off through the hills. . . . The hour was as gloomy as himself. Driving clouds hid the stars and the moon.

MUSIC: *Notes of worry.*

SOUND: *Crickets. One horse at walk. Crack of whip. Fade crickets and horse and hold.*

---

[2]**Major John André** a British spy who was caught, tried and hanged by the patriots near Tarrytown in 1780

ICHABOD: Get up, you crow's bait! Heaven have mercy on us! What's the matter with this animal?

SOUND: *Horse at walk. Horse stops. Crack of whip.*

ICHABOD: Giddap! Drat you, you one-eyed, knock-kneed, sway-backed nag!

SOUND: *Horse whinnies. Hoofs begin walk, hold briefly, and stop.*

ICHABOD (*in whisper*)**:** It's the hanging tree! It's the tree where they hanged André! Come, come, Gunpowder. If we're to get home before light, we've got to get by this tree somehow. I'll whistle to keep our courage up.

SOUND: *Whistling of "Yankee Doodle." Horse at walk again. Add whistling of "Yankee Doodle" in higher key and out of time with first. Then whistling stops.*

ICHABOD: Oooo . . . even the echo makes fun of me tonight!

SOUND: *Groans.*

ICHABOD: What was that?

VOICE (*ghostly*)**:** Ichabod! Ichabod Crane!

ICHABOD (*in whisper*)**:** W-w-who wants Ichabod C-c-crane?

SOUND: *Weird laughter.*

ICHABOD (*in whisper*)**:** I see it now, waiting beside the road—a man on horseback. Perhaps it's just one of the people going home from the Van Tassels' party. I'll speak to him. (*In a loud, cheerful tone*) Good evening, friend!

SOUND: *Add hoofs of second horse at walk more distant.*

ICHABOD (*afraid*)**:** W-w-who are you? Whoa, Gunpowder!

SOUND: *First horse stops. Second horse approaches.*

ICHABOD: If he's more than a human being, a hymn ought to drive him away. (*Singing through his nose in a shaky voice*) Praise God from whom all blessings flow. . . .

VOICE (*distant*)**:** Raise cod from tombs, small, large, or slow. . . .

ICHABOD: There goes that echo again, making fun of me. Oh, mercy! mercy! He's riding beside me!

SOUND: *As second horse grows louder, first horse begins walking again. Hold both low.*

ICHABOD (*in loud tone*)**:** Friend, since you don't seem any too polite tonight, I'll just take my leave of you. Giddap, Gunpowder!

SOUND: *Horse one, then horse two starts to trot.*

ICHABOD (*sadly*)**:** He's close on my heels! (*Calling*) Very well, friend, I have no mind to be polite myself, so I'll just drop behind, if you don't mind.

Mahantango Valley Farm c. 1860. Anonymous. The Granger Collection

SOUND: *Horse one, then horse two slows to walk.*

ICHABOD: He won't let me lag behind. Well, here comes the moon out from under the cloud. Now I'll get a glimpse of his face! Bless me, he hasn't any head! He's the headless horseman himself! And he's carrying his head in front of him on the saddle! Giddap, Gunpowder!

SOUND: *Horses begin to gallop. Fade into distance.*

ANNOUNCER: Away then they dashed, stones flying at every step. Ichabod's flimsy garments fluttered in the wind as he stretched his long, lean body over the horse's head in the eagerness of his flight.

SOUND: *Two horses at gallop, fade and hold.*

ICHABOD (*gasping*): There's the church bridge ahead, Gunpowder! Ghosts can't stand . . . churches! Just reach the bridge and we'll be safe!

SOUND: *Two horses galloping on dirt road, then on bridge, then on road again. A rooster crows in the distance. Hold horses low.*

ICHABOD: A rooster! Ghosts always vanish when they hear the first crowing! Let's see . . . if he's gone. (*Gasping*) He hasn't vanished! He's right behind me! (*Shouting*) He's going to throw his head at me! (*Screaming*) Ahhhh!

SOUND: *Horses fade quickly following scream to silence. Hold silence five seconds.*

ANNOUNCER: The next morning the old horse was found without his saddle, and with the bridle under his feet, quietly eating the grass at his master's gate. And where was Ichabod Crane? That worried Frow Van Ripper, too (*Fade*) as she said . . .

FROW VAN RIPPER: (*Fade in*) Hans Van Ripper, please to call Master Crane to breakfast. He's late for school now. And breakfast is spoiling. Hurry now!

HANS: Ja, Ja.

SOUND: *Chair scraped wood floor.*

HANS (*surprised*): Why, Frow, look out the window yet. That's Gunpowder. But where is my saddle? And look at that bridle!

SOUND: *Footsteps on wood. Door opens.*

HANS (*calling*): Ichabod Crane, why didn't you put Gunpowder in the barn last night? (*Short pause*) Ichabod, why don't you answer?

FROW VAN RIPPER: But, Hans, has something happened to School-master? Where is he?

MUSIC: *Up and fade out under.*

ANNOUNCER: Over at the schoolhouse the boys and girls gathered at the usual hour. As time went by and Master Crane did not appear, groups formed on the steps and in the yard. Several of the older boys strolled about the banks of the brook, while the younger ones played in the schoolyard. But still no schoolmaster! Later in the day small groups of neighbors gathered (*Fading*) to discuss the strange disappearance.

MAN 1: Ach, the poor schoolmaster. He's a strange one!

MAN 2: Wasn't he now? You should'a seen him doing the shake-down with Miss Katrina. And eat—where does he put it?

VAN TIL: Well, then, he would have to come home by the bridge and the church road. He was on Gunpowder, wasn't he, Hans?

HANS: Ja, neighbor. I lent him my horse and my best saddle to help him win Miss Katrina. (*Laughter from group*) And it looks as if we both lost! (*Laughter up and under*)

MAN 2: Let's walk down to the bridge anyhow. Maybe we can see the horse's hoofprints.

MUSIC: *Up and fade out under.*

ANNOUNCER: And so the neighbors followed slowly after Ichabod's landlord, Hans Van Ripper, as he walked with bent head and searching eyes toward the Sleepy Hollow bridge. Hans noticed that the tracks of the horse's hoofs could be seen clearly in the road, and he knew that meant terrific speed. When he found his best saddle in the mud, he was speechless with anger. (*Fading*) But as the men reached the bridge . . .

MAN 1 (*excited*): Hans! There! On the bank near the water. It's Ichabod's hat!

VAN TIL: And that smashed pumpkin! Where did it come from?

HANS (*shocked*): Ichabod's hat! And so close to the water, too. We must look for his body. . . . (*Voice fading*) He must be buried in the proper way . . .

ANNOUNCER: And so the good neighbors searched the brook, but the body of the schoolmaster was not to be found. When Hans Van Ripper got home, he went to Ichabod's room. His tuning fork, his books, clothes—all were there. As he was a bachelor and had no debts, no one troubled his head any more about him. But as winter approached and the time came for stories by the fireside, the story of Ichabod's disappearance was told again and again. (*Fading*) And the legend grew until one day . . .

MUSIC: *Wedding march up and out under.*

MINISTER: Brom Van Brunt, wilt thou have this woman to be thy wedded wife . . . (*Fading to murmur, then up*) so long as ye both shall live?

VAN BRUNT: I will.

MINISTER: Katrina Van Tassel, wilt thou have this man to be. . . . (*Fading, then up*) I now pronounce that they are husband and wife.

MUSIC: *Wedding march up, fade slowly and out under.*

ANNOUNCER: At the wedding breakfast at the Van Tassel home, the conversation naturally turned to Ichabod (*Fading*) as the guests thought about the past.

SOUND: *Small crowd at breakfast. Fade and hold.*

WOMAN: Have another piece of cake, Hans.

HANS: That I will. Say, wasn't this Ichabod's favorite cake? Wonder what's become of him?

VAN TIL: Why, I saw Ichabod Crane in New York when I was in the city last week.

HANS (*amazed*): No . . .Van Til. You mean our Ichabod? Yi, yi, yi.

VAN TIL: You know, Hans, I've been thinking about that ride of Ichabod's. Seems to me that pumpkin we found beside his hat was more important than we thought. Whenever that story is told with Brom Van Brunt around, he always laughs fit to kill. I'm not sure about this headless horseman. (*Fade*)

SOUND: *Fade crowd noise to silence. Five seconds.*

ANNOUNCER: Although Hans Van Ripper and Farmer Van Til questioned the method of Ichabod's disappearance, a lot of people said for years that the schoolmaster had been the victim of the headless horseman. The bridge became more than ever an object of great wonder. The schoolhouse, which was never used again, was reported as haunted by Ichabod Crane's ghost. And the plowboy swore that on a still summer evening he could hear Ichabod's voice singing a sorrowful hymn among the peaceful groves of Sleepy Hollow.

MUSIC: *Up to end.*

Washington Irving (1783–1859)

Washington Irving has often been called America's first great writer, a title he well deserves. Even people who have not read "Rip Van Winkle" seem to know about the character of the same name, the man who slept for twenty years. Other characters are just as famous. Irving's headless horseman, some say, still rides about Sleepy Hollow on gloomy, gray days. And what would New York City be without the Knicks, or the name "Knickerbocker"? The first Knickerbocker was one "Diedrich Knickerbocker," a name Irving invented for the author of his make-believe *History of New York*.

There is a stereotyped character known as "the typical American author" whose life goes like this. The author is born poor, struggles through early hardships, risks all to be a writer, and finally achieves success. Only the last of these is true for Irving. He was born into a comfortable business family. Instead of going to college, he traveled through Europe. At first his writing was just a hobby, and he always took a relaxed approach to his work. He defined the "happy age" of life as the time when a person can be idle and not feel guilty about it. A very social man, Irving could appreciate a well-set table and a good cigar.

Yet Irving did achieve great success. His easy, effortless style transformed all that it touched. He was equally good at humor (*Knickerbocker's History*) and horror ("The Adventure of the German Student"). In addition to many short stories, he wrote travel books, histories, and biographies. He even wrote a hit play. If Mark Twain was "the Lincoln of our literature," Irving was definitely the Washington. What is unusual about the way Washington Irving got his start as a writer?

Review the Selection

UNDERSTAND THE SELECTION

Recall

1. Who was Ichabod Crane?

2. Who was the daughter of the wealthiest Dutch farmer?

3. What two items did the villagers find on the bank near the water?

Infer

4. Who was pretending to be the headless horseman? Why?

5. What answer did Katrina give Ichabod the night of the party? Explain.

6. Did Brom Van Brunt really see the headless horseman? Explain.

7. How do you think the school children reacted to Ichabod's disappearance?

Apply

8. How does Ichabod's behavior in the scenes with the school children differ from his other behavior?

9. What admirable qualities do you see in either Brom or Ichabod? Explain.

10. Suppose that Ichabod and Katrina did marry. Describe their conversations.

Respond to Literature

Each character in this story has a story of his or her own to tell. Choose a character and explain what happens to him or her after this play ends.

WRITE ABOUT THE SELECTION

At the end of the original story, Irving leaves his readers with the strong impression that Brom Van Brunt was really the one who had scared away Ichabod Crane. Still, there were others who believed the "headless horseman" had gotten him. Where had Ichabod gone? What had happened to him? Your assignment is to solve the mystery of that fateful evening.

Write one or more scenes to this play giving your solution to this mystery. Create new characters, if you wish. Write the dialogue in play form using the selection as a guide.

Prewriting Decide on an outcome for Ichabod. Write an informal outline about what happened to Ichabod and where he could be found after the story ended. In this sequel, add characters that you feel are necessary to your conclusion.

Writing Use your outline as a guide. List your characters. As you write the play, be sure each character speaks in the proper sequence to make your plot have a logical beginning, middle, and conclusion.

Revising When you revise, add details to support your solution to this mystery. Be sure each character has said exactly what you intended. Check to see that the characters do not all sound the same.

Proofreading Be sure your play is written in the correct format. Check to see that you have listed characters and have written dialogue and stage directions correctly. Check your punctuation.

THINK ABOUT PLOT

In designing the plot of a work, an author will try to keep the audience's curiosity alive and build suspense. In a carefully worked-out plot, each event serves as the cause of the next event. Cause-and-effect relationships are especially important in dramas, which have only a short time to set up the action and advance the plot.

1. What is the central conflict in the dramatization of "The Legend of Sleepy Hollow"? What questions come to mind at the beginning of the play?

2. Which character is the protagonist in the play? Which character is the antagonist? How do they relate to one another?

3. At what point in the play does the climax come?

4. What is the purpose of the announcer in this radio drama?

5. What clues do you find in the play to show that Ichabod believes the headless horseman really exists?

READING FOCUS

Identify Hyperbole Choose two instances where the author used hyperbole. Write the phrases. How did Irving's use of hyperbole make the story more interesting to you?

DEVELOP YOUR VOCABULARY

Some words imitate the natural sounds they represent. For example, when you read "clanging bells," the word "clanging" imitates the sound of a bell. The formulation of words in this way is **onomatopoeia** (AHN-uh-MAT-uh-PEE-uh). Onomatopoeia can be a particularly useful tool to the radio dramatist, who must communicate the setting to the listeners through sounds. In this selection, you have seen onomatopoeia used for this purpose.

Following are phrases that were used in this selection. Choose the word in each phrase that illustrates onomatopoeia. Then, use each word to write an original sentence.

1. Indian war whoops
2. odd shrieks
3. smacking lips
4. hoot of owl
5. bullfrogs croaking
6. clapping hands
7. stamping feet
8. chattering teeth
9. crack of whip
10. horse whinnies

NARRATION

Narration, as you have learned, is one of the four forms of discourse. One of its purposes is to describe an event or a series of events.

Ordinarily, narration is an end in itself. Its main purpose is to interest and entertain. This is the case for short stories and novels. However, narration can also be used for other purposes. Sometimes narration is used to explain; that is, its intent is **expository**. It may also be used to present a plea for a change in attitude or to support a particular action. In this case, its purpose is **persuasive**.

The narrative itself, therefore, becomes a means to an end. Like a fable or parable in fiction, a factual narrative can also serve to illustrate a point—to teach a lesson or to seek a change in the attitudes of readers or listeners.

As you read this selection, ask yourself:
1. What is the intent of Chief Joseph's speech?
2. Is his aim well supported by his narrative?

WRITING CONNECTION

Write a narrative paragraph about an injustice that you know about that was done to an individual or a group.

READING FOCUS

Understand Sequence of Events The sequence, or order, of events can be very important to understanding a selection. Often, an event only makes sense if you know what preceded it. As you read "No More Forever," think about the sequence of events and how they are related.

NO MORE FOREVER

by Chief Joseph
(In-mut-too-yah-lat-lat)

ADAPTED

My friends, I have been asked to show you my heart. I am glad to have a chance to do so. I want the white people to understand my people. I believe much trouble and blood would be saved if we opened our hearts more. I will tell you in my way how the Indian sees things. What I have to say will come from my heart, and I will speak with a straight tongue.

My name is In-mut-too-yah-lat-lat (Thunder Traveling over the Mountains). I am chief of a band of Nez Percé (Nose Pierced). I was born in eastern Oregon, 38 winters ago. My father (also called Joseph by white men) was chief before me. He died a few years ago. There was no stain on his hands of the blood of a white man. He left a good name on the earth. He advised me well for my people.

Our fathers gave us many laws, which they had learned from their fathers. These laws were good. They told us to treat all men as they treated us; that we should never be the first to break a bargain; that it was a disgrace to tell a lie; that it was a shame for one man to take from another his wife, or his property without paying for it. We were taught to believe that the Great Spirit sees and hears everything, and that he never forgets. Hereafter, he will give every man a spirit-home according to his deserts: if he has been a good man, he will have a good home; if he has been a bad man, he will have a bad home. This I believe, and all my people believe the same.

We did not know there were other people besides the Indian until about one hundred winters ago, when some men with white faces came to our country. They brought many things with them to trade for furs and skins. These men were French, and they called our people "Nez Percé," because some wore rings in their noses. Although very few of our people wear them now, we are still called by the same name.

The first white men of your people who came to our country were named Lewis and Clark. They also brought many things that our people had never seen.

---

deserts (dih ZURTS) reward or punishment; what is deserved

They talked straight, and our people gave them a great feast, as a proof that their hearts were friendly. These men were very kind. They made presents to our chiefs and our people made presents to them. We had a great many horses, of which we gave them what they needed. They gave us guns and tobacco in return. All the Nez Percé made friends with Lewis and Clark, and agreed to let them pass through their country, and never to make war on white men. This promise the Nez Percé has never broken.

It has always been the pride of the Nez Percé that they were the friends of the white men. But about twenty winters ago, a number of white people came into our country and built houses and made farms. At first our people made no complaint. They thought there was room enough for all to live in peace, and they were learning many things from the white men that seemed to be good. But we soon found that the white men were growing rich very fast, and were greedy to possess everything the Indian had. My father was the first to see through the schemes of the white men. He warned his tribe to be careful about trading with them. He had suspicion of men who seemed so anxious to make money. I was a boy then, but I remember well my father's caution. He had sharper eyes than the rest of our people.

Next there came a white officer (Governor Stevens), who invited all the Nez Percé to a treaty council. He said there were a great many white people in the country, and many more would come. He wanted the land marked out so that the Indians and white men could be separated. If they were to live in peace, that was necessary, he said. The Indians should have a country set apart for them, and in that country they must stay. My father, who represented his band, refused to have anything to do with the council. He wished to be a free man. He claimed that no man owned any part of the earth, and a man could not sell what he did not own.

Governor Stevens urged my father to sign his treaty, but he refused. I will not sign your paper," he said. "You go where you please, so do I. You are not a child. I am no child. I can think for myself. No man can think for me. I have no other home than this. I will not give it up to any man. My people would have no home. Take away your paper. I will not touch it with my hand."

My father left the council. Some of the chiefs of the other bands of the Nez Percé signed the treaty. (The lands of these bands, however, were already inside the newly created reservation assigned to the Nez Percé.) Two-thirds of the Nez Percé did *not* sign. Then Governor Stevens gave them presents of blankets. My father cautioned his people to take no presents. "After a while," he said, "they will claim that you have accepted pay for your country." Since that time four bands of the Nez Percé have received annuities from the United States.

---

annuity (un NOO uh tee) regular payment

Eight years later (1863) was the next treaty council. A chief called Lawyer, because he was a great talker, took the lead in this council. He sold nearly all the Nez Percé country. My father was not there. He said to me: "When you go into council with the white man, always remember your country. Do not give it away. I have taken no pay from the United States. I have never sold our land." In this treaty Lawyer acted without authority from our band. He had no right to sell our Wallowa River country (in Oregon). That had always belonged to my father's own people, and the other bands had never disputed our right to it. No other Indians ever claimed Wallowa.

The United States claimed they had bought all the Nez Percé country outside of Lapwai Reservation (in Idaho) from Lawyer and other chiefs. But we continued to live on this land in peace until eight years ago, when many white men began to come. We warned them against this great wrong, but they would not leave our land. The United States Government again asked for a treaty council. My father had become blind and feeble. He could no longer speak for his people. It was then that I took my father's place as chief. In this council I made my first speech to white men. I said to the agent who held the council:

"I did not want to come to this council, but I came hoping that we could save blood. The white man has no right to come here and take our country. We have never accepted any presents from the government. Neither Lawyer nor any other chief had authority to sell this

Chief Joseph, 1878, Cyrenius Hall. The Granger Collection

land. We will defend this land as long as a drop of Indian blood warms the hearts of our men."

The agent said he had orders, from the Great White Chief at Washington, for us to go upon the Lapwai Reservation. If we obeyed he would help us in many ways. "You *must* move," he said. I answered him, "I will not. I do not need your help. We have plenty, and we are contented and happy if the white man will let us alone.

The reservation is too small for so many people with all their stock. We are free now; we can go where we please. Our fathers were born here. Here they lived, here they died, here are their graves. We will never leave them." The agent went away, and we had peace for a little while.

Soon after this my father sent for me. I saw he was dying. I took his hand in mine. He said, "My son, my body is returning to my mother earth, and my spirit is going very soon to see the Great Spirit Chief. When I am gone, think of your country. You are the chief of these people. They look to you to guide them. Always remember that your father never sold his country. You must stop your ears whenever you are asked to sign a treaty selling your home. A few years more, and white men will be all around you. They have their eyes on this land. My son, never forget my dying words. This country holds your father's body. Never sell the bones of your father and your mother." I pressed my father's hand and told him I would protect his grave with my life. My father smiled and passed away to the spirit-land.

I buried him in that beautiful valley of winding waters. I love that land more than all the rest of the world. A man who would not love his father's grave is worse than a wild animal.

For a short time we lived quietly. But this could not last. White men stole a great many horses from us, and we could not get them back. The white men told lies for each other. They drove off a great many of our cattle. Some white men branded our young cattle so they could claim them. It seemed to me that some of the white men in Wallowa were doing these things on purpose to get up a war. They knew that we were not strong enough to fight them. They forgot that years before, when the white men were few and we were strong, we could have killed them all off. But the Nez Percé wished to live at peace.

Because we did not do so, we have not been to blame. I believe that the old treaty has never been correctly reported. If we ever owned the land we own it still, for we never sold it. Suppose a white man should come to me and say, "Joseph, I like your horses, and I want to buy them." I say to him, "No, my horses suit me, I will not sell them." Then he goes to my neighbor, and says to him, "Joseph has some good horses. I want to buy them, but he refuses to sell." My neighbor answers, "Pay me the money, and I will sell you Joseph's horses." The white man returns to me, and says, "Joseph, I have bought your horses, and you must let me have them." If we sold our lands to the government, this is the way they were bought.

On account of the treaty made by the other bands of the Nez Percé, the white men claimed our lands. We were troubled greatly by white men crowding over the line. Some of these were good men, and we lived on peaceful terms with them, but they were not all good.

---

stock (STOK) farm animals

Nearly every year the agent came over from Lapwai and ordered us on to the reservation. We always replied that we were satisfied to live in Wallowa. We were careful to refuse the presents or annuities which he offered.

Through all the years since the white men came to Wallowa we have been threatened by them. They have given us no rest. We have had a few good friends among white men, and they have always advised my people to bear these threats without fighting. Our young men were quick-tempered, and I have had great trouble in keeping them from doing rash things.

Year after year we have been threatened, but no war was made upon my people until General Howard came two years ago and told us that he was the white war-chief of all that country. He said: "I have a great many soldiers at my back. I am going to bring them up here, and then I will talk to you again. The country belongs to the government, and I intend to make you go upon the reservation."

General Howard sent out runners and called all the Indians in to a grand council. I was in that council. I said to General Howard, "I am ready to talk. I have been in a great many councils, but I am no wiser. We are all sprung from a woman, although we are unlike in many things. We cannot be made over again. You are as you were made, and as you were made you can remain. We are just as we were made, and you cannot change us. Why should children of one mother and one father quarrel—why should one try to cheat the other? I do not believe that the Great Spirit Chief gave one kind of men the right to tell another kind of men what they must do."

General Howard replied. "You deny my authority, do you? You want to dictate to me, do you?"

Then one of my chiefs—Too-hool-hool-suit—rose in the council and said to General Howard, "The Great Spirit Chief made the world as it is, and as he wanted it. He made a part of it for us to live upon. I do not see where you get authority to say that we shall not live where he placed us."

General Howard lost his temper and said, "Shut up! I don't want to hear any more of such talk. The law says you shall go upon the reservation to live, and I want you to do so."

Too-hool-hool-suit answered, "Who are you, that you ask us to talk, and then tell me I shan't talk? Are you the Great Spirit? Did you make the world? Did you make the sun? Did you make the rivers to run for us to drink? Did you make the grass to grow? Did you make all these things, that you talk to us as though we were boys? If you did, then you have the right to talk as you do."

General Howard replied, "You are an impudent fellow, and I will put you in the guardhouse."

The soldiers came forward, seized my friend, and took him to the guardhouse.

---

rash (RASH) reckless; foolhardy
impudent (IM pyoo dunt) rude; insulting

My men whispered among themselves, whether they should let this thing be done. I counseled them to submit. I knew if we resisted that all the white men present, including General Howard, would be killed in a moment, and we would be blamed. While they dragged Too-hool-hool-suit to prison, I arose and said, *"I am going to talk now. I don't care whether you arrest me or not."* I turned to my people and said: "The arrest of Too-hool-hool-suit was wrong, but we will not resent the insult. We were invited to this council to express our hearts, and we have done so." Too-hool-hool-suit was prisoner for five days before he was released.

The council broke up for that day. Next day, General Howard informed me that he would give my people *thirty days* to go back home, collect all their stock, and move onto the reservation. "If you are not there in that time, I shall consider that you want to fight, and will send my soldiers to drive you on."

I said, "War can be avoided, and it ought to be avoided. I want no war. My people have always been the friends of the white man. Why are you in such a hurry? I cannot get ready to move in thirty days. Our stock is scattered, and Snake River is very high. Let us wait until fall, when the river will be low. We want time to hunt up our stock and gather supplies for winter."

General Howard replied, "If you let the time run over one day, the soldiers will be there to drive you on the reservation.

And all your cattle and horses outside of the reservation at that time will fall into the hands of the white men."

I knew I had never sold my country, and that I had no land in Lapwai. But I did not want bloodshed. I did not want my people killed. I did not want anybody killed. I said in my heart that, rather than have war, I would give up my country. I would give up my father's grave. I would give up everything rather than have the blood of white men upon the hands of my people.

General Howard refused to allow me more than thirty days to move my people and their stock. I am sure that he began to prepare for war at once.

When I returned to Wallowa, I found my people very much excited. The soldiers were already in the Wallowa Valley. We held a council, and decided to move immediately, to avoid bloodshed.

Too-hool-hool-suit, who felt outraged by his imprisonment, talked for war. He made many of my young men willing to fight rather than be driven like dogs from the land where they were born. It required a strong heart to stand up against such talk, but I urged my people to be quiet, and not to begin a war.

We gathered all the stock we could find, and made an attempt to move. We left many of our horses and cattle in Wallowa, and we lost several hundred in crossing the river. All of my people succeeded in getting across in safety. Many of the Nez Percé came together in Rocky Canyon to hold a grand council.

---

outraged (OUT rayjd) insulted; made very angry

I went with all my people. This council lasted ten days. There was a great deal of war talk, and a great deal of excitement. There was one young brave present whose father had been killed by a white man five years before. This man's blood was bad against white men, and he left the council calling for revenge.

Again I counseled peace, and I thought the danger was past. We had not complied with General Howard's order because we could not, but we intended to do so as soon as possible. I was leaving the council to kill beef for my family, when news came that the young man whose father had been killed had gone out with several other hot-blooded young braves and killed four white men. He rode up to the council and shouted, "Why do you sit here? The war has begun already!"

I heard then that Too-hool-hool-suit had succeeded in organizing a war party. I knew that their acts would involve all my people. I saw that the war could not then be prevented. That time had passed.

I had counseled peace from the beginning. I knew that we were too weak to fight the United States. I admit that my young men did a great wrong, but I ask, who was first to blame? They had been insulted a thousand times. Their fathers and brothers had been killed. They had been told by General Howard that all the horses and cattle they had been unable to drive out of Wallowa were to fall into the hands of white men. And, added to this, they were homeless and desperate.

I would have given my own life if I could have undone the killing of white men by my people. I blame my young men and I blame the white men. I blame General Howard for not giving my people time to get their stock away from Wallowa. I do not acknowledge that he had the right to order me to leave Wallowa at any time. I deny that either my father or myself ever sold that land. It is still our land. It may never again be our home, but my father sleeps there, and I love it as I love my mother. I left there, hoping to avoid bloodshed.

I would have taken my people to the buffalo country (Montana) without fighting, if possible. I could see no other way to avoid a war. We moved over to Whitebird Creek, sixteen miles away, intending to collect our stock before leaving. But the soldiers attacked us, and the first battle was fought. We numbered in that battle sixty-six men, and the soldiers one hundred. The fight lasted but a few minutes, when the soldiers retreated before us for twelve miles. They lost thirty-three killed, and had seven wounded.

Seven days after the first battle, General Howard arrived, bringing more soldiers. It was now war in earnest. We crossed over Salmon River, hoping General Howard would follow. We were not disappointed. We got back between him and his supplies. The battle lasted all day, and was renewed next morning. We killed four and wounded seven or eight.

Five days later General Howard attacked us with 350 soldiers and settlers. We had 250 warriors. The fight lasted twenty-seven hours. We lost four killed and several wounded. General Howard's loss was twenty-nine men killed and sixty wounded.

Trail of Tears, Robert Lindneux. Corbis Bettmann

The following day the soldiers charged upon us, and we retreated with our families and stock a few miles, leaving eighty lodges to fall into General Howard's hands.

Finding that we were outnumbered, we retreated to Bitterroot Valley. Here another body of soldiers and settlers came upon us and demanded our surrender. We refused. They said, "You cannot get by our fort (later called 'Fort Fizzle')." We answered, "We are going by it without fighting if you will let us, but we are going by anyhow." We then made a treaty with these settlers. We agreed not to molest anyone, and they agreed that we might pass through the Bitterroot country in peace. We bought provisions and traded stock with white men there.

We understood that there was to be no more war. We intended to go peaceably to the buffalo country, and leave the question of returning to our country to be settled afterward.

With this understanding we traveled on for four days. Thinking that the trouble was all over, we stopped and prepared tentpoles to take with us. We started again, and at the end of two days we saw three white men passing our camp. Thinking that peace had been made, we did not molest them. We could have killed or taken them prisoners, but we did not suspect them of being spies, which they were.

That night the soldiers surrounded our camp (near Big Hole, Montana). About daybreak one of my men went out to look after his horses. The soldiers saw him and

---

molest (muh LEST) bother; annoy

shot him down like a coyote. I have since learned that these soldiers were not those we had left behind. They had come upon us from another direction. The new white war-chief's name was Gibbon. He charged upon us while some of my people were still asleep. We had a hard fight. Some of my men crept around and attacked the soldiers from the rear. In this battle we lost nearly all our lodges, but we finally drove General Gibbon back. In the fight we lost fifty women and children and thirty fighting men. We remained long enough to bury our dead. The Nez Percé never make war on women and children. We could have killed a great many women and children while the war lasted, but we would feel ashamed to do so cowardly an act.

We retreated as rapidly as we could toward the buffalo country. After six days General Howard came close to us, and we went out and attacked him. We captured nearly all his horses and mules (about 250 head). We then marched on to the Yellowstone Basin (Wyoming).

On the way we captured one white man and two white women. We released them at the end of three days. They were treated kindly. The women were not insulted. Can the white soldiers tell me of one time when Indian women were taken prisoners, and held three days and then released without being insulted? Were the Nez Percé women who fell into the hands of General Howard's soldiers treated with as much respect? I deny that a Nez Percé was ever guilty of such a crime.

Nine days' march brought us to the mouth of Clark Fork of the Yellowstone. We did not know what had become of General Howard, but we supposed that he had sent for more horses and mules. He did not come up, but another new war-chief (General Sturgis) attacked us. We held him in check while we moved all our women and children and stock out of danger, leaving a few men to cover our retreat.

Several days passed, and we heard nothing of General Howard, or Gibbon, or Sturgis. We had repulsed each in turn, and began to feel secure, when another army, under General Miles, struck us (near Bearpaw, Montana). This was the fourth army, each of which outnumbered our fighting force, that we had encountered within sixty days.

We had no knowledge of General Miles's army until a short time before he made a charge upon us. He cut our camp in two, capturing nearly all of our horses. About seventy men, myself among them, were cut off. My little daughter, twelve years of age, was with me. I gave her a rope, and told her to catch a horse and join the others who were cut off from the camp. I have not seen her since, but I have learned that she is alive and well.

I thought of my wife and children, who were now surrounded by soldiers. I resolved to go to them or die. With a prayer in my mouth, I dashed unarmed through the line of soldiers. It seemed to me that there were guns on every side,

---

repulsed (rih PULST) drove back; repelled
resolved (rih ZOLVD) determined; decided

before and behind me. My clothes were cut to pieces and my horse was wounded, but I was not hurt. As I reached the door of my lodge, my wife handed me my rifle, saying: "Here's your gun. Fight!"

The soldiers kept up a continuous fire. Six of my men were killed in one spot near me. We fought at close range, not more than twenty steps apart, and drove the soldiers back, leaving their dead in our hands. We lost, the first day and night, eighteen men and three women. General Miles lost twenty-six killed and forty wounded. The following day General Miles sent a messenger into my camp under protection of a white flag. I sent my friend Yellow Bull to meet him.

Yellow Bull understood the messenger to say that General Miles did not want to kill my people unnecessarily. Yellow Bull understood this to be a demand for me to surrender and save blood. I sent him back with my answer, that I had not made up my mind, but would think about it and send word soon. A little later I walked to General Miles's tent. He met me and we shook hands. He said, "Come, let us sit down by the fire and talk this matter over." I remained with him all night. Next morning Yellow Bull came over to see if I was alive, and why I did not return.

General Miles would not let me leave the tent to see my friend alone.

Yellow Bull said to me, "They have got you in their power, and I am afraid they will never let you go again. I have an officer in our camp, and I will hold him until they let you go free."

I said, "I do not know what they mean to do with me, but if they kill me you must not kill the officer. It will do no good to avenge my death by killing him."

Yellow Bull returned to my camp. I did not make any agreement that day with General Miles. I was very anxious about my people. I knew that we were near Sitting Bull's camp in King George's land (Canada), and I thought maybe the Nez Percé who had escaped would return with assistance. No great damage was done to either party during the night.

On the following morning I returned to my camp by agreement, meeting the officer who had been held prisoner in my camp at the flag of truce. My people were divided about surrendering. We could have escaped from Bearpaw Mountain if we had left our wounded, old women, and children behind. We were unwilling to do this. We had never heard of a wounded Indian recovering while in the hands of white men.

On the evening of the fourth day, General Miles said to me in plain words, "If you will come out and give up your arms, I will spare your lives and send you to your reservation."

I could not bear to see my wounded men and women suffer any longer; we had lost enough already. General Miles had promised that we might return to our own country with what stock we had left. I thought we could start again. I believed General Miles, or *I never would have surrendered*.

On the fifth day I went to General Miles, gave up my gun, and said:

Tell General Howard that I know his heart. What he told me before I have in my heart. I am tired of fighting. Our chiefs are killed. Looking Glass is dead. Too-hool-hool-suit is dead. The old men are all dead. It is the young men who say yes or no. Ollokot is dead. It is cold and we have no blankets. The little children are freezing to death. My people, some of them, have run away to the hills, and have no blankets, no food; no one knows where they are—perhaps freezing to death. I want to have time to look for my children and see how many of them I can find. Maybe I shall find them among the dead. From where the sun now stands I will fight no more forever.

I was told we could go with General Miles to Tongue River and stay there until spring, when we would be sent back to our country. We had nothing to say about it. After our arrival at Tongue River, General Miles received orders to take us to Bismarck (North Dakota). General Miles was opposed to this order. He said, "You must not blame me. I have endeavored to keep my word, but the chief who is over me has given the order. I must obey it or resign. That would do you no good. Some other officer would carry out the order."

I believe General Miles would have kept his word if he could have done so. I do not blame him for what we have suffered since the surrender. I do not know who is to blame.

We were taken to Bismarck. Captain Johnson, who now had charge of us, received an order to take us to Fort Leavenworth (Kansas). At Leavenworth we were placed on a low river bottom, with no water except river water to drink and cook with. We had always lived in a healthy country, where the mountains were high and the water was cold and clear. Many of my people sickened and died, and we buried them in this strange land. I cannot tell how much my heart suffered for my people, while at Leavenworth.

During the hot days (July 1878) we received notice that we were to be moved farther away from our own country. We were not asked if we were willing to go. We were ordered to get into the railroad cars. Three of my people died on the way to Baxter Springs (Kansas). It was worse to die there than to die fighting in the mountains.

We were moved from Baxter Springs to the Indian Territory (Oklahoma). We had but little medicine, and we were nearly all sick. Seventy of my people have died since we moved there.

We have had a great many visitors who have talked many ways. Some of the chiefs (General Fish and Colonel Stickney) from Washington, D.C., came to see us, and selected land for us to live upon. We have not moved to that land, for it is not a good place to live.

The Commissioner Chief (E. A. Hayt) came to see us. I told him, as I told everyone, that I expected General Miles's word would be carried out. He said it could not be done. White men now lived in my country, and all the land was taken up. If I returned to Wallowa, I could not live in peace, and the government could not protect my people. This talk fell like a heavy stone upon my heart. I saw that I could not gain anything by talking to him.

Then the Inspector Chief [General McNiel] came to my camp and we had a long talk. He said I ought to have a home in the mountain country north, and that he would write a letter to the Great Chief at Washington. Again the hope of seeing the mountains of Idaho and Oregon grew up in my heart.

At least I was granted permission to come to Washington, D.C., and bring my friend Yellow Bull with me. I am glad we came. I have shaken hands with a great many friends, but there are some things I want to know which no one seems able to explain. I cannot understand how the government sends a man out to fight us, as it did General Miles, and then breaks his word. Such a government has something wrong about it. I cannot understand why so many chiefs are allowed to talk so many different ways, and promise so many different things. I have seen the Great Father Chief (the President), the next Great Chief (Secretary of the Interior), and many other law chiefs (congressmen). They all say they are my friends, and that I shall have justice. But while their mouths all talk right I do not understand why nothing is done for my people. I have heard talk and talk, but nothing is done.

If the white man wants to live in peace with the Indian, he can live in peace. There need be no trouble. Treat all men alike. Give them all the same law. Give them all an even chance to live and grow. They are all brothers. The earth is the mother of all people, and all people should have equal rights upon it. You might as well expect the rivers to run backward as that any man who was born free should be contented when penned up and denied liberty.

I only ask of the government to be treated as all other men are treated. If I cannot go to my own home, let me have a home in some country were my people will not die so fast. I would like to go to Bitterroot Valley. There my people would be healthy. Where they are now they are dying. Three have died since I left my camp to come to Washington.

We only ask an even chance to live as other men live. We ask to be recognized as men. We ask that the same law shall work alike on all men. If the Indian breaks the law, punish him by the law. If the white man breaks the law, punish him also.

Let me be a free man—free to travel, free to stop, free to work, free to trade where I choose, free to choose my own teachers, free to follow the religion of my fathers, free to think and talk and act for myself—and I will obey every law, or submit to the penalty.

Whenever the white man treats the Indian as they treat each other, then we will have no more wars. We shall all be alike—brothers of one father and one mother, with one sky above us, one country around us, and one government for all. I hope that no more groans of wounded men and women will ever go to the ear of the Great Spirit Chief above, and that all people may be one people.

In-mut-too-yah-lat-lat has spoken for his people.

Chief Joseph (1840–1904)

By the end of the 1870s, nearly all Native Americans in the United States had been forced onto reservations. The famous Sitting Bull had escaped to Canada. The Apache chief Geronimo was in Mexico. Then quite suddenly, in 1877, another great leader—called "Chief Joseph" by the white settlers—gained wide attention.

According to newspaper stories, Chief Joseph was the leader of the "unruly" Nez Percé (NEZ PURS) "troublemakers" in the northwestern United States. The papers claimed that rather than move onto a reservation, Joseph and his people decided to take on the U.S. Army. Retreating over a 1300-mile path through four western states, he fought off attack after attack, in each of which his force was greatly outnumbered. Moreover, all this was done while protecting hundreds of women and children and thousands of horses and cattle. Chief Joseph was not stopped until he was about 30 miles from his goal—Canada and freedom.

Once the Nez Percé War was over, however, quite a different story came out. Chief Joseph's people were not rebels but in the right: they had twice been guaranteed their homeland in the Wallowa Valley of Oregon (in 1855 and 1873). Moreover, Joseph was only one of several Nez Percé chiefs, and because he had always been a man of peace, he had lost much of his influence when the war started. In fact, during the months of the long march, Joseph's job had been to protect the women, children, and elderly, not to engage in combat. Only after the war did he emerge as *the* leader.

His hopes were never fully realized. Not until 1885 was he permitted to return to the Northwest, and then to a reservation in Washington, not to his Oregon homeland. He died on September 21, 1904.

Review the Selection

Recall

1. To which tribe did Chief Joseph belong?

2. Where did Chief Joseph surrender?

3. Who were the first American white men that the Nez Percé ever saw?

Infer

4. Why did Chief Joseph say the government was being unfair?

5. What does Chief Joseph mean by "talking with a straight tongue"?

6. Why did the government not keep its agreement with Chief Joseph?

7. Why did Chief Joseph stop fighting?

Apply

8. If you were an Indian in Chief Joseph's band, would you have favored surrender?

9. What would have happened if Chief Joseph's band continued fighting?

10. Do you think Chief Joseph's father would have been proud of his son?

Respond to Literature

Was the treatment the Native Americans received a good example of the beliefs on which the United States was founded?

WRITE ABOUT THE SELECTION

In this selection, you have read about the plight of Chief Joseph and the Nez Percé. He had always wanted two things: peace and the land that belonged to his people. Chief Joseph surrendered believing that the United States Government had agreed to these wishes and would honor them. The government officials did not keep their word.

Before Chief Joseph surrendered, he had one other option. He could have fled into Canada. Would they have fared better or worse? Assume that he had chosen to lead his people there.

Prewriting Freewrite about what you think would have happened to Chief Joseph's group in Canada. Include details of the attitudes they might have encountered. Speculate about how they would provide food and shelter for themselves and about difficulties they might face. Then organize your notes into a brief outline.

Writing Use your outline to write a paragraph explaining what Chief Joseph's group might have experienced in Canada and how they might have been treated there.

Revising When you revise your paragraph, add details to make your ideas more vivid.

Proofreading Read over your selection and check your spelling.

THINK ABOUT NARRATION

In nonfiction, narration is concerned with personal and historical events. The intention of the narrative, however, may be **expository** (to explain) or **persuasive** (to persuade). In such writing, the narrative serves as a long example to support the point that the author wishes to make.

1. Was Chief Joseph's intention in relating the history of the Nez Percé band expository or persuasive?

2. Does Chief Joseph make a thesis statement in his speech? If so, what is it?

3. Tell where the introduction, body, and conclusion of Chief Joseph's speech occur.

4. How did Chief Joseph establish with the reader or listener that he was honest and that he spoke truthfully?

5. What is the lesson that Chief Joseph's narrative best illustrates?

READING FOCUS

Understand the Sequence of Events List three key events in this selection. Explain the order in which they occur and how they are related to one another.

DEVELOP YOUR VOCABULARY

Words sometimes have several meanings. If you are not sure of the meaning of a word, context clues may help. Look at the words surrounding the unfamiliar word; they may give you a hint of its meaning. Chief Joseph explains, "I am chief of a *band* of Nez Percé." The word *chief* suggests that *band* means "a group."

Read each item below. Use the context to try to figure out the meaning of each italicized word. Check your meaning in a dictionary to see that it is correct. Write an original sentence using each word.

1. The *reservation* is too small for so many people with all their stock.

2. No, my horses *suit* me, I will not sell them.

3. . . . I have had great trouble in keeping them from doing *rash* things.

4. We are all *sprung* from a woman. . . .

5. We held him in *check*, while we moved our women and children. . . .

Learn About

METER

You have learned that all poetry has **rhythm**. It is the natural sense of movement that occurs when successive syllables are stressed or not stressed. It comes from the natural rise and fall of language.

Poets often build into their poems a strong pattern of stressed and unstressed syllables. The rhythmic pattern is so pronounced that the reader may tap a pencil to its beat. Such a pattern is called **meter**. The difference between natural rhythm and meter is that in natural rhythm, the accented syllables are random; in metrical lines of poetry, the accents come at regular intervals. Meter carries a reader along toward a planned conclusion.

The music of poetry can be enhanced by other means, too. The repetition of words and phrases and the use of rhyme add to the flow of sound.

As you read this selection, ask yourself:

1. What kind of meter can I detect in this poem?
2. Does the poet use repetition and rhyme for musical effects?

READING FOCUS

Identify Cause and Effect A cause-and-effect relationship is one in which one event (the cause) is responsible for another event (the effect). An author connects thoughts and actions by showing a cause-and-effect relationship. This helps the reader better understand the reasons why things happen. As you read this poem, note the effects, or what happens. As you reread the poem, look for the causes of each effect you noted.

WRITING CONNECTION

Write down four lines of lyrics from a favorite song. Can you detect a metrical pattern? Write a paragraph about it.

Annabel Lee

by Edgar Allan Poe

It was many and many a year ago,
    In a kingdom by the sea,
That a maiden there lived whom you may know
    By the name of Annabel Lee;
5   And this maiden she lived with no other thought
    Than to love and be loved by me.

I was a child and *she* was a child,
    In this kingdom by the sea,
But we loved with a love that was more than love—
10   I and my Annabel Lee;
With a love that the wingèd seraphs of heaven
    Coveted her and me.

And this was the reason that, long ago,
    In this kingdom by the sea,
15   A wind blew out of a cloud, chilling
    My beautiful Annabel Lee;
So that her high-born kinsman came
    And bore her away from me,
To shut her up in a sepulcher
20   In this kingdom by the sea.

The angels, not half so happy in heaven,
    Went envying her and me—
Yes!—that was the reason (as all men know,
    In this kingdom by the sea)
25   That the wind came out of the cloud by night,
    Chilling and killing my Annabel Lee.

---

seraph (SER uf) kind of heavenly being; winged angel
covet (KUV it) desire what belongs to another
high-born (HY bawrn) of noble birth
sepulcher (SEP ul kur) tomb; burial place

But our love it was stronger by far than the love
    Of those who were older than we—
    Of many far wiser than we—
30   And neither the angels in heaven above
    Nor the demons down under the sea,
Can ever dissever my soul from the soul
    Of the beautiful Annabel Lee,

For the moon never beams, without bringing me dreams
35   Of the beautiful Annabel Lee;
And the stars never rise, but I feel the bright eyes
    Of the beautiful Annabel Lee;
And so, all the night-tide, I lie down by the side
Of my darling—my darling—my life and my bride,
40   In the sepulcher there by the sea,
    In her tomb by the sounding sea.

---

dissever (dih SEV ur) separate
night-tide (NYT tyd) nighttime

Edgar Allan Poe (1809–1849)

For some authors, writing is a carefully studied skill. For others, writing is a refined art. But for a very few, writing seems the outpouring of genius that cannot be contained. Edgar Allan Poe was such an author. His life proves that true talent is a powerful force indeed.

Born in 1809, Edgar Poe never knew his father, an actor who left his family and simply disappeared. Death claimed Poe's mother, an actress, when the boy was two. But luckily, the child was taken in by John Allan, a wealthy tobacco dealer. In 1815 the Allans went to England on business, and for five years Edgar went to a private school there.

Poe's luck, however, was not to continue. He quarreled violently with John Allan. He was forced to leave the University of Virginia because of gambling debts. He joined the army for a time and then drifted here and there, unable to settle down. He got a number of jobs as an editor but lost them because of excessive drinking.

In midlife Poe was taken in by an aunt, Maria Clemm. She gave him the comfort he needed, and he began to write—and sell!—the fantastic stories that made him famous. He married Mrs. Clemm's daughter, Virginia, a girl of 13.

Troubles continued to follow the struggling author. He could not hold a job for long. His stories and poems brought in some money, but never enough for a comfortable life. He, Virginia, and Mrs. Clemm drifted into poverty. Virginia died in 1847. Two years later Poe himself was found near death in Baltimore, Maryland. He died four days later. In your opinion, what were the two worst misfortunes in Poe's unhappy life?

Review the Selection

UNDERSTAND THE SELECTION

Recall

1. Where did Annabel Lee live?

2. Where did her kinsmen bury her?

3. What killed Anabell Lee?

Infer

4. What may have been the real cause of Annabel Lee's death?

5. What made Annabel Lee's death so difficult for the author?

6. Why was it necessary for her kinsmen to take her away to be buried?

7. Do you think the narrator accepted her death after a short period of time?

Apply

8. Suppose that Annabel Lee could speak from the grave. What might she say to the narrator?

9. Assume that you are one of the residents of this kingdom. Would you visit the narrator? Why or why not?

10. Do you think Annabel Lee's family opposed this marriage? Why?

Respond to Literature

Most of the literature of this period had an American setting. What about this selection is typical of the period?

WRITE ABOUT THE SELECTION

In this poem, Annabel Lee and the narrator live "in a kingdom by the sea." That kingdom is never described, but it serves to have a mysterious and fantastic quality about it. Picture the dwelling of Annabel Lee and the narrator. Is it a palace? Is it a humble house, since his social status may be lower than hers? Is it a romantic place with rich furnishings or a hovel where possessions mean nothing? Dream up the fantasy house of Annabel Lee. Think about how it is constructed, how large it is, and what kind of views it has. Think about the mood it creates as well.

Prewriting   Create a web describing the surroundings in which the couple lives. Include details of the rooms and what they contain. Freewrite any conversation you can come up with between Annabel Lee and the narrator. Make some notes about how their house might affect their lives.

Writing   Use your web to write a paragraph describing Annabel Lee's fantasy house.

Revising   When you revise your paragraph, be sure to add details that illustrate the richness or lack of richness in the house and grounds.

Proofreading   Read over your selection. Be sure to check the spelling of any unusual words you might have used.

THINK ABOUT METER

Meter refers to a pattern of stressed and unstressed syllables in poetry. It is distinguished from rhythm by its use of regularly recurring accented and unaccented syllables. Each patterned group of syllables has a name. For example, one unstressed syllable followed by one stressed syllable (as in kon-TROL) is called an **iamb**. Similarly, two unstressed syllables followed by a stressed syllable (as in kontruh-DIKT) is called an **anapest**.

1. Which meter is the basic one in "Annabel Lee"—an iamb or an anapest? Why do you say so?

2. The first two lines of the poem have been likened to the opening of a fairy tale. Do you agree? Why or why not?

3. In line 15, the meter is broken temporarily by the word *chilling*. Why do you think Poe did this?

4. What other "musical" effects did Poe use in the poem?

5. What words and phrases did Poe often repeat in the poem?

READING FOCUS

Identify Cause and Effect "Annabel Lee" describes the death of someone the speaker loved deeply. What two things does the speaker say caused Annabel Lee's death?

DEVELOP YOUR VOCABULARY

An **antonym** is a word that has a meaning opposite or nearly opposite to that of another word. For example, in this selection, Poe refers to "the angels . . . in heaven" and "the demons down under the sea." *Angels* and *demons* are antonyms, or words that are opposite in meaning to each other.

Following are words used in this selection. Read the words, review the meaning of each word whose meaning is not clear to you. Some of the words are not in common use today. Check the poem to help you figure out the meanings of these words.

Select an antonym for each word. Check in a dictionary for the meaning of each antonym you have selected. Double check to be sure it has a meaning opposite to that of the original word. Then, use each antonym to write an original sentence. Be sure that your sentences include context clues to the words' meanings.

1. love
2. beautiful
3. highborn
4. shut
5. chilling
6. wise
7. dissever
8. bright

Suspense is the growing excitement that a reader or listener feels while waiting for the climax or resolution of the events in a work of fiction. There are two kinds of suspense. In one kind, the author leaves the outcome in doubt until the very end so that the audience will wonder *who*, *what*, or *how*. In the other kind, the author lets the audience know about the outcome before the end. The big suspense is then focused on *when*.

Authors have ways of building suspense. They can create an atmosphere that contributes to it and they can **foreshadow** events, that is, they can give tantalizing hints of what may happen in the plot.

Suspense plays a part in all fiction—short stories, novels, and plays. In some works, however, it is the main ingredient.

As you read this selection, ask yourself:

1. Which of the two kinds of suspense does Poe use in this story?
2. What details besides the plot contribute to the suspense?

READING FOCUS

Identify Signal Words Authors use the relationships between events to string together a story in a believable way. They often use signal words to suggest a cause-and-effect relationship or time order. As you read "The Tell-Tale Heart," look for words that signal cause and effect, such as *because*, *so*, and *since*. Also look for and words that signal a time order, such as *first*, *next*, *last*, *finally*, and *soon*.

WRITING CONNECTION

In a paragraph, describe a movie thriller you have seen recently. Explain how the suspense was achieved.

THE TELL-TALE HEART

ADAPTED

by Edgar Allan Poe

True!—nervous—very, very dreadfully nervous I have been and am. But why *will* you say that I am mad? The disease has sharpened my senses—not destroyed—not dulled them. Above all was my sense of hearing acute. I heard all things in the heaven and in the earth. I heard many things in hell. How, then, am I mad? Listen! and observe how clearly—how calmly I can tell you the whole story.

It is impossible to say how the idea first entered my brain. But once conceived, it haunted me day and night. There was no good reason. There was no real hatred. I loved the old man. He had never wronged me. He had never given me insult. For his gold I had no desire. I think it was his eye! Yes, it was this! One of his eyes resembled that of a vulture—a pale blue eye, with a film over it. Whenever it fell upon me, my blood ran cold. And so little by little—very gradually—I made up my mind to take the life of the old man, and thus rid myself of the eye forever.

Now this is the point. You think I am mad. Madmen know nothing. But you should have seen me. You should have seen how wisely I proceeded—with what caution—with what skill—with what secrecy I went to work! I was never kinder to the old man than during the whole week before I killed him. And every night, about midnight, I turned the latch of his door and opened it—oh, so gently! And then, when I had made an opening the size of my head, I put in a dark lantern, all closed up, closed up so that no light shone out, and then I thrust in my head. Oh, you would have laughed to see how cunningly I did it! I moved my head slowly—very, very slowly, so that I might not disturb the old man's sleep. It took me an hour to move my head so far that I could see him as he lay upon his bed. Ha!—would a madman

---

acute (uh KYOOT) sharp, sensitive
conceived (kun SEEVD) thought of; imagined
cunningly (KUN ing lee) slyly

have been so wise as this? And then, when my head was well into the room, I undid the lantern cautiously. Oh, so cautiously—cautiously (for the hinges squeaked) I undid it just so much that a single thin ray of light fell upon the vulture eye.

This I did for seven long nights—every night just at midnight—but I found the eye always closed. And so it was impossible to do the deed. For it was not the old man who vexed me, but his Evil Eye. And every morning, when the day broke, I went boldly into the room, and spoke courageously to him. I called him by name in a cheerful tone, and asked how he had passed the night. So you see he would have been a very profound old man, indeed, to suspect that every night, just at twelve, I looked in upon him while he slept.

Upon the eighth night I was more than usually cautious in opening the door. A watch's minute hand moves more quickly than did mine. Never before that night had I really *felt* just how powerful I was—just how wise. I could hardly contain my feeling of triumph. To think that there I was, opening the door, little by little. And he not even dreaming of my secret purpose or thought! I nearly chuckled at the idea—and perhaps he heard me! For he moved on the bed suddenly, as if startled. Now you may think that I drew back—but no. His room was black as pitch with the thick darkness (the shutters were fastened tight, for fear of robbers). So I knew that he could not see the opening of the door, and I kept pushing it on steadily, steadily.

I had my head in, and was about to open the lantern. All at once my thumb slipped on the tin, and the old man sprang up in the bed, crying out—"Who's there?"

I kept quite still and said nothing. For a whole hour I did not move a muscle. And in the meantime I did not hear him lie down. He was still sitting up in the bed listening—just as I have done, night after night, listening—waiting—for Death.

Then I heard a little groan, and I knew it was the groan of mortal terror. It was not a groan of pain or of grief—oh, no! It was the low stifled sound that comes from the bottom of the soul when overfilled with fear. I knew the sound well. Many a night, just at midnight, when all the world slept, it was sprung up from the bottom of my own soul, deepening, with its dreadful echo, the terrors that held me. I say I knew it well. I knew what the old man felt, and pitied him—although I chuckled at heart. I knew that he had been lying awake ever since the first slight noise, when he had turned in the bed. His fears had ever since been growing on him. He had been trying to ignore them, but could not. He had been saying to himself—"It is nothing but the wind in the chimney," or

---

vexed (VEKST) disturbed; annoyed; irritated
profound (pruh FOUND) wise; intellectually deep
pitch (PICH) a black, sticky substance formed from distilling of tar
mortal (MAWR tul) fatal; causing death
stifled (STY fuld) muffled, smothered

"It is only a mouse crossing the floor." Yes, he had been trying to comfort himself with these lies. But he had found all in vain. *All in vain.* For Death, in approaching him, had walked with his black shadow before him, and surrounded the old man. And it was that unseen shadow that made him feel, yes *feel*, the presence of my head within the room.

By then I had waited a long time, very patiently, without hearing him lie down. I decided to open a little, a very, very little crack in the lantern. So I opened it—you cannot imagine how slowly, slowly.

Suddenly a single dim ray, like the thread of a spider, shot out from the crack and fell upon the vulture eye.

It was open—wide, wide open. I grew furious as I gazed upon it. I saw it clearly, so clearly—all a dull blue, with a hideous film over it. A hideous film that chilled me to the very bones. But I could see nothing else of the old man's face or body; for I had pointed the ray as if by instinct, exactly upon the damned spot.

And now—have I not told you about my most acute senses? Now, I say, there came to my ears a low, dull, quick sound.

---

vain (VAYN) without success; useless
hideous (HID ee us) very ugly or frightening

It was a sound such as a watch makes when enveloped in cotton. I knew *that* sound well too. It was the beating of the old man's heart. It increased my anger, as the beating of a drum increases a soldier's courage.

But even yet I held back, I kept still. I hardly breathed. I held the lantern motionless. I tried to see how steadily I could keep the ray upon the eye. Meantime the hellish drumbeat of the heart increased. It grew quicker and quicker, and louder and louder every instant. The old man's terror *must* have been great! It grew louder, I say, louder every moment! —do you hear me well? I have told you that I am nervous. So I am. And now at the dead hour of the night, in the dreadful silence of that old house, so strange a noise as this excited me to uncontrollable terror. Yet, for some minutes longer I held back and stood still. But the beating grew louder, louder! I thought the heart must burst. And now a new anxiety seized me —the sound would be heard by a neighbor! The old man's hour had come! With a loud yell, I threw open the lantern. I leaped toward him. He shrieked once— once only. In an instant I dragged him to the floor, and pulled the heavy mattress over him. I then smiled, to find the deed so far done. But for many minutes, the heart beat on with a stifled sound. This, however, did not worry me. It would not be heard through the wall. At length it stopped. The old man was dead. I removed the mattress and examined the corpse. Yes, he was stone, stone dead. I placed my hand upon the heart and held it there many minutes. There was no pulse. He was stone dead. His eye would trouble me no more.

If you still think me mad, you will think so no longer when I describe the wise steps I took to hide the body. The night went on, and I worked quickly, but in silence. First of all I cut up the corpse. I took off the head and the arms and the legs.

I then took up three wide boards from the floor of the room, and put all underneath. I then put the boards back so cleverly, so skillfully, that no human eye —not even *his*—could have noticed anything wrong. There was nothing to wash out—no stain of any kind, no blood-spot whatever. I had been too careful for that. A tub had caught all—ha! ha!

When I had made an end of these labors, it was four o'clock—still dark as midnight. As the bell sounded the hour, there came a knocking at the street door. I went to open it with a light heart—for what had I *now* to fear? There entered three men, who introduced themselves, with perfect courtesy, as officers of the police. A shriek, they said, had been heard by a neighbor during the night. The neighbor had been suspicious. The information had been brought to the police office. And now they (the officers) had been sent to search the house.

I smiled—for *what* had I to fear? I made the gentlemen welcome. The shriek, I said, was my own in a dream.

---

enveloped (en VEL upd) wrapped up
anxiety (ang ZY uh tee) worry

The old man, I added, was absent in the country. I took my visitors all over the house. I told them to search—search *well*. I led them, finally, to *his* bedroom. I showed them his treasures, safe, undisturbed. In the excitement of my confidence, I brought chairs into the room. I asked them *here* to rest from their work, while I myself, in the wild audacity of my perfect triumph, placed my own chair upon the very spot that lay over the corpse of the victim.

The officers were satisfied. My *manner* had convinced them. I was strangely at ease. They sat there, and after I answered their questions happily, they talked about familiar things. But, before long, I felt myself growing pale. I wished them gone. My head ached, and I imagined a ringing in my ears; but still they sat, and still they chatted. The ringing became more distinct—it continued and became ever more distinct. I talked more freely to get rid of the feeling; but the ringing went on, ever louder—until, at length, I found that the noise was *not* within my own ears.

No doubt I now grew *very* pale. But I talked more fluently, and with a louder voice. Yet the sound increased—and what could I do? It was *a low, dull, quick sound—a sound such as a watch makes when enveloped in cotton.* I gasped for breath—and yet the officers heard it not. I talked more quickly—more excitedly. But the noise steadily increased. I stood up and argued about trifles, in a high voice and with wild movements. But the noise steadily increased. Why *would* they not be gone? I paced the floor with heavy steps—but the noise steadily increased. Oh what *could* I do? I shouted—I swore! I took the chair upon which I had been sitting and pushed it loudly upon the boards, but the noise rose up over all and continued to increase. It grew louder—and louder—*louder!* And still the men chatted pleasantly, and smiled. Was it possible they heard it not? No, no! They heard! —they suspected—they *knew!* They were making a mockery of my horror!—this I thought, and this I think. But anything was better than this agony! Anything was better than this mockery! I could bear those hypocritical smiles no longer! I felt that I must scream or die! —and now—again! —listen! —louder! louder! *louder!*—

"Villains!" I shrieked. "Pretend no more. I admit the crime! Tear up the boards! —here, here!—it is the beating of his hideous heart!"

---

audacity (aw DAS uh tee) boldness; daring
fluently (FLOO unt lee) easily (of talking)
trifle (TRY ful) unimportant thing
mockery (MOK uh ree) person or thing made fun of
hypocritical (hip uh KRIT ih kul) false; not sincere

Review the Selection

UNDERSTAND THE SELECTION

Recall

1. At what hour every night did the narrator enter the old man's room?

2. What vexed the narrator?

3. Why did the policemen come?

Infer

4. Why do you think the narrator acted more kindly toward the old man for a week prior to the murder?

5. Who might the old man have been?

6. What do you think might have caused the glaze on the old man's eye that the narrator thought was evil?

7. Why did the policemen stay after the narrator answered their questions?

Apply

8. How does the expression "You protest too much," apply to the narrator's comments about his sanity?

9. What questions might the police ask the narrator?

10. Assume you are the old man. You sense something sinister. Who do you think has entered the room? Why?

Respond to Literature

Is Poe's suspenseful tale typical of the literature of this period? Explain.

WRITE ABOUT THE SELECTION

Edgar Allan Poe has been called the master of suspense. "The Tell-Tale Heart" illustrates his ability to keep a reader "on the edge of a seat." In this selection, the main character, a madman, relates his tale of horror and suspense. The madman presents the tale in a logical manner—insisting that he is not crazy.

Suppose that you are one of the policemen who has answered the neighbor's complaint. You are sitting and chatting with this madman. Suddenly he confesses to the murder and begins to rip up the floor boards looking for the "beating heart." How do you maintain your composure? What do you say? Add an episode to this tale describing the events that follow the madman's confession.

Prewriting Freewrite your ideas about what happened and how you reacted. Include details of how the madman acted.

Writing Write at least one paragraph describing the new sequence of events. Explain how you handled the situation and the madman. Remember, you are writing from the point of view of a policeman in the 19th century.

Revising When you revise your tale, add details that help keep up the element of suspense.

Proofreading Read over your selection. Be sure each of your sentences begins with a capital letter.

THINK ABOUT SUSPENSE

To achieve suspense in a story, an author may foreshadow events, create atmospheric details, add events that heighten the tension the reader feels, and use character traits that make the reader feel strongly, one way or another, about a character.

1. Who is the narrator of the story?

2. How does Poe make it clear from the outset that the narrator is insane?

3. There are two kinds of suspense, one that leaves the outcome in doubt until the end of the story and one in which the outcome is known but not when it will happen. Which type does Poe use in this story?

4. What are some details that Poe uses to build suspense in the story?

5. Why did the narrator think he heard the old man's heart beating under the floor?

READING FOCUS

Identify Signal Words As you read this selection, you identified cause-and-effect relationships and the sequence of events by using signal words. Choose a series of events from the story. Write the signal words you identified. Tell why you think these words make the relationships among these events clear.

DEVELOP YOUR VOCABULARY

You will find it difficult to understand and appreciate any literary work if you do not understand the vocabulary used by the author. Sometimes you may be able to figure out the meaning of a word from **context clues**—from the words that surround the unfamiliar word. However, it is always wise to check the meaning of the unfamiliar word in a dictionary as well. At times, unfamiliar words will be defined within or following a selection. This is true in this text. Be sure to check these definitions as you read.

Review the meanings of the following words from "The Tell-Tale Heart." When you are sure you understand the words, write an original sentence for each one that shows you understand the meaning.

1. vexed
2. pitch
3. enveloped
4. audacity
5. acute
6. fluently
7. mockery
8. hypocritical
9. stifled
10. mortal

Focus ON FICTION

*F*iction has several recognizable elements. Knowing them will help you to understand fictional works better. The most basic elements are setting, characters, plot, theme, and point of view.

Setting Setting is the physical place, the time, and the general background against which the action or events in a story take place. The physical place might be the great outdoors or a single room. It might be a city street or a country estate. The time might include the time of day, a particular season, or a period in history. The general background often includes a specific kind of weather or the general climate of a region.

The action of a novel, play, or short story may be set in more than one place. One part of the work may take place in one setting; another part in another setting.

Sometimes a setting can be a major force affecting events of the story. A blizzard, for example, may change the plans the characters had for going on a journey. The setting may also help the reader to understand a character better. A character who lives on a houseboat, for example, is likely to be accustomed to water and self-reliance.

Characters Characters are the inhabitants of the fictional world the author creates. Characters have physical features and personalities. The author may use physical features to shed light on a character's personality. Usually, the characters are human. Occasionally, an animal may be given a personality. Then, that animal becomes a character.

The author creates personality through the character's thoughts, words, and deeds. A character's personality may also be revealed through the opinions and attitudes expressed by other people in the story. Some characters are well-rounded and believable. A **well-rounded** character has strengths and weaknesses, as real people do. Minor characters are often **flat**, not round. They have one-dimensional personalities and may even be stereotypes.

Plot   Plot is the series of events in a literary work. Conflict provides the dramatic action that advances the plot. Conflict arises when two characters important to the story struggle against one another. The main character is called the **protagonist**. His or her rival is called the **antagonist**. Conflict may also arise when one character struggles within his or her own mind about something. This kind of struggle is called **internal conflict**.

The **climax** is the decisive turning point in the action of the story. The dramatic tension, caused by the conflict, reaches its highest point at the climax. At that moment, the conflict begins to be resolved. The tension is released, and the **dénouement**, or conclusion, follows.

Theme   Theme is the central or dominating idea of a literary work. In nonfiction, the theme is often stated as a topic. Theme is rarely stated in fiction. Instead, the author uses the other elements of fiction, such as plot, character, and setting, to communicate an idea or concept to the reader.

Point of View   Point of view is the position from which the story is told. A fictional story may be told from the first-person or the third-person point of view.

In **first-person** point of view, the narrator is a participant in the action. He or she has a limited view of the action, and can tell the reader only what he or she sees, hears, and knows.

In **third-person** point of view, the narrator is an observer who stands outside the action. A third person narrator might be able to see, hear, and know everything that happens to all the characters or a third person narrator's point of view might be limited to the information experienced by just one character.

When the narrator can tell the innermost feelings and thoughts of only one character, the point of view is called **third-person limited**. When the third person narrator is all-knowing, the point of view is called **omniscient**. An omniscient narrator can tell the reader what the characters are thinking.

from
The Prairie

by James Fenimore Cooper

In the following excerpt, Natty Bumppo is
close to death. He is visited by Duncan
Uncas Middleton, an army officer whose life
Bumppo had saved a year earlier, and by
Middleton's scouting party. Bumppo has
been living with the tribe of Hard-Heart,
a young Pawnee chief, whom Bumppo
had adopted as a son. As Bumppo's death
approaches, the Pawnee chief and the army
officer both share a deep sadness.

When the scouting party entered the village, its inhabitants
were gathered in an open space. The Indians formed a large
circle with perhaps a dozen of the principal chiefs at the center.
Around them were the others arrayed, as was their custom,
by age and rank. Hard-Heart waved his hand as Middleton
approached. The circle parted to let him and his companions pass

through. At the center, they dismounted. As their horses were led
away, the strangers found themselves surrounded by a thousand
grave, concerned faces.

Middleton gazed about him, troubled. No song or shout
had welcomed him among these people, with whom he was on
the best of terms. His followers shared his apprehensions. Deter-
mination replaced anxiety in their eyes. Each man felt silently
for his weapons. Yet there was no sign of hostility on the part of
their hosts.

---

grave (GRAYV) serious
apprehension (ap rih HEN shun) fear, dread

Hard-Heart beckoned for Middleton to follow him. He led the way toward the cluster of chiefs that stood at the center. Here the visitors found the solution to the mystery.

Bumppo sat on a homemade seat. The chair, though crudely made, had been carefully designed to support his frame in an upright and comfortable posture. It was apparent at first glance that the old man was dying. His eyes were glazed, unseeing and expressionless. His skin was more sunken than before, but there all outward change ended.

> The author gives details of the setting.

> The author describes the character's physical appearances.

He did not suffer from any particular disease. His body had, with time, simply worn out. Life still lingered in his system. It seemed as though the spirit knew it was time to leave. Yet, it was reluctant to depart from a shell that had for so long provided honorable shelter. Middleton could almost imagine he could see the spirit fluttering about the placid lips of the old woodsman.

> The conflict is revealed— Bumppo *vs.* death.

The light from the setting sun fell full upon Bumppo's solemn features. His head was bare, and his long gray hair stirred lightly in the evening breeze. His rifle lay upon his knee. The other tools of a hunter were at his side, within easy reach. The figure of a hound crouched at his feet, as if asleep. So natural was its position that Middleton had to look closely before he realized it was not alive. The Indians had, with tenderness and ingenuity, stuffed the skin of Hector, Bumppo's dead dog, and placed it there.

> The character of Bumppo is slowly revealed.

Le Balafre, the old Pawnee chief, sat beside the dying trapper. His own hour of departure did not appear far off. Nearby stood other old men. They had come to watch how a just and fearless warrior would approach life's greatest journey.

Bumppo had lived a life uncorrupted by vice. The reward for his temperance was a peaceful death. His vigor had endured to the end. Decay, when it did occur, was rapid and painless.

> The author sets limits on the conflict.

He had hunted with the tribe throughout the Spring and Summer. As Fall approached, his limbs suddenly became paralyzed. Soon after that, he fell into a coma. The Pawnees believed that they were going to lose, so unexpectedly, the wise friend they had come to love and respect. But, as we have already said, the soul seemed reluctant to depart. The lamp of life flickered but would not go out.

---

placid (PLAS id) quiet
ingenuity (in juh NOO uh tee) cleverness; originality
temperance (TEM pur uns) self-restraint in conduct, appetite, etc.

The author continues the omniscient point of view.

On the day of Middleton's arrival, the old man regained consciousness. He spoke coherently. From time to time his sight returned, and he recognized those about him. It was not recovery, but a final rally before death.

Hard-Heart, leaning forward, asked sadly and politely:

Bumppo and the Pawnee speak to each other with respect.

"Does my father hear the words of his adopted son?" Hard-Heart spoke in Pawnee.

"Speak," replied the trapper in the same language. His voice was weak but the words were distinct. "I am about to depart from the Pawnee village. I shall soon be beyond the reach of your voice."

"Let the wise chief have no cares for his journey. The spirits of a hundred dead Pawnee warriors await you in the next world. They will ride at your side." In his concern for the old man, Hard-Heart had forgotten that others were waiting to speak with Bumppo.

The author hints at theme through dialogue.

"Pawnee, I die, as I have lived, a Christian," the frontiersman answered. His voice was now strong. Its force startled his listeners. "I will leave life as I came into it. Horses and arms are not needed to stand in the presence of the Great Spirit of my people. He will judge me by my deeds."

"My father will tell my young men how many enemy warriors he has defeated. He will tell what acts of valor and justice he has done so they will know how to imitate him."

"A boastful tongue is not heard in the heaven of a white-man!" Bumppo spoke solemnly. "What I have done, God has seen. What I have done well, he will remember. He will chastise me for my sins, but he will do so with mercy. No, my son, a paleface is not allowed to sing his own praises before his God."

Notice the omniscient point of view.

Hard-Heart was a little disappointed but did not want to argue. He stepped back modestly and allowed the others to approach. Middleton took Bumppo's hand in his own. He had difficulty controlling his emotions. The old man seemed lost in thought, but a joyful expression crossed his faded features at the sound of Middleton's voice.

"I hope you have not forgotten him whose life you saved."

---

coherently (koh HIR unt lee) clearly speaking
chastise (chas TYZ) punish

Sunset over the Marshes, Martin Johnson Heade. Corbis Bettmann

"I have forgotten very little that I have seen," the trapper replied in English. "I am at the end of many weary days, but there is not one of them that I would choose to forget. I remember you and your whole party. I remember your grandfather dead these many years. I am glad that you have come. Will you do a favor for an old and dying man?"

The tension relaxes as the old man finds the strength to let his last wishes be known.

"Name it," said Middleton, "and it shall be done."

"Kindness and friendship should not be forgotten. There is a settlement in the Ostego hills. It is a long journey—"

The old man's strength was fading; his breathing was labored. He spoke at short intervals. Middleton interrupted to spare him further effort.

"I know the place. Tell me what you want done."

"Take this rifle, bullet pouch, and powder horn. Send them to the person whose name is engraved on the rifle. I had the letters put there. I have long intended that he should inherit my rifle."

"He shall have it. Is there anything else I can do?"

"I have few other possessions. I have given my traps to Hard-Heart. He has been a good son. Let him come closer."

Middleton explained to the Indian chief what the trapper had said. He stood back to let Hard-Heart approach.

"Pawnee," continued the old man, changing his language to suit the need. "My people have a custom. The father always leaves his son a blessing before he shuts his eyes forever. This blessing I give you. Take it for we are all children of the same God. May God look on your deeds with friendly eyes. May you never commit an act that angers him.

"I do not know if we shall ever meet again. There are many beliefs about an afterlife. You believe in the blessed prairies. I have faith in the sayings of my fathers. This parting may be final. Then again, we may both stand together before the face of one God.

"There is much good in both religions. Each seems suited to its own people. I go contented. Still, it is a little painful to give up the pleasures of the hunt."

Bumppo leaned forward, feeling for his dog. "Aye, Hector," he said, "we must part at last. You've been a faithful hound. Pawnee, you cannot slay the dog on my grave, as is your custom. That is not my way. If you love me, be kind to him after I have gone.

"I hear the words of my father."

"Do you hear the chief's promise, dog?" asked the trapper. Hearing no response, the old man felt for the dog's mouth. Touching its cold lips, he realized the truth. Falling back in the seat, he hung his head, as though in shock. Two young Indians took advantage of his momentary distraction. They removed the stuffed dog with the same sensitivity that had tempted them to try the deception.

After a few minutes, Bumppo raised his head. "The dog is dead," he said. "A hound has his time, just as men do." He called for Middleton.

"Captain," he said, "I am glad you have come. These Indians mean well, but they do not understand our ways. Bury the dog with me."

"As you wish."

The old man retreated into his own thoughts. At times, he raised his eyes wistfully. It seemed as though he had more to say,

The old hunter shows his understanding of both cultures.

The author takes pains to show the Indians' sensitivity and respect for Bumppo.

The stuffed dog is used as a symbol for the mortality of all creatures.

but no words passed his lips. Noting this, Middleton asked if there was anything else he could do.

"I have no kith or kin," the trapper said. "My blood line dies with me. We Bumppos have never been chiefs. We were honest and useful in our own way. My father lies buried near the sea, but the bones of his son will whiten on the prairie."

The author gives more clues to Bumppo's character.

"Name the spot, and your remains will be buried by your father's side," said Middleton.

"No, let me sleep where I have lived, far from the din of cities. I would not like an unmarked grave, though. These redskins, fearing grave robbers, hide their dead. I paid a man in the settlements to put a tombstone on my father's grave. I paid him in beaver skins. It told passersby that a Christian lay under that ground. The words on the stone were few, but enough to tell of his manner of life, his years, his honesty."

"Would you like such a stone at your grave?"

"I! No. Hard-Heart is my only son. He knows little of white man's ways. Besides, I am already in his debt. I have been of little help to the tribe. I have no money. The rifle has some value, but I have promised it to the boy whose name is engraved on it."

"You saved my life. Many years before, you saved my grand-father's. Let me show my gratitude. A stone shall be put at the head of your grave."

The old man extended an emaciated hand and gave Middleton a squeeze of thanks.

"I thought you would be willing to do it. I was reluctant to ask since you are not my kin. Put no boastful words on the stone. My name and age, year of death, and a few words from the Bible will do. Then my name will not be altogether lost on earth. I need no more."

"It will be done," Middleton said.

Those words seemed to close the old man's accounts with this world. He drew back within himself. Middleton and Hard-Heart stood on either side of the chair. Two hours passed. Occasionally, the old man spoke, but his words were distant. He spoke of events they had not seen. The circle Middleton had ridden into

The plot is advanced through a change in Bumppo's condition.

---

kith (KITH) archaic meaning for friends
kin (KIN) relatives
emaciated (ih MAY see ayt id) abnormally lean

that morning remained unbroken. When the old man spoke, the Indians bent forward to listen. When he finished, they stood in thoughtful silence.

As the flame of life grew dimmer, his voice became hushed. His weather-beaten face often changed expression. At times, Middleton imagined he could see the workings of the old man's soul in his alternating facial expressions. Perhaps, he did. Who among the living can say? Without pretending to explain that mystery, we shall simply tell what he saw.

Another hour went by. The trapper's eyes opened and shut occasionally. When open, his eyes appeared to focus on the western horizon and the glorious colors of an American sunset. Nature and the event seemed to fill the observers with solemn awe.

Suddenly, the old man grasped Middleton's hand with incredible power. Supported on either side by his friend and his adopted son, Bumppo rose to his feet. Erect, he looked about him. In a voice heard throughout the surrounding throng, he pronounced one word:

"Here!"

The sudden action and the uncommon force of his utterance took all present by surprise. Middleton and Hard-Heart, each of whom had reflexively extended a supporting hand, turned to look at their aged friend. As they did, they realized he was beyond their care. They placed the body gently in the seat. Le Balafre stood and made an announcement to the tribe. The voice of the old Indian seemed to be an echo from another world.

"A valiant, just, and wise warrior has gone to the blessed lands of his people. When the call came, he was ready to answer. Go my children. Remember the just chief of the palefaces, and imitate his ways!"

A grave was dug beneath the shade of some noble oaks. The Pawnee keep careful watch over it. Passing travelers are shown the spot where a just white man sleeps. A stone was placed at its head with the simple inscription the trapper had requested. Middleton took only one liberty. He added, "May no wanton hand ever disturb his remains!"

Notice that the narrator, using the editorial we, demonstrates his omniscience.

The author hints at theme through setting and symbol. What does the sunset stand for?

The climax has arrived.

The dénouement begins.

Bumppo's character is revealed through the opinion of another.

---

utterance (UT ur uns) expressing by voice
reflexively (rih FLEK siv lee) an action done automatically
grave (GRAYV) burial plot
wanton (WAHN tun) mischievous, unruly

Chief Tustennuggee, 19th century. Corbis Bettmann

Review the Selection

UNDERSTAND THE SELECTION

Recall

1. Who was Bumppo's adopted son?

2. What was the name of Bumppo's dog?

3. Where was Bumppo's father buried?

Infer

4. Why did the Indians respect Bumppo?

5. Why did Bumppo want a tombstone?

6. Why was Middleton afraid when he first rode in to camp?

7. Why does the author say the reward for Bumppo's temperance was a peaceful death?

Apply

8. Suppose that you are the person whose name had been engraved on Bumppo's rifle. How would you have reacted when Middleton delivered it?

9. Suppose Hard-Heart died. Does he leave the world with as much grace as Bumppo did?

10. Suppose that you are one of the Indians present when Bumppo spoke of past events. What did he talk about?

Respond to Literature

What does Bumppo's life and death on the prairie symbolize?

WRITE ABOUT THE SELECTION

In this excerpt from *The Prairie*, Natty Bumppo asked his friend Middleton to take care of his funeral arrangements. In addition to the things Bumppo actually asked of him, Middleton probably delivered a short eulogy at Bumppo's gravesite. A **eulogy** is a speech praising a dead person. Suppose that you are Middleton and that you deliver Bumppo's eulogy. What would you say?

Prewriting Skim the story to gather data you might use in your eulogy. Organize the data as best you can and write an informal outline of the main points you would make. Tell about Bumppo's life and the example he gave to others. Include details about his personal achievements and his friendship with the Pawnees.

Writing Use your informal outline to write the eulogy. Remember to write in the first person (I) as you are supposedly Middleton. In the eulogy, include details that a friend might think important.

Revising When you revise your eulogy, be sure you have included all the points you would like people to remember about Bumppo. Add details to make the description more vivid. For each point you make, include an example from the story that illustrates your point.

Proofreading Read over your selection. Be sure each sentence is a complete thought with a subject and a predicate.

THINK ABOUT FICTION

Fiction is primarily narrative writing that comes from the imagination of an author. Unlike nonfiction narrative, it is not based on history or fact. Stories, told in novels, short stories, and plays, make up the category of fictional narrative. Through fiction, the reader experiences sadness, joy, humor, and other emotions common to human life and watches the resolution of lifelike conflicts and struggles.

1. Who is the protagonist in the excerpt you read? Who is the antagonist? Are they in conflict? Explain.

2. Does the setting of the excerpt contribute to your understanding of Bumppo's character?

3. What element of plot follows the climax?

4. What is an omniscient narrator able to do that narrators using other points of view cannot? Is this an advantage? Explain.

5. What do you think the theme of the excerpt is?

DEVELOP YOUR VOCABULARY

Root words are English words that have no letters or syllables added to them. **Suffixes** are word parts that can be added to base words to change their part of speech. For example, *-ful* is a commonly used suffix. Add it to *care* or *pain*, both nouns, and you have formed *careful* or *painful*, both adjectives. Here are some other suffixes and what they do:

Noun-forming suffixes: *-ance, -ion, -ity, -ment, -ness, -or, -ship*
Adjective-forming suffixes: *-able, -ful, -less*
Adverb-forming suffixes: *-ly, -ward*

Write the following words from *The Prairie*. Circle each suffix and write whether the word is a noun, an adjective, or an adverb.

1. visitor
2. comfortable
3. settlement
4. boastful
5. politely
6. kindness
7. friendship
8. modestly
9. fearless
10. outwardly
11. utterance
12. sensitively

Learn About

THE LYRIC

A **lyric** is a short poem usually expressing intense personal feeling. A lyric is like a still photograph as opposed to a movie. The lyric does not have a plot that is advanced through a series of events. Instead, it captures a moment in time and focuses on it very closely.

The lyric poet attempts to create a specific emotional response in the reader. The poet achieves this effect through the details, impressions, and insights that a heightened awareness makes him or her capable of expressing. The result is a vivid word picture of an experience to which the poet may give new meaning for the reader.

As you read "To a Waterfowl," ask yourself:

1. What lesson or new meaning does the author find in the migration of the bird?
2. In what way does this poem illustrate the poet's heightened awareness?

READING FOCUS

Draw Conclusions Sometimes you must think beyond the words on the page to get a full meaning of the author's intent. Readers draw conclusions by using prior knowledge to arrive at a decision or judgment. As you read "To a Waterfowl," draw conclusions about what the author might think of his own life, as well as how he views birds.

WRITING CONNECTION

Select a common experience in nature, for example, leaves falling from a tree in autumn or a deer running across a green meadow. In a prose paragraph, use details, impressions, or insights to give this experience a new meaning.

TO A WATERFOWL

by William Cullen Bryant

Whither, midst falling dew,
While glow the heavens with the last steps of day,
Far, through their rosy depths, dost thou pursue
    Thy solitary way?

5   Vainly the fowler's eye
Might mark thy distant flight to do thee wrong,
As, darkly seen against the crimson sky,
    Thy figure floats along.

       Seek'st thou the plashy brink
10   Of weedy lake, or marge of river wide,
Or where the rocking billows rise and sink
    On the chafed ocean-side?

There is a Power whose care
Teaches thy way along that pathless coast—
15   The desert and illimitable air—
    Lone wandering, but not lost.

---

whither (HWI*TH* ur) to what place, point, etc.
fowler (FOUL ur) hunter of wildfowl
plashy (PLASH ee) marshy; wet
marge (MAHRJ) edge or border
chafed (CHAYFT) to have been worn away; eroded
illimitable (ih LIM ih tuh bul) endless

All day thy wings have fanned,
At that far height, the cold, thin atmosphere,
Yet stoop not, weary, to the welcome land,
20   Though the dark night is near.

And soon that toil shall end;
Soon shalt thou find a summer home, and rest,
And scream among thy fellows; reeds shall bend,
       Soon, o'er thy sheltered nest.

25   Thou'rt gone, thy abyss of heaven
Hath swallowed up thy form; yet, on my heart
Deeply has sunk the lesson thou hast given,
       And shall not soon depart.

He who, from zone to zone,
30   Guides through the boundless sky thy certain flight,
In the long way that I must tread alone,
       Will lead my steps aright.

---

abyss (uh BIS) a thing too big for measurement

Review the Selection

UNDERSTAND THE SELECTION

Recall

1. What color was the sky? How does the bird show up against it?

2. Was the bird alone or was it part of a flock?

3. What will the bird soon find?

Infer

4. At what time of day did Bryant observe the bird?

5. Why could a hunter not harm the bird?

6. Where was the bird headed?

7. What type of bird was this?

Apply

8. What lesson did Bryant learn from observing the bird?

9. Predict what might have happened if Bryant had found an injured waterfowl. Explain why.

10. Suppose that Bryant was a hunter. Do you think he would have seen the bird any differently? Compare and contrast the two viewpoints.

Respond to Literature

What characteristics do Bumppo and the speaker of this poem share?

WRITE ABOUT THE SELECTION

In this lyric poem, Bryant captured his momentary impressions of a waterfowl. Had this been a narrative poem, he would have continued to follow the bird, requiring him to write additional stanzas. Imagine that you are watching this same bird. How far does it fly? What dangers does it encounter? What is the climax of its story? Write a prose paragraph telling where you think the bird goes and what it does. The paragraph should contain a sequence of events that tell a story.

Prewriting Let your mind run free. Make a list of places the bird might go. Invent some adventures for the bird. Organize your list into an informal outline of what you envision happens to the bird. Include details of what you feel the bird might encounter. For example, it might have to escape from hunters, it might look for food, or it might have to find shelter in a storm.

Writing Use your informal outline to write a paragraph or two, telling of the bird's adventures. In your composition, briefly explain the setting where its adventure ends.

Revising When you revise, be sure to add specific details that allow others to visualize your impressions of the bird and of the setting that you chose.

Proofreading Read over your selection. Be sure all your words are spelled correctly.

THINK ABOUT LYRIC

A **lyric** is a poem that usually expresses intense personal feeling. The poet tries to create a specific emotional response in the reader. Through this response, the poet hopes the reader will share his or her intense feeling for the experience.

1. Why do you think the poet describes a "solitary" bird rather than a flock?

2. The bird is flying too high to be shot by hunters. How did you react when you read that? Why?

3. What is meant by "There is a Power whose care/Teaches thy way along that pathless coast"?

4. In stanza 8, do you think the poet's "long way" refers to his journey home or his life? Why?

5. The English poet William Wordsworth said that "poetry . . . takes its origin from emotion recollected in tranquility." How does this describe the way Bryant wrote "To a Waterfowl"? Why?

READING FOCUS

Draw Conclusions Tell about one conclusion that you drew about the deeper meaning of the poem. What details in the poem led you to this conclusion?

DEVELOP YOUR VOCABULARY

A poet must carefully select words to fit the meter of a poem as well as to express his or her thoughts and feelings. The **meter** is the pattern of stressed and unstressed syllables in each line of the poem.

Poets sometimes shorten words to keep the meter. They may make a contraction of a word or words not commonly used as contractions. A contraction is a shortened form of one or two words. Letters are removed. An apostrophe takes the place of the missing letter or letters. For example, *'twas* is a contraction of *it was*; *o'er* is the poetic contraction of *over*.

Following is a list of several contractions poets sometimes use. Study each contraction. Write the word or words you think the contraction represents. Check in a dictionary to be sure you are correct. (Not all the contractions will be found there, however.) Then use each contraction in an original sentence.

1. e'en
2. 'twill
3. shall't
4. 'tween
5. e'er
6. 'twixt

Learn About

DIALOGUE

The written conversation of two or more people is called **dialogue**. Although it is used most often in fiction, dialogue is also used in nonfiction.

The writer of an autobiographical narrative may use dialogue to help give an easy, natural flow to the work. The people who were a part of the author's life are allowed to speak in their own words as the author remembers them. Their dialogue advances the narrative and shows events as they were.

Conversational give-and-take helps to define the personality and develop the character of each speaker. Using the direct words of people makes the writing seem more realistic.

As you read this selection, ask yourself:

1. How is dialogue used in Alcott's autobiographical narrative?
2. Does the dialogue help to make the people she worked with seem more real?

WRITING CONNECTION

Think of a conversation you recently had with a friend. Try to recall exact words. Write your conversation as accurately as you can, using each person's words in quotation marks.

READING FOCUS

Make Inferences Authors often do not explain the thoughts, feelings, and personalities of the characters in a story. Instead, the reader infers, or guesses, what the characters are like based on their words.

As you read this text, make inferences about each of these characters: the narrator, Teddy, John, and the doctor. Think about how the dialogue reveals aspects of them.

A Night

from Hospital Sketches

by Louisa May Alcott

The hours I like best are at night, and so I was soon promoted to night nurse. I usually found the men in the most cheerful state of mind their condition allowed.

The evenings were spent in reading aloud and writing letters. I waited on and amused the men, and went with Dr. P. as he made his second daily rounds. I cared for my dozens of wounds, giving last doses of medicine and making the men cozy for the long hours to come.

I had managed to sort out the patients in the ward into three rooms. One I visited with a tray full of bandages and pins. Another I visited with books, flowers, games, and happy talk. To the third room I brought lullabies, kind words, and sometimes a helping hand in time of death.

The night I am writing about opened with a little comedy and closed with a little tragedy. I was watching beside the bed of a 12-year-old drummer boy who had come to us after a dreadful battle. A slight wound in the knee brought him there, but his mind had suffered more than his body. For days he had been reliving in his thoughts the scenes he could

not forget. Then he would break out in terrible sobs which were pitiful to hear.

As I sat by him, I tried to soothe his poor brain by the constant touch of my hands over his hot forehead. In his mind he was cheering his comrades on, then counting them as they fell around him. He often grabbed my arm to drag me from the neighborhood of a bursting shell. His face burned with fever, his eyes were restless, and his head was never still. A constant stream of shouts, warnings, and broken cries poured from his lips.

It was past 11:00 and my patient was slowly wearing himself into periods of quiet. In one of these pauses, I heard a curious sound. I looked over my shoulder and saw a one-legged man hopping around the room. I recognized a soldier whose fever had taken a turn for the worse and left his mind in a state of confusion. At this point he informed me he was heading for home. When his mind was clear, the least movement produced a roar of pain. But the loss of reason seemed to have caused a change in the man and in his manner. He balanced himself on one leg like a stork and refused any suggestion of mine to return to bed.

I couldn't think what to do with this creature. I was about to run for help when another wounded soldier came to the rescue. He put an end to the crisis by carrying the lively one-legged man to his bed. The one-legged soldier was worn out from his efforts and soon fell asleep.

My rescuer and I enjoyed a great laugh together, then returned to our places. Then the sound of a sob came from a bed in the corner. It was the little drummer boy. He was trying to control the sad sounds that kept breaking out.

"What is it, Teddy?" I asked, as he rubbed the tears away.

"I've got pain, ma'am, but I'm not crying for that, because I'm used to it. I dreamed Kit was here, and when I woke up he wasn't, and I couldn't help it then."

Kit was a good friend, badly hurt himself, who would not leave the drummer behind. He had wrapped him in his own blanket and carried him in his arms to the ambulance. Kit died at the door of the hospital which promised care and comfort for the drummer boy.

For ten days Teddy refused to be comforted because he had not been able to thank Kit for his protection, which may have cost him his life. This thought had been troubling him in secret. I told him that his friend probably would have died in any case, but I couldn't end his sorrow.

As I was comforting him, a message I had been fearing came for me.

"John is going, ma'am, and wants to see you, if you can come."

"I'll be there the moment this boy is asleep. Tell John so, and let me know if I am in danger of being too late."

The messenger left and while I quieted the drummer, I thought of John. He had come in a day or two after the others and was put in my "pitiful" room. He was a large man with a fine face and the most peaceful eyes I have ever seen.

When he came, I watched him for a night or two before I made friends with him. He seldom spoke and never complained. He was thoughtful and concerned while watching the suffering of others, as if he forgot his own.

One night, as I went on my rounds with Dr. P., I asked which man in the room probably suffered most. To my great surprise, the doctor glanced at John.

"Every breath he draws is like a stab, for the bullet went into his left lung and broke a rib. The poor man can find no rest because he must lie on his wounded back or else he can't breathe. It will be a long, hard struggle because of his great strength, but even this can't save him."

"You don't mean he must die, Doctor?"

"There's not the slightest hope for him, and you'd better tell him so before long. You have a way of doing such things comfortably, so I leave it to you. He won't last more than a day or two at the most."

I could have sat down on the spot and cried if I had not learned to save my tears

---

draw (DRAW) to take air into the lungs; inhale

for spare moments. Such an end seemed very hard for such a fine man. The army needed men like John who fight for freedom with both heart and hand. I could not give him up so soon. It was an easy thing for Dr. P. to say, "Tell him he must die," but a hard thing to do. I didn't have the heart to do it then, and I hoped that some change for the better might take place in spite of what Dr. P. had said.

A few minutes later I came in and saw John sitting up with no one to support him. The doctor was changing the bandage on his back.

The doctor's words made me feel sad that I had not given John those little cares and kindnesses that make the heavy hours pass earlier. He looked very lonely just then, as he sat with bent head and hands folded on his knees. I saw no sign of suffering till I looked nearer. Then I saw great tears roll down and drop upon the floor. It was a new sight there. Though I had seen many men suffer in silence or with groans of pain, none of them cried. It did not seem weak, only very moving. My heart opened wide and took him in. I gathered the bent head in my arms as freely as if he had been a little child and said, "Let me help you bear it, John."

Never on any human face have I seen so beautiful a look of thanks, surprise, and comfort, as that which he gave me.

"Thank you, ma'am," he whispered. "This is just what I wanted!"

"Then why not ask for it before?"

"I didn't like to be a trouble. You seemed so busy, and I could manage to get on alone."

"You shall not want it anymore, John."

Now I understood the sad look he sometimes gave me as I went out after a brief pause beside his bed. I had been used to stopping with those who seemed to need me more than he did. But now I knew that I brought as much comfort to him as to the others. I took the place of his mother, wife, or sister. Now while I cared for his wounds, he leaned against me, holding my hand tightly. If pain brought forth tears from him, no one saw them fall but me. I found him the manliest man of all of them, shy and brave and natural. I saw his goodness and his dreams, which had helped to make him what he was.

After that night I gave an hour of each evening that remained of his life to his comfort and pleasure. He could only speak in whispers, but what he told me added to the warmth and respect I felt for him.

Once I asked him, "Do you ever regret that you came, when you lie here suffering so much?"

"Never ma'am," he answered. "I have not helped a great deal, but I've shown I was willing to give my life, and maybe I have to. But I don't blame anybody, and if it was to do over again, I'd do it."

Then he suddenly asked: "This is my first battle. Do they think it's going to be my last?"

"I'm afraid they do, John."

It was the hardest question I ever had been called upon to answer. His clear eyes were fixed on mine, forcing a truthful answer by their own truth. He seemed a little surprised at first, as he considered the terrible fact. Then he shook his head and spoke.

"I'm not afraid, but it's difficult to believe all at once. It doesn't seem possible for such a little wound to kill me."

But John had never seen the great holes between his shoulders. He saw only the awful sights about him, and he could not believe his own wound was worse than these.

"Shall I write your mother now?" I asked, thinking that the news I had just given him might change all his plans. But I think I should have guessed his answer, knowing him as I did.

"No, ma'am, to my brother just the

same. He'll break the news to her best, and I'll add a line to her myself when you get done. I hope the answer will come in time for me to see it."

These things had happened two days earlier. Now John was dying, and the letter had not come. I had been called to many deathbeds in my life, but to none that made my heart ache as it did then. As I went in, John stretched out both hands.

"I knew you would come! I guess I'm moving on, ma'am."

He was dying so quickly that even as he spoke I saw his face grow paler. I sat down by him and wiped the drops from his forehead. I stirred the air about him with a slow wave of the fan, and waited to help him die. He stood in need of help, and I could do so little. As the doctor had said, the strong body fought against death every inch of the way. He was forced to draw each breath with pain. For hours he suffered, yet through it all, his eyes never lost their perfect calm, and his strong spirit showed in them.

Suddenly he rose up in his bed and cried out with a bitter cry that broke the silence with its terrible suffering: "For God's sake, give me air!"

It was the only cry that pain or death had squeezed from him, the only favor he had asked. None of us could grant it, for all the airs that blew were useless now. We threw up the window. The first red light of dawn was warming the sky, and we could see the rising sun. John saw it, and laid himself gently down and sighed deeply. We knew then that for him suffering was forever past. He died then, and though the heavy breaths still continued, he never spoke again. To the end he held my hand close, so close that when he was asleep at last, I could not draw it away. I felt glad that perhaps my touch had eased his hardest hour.

When they had gotten him ready for the grave, John looked to me like a hero. I felt a tender pride in my lost patient. The lovely expression on his face soon replaced the marks of pain. I longed for those who loved him best to see him as he had accepted Death.

As we stood looking at him, a letter was handed to me which had been forgotten the night before. It was John's letter, come just an hour too late for him to see it. Yet he did have it, for after I had cut some of his hair for his mother, I took off his ring to send her. Then I kissed him for her sake, and laid the letter in his hand. I felt that its place was with him. I made myself happy with the thought that even now he would have some token of the love which makes life beautiful and lives on past death.

Then I left him, glad to have known so fine a man, and carrying with me a lasting memory of him. I remembered John as he lay calmly waiting for the dawn of that long day which knows no night.

Review the Selection

UNDERSTAND THE SELECTION

Recall

1. What is the setting of this selection?

2. How old is the youngest patient?

3. What patient does Alcott most admire?

Infer

4. Why did Teddy dream about Kit?

5. Why did John think his wound was not serious?

6. Why did Alcott have difficulty answering when John asked if he had been in his last battle?

7. Why did Alcott admire John so much?

Apply

8. Suppose you have to explain to John that he will die. How would you feel?

9. Suppose you were John's brother. How would you tell your mother about his death?

10. Is the suffering the same in every war?

Respond to Literature

Realism in literature is the attempt to picture things as they really are. How does this selection illustrate that trend?

WRITE ABOUT THE SELECTION

In this selection, John's mother wrote a letter to her dying son. It arrived one hour too late for John to read it. Alcott did not open it or return it; she had it buried with John. Its contents were never revealed. How do you think John's mother reacted when she learned her son was dying? Would she blame the war? What would she say to a son she would never see again? How would she comfort him?

Assume that you are that mother. You have very little time and only this letter to express your feelings to your son. Write a letter to him.

Prewriting Write an informal outline of the main points you want to include in your letter. Include details of past events you think important. You will have to assume what the relationship was between John and his mother. Think about the kind of mother such a man might have had. Also think about what John was like as a child.

Writing Use your informal outline to write your letter. In it, express your feelings for your son. As you write, keep in mind that you are writing from the perspective of a woman who is living during the time of the Civil War.

Revising When you revise your letter, be sure to include comforting thoughts.

Proofreading Read over your letter. Be sure you have used the proper punctuation for the greeting, each sentence, and the closing of the letter.

THINK ABOUT DIALOGUE

Dialogue is the words of real people or fictional characters. Thus, it is a conversation between two or more people. In drama, it can be the main way that the plot is developed. In nonfiction, it allows participants in a narrative to speak for themselves.

1. How does the use of dialogue in "A Night" make the people seem real?

2. Cite one example of how a speaker revealed his or her personality in dialogue.

3. Do you think Alcott understates or exaggerates the horrors of life in a wartime hospital? Explain.

4. Where is the main focus in "A Night" —on Alcott or on the men in the hospital? Explain your answer.

5. Most of the activity Alcott discusses happened in one night. Why do you think she chose to write about such a short period of time?

READING FOCUS

Make Inferences As you read, you made inferences about the characters' personalities from the dialogue. What can you infer about the doctor's personality from his description of John's condition? Why do you think the author did not just report what the doctor said?

DEVELOP YOUR VOCABULARY

Sometimes a specialized vocabulary develops around a place or occupation. New words or new meanings for existing words become part of this specialized vocabulary, which is often called *jargon*. For example, if you hear the words *classroom*, *teacher*, or *schoolbus*, you immediately think of school. If you hear the words *backstage*, *cast*, or *script*, you immediately think of the theater. Can you think of other words related to the school or theater setting?

A hospital was the setting for this selection. Consequently, words commonly associated with the vocabulary of a hospital have been used. Following are words found in this selection. Review each word carefully. Look the words up in a dictionary, if necessary. Then write an original paragraph using each word at least once.

1. ambulance
2. hospital
3. medicine
4. bandage
5. rounds
6. nurse
7. doctor
8. wound

UNIT 2 *Review*

Write About Character

The characters in this unit came from different backgrounds and lived in different parts of the United States. Place any character from any selection in the setting of a different work. How would that character react? Describe that character's thoughts and words in the new setting. Include a conversation with one of the original characters from the chosen work.

Prewriting Before you begin to write, choose the character you will move. Review the setting of the selection into which you will place the character. Freewrite the character's thoughts and conversation.

Writing Introduce the work with a brief discussion of the setting. Use your freewriting as a basis for what takes place. Include physical reactions such as facial expressions, instinctive movements, and tone of voice to bring the characters to life.

Revising Be sure the setting is accurate. When describing thoughts or conversation, be sure the characters are consistent. They should not suddenly change character unless you have explained what brought about the change.

Proofreading Be certain that you have used capital letters and quotation marks correctly.

Write About Fiction

When people analyze writing, they often examine the elements of literature that apply. You have studied the elements of fiction—setting, character, plot, theme, and point of view. Choose one of the two fiction selections in this unit. Pick any three fictional elements. Decide how these elements played a role in forming your opinion of the work. You will use this information to write a critical essay.

Prewriting Write the name of the first fictional element you will discuss. List the reasons why you liked or disliked the author's use of that element. Repeat the process for the other elements you have chosen.

Writing Before you write, decide which literary elements played the most important and the least important role in forming your opinion of each work. Write about the most important element first and least important element last.

Revising Be sure that you completed each discussion of a literary element before going on to discuss the next one. If you did not write a conclusion summarizing your opinion, do so now.

Proofreading Make sure you wrote the author's name and the exact title of the selection correctly. If you used quotations, make sure they are accurate.

BUILD LANGUAGE SKILLS

Vocabulary

A **homophone** is one of two or more words pronounced alike but different in meaning and spelling. When reading the printed word, you can determine which homophone an author is using from the spelling and from the context in which the word is used. When listening to spoken words, your only clue is the context.

Examples: The *council* broke up for the day, and those who had attended the meeting went home.
Again, I *counseled* peace, and my advice was heeded.

Council and *counsel* are homophones. *Council* is a noun meaning an assembly or meeting. *Counsel* can be used as a noun or a verb. It means advice or to advise.

If you had heard the example sentences spoken, you would not have had the advantage of seeing the words spelled out. However, you would have understood from the context which homophone the speaker was using. Below is a group of homophones. Write a sentence using each word in a context that provides clues to its meaning. If you do not understand the meaning of any word, look it up in the dictionary.

1. week–weak
2. earn–urn
3. coward–cowered
4. colonel–kernel
5. fowl–foul

Grammar, Usage, and Mechanics

The first word in a direct quotation or a dialogue is capitalized. A divided quotation is one in which one sentence appears in two separated parts within a single sentence. The first part of the sentence appears before a reference to the speaker. The second part appears after it. Do not capitalize the first word in the second part of a divided quotation if it is only part of a sentence.

Example: "Name it," said Middleton, "and it shall be done."

Capitalize these sentences appropriately.

1. "the dog is dead," he said.

2. General Howard replied, "you deny my authority, do you?"

3. My wife said, "here's your gun."

4. "he has come," she said, "at last."

5. "villains," I shrieked. "run."

6. "aye, Hector," he said, "we go."

7. Ichabod shouted, "he's going to throw his head at me!"

8. It was an easy thing for Dr. P. to say, "tell him he must die," but a hard thing to do.

9. I gathered the bent head in my arms . . . and said, "let me help you bear it, John."

10. "shall I write your mother now?" I asked.

UNIT 2 *Review*

SPEAKING AND LISTENING

One of the goals of reading literature is to be able to talk about it with understanding and appreciation. You may want to discuss your reactions to a selection and explain why it is personally meaningful. Sometimes to discuss a selection from the point of literary analysis can be rewarding too. It can give you a deeper understanding of literature that will add to your scope of knowledge.

Your task now is to prepare a short talk about one of the fiction selections in this unit. You should center your talk around the elements of fiction: setting, characters, plot and conflict, theme, and point of view. The main purpose of your talk is to explain these elements as they relate to your selection.

To prepare your talk, review the following points:

1. Refresh your memory by reading Focus on Fiction on pp. 130–131 and understand the elements of the fiction.

2. Choose a selection that you are familiar with. Reread it and take notes on those elements that you may need to review, such as the names of characters or how the plot helps to express the theme of the story.

3. Think of a strong beginning for your talk. Try not to begin with the typical title-and-author sentence. Instead, begin in an unusual way so that your audience will be intrigued. Perhaps you will never divulge the author and title, but will ask your classmates to name them after your talk.

4. Practice your talk out loud. Stand in front of a mirror. Notice your body language. Pay attention to your posture and gestures.

5. Maintain a great attitude. Be positive. if you make a mistake in your talk, don't worry. Just go on gracefully.

Now, begin working on this assignment by choosing a selection you have enjoyed in this unit. Since you are centering this talk on the elements of the fiction, your choice will be limited. However, if your teacher doesn't object, you can go to another unit and make a selection from there. Your talk should be at least three minutes. You can share it with the whole class or with a small group as your teacher directs.

CRITICAL THINKING

Sequencing A **sequence** is a group of items organized according to a planned pattern. If you arrange the names of class members according to the grade each student made on a test, you have listed them in **numerical order**. A dictionary lists words according to their place in the alphabet, that is, in **alphabetical order**.

Literature often makes use of three other sequencing orders. Events in narratives, both fictional and nonfictional, are often written in the order in which the events occurred. That is, they are written in **chronological**, or **time order**. Descriptions are often written in **spatial order**. This means that the writer describes them according to how they are arranged physically, or according to their location, or place, in space.

In expository and persuasive writing, items are frequently arranged according to the **order of importance**. Reasons for an event or arguments in favor of a cause are given according to their importance.

Choose one selection you have recently read and ask these questions:

1. What order was used in organizing this narrative (or description or persuasive passage)?

2. Explain what other order may have worked as well or better.

EFFECTIVE STUDYING

Preparing for Tests A test measures your knowledge of certain subject material. Doing your best on a test requires both long-term and short-term planning and work. Doing well in a subject requires that follow certain guidelines

1. Long-term plan:
   - As you read, make an outline of the important points to remember.
   - Take notes in class as you listen carefully to the discussions.
   - Ask questions when you do not understand what has been discussed.
   - Always complete any assignment thoroughly and on time.

2. Short-term plan:
   - Be sure to understand exactly what material will be included in the test. If necessary, ask your teacher to clarify.
   - Briefly review the text by skimming reading selections you have read.
   - Thoroughly review all your outlines, notes, and the correct answers to your assignments.
   - On the day of the test, eat a good meal, relax, and do your best.

Test Preparation

When answering an essay test question, read the question more than once to make sure you know what is being asked. If possible, ask the teacher to clarify any words or questions you don't understand.

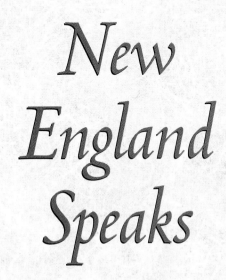

New England Speaks

We looked upon a world unknown,
On nothing we could call our own.
Around the glistening wonder bent
The blue walls of the firmament,
No cloud above, no earth below,—
A universe of sky and snow!
—John Greenleaf Whittier

Morning Light, Walter Elmer Schofield. Giraudon/Art Resource

1844 Sarah Margaret Fuller becomes first female journalist.

1849 Hawthorne begins writing *The Scarlet Letter*.

1851 Melville's *Moby-Dick* appears.

1854 Thoreau publishes *Walden*.

1855 Longfellow celebrates Native American legends.

1863 President Lincoln gives the "Gettysburg Address."

1840	1845	1850	1855	1860	1865

1848 First Women's Rights Convention held in Seneca Falls, NY.

1849 California "Gold Rush" attracts 80,000 prospectors.

1857 Supreme Court makes decision in Dred Scott case.

1865 Thirteenth Amendment abolishes slavery.

HISTORICAL HIGHLIGHTS

New England Speaks

The America of the 1800s was a land of great variation. Would you have preferred the wild West or the sophisticated East? If you like outdoor life, you would have enjoyed pioneering in the West. If you prefer to spend time discussing ideas, you would have been happy in the eastern part of the country.

■ THE IMPORTANCE OF AMERICAN IDEAS

In 1800, Thomas Jefferson was elected president. Jefferson dreamed of the United States as a strong nation of individuals. This thought helped to shape America over the next hundred years. Writers no longer turned to Europe for their ideas. Instead they wanted to write about their experiences in their own country.

■ THE TRANSCENDENTALISTS

New England, particularly the area around Boston, was especially famous for the number of writers it produced and the influence of their ideas. One Boston group, the Transcendentalists, often met at Ralph Waldo Emerson's home. The Transcendentalists believed that people should examine their innermost feelings. Returning to nature, they thought, would help them to do this. One member of the group, Henry David Thoreau, built a humble cabin at Walden Pond near Boston, where he lived alone for over two years. His book, *Walden*, about this experience is still read all over the world.

1886 Emily Dickinson dies, leaving 1,775 unpublished poems.

1895 Stephen Crane publishes *The Red Badge of Courage.*

| 1870 | 1875 | 1880 | 1885 | 1890 | 1895 |

1869 Transcontinental railroad completed at Promontory, UT.

1876 Alexander Graham Bell patents the telephone.

1896 Supreme Court approves "separate but equal" racial segregation.

The Transcendentalists influenced many writers who were not members of the group, including poet Emily Dickinson. Though only two of Dickinson's poems were published during her lifetime, today she is considered one of America's finest writers.

■ THE ABOLITIONISTS

Many 19th century writers were active in the movement to abolish slavery. Among the New England writers who protested slavery were Henry David Thoreau and the poets James Russell Lowell and John Greenleaf Whittier.

■ OTHER INFLUENCES

Some New England writers of the period did not belong to any particular group but rather based their themes on their personal experiences and interests. Nathaniel Hawthorne and Henry Wadsworth Longfellow, for example, both derived some of their inspiration from history. Herman Melville, a New Yorker, spent many years working on whaling ships. On these voyages, he gathered information for several of his books. Melville is included here because he was influenced by the Transcendentalists and because whaling is considered to be a New England topic.

The selections in this unit focus on literature from New England in the 1800s. As you read the selections, think about the ideas they contain. What thoughts and feelings do you share with the writers? Can you see how growing up in America shaped their writing?

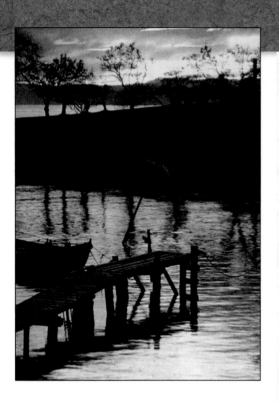

RHYME

Poets use various techniques to convey their ideas and feelings. One of the devices a poet uses is repetition of sounds to create rhyme. In poetry, **rhyme** is a regular repetition of sounds.

There are two ways in which a poet can use rhyme in a poem. The kind of rhyme most frequently used is **end rhyme**. End rhymes occur when words at the end of lines rhyme with each other. *Splash* and *crash* rhyme in these lines:

Tiny waves just splash
While giant waves do crash
Upon the silent shore.

However, some writers use internal rhymes; that is, words that rhyme within a single line. In this line, *Squirrels leaping and creeping on waving branches*, the words *leaping* and *creeping* are an example of internal rhyme.

As you read the following poems, ask yourself:

1. Would the flow of the poems change if Longfellow had not used rhyme?
2. How did Longfellow's use of rhyme contribute to the pace of the poem?

READING FOCUS

Understand Figures of Speech A simile is a comparison of two things using *like* or *as*. For example, "the pencil was red" might be written as "the pencil was as red as a licorice stick." A metaphor also compares but without the use of the words *like* or *as*. As you read "Paul Revere's Ride," look for these types of figures of speech. Think about how these figures of speech help create the mood, or feeling, of the poem.

WRITING CONNECTION

Make a list of six pairs of rhyming words. Then use one pair of words to write an end rhyme.

from
Paul Revere's Ride

by Henry Wadsworth Longfellow

Listen, my children, and you shall hear
Of the midnight ride of Paul Revere,
On the eighteenth of April, in Seventy-five;
Hardly a man is now alive

5   Who remembers that famous day and year.[1]

He said to his friend, "If the British march
By land or sea from the town to-night,
Hang a lantern aloft in the belfry arch
Of the North Church tower as a signal light,—

10   One, if by land, and two, if by sea;
And I on the opposite shore will be,
Ready to ride and spread the alarm
Through every Middlesex village and farm,
For the country folk to be up and to arm."

15   Then he said, "Good night!" and with muffled oar
Silently rowed to the Charlestown shore,
Just as the moon rose over the bay,
Where swinging wide at her moorings lay
The Somerset, British man-of-war;

20   A phantom ship, with each mast and spar
Across the moon like a prison bar,
And a huge black hulk, that was magnified
By its own reflection in the tide.

---

belfry (BEL free) bell tower
moorings (MUUR ingz) ropes to fasten a ship
man-of-war (man uv WAWR) warship
spar (SPAHR) pole attached to mast
hulk (HULK) old ship
[1]**famous day and year:** Longfellow's poem was written about 80 years after the events described.

Meanwhile, his friend, through alley and street,
25 Wanders and watches with eager ears,
Till in the silence around him he hears
The muster of men at the barrack door,
The sound of arms, and the tramp of feet,
And the measured tread of the grenadiers,
30 Marching down to their boats on the shore. . . .

On the opposite shore walked Paul Revere.
Now he patted his horse's side,
Now gazed at the landscape far and near,
Then, impetuous, stamped the earth,
35 And turned and tightened his saddle-girth;
But mostly he watched with eager search
The belfry-tower of the Old North Church,
As it rose above the graves on the hill,
Lonely and spectral and sombre and still.
40 And lo! as he looks, on the belfry's height
A glimmer, and then a gleam of light!
He springs to the saddle, the bridle he turns,
But lingers and gazes, till full on his sight
A second lamp in the belfry burns!

45 A hurry of hoofs in a village street,
A shape in the moonlight, a bulk in the dark,
And beneath, from the pebbles, in passing, a spark
Struck out by a steed flying fearless and fleet:
That was all! And yet, through the gloom and the light,
50 The fate of a nation was riding that night;
And the spark struck out by that steed, in his flight,
Kindled the land into flame with its heat. . .

It was twelve by the village clock,
When he crossed the bridge into Medford town. . . .

---

muster (MUS tur) roll call
grenadier (gren uh DIR) foot soldier
impetuous (im PECH oo us) eager; violent
girth (GURTH) strap that holds saddle on horse
spectral (SPEK trul) ghostlike
sombre (SOM bur) usually spelled somber; dark and gloomy
bulk (BULK) object; shape
fleet (FLEET) very fast

Paul Revere's Ride from Boston to Lexington, 19th century. The Granger Collection

55   It was one by the village clock,
When he galloped into Lexington. . . .

It was two by the village clock,
When he came to the bridge in Concord town.
He heard the bleating of the flock,
60   And the twitter of birds among the trees,
And felt the breath of the morning breeze
Blowing over the meadows brown.
And one was safe and asleep in his bed
Who at the bridge would be first to fall,

---

bleating (BLEET ing) cry of sheep

65   Who that day would be lying dead,
       Pierced by a British musket-ball.

       You know the rest. In the books you have read,
       How the British Regulars[2] fired and fled,—
       How the farmers gave them ball for ball,
70   From behind each fence and farm-yard wall,
       Chasing the red-coats down the lane,
       Then crossing the fields to emerge again
       Under the trees at the turn of the road,
       And only pausing to fire and load.

75   So through the night rode Paul Revere;
       And so through the night went his cry of alarm
       To every Middlesex village and farm, —
       A cry of defiance and not of fear,
       A voice in the darkness, a knock at the door,
80   And a word that shall echo forevermore!
       For, borne on the night-wind of the Past,
       Through all our history, to the last,
       In the hour of darkness and peril and need,
       The people will waken and listen to hear
85   The hurrying hoof-beats of that steed,
       And the midnight message of Paul Revere.

---

[2]**British Regulars:** These were regular army troops.

Twilight on the Shawangunk, 1865, T. Worthington Whittredge. The Granger Collection

from
THE DAY IS DONE

by Henry Wadsworth Longfellow

The day is done, and the darkness
Falls from the wings of Night,
As a feather is wafted downward
From an eagle in his flight.

5   I see the lights of the village
Gleam through the rain and the mist,
And a feeling of sadness comes o'er me
That my soul cannot resist:

A feeling of sadness and longing,
10   That is not akin to pain,
And resembles sorrow only
As the mist resembles the rain.

---

wafted (WAHFT id) blown along smoothly
akin (uh KIN) related

Come, read to me some poem,
Some simple and heartfelt lay,
15   That shall soothe this restless feeling,
And banish the thoughts of day.

Such songs have power to quiet
The restless pulse of care,
And come like the benediction
20   That follows after prayer.

Then read from the treasured volume
The poem of thy choice,
And lend to the rhyme of the poet
The beauty of thy voice.

25   And the night shall be filled with music,
And the cares, that infest the day,
Shall fold their tents, like the Arabs,
And as silently steal away.

---

heartfelt (HAHRT felt) sincere; meaningful
lay (LAY) short song or story poem
benediction (ben uh DIK shun) blessing
infest (in FEST) trouble; disturb

Henry Wadsworth Longfellow (1807–1882)

At the time of his death, and for years after, Henry Wadsworth Longfellow had no rival as America's best-loved poet. His poetry often appeared in magazines. His books were in constant demand. Schoolchildren read dozens of his poems and often had to memorize several.

Longfellow's popularity is easy to understand. He saw beauty everywhere—in an old ship against the moon in Boston Harbor, in the forests, in the fields. He was interested in the common life of the common people. He usually wrote rather simple, melodious poems that nearly everyone could understand. But most of all, he calmed the nerves of the nation. In an age when life was often hard, Longfellow told his American readers to work hard and to accept whatever fate had to offer.

Longfellow's life was mostly a comfortable one. He grew up in Maine, graduated from college at an early age, and went to Europe for further study. Afterwards, he kept two careers going at the same time—first as a poet, and second as a professor of foreign languages. He lived to see his poetry translated into 24 languages. But as he told his readers, "Into each life some rain must fall." In 1861, his wife burned to death when her dress accidentally caught fire. Longfellow's own struggle out of sorrow is reflected in some of his poems.

In his own day, what features of Longfellow's poetry do you think most appealed to his readers?

Review the Selection

UNDERSTAND THE SELECTION

Recall

1. When did Paul Revere make his ride?

2. Upon whom did he depend for information about the British troops?

3. What did the speaker in "The Day Is Done" like at the end of the day?

Infer

4. Paraphrase what Longfellow wrote about in "The Day Is Done."

5. Describe how you think the *Somerset* looked to Paul Revere as he rowed by.

6. Why do you think Longfellow wrote that "the fate of a nation was riding that night"?

7. Why do you think Longfellow wrote a poem about this night?

Apply

8. Predict what might have happened if the British had come by land.

9. What might Revere have thought while waiting for the signal?

10. Predict what you think happened to the speaker in "The Day Is Done" after hearing the poem.

Respond to Literature

How does "Paul Revere's Ride" reflect the feelings of Americans in the 1800s?

WRITE ABOUT THE SELECTION

At the conclusion of "Paul Revere's Ride," Longfellow wrote that there is "a word that shall echo forevermore!" What word was this? Remember that many colonists had fled from Europe to escape religious persecution, poverty, and oppression. What do you think freedom meant to the colonists? What does it mean to you? Suppose that you are one of those colonists who has come to America in search of freedom. Add a four-line stanza to the poem in which you write what freedom means to you.

Prewriting Jot down on a piece of paper in note form what freedom means to you. Include at least three ideas. Then, write pairs of rhyming words that relate to your ideas. Use your list to help you write the stanza.

Writing Use your notes and the list of rhyming words to write an additional stanza for "Paul Revere's Ride." Use this line to start: "Two hundred years later and no one need fear." Add four lines to this.

Revising Read your stanza several times to get a feel for the movement of the lines. Then delete or sharpen the wording of any lines that take away from the pace of the stanza.

Proofreading When writing poetry, be sure that each line begins with a capital letter and that the rhyming words are at the end of lines. Punctuate your verses as you would any prose sentence.

THINK ABOUT RHYME

Rhyme contributed greatly to the movement and pace of the two poems you have just read. Some words that rhyme have soft sounds that can make a poem seem to move slowly. Other words have crisp sounds that produce a steady pace. In "Paul Revere's Ride," the rhymes contribute to the feeling of urgency that Longfellow has written into the poem. How will the British advance? Will it be by land or sea? Will Paul Revere warn the colonists in time?

1. What kind of rhymes did Longfellow use in "Paul Revere's Ride"?

2. What was the pace of "Paul Revere's Ride"?

3. How did the pace of "The Day Is Done" differ from that of "Paul Revere's Ride"?

4. Which of the rhyming words in the second stanza of "Paul Revere's Ride" move the poem along at a steady pace?

5. Why do these words help move the poem along at a steady pace?

READING FOCUS
Understand Figures of Speech As you read "Paul Revere's Ride" and "The Day Is Done," you were asked to look for figures of speech. Choose your favorite simile or metaphor and explain how the comparison helped to create the mood of the poem.

DEVELOP YOUR VOCABULARY

Review the meanings of the vocabulary words from this selection. Context can often help you figure out the meaning of an unfamiliar word. Read this sentence: The captain gave his *heartfelt* thanks to the crew, and his warm sincerity touched them all. By the author's use of the words *warm sincerity* and *touched* you are better able to understand what *heartfelt* meant.

Read the following sentences. Use context clues to help you figure out the meaning of each italicized word. Underline the words that help you.

1. The *moorings* of the boat were not fastened tightly, and the ropes loosened.

2. The *spar* snapped in the rough winds, toppling the pole into the sea.

3. The leaves *wafted* gently through the air, moving slowly to the ground.

4. He watched the *belfry* closely, knowing at any moment he would hear the signal from the tower.

5. The *tempestuous* sea threw the boat violently in all directions.

6. The *grenadiers* moved slowly along on foot, not knowing that enemy soldiers were close behind.

Learn About

ESSAYS

Essays are nonfictional compositions. They are usually short and can be either formal or informal in style.

Formal essays are serious, very organized writings intended to inform or persuade. **Informal essays**, on the other hand, usually have a less serious purpose. They are not so rigorously organized and exhibit a more conversational style. These essays are usually meant to describe a personal experience.

There are many other classifications of essays. Sometimes essays are classified as narrative, descriptive, reflective, or editorial. These categories correspond roughly to the four types of writing: narrative, descriptive, expository, and persuasive.

As you read the following selections, ask yourself:

1. What purpose did each author have in writing the essay?
2. How would you classify each essay?

WRITING CONNECTION

Think of a prized possession that you own. Write a paragraph explaining your personal view or feeling about the object.

READING FOCUS

Identify Supporting Details Essays are an opportunity for authors to present their own opinions on a subject. They develop their ideas through the use of details, facts, and examples. As you read the selections from *Walden* and *Nature*, look for ways in which the authors support their opinions. Jot down each opinion and how it is supported by details.

from
WALDEN

ADAPTED

by Henry David Thoreau

At a certain season of our life we are accustomed to consider every spot as the possible site of a house. I have thus surveyed the country on every side within a dozen miles of where I live. In imagination I have bought all the farms in succession, for all were to be bought, and I knew their price. I walked over each farmer's land, tasted his wild apples, talked about farming with him, took his farm at his price, at any price, mortgaging it to him in my mind. I even put a higher price on it,—took everything but a deed of it. I took his word for his deed, for I dearly loved to talk. I cultivated it, and him too to some extent, I trust. Then I withdrew when I had enjoyed it long enough, leaving him to carry it on. This experience entitled me to be regarded as a sort of real-estate broker by my friends. Wherever I sat, there I might live, and the landscape radiated from me accordingly. What is a house but a *sedes*, a seat?— better if a country seat. I discovered many a site for a house not likely to be soon improved. Some might have thought it too far from the village, but to my eyes the village was too far from it. Well, there I might live, I said. And there I did live, for

an hour, a summer and a winter life; saw how I could let the years run off, buffet the winter through, and see the spring come in. The future inhabitants of this region, wherever they may place their houses, may be sure that they have been anticipated. An afternoon was enough time to lay out the land into orchard, woodlot and pasture, and to decide what fine oaks or pines should be left to stand before the door, and from where each blasted tree could be seen to the best advantage; and then I let it lie, fallow perhaps, for a man is rich in proportion to the number of things which he can afford to let alone.

My imagination carried me so far that I even had the refusal of several farms—the refusal was all I wanted—but I never got my fingers burned by actual possession. The nearest that I came to actual possession was when I bought the Hollowell Place. I had begun to sort my seeds, and collected materials with which to make a wheelbarrow to carry it on or off with. But before the owner gave me a deed of it, his wife changed her mind and wished to keep it, and he offered me ten dollars to release him. Now, to speak

---

cultivated (KUL tuh vayt id) prepared and cared for the land on which plants grow
fallow (FAL oh) land that is plowed, but not seeded

the truth, I had but ten cents in the world, and it surpassed my arithmetic to tell, if I was that man who had ten cents, or who had a farm, or ten dollars, or all together. However, I let him keep the ten dollars and the farm too, for I had carried it far enough; or rather, to be generous. I sold him the farm for just what I gave for it. As he was not a rich man, I made him a present of ten dollars, and still had my ten cents, and seeds, and materials for a wheelbarrow left. I found thus that I had been a rich man without any damage to my poverty. But I retained the landscape, and have since annually carried off what it yielded without a wheelbarrow. With respect to landscapes:

"I am monarch of all I *survey*,
    My right there is none to dispute."

I have frequently seen a poet withdraw, having enjoyed the most valuable part of a farm, while the crusty farmer supposed that he had got a few wild apples only. Why, the owner does not know it for many years when a poet has put his farm in rhyme, the most admirable kind of invisible fence, has fairly impounded it, milked it, skimmed it, and got all the cream, and left the farmer only the skimmed milk.

The real attractions of the Hollowell farm, to me, were: its complete retirement, being about two miles from the village, half a mile from the nearest neighbor, and separated from the highway by a broad field. A river bounded the farm, which the owner said protected

---

annually (AN you ul ee) occurring each year
crusty (KRUS tee) curt; rude

it by its fogs from frosts in the spring, though that was nothing to me. I was also attracted to the gray color and ruinous state of the house and barn, and the dilapidated fences, which put such an interval between me and the last occupant; the hollow and lichen-covered apple trees, gnawed by rabbits, showing what kind of neighbors I should have. But above all, the recollection I had of it from my earliest voyages up the river. The house was concealed behind a thick grove of red maples, through which I heard the house-dog bark. I was in haste to buy it, before the owner finished getting out some rocks, cutting down the hollow apple trees, and grubbing up some young birches which had sprung up in the pasture, or, in short, had made any more of his improvements. To enjoy these advantages I was ready to carry it on; like Atlas,[1] to take the world on my shoulders—I never heard what compensation he received for that—and do all those things which had no other motive or excuse but that I might pay for it and be unmolested in my possession of it. I knew all the while that it would yield the most plentiful crop of the kind I wanted if I could only afford to let it alone. But it turned out as I have said.

All that I could say, then, with respect to farming on a large scale (I have always cultivated a garden) was that I had had my seeds ready. Many think that seeds improve with age. I have no doubt that time can tell the difference between the good and the bad; and when at last I shall plant, I shall be less likely to be disappointed. But I would say to my fellows, once for all, as long as possible live free and uncommitted. It makes but little difference whether you are committed to a farm or the county jail.

Old Cato,[2] whose "Of Things Rustic" is my "Cultivator," says, and the only translation I have seen makes sheer nonsense of the passage, "When you think of getting a farm, turn it thus in your mind, not to buy greedily; nor spare your pains to look at it, and do not think it enough to go round it once. The oftener you go there the more it will please you, if it is good." I think I shall not buy greedily, but go round and round it as long as I live, and be buried in it first, that it may please me the more at last. . . .

I do not propose to write an ode to dejection, but to brag as lustily as chanticleer in the morning, standing on his roost, if only to wake my neighbors up.

When first I took up my home in the woods, that is, began to spend my nights as well as days there, which, by accident, was on Independence Day, or the fourth of July, 1845, my house was not finished for winter. It was merely a defense against the rain, without plastering or chimney. The walls were of rough weatherstained boards, with wide chinks,

---

chanticleer (CHAN tih klir) a rooster
[1]**Atlas:** from Greek mythology, a Titan who supported the heavens on his shoulders
[2]**Old Cato:** Roman statesman (234–149 B.C.)

Wisconsin Farm Scene, Paul Seifert. The Granger Collection

which made it cool at night. The upright white hewn posts and freshly planed door and window casings gave it a clean and airy look, especially in the morning, when its beams were saturated with dew, so that I fancied that by noon some sweet gum would exude from them. To my imagination it retained throughout the day more or less of this morning character. It reminded me of a certain house on a mountain which I had visited the year before. This was an airy and unplastered cabin. It was fit to entertain a traveling god, and where a goddess might trail her garments. The winds which passed over my home were such as sweep over ridges of mountains, bearing the broken strains, or heavenly parts only, of earthly music. The morning wind forever blows, the poem of creation is uninterrupted; but few are the ears that hear it. Olympus[3] is but the outside of the earth everywhere. . . .

I went to the woods because I wished to live thoughtfully, to face only the bare facts of life. I wanted to see if I could not learn what it had to teach, and not, when I came to die, discover that I had not lived. I did not wish to live what was not life, living is so dear. Nor did I wish to practice resignation, unless it was quite necessary. I wanted to live deep and suck out all the marrow of life, to live so sturdily and hardily as to crush all that was not life. I wanted to cut a broad path and shave close, to drive life into a corner,

---

[3]**Olympus:** in Greek mythology, the home of the gods

and reduce it to its lowest terms. If it proved to be mean, why then I wanted to eat the whole and genuine meanness of it, and publish its meanness to the world. If it were sublime, I wanted to know it by experience, and be able to give a true account of it in my next excursion. For most men, it appears to me, are in a strange uncertainty about it, whether it is of the Devil or of God. . . .

Still we live meanly, like ants; though the fable tells us that we were long ago changed into men. . . . It is an error upon error, and clout upon clout, and our best virtue has for its occasion a superfluous and evitable wretchedness. Our life is frittered away by detail. An honest man has hardly need to count more than his ten fingers, or in extreme cases he may add his ten toes, and lump the rest. Simplicity, simplicity, simplicity! I say, let your affairs be as two or three, and not a hundred or a thousand; instead of a million count half a dozen, and keep your accounts on your thumbnail. In the midst of this chopping sea of civilized life, such are the clouds and storms and quicksands and thousand-and-one items to be allowed for, that a man has to live, if he would not founder and go to the bottom and not make his port at all, by dead reckoning. He must be a great calculator indeed who succeeds. Simplify, simplify. Instead of three meals a day, if it be necessary eat but one. Instead of a hundred dishes, five; and reduce other things in proportion. Our life is like a German Confederacy,[4] made up of petty states, with its boundary forever changing, so that even a German cannot tell you how it is bounded at any moment. The nation itself, with all its so-called internal improvements, which, by the way, are all external and shallow, is just such an unwieldy and overgrown establishment, cluttered with furniture and tripped up by its own traps, ruined by luxury and heedless expense, by want of calculation and a worthy aim, as the million households in the land; and the only cure for it as for them is in a rigid economy, a stern and more than Spartan simplicity of life and elevation of purpose. It lives too fast. Men think that it is essential that the *Nation* have trade, and export ice, and talk through a telegraph, and ride thirty miles an hour, without a doubt, whether *they* do or not; but whether we should live like baboons or like men, is a little uncertain. If we do not get out railroad track ties and forge rails, and devote days and nights to the work, but go to tinkering upon our *lives* to improve *them*, who will build railroads? And if railroads are not built, how shall we get to heaven in season? But if we stay at home and mind our business, who will want railroads? We do not ride on the railroad; it rides upon us. . . .

Time is but the stream I go a-fishing in. I drink at it; but while I drink I see the

---

superfluous (suu PUR floo us) beyond what is required
dead reckoning (DED REK un ing) navigating without the assistance of stars
[4]**German confederacy:** At the time, Germany was a loose union of 38 independent states, with no common government.

sandy bottom and detect how shallow it is. Its thin current slides away, but eternity remains. I would drink deeper; fish in the sky, whose bottom is pebbly with stars. I cannot count one. I know not the first letter of the alphabet. I have always been regretting that I was not as wise as the day I was born. The intellect is a cleaver. It discerns and rifts its way into the secret of things. I do not wish to be any more busy with my hands than is necessary. My head is hands and feet. I feel all my best faculties concentrated in it. My inner feelings tell me that my head is an organ for burrowing, as some creatures use their snout and forepaws, and with it I would mine and burrow my way through these hills. I think that the richest vein is somewhere hereabouts.

I left the woods for as good a reason as I went there. Perhaps it seemed to me that I had several more lives to live, and could not spare any more time for that one. It is remarkable how easily and insensibly we fall into a particular route, and make a beaten track for ourselves. I had not lived there a week before my feet wore a path from my door to the pondside. Though it is five or six years since I trod it, it is still quite distinct. It is true, I fear that others may have fallen into it, and so helped to keep it open. The surface of the earth is soft and impressible by the feet of men; and so with the paths which the mind travels. How worn and dusty, then, must be the highways of the world, how deep the ruts of tradition and conformity! I did not wish to take a cabin passage, but rather to go before the mast and on the deck of the world, for there I could best see the moonlight amid the mountains. I do not wish to go below now.

I learned this, at least, by my experiment. If one advances confidently in the direction of his dreams, and endeavors to live the life which he has imagined, he will meet with a success unexpected in common hours. He will put some things behind and will pass an invisible boundary. New, universal, and more liberal laws will begin to establish themselves around and within him. Or the old laws will be expanded, and interpreted in his favor in a more liberal sense. He will live with the license of a higher order of beings. In proportion as he simplifies his life, the laws of the universe will appear less complex, and solitude will not be solitude, nor poverty poverty, nor weakness weakness. If you have built castles in the air, your work need not be lost; that is where they should be. Now put the foundations under them. . . .

Why should we be in such a desperate hurry to succeed, and in such desperate enterprises? If a man does not keep pace with his companions, perhaps it is because he hears a different drummer. Let him step to the music which he hears, however, measured or far away. It is not important that he should grow as soon as an apple tree or an oak. Shall he turn his

---

conformity (kun FAWR muh tee) behavior that is in agreement with current rules
common (KOM un) piece of public land

spring into summer? If the condition of things which we were made for is not yet, what were any reality which we can substitute? We will not be shipwrecked on a vain reality. Shall we with pains erect a heaven of blue glass over ourselves, though when it is done we shall be sure to gaze still at the true ethereal heaven far above, as if the former were not?. . . .

However mean your life is, meet it and live it; do not shun it and call it hard names. It is not so bad as you are. It looks poorest when you are richest. The fault-finder will find faults even in paradise. Love your life, poor as it is. You may perhaps have some pleasant, thrilling, glorious hours, even in a poorhouse. The setting sun is reflected from the windows of the poorhouse as brightly as from the rich man's home. The snow melts before its door as early in the spring. I do not see but a quiet mind may live as contentedly there, and have as cheering thoughts, as in a palace. The town's poor seem to me often to live the most independent lives of any. Maybe they are simply great enough to receive without misgiving. Most think that they are above being supported by the town; but it oftener happens that they are not above supporting themselves by dishonest means, which should be more disreputable. Cultivate poverty like a garden herb, like sage. Do not trouble yourself much to get new things, whether clothes or friends. Turn the old; return to them. Things do not change; we change. Sell your clothes and keep your thoughts. God will see that you do not want society. If I were confined to a corner of an attic

A Catskill Waterfall, Homer D. Martin.
Corbis Bettmann

all my days, like a spider, the world would be just as large to me while I had my thoughts about me. The philosopher said: "From an army of three divisions one can take away its general, and put it in disorder; from the man the most abject and vulgar one cannot take away his thought." Do not seek so anxiously to

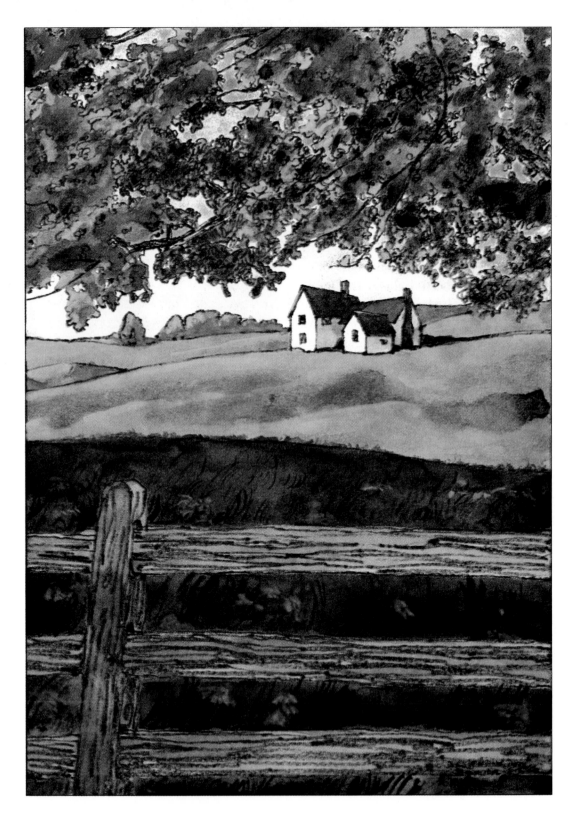

be developed, to subject yourself to many influences to be played on; it is all dissipation. Humility like darkness reveals the heavenly lights. The shadows of poverty and meanness gather around us, "and lo! creation widens to our view."[5] We are often reminded that if there were bestowed on us the wealth of Croesus[6], our aims must still be the same, and our means essentially the same. Moreover, if you are restricted in your range by poverty, if you cannot buy books and newspapers, for instance, you are but confined to the most significant and vital experiences. You are compelled to deal with the material which yields the most sugar and the most starch. It is life near the bone where it is sweetest. You are defended from being a trifler. No man loses ever on a lower level by magnanimity on a higher. Superfluous wealth can buy superfluities only. Money is not required to buy one necessary of the soul. . . .

The life in us is like the water in the river. It may rise this year higher than man has ever known it, and flood the dry uplands; even this may be the eventful year, which will drown out all our muskrats. It will not always be dry land where we dwell. I see far inland the banks which the stream anciently washed, before science began to record its freshets. Everyone has heard the story which has gone the rounds of New England.

A strong and beautiful bug came out of the dry leaf of an old table of apple-tree wood. It had stood in a farmer's kitchen for sixty years, first in Connecticut, and afterward in Massachusetts. An egg had been deposited in the living tree many years earlier still, as appeared by counting the annual layers beyond it. It was heard gnawing out for several weeks, hatched perhaps by the heat of an urn. Who does not feel his faith in a resurrection and immortality strengthened by hearing of this? Who knows what beautiful and winged life, whose egg has been buried for ages under many concentric layers of woodenness in the dead dry life of society, deposited at first in the soft wood of the green and living tree, which has been gradually converted into the semblance of its well-seasoned tomb—heard perhaps gnawing out now for years by the astonished family of man, as they sat round the festive board—may unexpectedly come forth from amidst society's most trivial and handselled furniture, to enjoy its perfect summer life at last!

I do not say that the average person will realize all this; but such is the character of that morrow which mere lapse of time can never make to dawn. The light which puts out our eyes is darkness to us. Only that day dawns to which we are awake. There is more day to dawn. The sun is but a morning star.

---

[5] **and lo! creation widens to our view:** from the sonnet "To Night" by British poet Joseph Blanco White
[6] **Croesus:** the king of Lydia (516 B.C.) thought to be the wealthiest person of his time

from

Nature

ADAPTED

by Ralph Waldo Emerson

Nature is a setting that fits equally well a funny or a sad piece. In good health, the air is a drink of incredible goodness. Crossing a bare common, in snow puddles, at twilight, under a clouded sky, without having in my thought any occurrence of special good fortune, I have enjoyed a perfect happiness. I am glad to the brink of fear. In the woods, too, a man casts off his years, as the snake sheds his skin, and at what period soever of life is always a child. In the woods is long lasting youth. Within these plantations of God, good behavior and holiness reign, a lasting festival is dressed. The guest sees not how he should tire of them in a thousand years. In the woods, we return to reason and faith. There I feel that nothing can happen to me in life—no disgrace, no accident (leaving me my eyes), which nature cannot repair. Standing on the bare ground—my head bathed by the care-free air and uplifted into infinite space—all mean self importance goes away. I become a transparent eyeball:

I am nothing: I am nothing: I see all. The currents of the Universal Being circulate through me; I am part or parcel of God. The name of the nearest friend sounds then foreign and accidental: to be brothers, to be acquaintances, master or servant, is then of little importance and a disturbance. I am the lover of uncontained and immortal beauty. In the wilderness, I find something more dear than in the streets or villages. In the peaceful landscape, and especially in the distant line of the horizon, man beholds something as beautiful as his own nature.

The greatest delight which the fields and woods give is the suggestion of a mysterious relation between man and vegetable. I am not alone and unacknowledged. They nod to me, and I to them. The waving of the boughs in the storm is new to me and old. It takes me by surprise, and yet is not unknown. Its effect is like that of a higher thought or a better emotion coming over me, when I considered I was thinking justly or doing right.

Pool in the Woods, George Inness. Corbis Bettmann

Yet it is certain that the power to produce this delight does not reside in nature, but in man, or in a harmony of both. It is necessary to use these pleasures with great moderation. For nature is not always dressed in holiday attire. The same scene which yesterday breathed perfume is overspread with sadness today. Nature always wears the colors of the spirit. To a man laboring under disaster, the heat of his own fire hath sadness in it. Then there is a kind of contempt of the landscape felt by him who has just lost by death a dear friend. The sky is less grand as it shuts down over less worth in the population.

Review the Selection

UNDERSTAND THE SELECTION

Recall

1. List two of Thoreau's examples that suggest that people live too fast.

2. When did Thoreau start living in the woods?

3. Where did Emerson find beauty?

Infer

4. Why did Thoreau live in the woods?

5. Why did Thoreau believe people should follow their dreams?

6. Briefly paraphrase how Emerson felt when he was in the woods.

7. How did nature help Emerson and Thoreau explore their feelings?

Apply

8. If you lived in the woods, would you spend a lot of time observing nature?

9. Predict what you think might happen if Thoreau had continued to live in the woods.

10. Select a line from one of the essays that you believe is a good and wise thought and tell why.

Respond to Literature

List several ways in which Thoreau's and Emerson's writings reflect the feelings of the time in which they wrote.

WRITE ABOUT THE SELECTION

Emerson and Thoreau make it very clear that nature and the wilderness were very important to them. They tell the reader that going to the country cleared their heads and made them forget their troubles. Where would you like to go to forget your troubles? Think about a special imaginary place where you would feel happy and forget your cares.

Prewriting Freewrite for a few sentences about an imaginary place where you could reflect quietly about your life. What would the place look like? How would it make you feel? How long do you think you would want to stay? You might want to jot down some extra words that describe your imaginary place.

Writing Use your ideas to write a descriptive paragraph about a wonderful place you can go when you want to forget your worries. Try to include words that consistently reflect your feelings about your special place.

Revising Reread your paragraph. When you revise, make sure you include several words that express your feelings accurately. Try to use vivid adjectives rather than settling for the first ones that come to mind.

Proofreading Read over your paragraph to check for errors. Check your punctuation and spelling, particularly the spelling of any new words you have chosen to use.

THINK ABOUT ESSAYS

Although the Thoreau essay is an excerpt from a full-sized book, his prose and purpose follow essay style. Emerson is perhaps better known for his essays than his poetry. A very wide variety of topics and types are included in the genre of essay—so many, in fact, that critics find it difficult to categorize them all.

1. How would you classify the Thoreau excerpt—as narrative, descriptive, reflective (expository), or editorial (persuasive)? Explain.

2. Which of Thoreau's ideas did you find most thought-provoking? Why?

3. A parable is a short simple story used to point out a moral lesson. What parable did Thoreau use in his essay? What did it teach?

4. How would you classify the Emerson excerpt—as narrative, descriptive, reflective, or editorial? Explain.

5. Are the essays you have read formal or informal in style? Explain.

READING FOCUS

Identify Supporting Details Writers can make readers agree with them more readily if they provide strong support for their opinions. Thoreau and Emerson state many opinions in their essays. Choose an opinion from one of their essays and list several supporting details provided.

DEVELOP YOUR VOCABULARY

An *allusion* is a reference in speech or writing to an event, person, place, or thing that presumably is familiar to the listener or reader. Thoreau makes several allusions in his essay—to the mythological giant Atlas, to the Roman statesman Cato, and to the extremely rich king of ancient Lydia, Croesus, to name three of them.

There are a large number of English words that allude to people and places. They are called **eponymous** words. They are words derived from the name of a real or mythical person. For example, *saxophone* comes from the name of its inventor, Adolphe Sax. *Panic*, the word for a sudden, unreasoning fear, comes from the mythical god Pan, who had a reputation for frightening travelers in woodland areas.

Look up the following words in a dictionary that has word histories. Identify the meaning and place or person each word comes from.

1. cardigan   4. quixotic
2. sandwich   5. watt
3. marathon   6. cereal

Learn About

THEME

The **theme** of a piece of literature is the message that the writer wants to convey to the reader. There are several reasons why it is important to understand the theme. First, theme helps you to understand how the writer feels about something. For example, it may be the writer's view of life. Second, theme underscores the relationship between character, events, and the outcome of the story. Finally, theme adds an extra dimension of interest to the story.

Sometimes, writers directly state the theme. However, if they do not, think about what the characters do and what happens to the characters as you read.

As you read "David Swan," ask yourself:

1. Is Hawthorne's message stated directly or indirectly?
2. What is Hawthorne's message to the reader?

WRITING CONNECTION

Suppose that you are a writer. Think of a message you would like to convey to readers. Then think about a character who might be able to carry your message to the readers. Write a brief paragraph describing the character.

READING FOCUS

Draw Conclusions When a character in a story does something, the reader can draw a conclusion about why the character acted in such a way. As you read "David Swan," think about the characters' motivation, or why they act as they do. Ask yourself: What motivates their actions? What do their actions tell about their personalities?

David Swan

by Nathaniel Hawthorne

We find David, at the age of 20, on the high road to the city of Boston, where an uncle was to take him behind the counter in his grocery store. Be it enough to say that he was a native of New Hampshire, born of good parents, and had received an ordinary school education. After traveling on foot from sunrise till nearly noon of a summer's day, his tiredness and the increasing heat forced him to rest. He looked ahead for a shady place where he could wait for the coming of the stagecoach. As if planted on purpose for him, there soon appeared a little tuft of maples. Then he noticed a fresh bubbling spring that seemed never to have sparkled for any traveler but David Swan. He kissed it with thirsty lips, and threw himself down on the bank. For a pillow he used some shirts and a pair of pants, tied up in a striped cotton hand-kerchief. The sunbeams could not reach him. The dust did not rise from the road after the heavy rain of yesterday. In short, his grassy bank suited the young man better than the softest of beds. The spring murmured sleepily beside him, and a deep sleep, perhaps hiding dreams within its depths, fell upon David Swan. But we are to relate events which he did not dream of.

While he lay sound asleep in the shade, other people were wide awake, and passed back and forth, on foot, on horseback, and in all sorts of vehicles. Some looked neither left nor right, and never knew that David was there. Some just glanced that way, without admitting the sleeper to their busy minds. Some laughed to see how soundly he slept. And several, whose hearts were full of scorn, ejected their venomous feelings on David Swan. A middle-aged widow, when no one else was near, told her-

---

tuft (TUFT) small bunch
relate (rih LAYT) tell
eject (ih JEKT) force out
venomous (VEN uh mus) poisonous; spiteful

self that the young fellow looked charming in his sleep. A temperance worker cursed him as an awful example of dead drunkenness by the roadside. But praise, laughter, curses, and even indifference were all one, or rather all nothing, to David Swan.

He had slept only a few minutes when a brown carriage, drawn by a handsome pair of horses, stopped nearly in front of David's resting place. A metal pin had fallen out, so that one of the wheels had slid off. The damage was slight, and brought only a moment's worry to an elderly merchant and his wife, who were returning to Boston in the carriage. While a servant started work on the wheels, the lady and gentleman sheltered themselves beneath the maple trees. There they saw the bubbling spring, and David Swan asleep beside it. The merchant stepped as lightly as he could, and his spouse tried not to rustle her silk dress.

"How soundly he sleeps!" whispered the old gentleman. "From what a depth he draws that easy breath! Such sleep as that would be worth to me more than half my income, for it would suppose good health and a mind free from troubles."

"And youth, besides," said the lady. "Even healthy and quiet old people do not sleep like this. Our slumber is no more like his than our wakefulness."

The longer they looked, the more they felt interested in the unknown youth, to whom the grassy bank and the maple shade were as a secret room. The woman suddenly perceived that a stray sunbeam fell down upon his face. She tried to push a branch to one side, so as to catch it. And having done this little act of kindness, she began to feel like a mother to him.

"Lady Luck seems to have laid him there," she whispered, "and to have brought us here to find him, after our disappointment with our cousin's son. I think I see a likeness to our departed Henry. Shall we waken him?"

"To what purpose?" said the merchant, pausing. "We know nothing about what he's really like."

"That open, honest face!" replied his wife. "This innocent sleep!"

---

temperance (TEM pur uns) belief that no one should drink alcohol
indifference (in DIF ur uns) lack of interest
spouse (SPOUS) husband or wife
perceive (pur SEEV) become aware of
departed (dih PAHRT id) dead

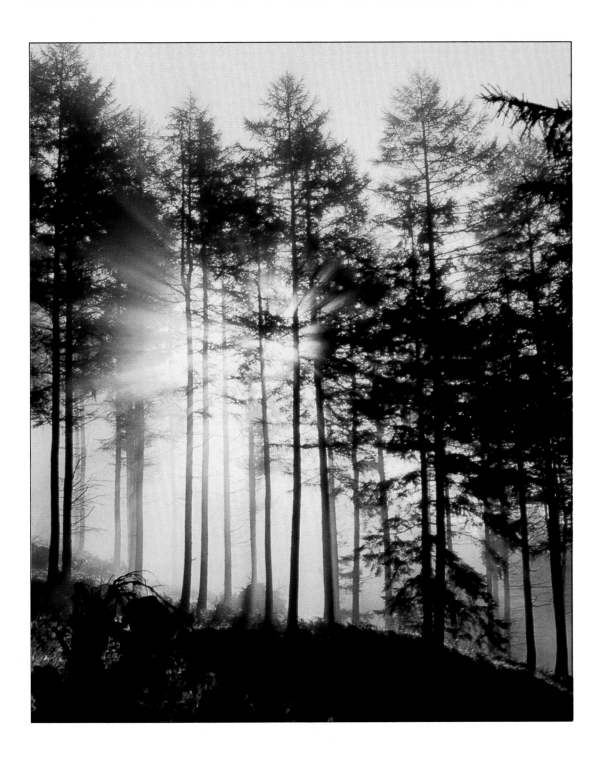

While these whispers were passing, the sleeper's breathing did not change, nor did his face show the least sign of interest. Yet Fortune was bending over him, just ready to let fall a shower of gold. The old merchant had lost his only son, and had no heir except a distant relative, with whose conduct he was dissatisfied. In such cases, people sometimes do stranger things than to act the magician and awaken this youth. He who fell asleep as a poor man would wake up to a rich life.

"Shall we not waken him?" repeated the lady, trying again.

"The coach is ready, sir," said the servant, behind.

The old couple jumped. With red faces, they hurried away. Waken the young man? Who would ever dream of doing anything so very ridiculous! The merchant threw himself back into the carriage, and filled his mind with business. Meanwhile, David Swan enjoyed his nap.

The carriage could not have gone more than a mile, when a charming young woman came along the road. Her lively step showed just how her happy heart was dancing. Perhaps it was this merry kind of motion that caused—is there any harm in saying it?—her garter to slip its knot. Knowing that the silken strap was relaxing its hold, she turned aside into the shelter of the maple trees, and there found a young man asleep by the spring!

Finding that she had stumbled into a gentleman's bedchamber, the girl blushed as red as any rose. "And for such a purpose, too!" she thought. She was about to make her escape on tiptoe— but there was peril near the sleeper. A monster of a bee had been wandering overhead—buzz, buzz, buzz—till finally it seemed to be settling on the eyelid of David Swan. The sting of a bee is sometimes deadly. The girl attacked the bee with her handkerchief, and drove it from beneath the maples. How sweet a picture! This done, with faster breath, and a deeper blush, she stole a glance at the youthful stranger for whom she had been battling with a dragon in the air.

"He is handsome!" thought she, and blushed redder yet.

How could it be that no dream of happiness should grow strong within him? How could it be that no such dream should wake him up, and allow him to see the girl? Why, at least, did no smile brighten upon his face? She had come, the maiden whose

---

peril (PER ul) danger

soul, according to the old and beautiful idea, had once been separated from his own. She had come, the one that he, unknowingly, had so hoped to meet. Her, only, could he love with a perfect love. Him, only, could she receive into the depths of her heart. And now her reflection was faintly blushing in the water, by his side. Should it pass away, its happy glow would leave his life forever.

"How sound he sleeps!" murmured the girl.

She departed, but did not skip along the road so lightly as when she came.

Now, this girl's father was a thriving merchant in the neighborhood, and at the time, he happened to be looking out for just such a man as David Swan. Had David become acquainted with the daughter, he would also have become her father's clerk—and all else in natural order. So here, again, had good Fortune come near David Swan. She had stolen so near that her garments touched him lightly, and he knew nothing of the matter.

The girl was hardly out of sight when two men turned aside beneath the maple shade. Both had evil faces, set off by cloth caps which slanted down over their foreheads. Their clothing was shabby, yet had a certain smartness. These were a couple of rascals who got their living by whatever the devil sent them. Now, having no other business, they had bet the profits of their next piece of villainy on a game of cards, which they planned to play here under the trees. But, finding David asleep by the spring, one of the rogues whispered to the other:

"Hist!—Do you see that bundle under his head?"

The other villain nodded, winked, and leered.

"I'll bet you," said the first, "that there's a nice fat wallet hidden there among his shirts. And if not there, in one of his pants pockets."

"But what if he wakes up?" asked the other.

His companion pushed aside his jacket, pointed at the handle of a large knife, and nodded.

"So be it!" muttered the second villain.

They approached the unconscious David. While one pointed the dagger towards his heart, the other reached for the bundle

---

thriving (THRYV ing) very successful
rogue (ROHG) rascal; villain

under his head. Their two faces, wrinkled and ghastly with guilt and fear, bent over David. They looked horrible enough to be mistaken for fiends, should he suddenly awake. But David Swan had never worn a more tranquil face, even when asleep in his mother's arms.

"I must take away the bundle," whispered one.

"If he moves, I'll strike," muttered the other.

But, at this moment, a dog, its nose to the ground, came in beneath the trees. It looked back and forth at the two evil men, and finally at the quiet sleeper. Then it lapped at the spring.

"Ah!" said one villain. "We can't do anything now. The dog's master must be close behind."

"Let's be off," said the other.

The man with the dagger put it away, and they left the spot joking together. As for David Swan, he still slept quietly, neither conscious of the shadow of death when it hung over him, nor of the glow of renewed life when the shadow departed.

He slept, but no longer so quietly as at first. An hour's repose had taken away his tiredness. Now he moved—first the lips, without a sound—and now he talked, in an inward tone, to the vanishing ghosts of his dream. But a noise of wheels came louder and louder along the road, until it smashed through the disappearing clouds of David's sleep. He jumped up, and there was the stagecoach.

"Hello, driver!" shouted he. "Take a passenger?"

"Room on top," answered the driver.

Up climbed David, and rode away toward Boston. He never glanced back at the spring. He knew not that Wealth had thrown a golden glow upon its waters, nor that Love had sighed softly to their murmurs, nor that Death had threatened to make them red with blood. Sleeping or waking, we never hear the silent footsteps of the things that almost happen. Yet these things are always right beside our paths. It is a wonder that there should still be order enough in human life to make the future even partially known.

---

tranquil (TRANG kwul) peaceful; at rest
repose (rih POHZ) rest

AUTHOR BIOGRAPHY

Nathaniel Hawthorne (1804–1864)

The life of the American writer Nathaniel Hawthorne is living proof that "practice makes perfect." Upon graduation from Bowdoin College in 1825, he made up his mind to be a writer. This was a courageous decision, for at the time the number of Americans who earned a living writing fiction could be counted on the fingers of one hand. Hawthorne knew what his decision would mean—practice, practice, and more practice. He returned to his mother's house in Salem, Massachusetts to write. A year passed and he was still at it. Another year went by, and then more years. After five years of effort, he had sold only one of his stories. Still more time passed. Hawthorne just wouldn't give up. Finally, after "twelve dark years" as he later called them, he published his first book, *Twice-Told Tales*.

But Hawthorne's practice paid off in perfection. Today he's recognized as one of the giants in American literature. Behind his polished sentences, the reader senses a kind, thoughtful man. Hawthorne wrote about the people of his time, of course, but first of all he wrote about ideas. What really makes a person a "criminal"? Is any person completely "good"? Which are more important to the individual, the dreams of youth or the rewards of age? Questions such as these will never die, and neither will the best of Hawthorne's stories.

What did the mature Hawthorne mean when he said there had been "twelve dark years" in his life?

Review the Selection

UNDERSTAND THE SELECTION

Recall

1. Where is David Swan going?

2. List three major events that occur.

3. How is this story like a fantasy?

Infer

4. How do the people who pass feel about David Swan?

5. Interpret "But praise, laughter, curses, and even indifference were all one, or rather all nothing, to David Swan."

6. Why doesn't the elderly merchant want to wake up David Swan?

7. Why are the girl's footsteps not so lively when she leaves?

Apply

8. Predict what might have happened if Swan had awakened.

9. Which event might Swan choose to wake up for? Why?

10. Explain this quote as it applies to the story: "Could we know all that *might* have happened, life would be too full of hope and fear to give us a single hour of true peace."

Respond to Literature

How does the theme of this story illustrate the writing style of the 1800s?

WRITE ABOUT THE SELECTION

At the conclusion of "David Swan," the young man wakes up and catches a stagecoach to Boston where he is to begin a new job at his uncle's grocery store. Because he had been napping, three events pass him by without his knowledge. Is it likely that more events pass him by in Boston? Why? Write a paragraph about something that happens to David Swan in Boston without his knowledge.

Prewriting Freewrite for a few minutes about an event that happens at David Swan's uncle's grocery store. Be sure to include what he was doing that prevents him from knowing about the event. Try to keep in mind that the event occurs in 1837.

Writing Use your freewriting as a basis for your paragraph. Be sure to make it clear that David Swan does not know that the event is taking place.

Revising When you revise, make sure that the details of the event are in keeping with 1837, the year the story takes place. If you have not, delete anything in the story that would not have happened in 1837.

Proofreading Read over your paragraph to check for errors. Be sure that all your sentences end with periods, question marks, or exclamation marks. Check that you have punctuated dialogue correctly and used new vocabulary words appropriately.

THINK ABOUT THEME

By understanding the theme, you can have a greater appreciation for stories you read. It also helps you to develop a clearer understanding of what a writer thinks and feels. Hawthorne introduces his own story, in which he gives the reader a clear picture of what the theme is. Then he explains that the story will illustrate this idea. In effect, he is saying to the reader: This is what I believe and now I am going to give you examples that support my idea.

1. What is the theme of "David Swan"?

2. By what means did Nathaniel Hawthorne illustrate the theme of his story?

3. What larger picture did the three events represent?

4. Did Hawthorne directly state his theme? If so, where?

5. How did the events help you understand the theme?

READING FOCUS

Draw Conclusions As you read "David Swan" you drew conclusions about each character. Choose two characters and describe the conclusions you drew about each one. On which of their actions did you base your conclusions?

DEVELOP YOUR VOCABULARY

A **synonym** is a word whose meaning is similar to, or the same as, another word. For example, *indifference* means "lack of interest." Words that have similar meanings are *disinterest, apathy,* and *unconcern.* Knowing synonyms for many words can make your writing more interesting.

Read the sentences below. Choose a word from the list that is a synonym for each italicized word.

melodious	venomous
peril	thriving
tuft	

1. The small *clump* of flowers caught his eye when he sat down by the pond.

2. Jeremy's *hostile* words hurt Kira.

3. Her antique business was *prospering* despite the business slump.

4. Because it was so cold on the mountain, the climbers were at great *risk*.

5. The parakeet imitated the *tuneful* music.

Learn About

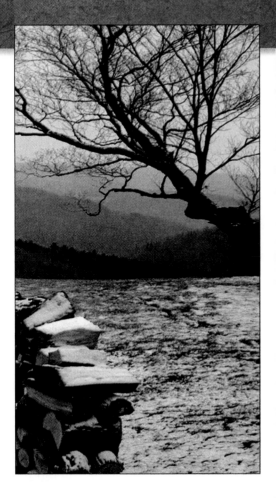

SOUNDS IN POETRY

Rhythm, meter, and rhyme all add musical effects to poetry, but they are not the only devices available to poets. The use of certain letters of the alphabet affects the sound of poetry. Some letters have a soft "liquid" sound: *l*, *m*, *n*, and *r*. Other letters have a more "explosive" sound: *b*, *d*, *g*, *k*, *p*, and *t*. Poets can manipulate the use of these sounds to create soothing or exciting lines.

Repetition is part of all music, and it plays a part in the music of poetry too. For example, the repetition of initial consonant sounds, as in "They *s*at in *s*olemn *s*ilence," is called **alliteration**. The repetition of vowel sounds, as in "*I* can f*i*nd the t*i*me," is called **assonance**. The repetition of final consonant sounds, as in "fir*st* and la*st*," is called **consonance**.

As you read the following poems, ask yourself:

1. Which sound devices did Dickinson use in her poems?
2. What effect do the devices have on the poems?

WRITING CONNECTION

Write a sentence using "liquid" letters and another using "explosive" letters. Explain the effect of each sentence on you.

READING FOCUS

Make Inferences An inference is a conclusion drawn from facts or evidence. You can use your own insights and knowledge of human behavior and the world around you in order to make inferences.

Reading poetry often requires the reader to infer meaning, or to think beyond the words on the page. As you read each poem, use your own knowledge and details in the poem to make inferences about the poem's meaning.

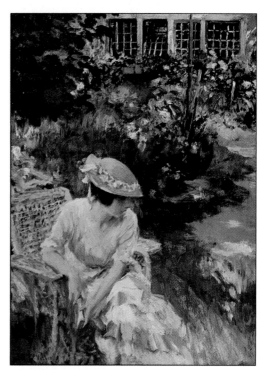

In the Garden, Irving Ramsay Wiles. Christie's Images

I'm nobody

by Emily Dickinson

I'm nobody! Who are you?
Are you nobody, too?
Then there's a pair of us—don't tell!
They'd banish us, you know.

How dreary to be somebody!
How public, like a frog
To tell your name the livelong day
To an admiring bog!

---

dreary (DRIR ee) dull; tiresome
bog (BOG) swamp; wet ground

A word is dead

by Emily Dickinson

A word is dead
When it is said,
Some say.
I say it just
Begins to live
That day.

I never saw a moor

by Emily Dickinson

I never saw a moor,
I never saw the sea;
Yet know I how the heather looks,
And what a wave must be.

I never spoke with God,
Nor visited in heaven;
Yet certain am I of the spot
As if the chart were given.

moor (MUUR) open wasteland
heather (HETH ur) low evergreen plant that often grows on moors

The sky is low

by Emily Dickinson

The sky is low, the clouds are mean,
A travelling flake of snow
Across a barn or through a rut
Debates if it will go.

A narrow wind complains all day
How some one treated him;
Nature, like us, is sometimes caught
Without her diadem.

Home at Montclair, George Inness. The Granger Collection

---

rut (RUT) a track made by a wheeled vehicle
diadem (DY uh dem) crown (more like halo here)

Some keep the Sabbath

by Emily Dickinson

Some keep the Sabbath going to church;
I keep it staying at home,
With a bobolink for a chorister,
And an orchard for a dome.

5   Some keep the Sabbath in surplice;
I just wear my wings,
And instead of tolling the bell for church,
Our little sexton sings.

God preaches,—a noted clergyman,—
10   And the sermon is never long;
So instead of getting to heaven at last,
I'm going all along!

---

bobolink (BOB uh lingk) kind of song bird
chorister (KAWR ih stur) singer in a choir
surplice (SUR plis) loose-fitting garment worn by members of the clergy and choirs
sexton (SEKS tun) church caretaker who rings the bells

Letter to Thomas Wentworth Higginson

by Emily Dickinson

Letter to Mr. T. W. Higginson
April 15, 1862

Mr. Higginson,

Are you too deeply occupied to say if my verse is alive?

The Mind is so near itself—it cannot see, distinctly—and I have none to ask. Should you think it breathed—and had you the leisure to tell me, I should feel quick gratitude—

If I make the mistake—that you dared to tell me— would give me sincerer honor toward you—

I enclosed my name—asking you. If you please— Sir- to tell me what is true? That you will not betray me—it is needless to ask—since honor is its own pawn—

Emily Dickinson (1830–1886)

"If I read a book," wrote Emily Dickinson, "and it makes my whole body so cold no fire can ever warm me, I know that is poetry. If I feel . . . as if the top of my head were taken off, I know that is poetry. These are the only ways I know it. Is there any other way?"

". . . *as if the top of my head were taken off*. . ."! Those are strong words, but Emily Dickinson knew what she was talking about. Today Emily Dickinson is considered one of the greatest American poets—if not *the* greatest.

Her story is a strange one. Nearly all her life was passed in a large house in Amherst, Massachusetts. As a girl she was active and fun-loving. She had a year of college. Then, in her early 20s, something happened that changed her life. It was probably a disappointing romance, but that may not be the whole story. At any rate, she started spending more and more time alone. She read a lot. She helped with family chores. She watched the wonders of nature in a private yard and garden. She stopped going to church. By and by her parents died, and her world grew smaller still. What happened outside this private world—even the Civil War—held little interest for her. She dressed only in white. She left chores outside the house to her unmarried sister, Vinnie. She refused to meet strangers. During the last ten years of her life she never went out.

Emily Dickinson died at the age of 55. Her relatives knew that poetry had been one of her interests. But she had written poetry mainly to please herself. During her lifetime, only seven of her poems had been published. Her family and a few friends had seen some others, but no one had dreamed of the surprise that came following her death. Her sister Vinnie entered her room to find drawers full of poems, trunks full of poems! In all, 1,775 were found! Most of them were arranged by year. In 1862, for instance, she had written 366 poems!

In a way, Emily Dickinson's world was small. But in another way, the world that she created was huge. Her mind stretched far, far out, beyond death—even beyond the world as we know it. Our world is richer for it.

In your opinion, what might have happened to make an active young woman slowly withdraw from society?

Review the Selection

UNDERSTAND THE SELECTION

Recall

1. Where does the speaker keep the Sabbath?

2. With whom does the speaker keep the Sabbath?

3. Who is the sexton in "Some keep the Sabbath" and what does it do?

Infer

4. Explain why you think the speaker in "I'm nobody" likes being nobody.

5. In "A word is dead," why does a word come alive when it is spoken?

6. Why did Dickinson write to Higginson?

7. In your opinion, what is the theme of "The sky is low"?

Apply

8. Select your favorite Dickinson poem. Explain why it is your favorite.

9. Suppose you are a poet. Name two things you have never seen or experienced about which you might write.

10. Why might Dickinson choose to use a frog as an example of somebody?

Respond to Literature

How does Dickinson's poetry reflect Emerson's group's transcendental idea about writing?

WRITE ABOUT THE SELECTION

In the poem "I'm nobody," the speaker makes it clear that she or he prefers to be nobody. Suppose that you can either be "nobody" or "somebody." Which would you choose to be? Why? Be sure to think about the various pros and cons of your choices before you finally make up your mind.

Prewriting   Write down on a piece of paper whether you want to be "nobody" or "somebody." Try to think about what each of these situations would be like and how you would feel about each. Then make a list of all the reasons you can think of for your choice.

Writing   Use your list to help you write a paragraph about why you chose to be "nobody" or "somebody." Include three or more reasons why you made your choice.

Revising   When you revise, make sure you have included two reasons for your choice. Then add one more reason from your list to your paragraph. Finally, reread your paragraph to make sure that your choices make sense. Revise as much as necessary to make sure that your reasons are clear.

Proofreading   Read over your paragraph to check for errors. Be sure that all your sentences end with the correct punctuation marks. Check your internal punctuation as well.

THINK ABOUT SOUNDS IN POETRY

Poetry has musical qualities that prose does not have. Repetition of initial consonant letters (**alliteration**), of vowel sounds (**assonance**), and of final consonant sounds (**consonance**) help the poet to create musical effects. The use of liquid and explosive letters of the alphabet can also add to the music of poetry.

1. Which musical device is used in the first two lines of "I'm nobody"? Cite the words that produce this device.

2. Which musical device is used in the first line of "A word is dead"? Cite the words that produce this device.

3. The use of one particular letter, especially at the beginning of words, is repeated in "Some keep the Sabbath." What letter is it, and what is the name of the device it represents?

4. Does "I never saw a moor" have more liquid or more explosive sounds in the first stanza? In the second stanza?

5. Which is more important in musical devices, spelling or sound? Why?

READING FOCUS

Make Inferences Choose one of Emily Dickinson's poems that you read in this selection. What inferences can you make about the poem's meaning based on your own experiences? What inferences can you make based on words or images in the poem?

DEVELOP YOUR VOCABULARY

Figurative language is the use of imagery, symbols, or other devices to create meaning beyond the dictionary meanings of the words used. For example, in the line "A narrow wind complains all day," Dickinson wrote words that do not mean exactly what they say. The wind makes a lot of noise all day; the word *complains* is used figuratively. In the line "I never saw the sea," however, Dickinson uses words with their exact dictionary meanings. The language is **literal**.

Read the sentences below. For each, indicate whether the figurative or literal meaning of the italicized word is used.

1. "How *dreary* to be somebody!"

2. "I never saw a *moor*, . . ."

3. "Nature, like us, is sometimes caught Without her *diadem*."

4. "Bell-shaped *heather* flowers were in bloom."

5. "And instead of tolling the bell for church, Our little *sexton* sings."

6. "They'd *banish* us, you know."

Focus ON POETRY

What is a poem, and what does a poem do? Poetry is writing in which imaginative, colorful language is used to paint a picture in the reader's mind. It can tell a story, express feelings and thoughts, or describe things.

You can tell a poem the minute you see it; its structure is different from prose. Thoughts and feelings are captured in a more concise way. The poems you have read in this unit are made up of stanzas. **Stanzas** are divisions in poems that are made up of two or more lines. The poets have chosen their words carefully to create rhythm and rhyme, two elements that convey thoughts and feelings and move the poem along at a steady pace.

There are a number of elements besides rhythm and rhyme that poets use to help them write poetry. These elements work together to make a poem come alive in the reader's mind. Let's look at some of these elements so that you can learn how to understand and enjoy poetry better.

Figurative Language Figurative language, such as simile, metaphor, personification, and hyperbole, is another device poets use to convey their feelings and thoughts. Figurative language paints a picture in the reader's mind that is different from that conveyed by the literal, or dictionary meaning, of individual words. It helps the reader think of something in a different way.

A **simile** compares two unlike objects using the words *like* or *as*. *She sang like a bird* is an example. A **metaphor** compares two unlike things, without using extra words to show that a comparison is being made. An example of a metaphor is: *The young dancer is a butterfly.* **Personification** gives human qualities to nonhuman objects. *The laughing brook* is an example of personification. **Hyperbole** is an exaggerated statement, such as: *That cat is as big as an elephant!* Uses of these different kinds of figurative language help to make poems more interesting and to describe things in a different way. Simile and metaphor make a connection between two unlike things that the reader might never have thought about before. On the other hand, personification and hyperbole can be used in a humorous way or for exaggeration.

Character/Speaker The voice or narrator of a poem is not necessarily the real voice of the poet. Often, poets put on a mask. They create a voice, separate from their own, to express their thoughts. The poet can write in the voice of a child, a father, a nation, or even the world.

Connotation and Denotation A reader should look closely at how poets use words. Often, writers use words that have two kinds of meanings. The connotation of a word suggests its emotional meaning—the feeling the word suggests to the reader. The denotation of a word is the actual meaning of a word as given in a dictionary. In the poem "I'm nobody" Dickinson wrote:

> How dreary to be somebody!
> How public, like a frog
> To tell your name the livelong day
> To an admiring bog!

Bog has an emotional meaning here. Dickinson did not use it to mean *swamp*, which is its dictionary meaning. She used it connotatively to imply a group of nameless, faceless people.

Sound Devices Poets also use sound devices, such as onomatopoeia and alliteration. **Onomatopoeia** is the use of words that sound like their meaning. *Splash* is an example. **Alliteration** is the repetition of initial consonant sounds in a line of poetry. *Some keep the Sabbath in surplice* is an example of alliteration. Poets use different elements because they want to share their thoughts in ways that will appeal to the imagination.

THE FIRST SNOW FALL

by James Russell Lowell

FOCUS ON POETRY
STUDY HINTS

Notice how Lowell
uses end rhymes
to link thoughts.

Think about the
connotation of the
words *ermine* and
pearl. What feelings
do they suggest
to you?

The poet uses
onomatopoeia.
Which word is it?

Lowell uses a simile
here. What is it?

The snow had begun in the gloaming,
　　And busily all the night
Had been heaping field and highway
　　With a silence deep and white.

5　Every pine and fir and hemlock
　　Wore ermine too dear for an earl,
And the poorest twig on the elm-tree
　　Was ridged inch deep with pearl.

From sheds new-roofed with Carrara
10　Came Chanticleer's muffled crow,
The stiff rails softened to swan's-down,
　　And still fluttered down the snow.

I stood and watched by the window
　　The noiseless work of the sky,
15　And the sudden flurries of snow-birds,
　　Like brown leaves whirling by.

---

gloaming (GLOHM ing) twilight
ermine (UR min) a weasel whose fur turns to white in the winter
Carrara (kuh RAHR uh) fine, white marble
chanticleer (CHAN tih klir) a rooster

I thought of a mound in sweet Auburn[1]
    Where a little headstone stood;
How the flakes were folding it gently,
20   As did robins the babes in the wood.

Create a picture in your mind of what these words are saying.

Up spoke our own little Mabel,
    Saying, "Father, who makes it snow?"
And I told of the good All-father
    Who cares for us here below.

Here, you find out who the speaker is. Who is it?

25 Again I looked at the snow-fall,
    And thought of the leaden sky
That arched o'er our first great sorrow,
    When that mound was heaped so high.

Here, the speaker shares his feelings of grief.

I remembered the gradual patience
30   That fell from that cloud like snow,
Flake by flake, healing and hiding
    The scar that renewed our woe.

What simile does Lowell use here?

And again to the child I whispered,
    "The snow that husheth all,
35 Darling, the merciful Father
    Alone can make it fall!"

Think about the connotation of the words in this stanza.

Then, with eyes that saw not, I kissed her;
    And she, kissing back, could not know
That *my* kiss was given to her sister,
    Folded close under deepening snow.

Finally the speaker reveals for whom he grieves and how much he misses her.

---

leaden (LED un) dull, dark gray
[1]**Mt. Auburn:** a cemetery in Cambridge, Massachusetts

Review the Selection

UNDERSTAND THE SELECTION

Recall

1. When had the snow begun to fall?

2. What is the speaker watching?

3. What are the speaker's feelings, and what caused them?

Infer

4. Describe in your own words how the landscape looks outside the window.

5. How do you know the speaker has tried to hide his grief?

6. Explain in your own words what the speaker is saying in this poem.

7. Discuss why Mabel could not know what her father was thinking.

Apply

8. Select three words from the poem that describe the speaker's voice.

9. Suppose that you are the speaker in this poem. You are looking out the window at the snow. How does the snow make you feel?

10. Select the stanza from the poem that tells the reader the speaker may be recovering from his great sorrow.

Respond to Literature

How does Lowell use nature to share his feelings with the reader?

WRITE ABOUT THE SELECTION

Has James Russell Lowell written a good poem? Think about what a poem is and what it is supposed to accomplish for a few minutes. Then suppose that you are a literary critic for the school literary magazine. Your assignment is to review "The First Snow Fall." What do you feel about the poem? Does the poet successfully express his thoughts through the speaker? Is the poet's use of figurative language successful? Does it make the poem vivid in your mind? Read the poem again.

Prewriting Freewrite for a few minutes on your feelings about this poem. Look at the annotations to help you. Ask yourself: Did I enjoy reading the poem? Is it well written? Is the poet's choice of words colorful?

Writing Write a short literary criticism of "The First Snow Fall." Be sure to include terms such as *figurative language*, *speaker*, and *sound devices* in your review.

Revising When you revise, make sure you have used concrete examples from the poem in your criticism. If you haven't, go back and include them.

Proofreading Reread your criticism to check for errors. Make sure that you have spelled all the words correctly, paying particular attention to the poetry terms. Look at your sentences. Does each of them express a complete thought? If not, rewrite them.

THINK ABOUT POETRY

Various elements of poetry work together to make a poem stimulating and interesting to read. Poets work hard to choose colorful words that will express their thoughts, feelings, and ideas in an imaginative way.

In the first stanza of "The First Snow Fall," you learn the snow began at twilight. Then, through a choice of such words as *busily*, *heaping*, and *silence*, a picture begins to emerge of how the snow must have looked. Lowell's choice of words creates a quiet, rhythmic feeling, similar to a gentle snowfall.

1. Whose voice does Lowell create in this poem?

2. Which kind of figurative language does Lowell use?

3. What is being compared in the simile "And the sudden flurries of snowbirds, Like brown leaves whirling by"?

4. What is the connotation of the word "husheth" in the line "The snow that husheth all, . . ."?

5. Name the sound device that Lowell uses and give two examples of it.

DEVELOP YOUR VOCABULARY

Homophones are words that sound the same when you say them but have different meanings and spellings. For example, the words *throne* and *thrown* are homophones.

Read the following sentences. Think of a homophone for each italicized word. Then use it in an original sentence.

1. The *beech* tree my grandfather planted last year has grown a lot.

2. Samantha read her report *aloud* to the other students.

3. Christopher put a lot of hot spices in the *chili* he made last night.

4. The *herd* of wolves moved quickly through the storm to nearby caves.

5. Rosa and Luke *rowed* across Rainbow Lake to a small island where they had a picnic.

6. The best time to look for shells is when the *tide* has gone out.

7. The *weight* of the package made me think it held the books I ordered.

8. How long does Becky have to *beat* the egg whites?

Learn About

CONFLICT

Plot, as you know, consists of a conflict, an attempt to resolve the conflict, a climax (or turning point in the events), and the dénouement, the final resolution, or outcome, of the events.

The essential element in any plot, however, is the conflict. A plot cannot exist without it. The conflict is what sets off the interplay of forces that make up the events that occur.

The conflict may be of several kinds. It may be between the main character and the forces of nature, another person, or social forces, or even between opposing sides of the character's own personality.

In weaving the events of a plot, an author must arrange incidents so that they seem to grow inevitably out of the conflict. Each incident must be the cause of the next one, down to the very end.

As you read the excerpts from *Moby-Dick*, ask yourself:

1. What is the main conflict in the story?
2. Where is the turning point in the events?

WRITING CONNECTION

Think of a conflict that might set up a series of events that must be resolved. Describe that conflict in a paragraph.

READING FOCUS

Visualize One of the things that makes a story exciting is the picture that you build in your mind from the details the author provides. When an author uses imagery—words that describe the sights, tastes, smells, sounds, and feelings—in a story, you can use your mind's eye to visualize more clearly what is happening. As you read this excerpt from *Moby-Dick*, use the imagery to visualize the events.

from
MOBY-DICK

ADAPTED

by Herman Melville

It was quite late in the evening when the little Moss came snugly to anchor. Queequeg and I went ashore. We didn't want to attend to any business that day, at least none but a supper and a bed. The landlord of the Spouter Inn had recommended us to his cousin Hosea Hussey of the Try Pots. He said that Hussey was the proprietor of one of the best-kept hotels in all Nantucket.[1] He had also assured us that Cousin Hosea, as he called him, was famous for his chowders. In short, he plainly hinted that we could not possibly do better than try potluck at the Try Pots. He had given us the following directions: keep a yellow warehouse on your right hand till you see a white church to the left. Then keep that on the left hand till you make a corner three points to the right. When that is done, ask the first man you meet where the place is. These crooked directions of his very much puzzled us at first, especially as, at the outset, Queequeg insisted that the yellow warehouse—our first point of departure—must be on the left side. I had understood Peter Coffin to say it was on the right. However, by walking around a little in the dark, and now and then knocking up a peaceful resident to inquire the way, we at last came to something which there was no mistaking.

Two enormous wooden pots painted black swung from the crosstrees of an old topmast and were planted in front of an old doorway. The horns of the crosstrees were sawed off on the other side, so that this old topmast looked not a little like a gallows. Perhaps I was oversensitive to such impressions at the time, but I could not help staring at this gallows with a vague misgiving. A sort of crick was in my neck as I gazed up to the two remaining horns; yes, two of them, one for Queequeg, and one for me. It's ominous, thinks I. A coffin was my innkeeper upon landing in my first whaling port. Tombstones were staring at me in the whalemen's chapel; and here a gallows! and a pair of very large black pots too! Are these last throwing out indirect hints?

I was interrupted from these thoughts

---

ominous (OM uh nus) dangerous; threatening
[1]**Nantucket:** an island, off the coast of Massachusetts, that was a huge whaling community

by the sight of a freckled woman with yellow hair and a yellow gown. She was standing in the porch of the inn, under a dull red lamp swinging there. It looked much like an injured eye, and she was carrying on a brisk scolding with a man in a purple woolen shirt.

"Get along with you," she said to the man, "or I'll be combing you!"

"Come on, Queequeg," said I, "all right. There's Mrs. Hussey."

And so it turned out; Mr. Hosea Hussey was not at home, but had left a very competent Mrs. Hussey to attend to all his affairs. Upon making known our desires for supper and a bed, Mrs. Hussey, postponing further scolding for the present, ushered us into a little room, and seating us at a table spread with the leftovers of a recently concluded meal, turned round to us and said "clam or cod?"

"What's that about cods, ma'am?" said I, with much politeness.

"Clam or cod?" she repeated.

"A clam for supper? a cold clam; is *that* what you mean, Mrs. Hussey?" says I! "but that's a rather cold and clammy reception in the winter time, isn't it, Mrs. Hussey?"

But being in a great hurry to resume scolding the man in the purple shirt who was waiting for it in the entry, and seeming to hear nothing but the word "clam," Mrs. Hussey hurried towards an open door leading to the kitchen, and bawling out "clam for two," disappeared.

"Queequeg," said I, "do you think that we can make a supper for us both on one clam?"

The Whale Fishery "Laying On," 1852, Nathaniel Currier. The Granger Collection

However, a warm savory steam from the kitchen served to confuse us regarding the clam on the table. But when that smoking chowder came in, the mystery was delightfully explained. Oh, sweet friends, listen to me. It was made of small juicy clams, scarcely bigger than hazel nuts, mixed with pounded ship biscuits, and salted pork cut up into little flakes! The chowder was enriched with butter, and it was generously seasoned with pepper and salt. Our appetites had been sharpened by the frosty voyage. In particular, Queequeg seeing his favorite fishing food before him, and the chowder being surpassingly excellent, we started to eat very quickly. Then leaning back for a moment, I thought I would try a little experiment. Stepping to the kitchen door, I uttered the word "cod" with great emphasis, and resumed my seat. In a few moments the savory steam came forth again, but with a different flavor, and in good time a fine cod chowder was placed before us.

Finally, supper concluded, we received a lamp, and directions from Mrs. Hussey about how to find our beds. As Queequeg was about to precede me up the stairs, the lady reached toward him, and demanded his harpoon. She allowed no harpoon in her chambers. "Why not?" said I; "every true whaleman sleeps with his harpoon—but why not?" "Because it's dangerous," says she. "Ever since young Stiggs coming from that unfortunate voyage of his, when he was gone four years and a half, with only three barrels of oil was found dead in my first floor back, with his harpoon in his side. Ever since then I allow no boarders to take such dangerous weapons in their rooms at night. So, Mr. Queequeg" (for she had learned his name), "I will just take this here iron, and keep it for you till morning. But the chowder; clam or cod tomorrow for breakfast, men?"

"Both," says I, "and let's have a couple of smoked herring by way of variety."

When the crew signed aboard the Pequod, *the voyage was to be nothing more than a business venture. However, early in the voyage, Ahab makes clear to the crew that his purpose is to seek revenge against Moby-Dick.*

One morning shortly after breakfast, Ahab, as was his habit, climbed up the cabin gangway to the deck. There most sea captains usually walk at that hour, as country gentlemen, after the same meal, take a few turns in the garden.

Soon his steady, ivory stride was heard. To and fro he paced on his old rounds. The wood was so familiar to his step, that they were all over dented with the peculiar mark of his walk. If you looked, too, upon that ribbed and dented brow, you would also see still stranger footprints—the footprints of his one unsleeping, ever-pacing thought.

But on the occasion in question, those dents looked deeper, even as his nervous

---

savory (SAY vur ee) appetizing smell

step that morning left a deeper mark. Ahab was so deep in thought that at every uniform turn that he made, now at the mainmast and now at the compass, you could almost see that thought turn in him as he turned, and pace in him as he paced. It was so completely possessing him, indeed, that it all but seemed that every move he made was based on an inner thought.

"Do you see him, Flask?" whispered Stubb; "the chick that's in him pecks the shell. It will soon be out."

The hours wore on—Ahab was now shut up within his cabin. Then later he was pacing the deck, with the same single-mindedness as before.

It drew near the close of day. Suddenly he stopped by the side of the ship on the upper deck. Inserting his bone leg into the harpoon hole there, and with one hand grasping a set of ropes, he ordered Starbuck to send everybody to the back of the boat.

"Sir!" said the mate, surprised at an order seldom or never given on shipboard except in some extraordinary case.

"Send everybody to the back," repeated Ahab. "Mastheads, there! come down!"

When the entire ship's company were assembled, the curious and fearful faces eyed him. He looked not unlike the weather horizon when a storm is coming up. Ahab rapidly glanced over the sides of the ship. Then he looked back and forth at the crew. Then acting as if not a soul were present, he continued to pace with his head bent. He was unmindful of the wondering whispering among the men.

Then Stubb cautiously whispered to Flask, that Ahab must have summoned them there for the purpose of watching this ordinary event. But this did not last long. Suddenly stopping, he cried:

"What do you do when you see a whale, men?"

"Sing out for him!" was the quick answer from a score of clubbed voices.

"Good!" cried Ahab, with a wild approval in his tones. He liked the hearty reply to his unexpected question.

"And what do you next, men?"

"Lower the boats and go after him."

"And what tune is it you pull to, men?"

"A dead whale or a smashed boat!"

More and more strangely and fiercely glad and approving, grew the face of the old man at every shout. The crew began to look curiously at each other. They began to marvel at how they had become so excited at such seemingly purposeless questions.

But they were all eagerness again. Then Ahab, now with one hand reaching high up to a set of ropes, and tightly grasping it, addressed them:

"All you mastheaders have before now heard me give orders about a white whale. Look at this! Do you see this Spanish ounce of gold?"—holding up a broad bright coin to the sun—"it is a sixteen-dollar piece, men. Do you see it? Mr. Starbuck, hand me your hammer."

While the mate was getting it, Ahab, without speaking, was slowly rubbing the gold piece against the skirts of his jacket, as if to heighten its shine. Without using any words, he was humming to himself,

Whalers Capturing a Sperm Whale, 1847. The Granger Collection

producing a sound that was strangely muffled. It seemed like the mechanical humming of his mind.

Receiving the hammer from Starbuck, he advanced towards the mainmast. The hammer was uplifted in one hand, while he exhibited the gold with the other. With a high raised voice he exclaimed: "Whosoever of you kills me a white-headed whale with a wrinkled brow and a crooked jaw; whosoever of you kills that white-headed whale for me, with three holes punctured in his tail—look here, whosoever of you kills that same white whale for me, he shall have this gold ounce, my boys!"

"Huzza! huzza!" cried the seamen. Then with swinging canvas sails they cheered the act of nailing the gold to the mast.

"It's a white whale, I say," resumed Ahab, as he threw down the hammer: "a white whale. Keep your eyes peeled for him, men; look sharp for white water; if you see but a bubble, sing out."

All this while Tashtego, Daggoo, and Queequeg had looked on with even more intense interest and surprise than the rest. At the mention of the wrinkled brow and crooked jaw, they had jumped as if each was separately touched by some specific recollection.

"Captain Ahab," said Tashtego, "that white whale must be the same that some call Moby-Dick."

"Moby-Dick?" shouted Ahab. "Do you know the white whale then, Tash?"

"Does he spread his tail out like a fan before he goes down?" said the Gay-Header[2] deliberately.

"And has he a curious spout, too," said Daggoo, "very bushy, and mighty quick, Captain Ahab?"

"And he has one, two, three—oh! a good many irons in his hide, too, Captain," cried Queequeg disjointedly, "all twiske-tee betwisk, like him—him—" faltering hard for a word, and screwing his hand round and round as though uncorking a bottle—"like him—him—"

"Corkscrew!" cried Ahab, "aye, Queequeg, the harpoons lie all twisted and wrenched in him. Aye, Daggoo, his spout is a big one, like a whole shock of wheat, and white as a pile of Nantucket wool after the great annual sheepshearing. Aye, Tashtego, he spreads his tail out like a fan. Death and devils! men, it is Moby-Dick you have seen—Moby-Dick—Moby-Dick!"

"Captain Ahab," said Starbuck, who, with Stubb and Flask, had been looking at the captain with increasing surprise. He at last seemed struck with a thought which somewhat explained all the wonder, "Captain Ahab, I have heard of Moby-Dick —but it was not Moby-Dick that took off your leg?"

"Who told you that?" cried Ahab; then pausing, "Aye, Starbuck; aye, my congratulations all around. It was Moby-Dick that dismasted me. It was Moby-Dick that brought me to this dead stump I stand on now. Aye, aye," he shouted with a terrific, loud, animal sob, like that of a heart-stricken moose. "Aye, aye! It was that hateful white whale that destroyed me and made me so clumsy forever and a day!" Then tossing up both arms, he shouted out: "Aye, aye! and I'll chase him round Good Hope, and round the Horn[3] before I give him up. And this is what you have shipped for men! We are going to chase that white whale on both sides of land, and over all sides of earth, till he spouts black blood and rolls fin out. What say you, men, will you join hands on it, now? I think you do look brave."

"Aye, aye!" shouted the harpooneers and seamen, running closer to the excited old man: "A sharp eye for the white whale; a sharp harpoon for Moby-Dick!"

"God bless you," he seemed to half sob and half shout. "God bless you, men. Steward! go get something to drink. But what's this long face about, Mr. Starbuck; don't you want to chase the white whale? you're not willing?"

"I am willing for his crooked jaw, and

---

[2]**Gay-Header:** Gay Head is a town on Martha's Vineyard, another island off the coast of Massachusetts that had a large whaling community.
[3]**Good Hope** and **the Horn:** two of the most dangerous sea passages in the world

for the jaws of Death too, Captain Ahab, if it fairly comes in the way of the business we follow. I came here to hunt whales, not my commander's vengeance. How many barrels will your harm yield you even if you catch it, Captain Ahab? it will not get much in our Nantucket market."

"Nantucket market! Hoot! But come closer, Starbuck. If money's to be the measurer, man, and the accountants have worked out that their great countinghouse is the globe, by surrounding it with money, then, let me tell you, that my vengeance will get a great price *here*!"

"He strikes his chest," whispered Stubb, "what's that for? He has said a lot but it doesn't mean much."

"Vengeance on a dumb animal!" cried Starbuck, "that simply doesn't make any sense! Madness! To be angry with a dumb thing, Captain Ahab, seems disrespectful."

"Listen again—a little more closely. All visible objects, man, are but as pasteboard masks. But in each event there is some unknown but still reasoning thing that puts forth its features from behind the unreasoning mask. If man will strike, strike through the mask! How can the prisoner reach outside except by breaking through the wall? To me, the white whale is that wall, shoved near to me. Sometimes I think there's nothing beyond. But it's enough. He tasks me; he heaps me; I see in him outrageous strength, with a mysterious meanness to him. That mysterious thing is chiefly what I hate. And whether I kill the white whale for money or not, I will do it because I hate him. Talk not to me of disrespect, man; I'd strike the sun if it insulted me. If the sun struck me, I'd strike back. There is ever a sort of fair play on earth because jealousy has control over all creations. But not my master, man, is even that fair play. Who's over me? Truth hath no boundaries. Don't look at me like that! You are furious. My words have enraged you. But listen, Starbuck, what is said in anger can be undone. I meant not to make you angry. Let it go. Look! Look at the crew. Don't they all agree with Ahab, in this matter of the whale? See Stubb! he laughs! See yonder Chilean! he snorts to think of it. Don't you be the only one who disagrees. You can't win, Starbuck! Deal with it. I only want you to help strike a fin; that's no wondrous accomplishment for Starbuck. You are the best lance out of all Nantucket, surely you will not hang back, when every foremasthand has clutched a whetstone. Ah! you feel uneasy. You're changing your mind. Speak, but speak!—Aye, aye! Your silence says more than words. (*Aside*) He is thinking about what I said. He's changing his mind. Starbuck now is mine. He cannot oppose me now."

"God keep me!—keep us all!" murmured Starbuck, lowly.

But in his joy at the understood

---

vengeance (VEN juns) causing harm to something in return for an injury or harm done
whetstone (HWET stohn) a stone used for sharpening tools

obedience of the mate, Ahab did not hear the warnings in the laughter from the hold; nor yet the warning sounds of the winds in the ropes; nor yet the hollow flap of the sails against the masts. For a moment their hearts sank in. For again Starbuck's downcast eyes lighted up with the stubbornness of life. The hidden laugh died away. The winds blew on. The sails filled out. The ship heaved and rolled as before. Ah, the warnings were everywhere. Actually, they were more predictions than warnings! Yet not so much predictions from nature, as proof of the foregoing things within the mind. With not much to hold us back, the innermost necessities in our being still drive us on.

"The cup! the cup!" cried Ahab.

Receiving the brimming pewter, and turning to the harpooneers, he ordered them to produce their weapons. Then arranging them before him with their harpoons in their hands, his three mates stood at his side with their lances. The rest of the ship's company formed a circle around the group. He stood for an instant looking directly at every man of his crew. Those wild eyes met his. They were like the bloodshot eyes of the prairie wolves when they meet the eye of their leader before he rushes on at their head in the trail of the bison. Alas, only to be caught by the hidden traps of hunters.

"Advance, mates! cross your lances full before me. Well done! Let me touch the center." He said that and then he grasped the lances at their crossed center. While so doing, he suddenly and nervously twitched them. Meanwhile he glanced intently from Starbuck to Stubb; from Stubb to Flask. It seemed as though, by some nameless, inside willpower, he wanted to shock them into having the same fiery feelings that he had within himself. The three mates quailed before his strong, mysterious presence. Stubb and Flask looked away from him. The honest eye of Starbuck fell downright.

"In vain!" cried Ahab; "but, maybe it's just as well. For if I gave you my stored, strong feelings, then I might have lost them for myself. Perhaps, too, it might have caused me to drop dead. Perhaps you don't need them. Put your lances down! And now, mates, I need to choose three men to help my brave harpooneers. Don't look down on the job. Remember that the great Pope washes the feet of beggars, using his crown for a pitcher. It is your own superiority that will make you do it. I do not order you; you make it happen to yourselves. Cut your lines and draw the poles, harpooneers!"

Silently obeying the order, the three harpooneers, now stood with the detached iron part of their harpoons, some three feet long, held, barbs up, before him.

"Do not stab me with that sharp steel! Turn them; turn them over! Don't you know the goblet end? Turn up the socket! So, so; now, advance. The irons! take them;

---

quailed (KWAYLD) lost courage; cowered

hold them while I fill!" He immediately went from one officer to the other, filling the harpoon sockets with the fiery waters from the pewter.

"Now, three to three, you stand. Raise the murderous cups! Present them, you who are now part of this permanent group. Ha! Starbuck! but the deed is done! Drink, you harpooneers! drink and swear, you men that man the deathful whaleboat's bow—Death to Moby-Dick! God will hunt us all, if we do not hunt Moby-Dick to his death!" The long, barbed steel goblets were lifted; and to cries and curses against the white whale, the drinks were all at once drunk down. Starbuck paled, and turned, and shivered. Once more, and finally, the refilled pewter went the rounds among the desperate crew; when, waving his free hand to them, they all went their separate ways; and Ahab retired within his cabin.

After Moby-Dick has been sighted in the Pacific Ocean, the Pequod's boats follow the whale for two days. One of the boats has been sunk, and Ahab's ivory leg has been broken off. However, as the next day dawns, the chase continues.

The morning of the third day dawned fair and fresh, and once more the solitary night man at the foremasthead was relieved by crowds of the daylight lookouts, who were on every mast and almost every pole.

"Do you see him?" cried Ahab; but the whale was not yet in sight. "Aloft there! What do you see?"

"Nothing, sir."

"Nothing! and noon at hand! The gold coin goes a-begging! See the sun! Aye, aye, it must be so. I've sailed past him. How, got the start? Aye, he's chasing *me* now; not I, *him*—that's bad. I might have known it, too. Fool! the lines—the harpoons he's towing. Aye, aye, I have run him by last night. About! about! Come down, all of you, but the regular lookouts! Make preparations to turn!"

Steering as she had done, the wind had been somewhat on the *Pequod*'s quarter. Now that the ship was being pointed in the reverse direction, she sailed hard upon the breeze as she rechurned the cream in her own white wake.

"Against the wind he now steers for the open jaw," murmured Starbuck to himself. "God keep us, but already my bones feel damp within me, and from the inside wet my flesh. I fear that I disobey my God in obeying him!"

"Stand by to help me up!" cried Ahab, advancing to the rope basket. "We should meet him soon."

"Aye, aye, sir," and straightway Starbuck helped him, and once more Ahab swung on high.

A whole hour now passed: goldbeaten out to ages. Time itself now held long breaths with sharp suspense. But at last, some three points off the weather bow,

---

suspense (suh SPENS) uncertainty about what will happen

Ahab descried the spout again. Instantly from the three mastheads three shrieks went up as if the tongues of fire had voiced it.

"Forehead to forehead I meet you, this third time, Moby-Dick! On deck there!—turn her; turn her into the wind's eye. He's too far off to lower yet, Mr. Starbuck. The sails shake! Stand over that helmsman with a topmaul! So, so; he travels fast, and I must get down. But let me have one more good round look at the sea while I'm up here. There's time for that. An old, old sight, and yet somehow it's so young; aye, and it hasn't changed a wink since I first saw it as a boy from the sand hills of Nantucket! The same!—the same! There's a soft shower downwind. Such lovely downwinds! They must lead somewhere—to something more than common land. Downwind! the white whale goes that way; look to windward. Good-bye, goodbye, old masthead! What's this?—green: aye, tiny mosses in these warped cracks. No such green weather stains on Ahab's head! There's the difference now between man's old age and a boat's old age. But yes, old mast, we both grow old together. We are sound in our hulls, though, are we not, my ship? Yes, minus a leg, that's all. This dead wood has the better of my live flesh in every way. I can't compare with it. I've known some ships made of dead trees that outlast the lives of men made of the most vital stuff. What's that he said? he should still go before me, my pilot; and yet to be seen again? But where? Will I have eyes at the bottom of the sea?

Suppose I descend those endless stairs? All night I've been sailing from him, wherever he did sink to. Good-bye, masthead—keep a good eye upon the whale while I'm gone. We'll talk tomorrow, no, tonight, when the white whale lies down there, tied by head and tail."

He gave the word. And then still gazing around him, he was steadily lowered through the blue air to the deck.

In due time the boats were lowered. While standing in his boat's stern, Ahab seemed to hold back from leaving. He waved to the mate—who held one of the tackle ropes on deck—and bade him pause.

"Starbuck!"

"Sir?"

"For the third time my soul's ship starts upon this voyage, Starbuck."

"Aye, sir, that's what you want."

"Some ships sail from their ports, and ever afterwards are missing, Starbuck!"

"Truth, sir; saddest truth."

"Some men die at ebb tide; some at low water; some at the full of the flood—and I feel now like a wave that's reached its height, Starbuck. I am old—shake hands with me, man."

Their hands met. Their eyes fastened. Starbuck spoke rapidly.

"Oh, my captain, my captain!—noble heart—go not—go not!—see, it's a brave man that knows how to weep!"

"Lower away!"—cried Ahab, tossing the mate's arm from him. "Stand by the crew!"

In an instant the boat was pulling round close under the stern.

Florida, John White. John R. Freeman & Co./The Fotomas Index

"The sharks! the sharks!" cried a voice from the low cabin window there; "O master, my master, come back!"

But Ahab heard nothing. His own voice was high-lifted then; and the boat leaped on.

The boats had not gone very far, when by a signal from the mastheads—a downward pointed arm, Ahab knew that the whale had sounded. He intended to be near him at the next rising. He held on his way a little sideways from the vessel. The crew maintained a profound silence, as the head-beat waves hammered and hammered against the opposing bow.

Suddenly the waters around them slowly swelled in broad circles. Then it quickly upheaved, as if sideways sliding from a submerged berg of ice, swiftly rising to the surface. A low rumbling sound was heard, a deep hum. They all held their breaths. A vast form shot lengthwise from the sea, wet with trailing ropes, harpoons, and lances. Covered in a thin drooping veil of mist, it hovered for a moment in the rainbowed air. Then it fell swamping back into the deep. Crushed thirty feet upwards, the waters flashed for an instant like heaps of fountains. Then they brokenly sank in a shower of flakes, leaving the circling surface creamed like new milk around the marble trunk of the whale.

---

sounded (SOWND ed) dove deeply downward (by a whale or fish)

"Give way!" cried Ahab to the oars-men. The boats darted forward to the attack. Maddened by yesterday's fresh irons that rotted in him, Moby-Dick seemed absolutely sure of what he was doing. The wide layers of welded tendons overspreading his broad white forehead looked knitted together beneath the transparent skin. Head on, he came churning his tail among the boats. And once more he beat them apart. The irons and lances spilled out from the two mates' boats. And one side of their boat was caved in at the bow. But Ahab's boat was left almost without a scar.

Daggoo and Queequeg were stop-ping the trained planks. The whale swam out from them, turned, and showed one entire flank as he shot by them again. At that moment a quick cry went up. Lashed round and round to the fish's back; bound up in the turns upon turns in which, during the past night, the whale had reeled the lines around him, the half-torn body of a sailor was seen. His clothes were torn to shreds; his swollen eyes turned full upon old Ahab.

The harpoon dropped from his hand.

"You have fooled me!"—drawing in a long lean breath—"Aye, this, *this* then is the hearse that you promised. Away, mates, to the ship! Those boats are useless now. Repair them if you can in time, and return to me. If not, Ahab is sure enough to die—Down, men! If anything jumps from this boat I stand in, I shall harpoon it. You are not other men, but my arms and my legs; and so obey me—Where's the whale? gone down again?"

But he looked too near the boat. As if bent upon escaping with the corpse he bore, Moby-Dick was now again steadily swimming forward. He had almost passed the ship—which thus far had been sailing in the opposite direction to him. He seemed swimming with his utmost speed. He was now only intent upon pursuing his own straight path in the sea.

"Oh! Ahab," cried Starbuck, "not too late is it, even now, the third day, to stop. See! Moby-Dick is not after you. It is you, you, who is madly after him!"

Setting sail to the rising wind, the only boat was swiftly going downwind. And at last when Ahab was sliding by the vessel, close enough to distinguish Star-buck's face as he leaned over the rail, he hailed him to turn the vessel about. Then he asked him to follow, not too swiftly, but at a good distance behind. Glancing upwards he saw Tashtego, Queequeg, and Daggoo, eagerly mount-ing to the three mastheads. The oarsmen were rocking in the two wooden boats which had just been lifted to the side. They were busily at work repairing them. One after the other, through the portholes, as he sped, he also caught flying glimpses of Stubb and Flask, busying themselves on deck among bundles of new irons and lances. As he saw all this; as he heard the hammers in the broken boats; far other hammers seemed driving a nail into his heart. But he rallied. And now he noticed that the vane or flag was gone from the main masthead, he shouted to Tashtego, who had just gained that perch, to descend again for another flag, and a hammer and nails, and so nail it to the mast.

Whether exhausted by the three days' running chase, and the resistance to his swimming because of the knotted ropes around him, or whether it was some inactive dishonesty and malice in him: whichever was true, the White Whale's way now began to lessen. The boat was rapidly nearing him once more. The whale's last start, however, had not been so long a one as before. And still as Ahab glided over the waves the unpitying sharks accompanied him; and so stubbornly stuck to the boat; and so continually bit at the plying oars, that the blades became jagged and crunched. They left small splinters in the sea, at almost every dip.

"Heed them not! those teeth but give new rowlocks to your oars. Pull on! 'tis the better rest, the sharks' jaw than the yielding water."

"But at every bite, sir, the thin blades grow smaller and smaller!"

"They will last long enough! pull on!—But who can tell"—he muttered—"whether these sharks swim to feast on the whale or on Ahab?—But pull on! Aye, all alive, now—we near him. The helm! take the helm! let me pass"—and so saying, two of the oarsmen helped him forward to the bows of the still flying boat.

As the boat was cast to one side, it landed next to the White Whale's body. The White Whale seemed strangely oblivious of the boat's advance. Sometimes whales act that way. Ahab was fairly within the smoky mountain mist, which, thrown off from the whale's spout, curled round his great mountainous hump. He was very close to him; when, with body arched back, and both arms lifted high, he darted his fierce iron and his far fiercer curse into the hated whale. As both steel and curse sank to the socket, as if sucked into a swamp, Moby-Dick twisted and turned. He rolled the top part of his body against the bow. And, without putting a hole in the boat, he suddenly turned it over. If it had not been for the upper part of the side of the boat to which he then clung, Ahab would once more have been tossed into the sea. As it was, three of the oarsmen had no idea that Ahab had attacked the whale. They were therefore unprepared for its attack and were flung out of the boat. Two of them clutched the side of it and hurled themselves bodily inboard again. The third man helplessly dropped behind the boat but he was still afloat and swimming.

Almost at the same moment, with amazing speed, the White Whale swam through the rolling sea. But when Ahab cried out to the steersman to take new turns with the line, and hold it so; and commanded the crew to turn round on their seats, and tow the boat up to the mark; the moment the undependable line felt that double strain and tug, it snapped in the empty air!

---

malice (MAL is) desire to see others harmed

"What breaks in me? My strength cracks!—it's whole again; oars! oars! Row towards him!"

Hearing the tremendous rush of the sea-crashing boat, the whale wheeled around to present his blank forehead. In that turn, he caught sight of the nearing black hull of the ship. He may have believed it was the source of all his trouble. He also may have thought it was a noble enemy. Whatever, all of a sudden, he bore down upon its advancing bow, clamping his jaws amid fiery showers of foam.

Ahab staggered; his hand struck his forehead. "I grow blind; hands! stretch out before me that I may yet find my way. Isn't it night?"

"The whale! The ship!" cried the fearful oarsmen.

"Oars! oars! Row the boat. It may be too late for Ahab to make his mark this one last time! I see: the ship! the ship! Go on, my men! will you not save my ship?"

But as the oarsmen violently forced their boat through the sledge-hammering seas, two planks burst through the bow of the boat. In an instant almost, the temporarily weakened boat lay nearly level with the waves. Its half-wading, splashing crew, tried hard to stop the gap and bail out the pouring water. But it didn't work.

From the ship's bows, nearly all the seamen now hung inactive. They still held hammers, bits of plank, lances, and harpoons in their hands, just as if they had come from their various employments. All their spellbound eyes looked at the whale. On either side of him was a huge semicircle of foam as he rushed toward them. Punishment, swift vengeance, everlasting harm were in his whole being. In spite of all that living man could do, his forehead hit the ship's right bow. The men and wood reeled. Some fell flat upon their faces. Like dislodged trucks, the heads of the harpooneers aloft shook on their bull-like necks. Through the hole, they heard the water pour, as a mountain stream pours down a narrow gorge.

"The ship! The hearse!—the second hearse!" cried Ahab from the boat; "its wood could only be American!"

Diving beneath the settling ship, the whale ran quivering along its keel. Then turning under water, he swiftly shot to the surface again. Then he stopped within a few yards of Ahab's coat, where, for a time, he lay quiet.

"I turn my body from the sun. Where are you, Tashtego? Let me hear your hammer. Oh! my wonderful boat, masts that did not surrender, the uncracked keel, and only god-bullied hull. The firm deck, and proud steering gear, and Polepointed bow—death-glorious ship! Must you then sink, and without me? Am I cut off from the last fond pride of meanest shipwrecked captains? Oh, lonely death

---

quivering (KWIV ur ing) trembling; slight vibrating motion
keel (KEEL) a piece of wood that runs along the center line from front of the boat to the back

on lonely life! Oh, now I feel my most incredible greatness lies in my most incredible grief. This is the greatest moment of my life and now that it has reached its peak there is nothing left for me but death. Towards you I roll, you all-destroying but unconquering whale; to the last I fight with you. From the bottom of my heart I stab at you; for hate's sake I spit my last breath at you. Sink all coffins and all hearses to one common pool! Since neither can be mine, let me then tow to pieces, you damned whale! *Thus,* I give up the spear!"

The harpoon was darted; the stricken whale flew forward; with igniting speed the line ran through the groove;—ran afoul. Ahab stooped to clear it. He did clear it. But the flying turn caught him round the neck, and voicelessly he was shot out of the boat. Not even the crew knew he was gone. In the next instant, the whale broke the rope, knocked down an oarsman, and striking the sea, disappeared in its depths.

For an instant, the dazed boat's crew stood still. Then they turned. "The ship? Great God, where is the ship?" Soon they saw her. She was a fading phantom, as in a mirage. Only the uppermost masts were out of the water; however, the loyal harpooneers still maintained their sinking lookouts on the sea. And now, circles grabbed hold of the lone boat itself. All its crew, and each floating oar, and every lance pole, and spinning, living and not living thing, all round and round in one circle, carried the smallest chip of the *Pequod* out of sight.

Now small birds flew screaming over the yet yawning gulf; a sullen white surf beat against its steep sides; then all collapsed, and the great shroud of the sea rolled on as it rolled five thousand years ago.

---

phantom (FAN tum) an unreal mental image
sullen (SUL un) sulky and brooding; moody
shroud (SHROWD) something that hides or protects

Review the Selection

UNDERSTAND THE SELECTION

Recall

1. Why did Ahab seek revenge?

2. What did Ahab offer the men if they killed Moby-Dick?

3. Where did Ahab say he would go to search for Moby-Dick?

Infer

4. Why did Starbuck protest Ahab's intention to kill Moby-Dick?

5. Give a brief description of Ahab telling what kind of man he was.

6. What might the fight between Ahab and Moby-Dick really represent?

7. Read the last paragraph of *Moby-Dick* again. Then use your own words to tell what Melville meant.

Apply

8. How might Ahab have felt upon first seeing Moby-Dick?

9. Suppose that you are Moby-Dick. Describe your feelings about human beings.

10. Select an important event from *Moby-Dick* and tell why it made the story more interesting.

Respond to Literature

Explain how Emerson's influence on Melville is reflected in *Moby-Dick*.

WRITE ABOUT THE SELECTION

Herman Melville spent a lot of time on whaling ships where he gathered information for several books, including *Moby-Dick*. It is possible that he kept a journal to record his thoughts and observations about whaling and the sea. Imagine it is 1838, and you are on a whaling ship. How do you feel about the ocean? How do you feel about hunting whales? What is the weather like? What is life like aboard a whaling ship? Write a journal entry.

Prewriting   Freewrite for a few minutes to explore what you want to include in your journal entry. Describe what the ocean looked like, how it smelled, and what sea life you saw. You might want to include a whale sighting or a whale hunt. Try to capture the excitement and the danger of your situation.

Writing   Write a journal entry about a day at sea on a whaling boat. Include your thoughts and recollections of the day.

Revising   When you revise, make sure that you have included several observations about sea life. If you have not, be sure to include them during your revision. Conversely, if you have included any passages that do not relate to ocean life, eliminate these when you revise.

Proofreading   Reread your journal entry to check for errors. Be sure all your sentences end with periods, question marks, or exclamation points.

THINK ABOUT CONFLICT

One type of conflict in literature is the struggle that results from the interaction between characters representing opposite forces in a plot. The main character is called the **protagonist**; the rival character is called the **antagonist**. The protagonist and the antagonist struggle against each other. Each should be motivated to resolve the conflict. If the characters lack purpose or other motivation, the plot will seem amateurish to the reader or listener. If the characters are well-motivated, the plot will be more satisfying.

1. Who is the protagonist in the excerpts? Who is the antagonist? Describe the main conflict between them.

2. At what point does the climax, or the turning point, of the story come?

3. In the madness of the pursuit, one character was the voice of reason. Whose voice was that?

4. Why did Ahab not heed the warnings of the voice of reason? What was driving him?

5. What was the resolution of the story?

READING FOCUS

Visualize As you read this excerpt from *Moby-Dick*, you were able to visualize certain scenes from the story. What scene in this story remains most vivid to you? Give some examples of the imagery that helped you visualize this scene.

DEVELOP YOUR VOCABULARY

An **antonym** is a word that has a meaning opposite, or almost opposite, to that of another word. For example, *enormous* means "huge" or "very big." Words that mean the opposite are *tiny* and *little*.

Read the sentences below. Choose a word from the list that is an antonym for each italicized word. Then write a sentence using the word.

malice	effortless
vague	vengeance
ominous	calm

1. The weather was *favorable* for an afternoon sail.

2. No *mercy* was shown to the defendant when his sentence was given.

3. Your *kindness* during this difficult time is greatly appreciated.

4. Lucy gave a *specific* description of the house so they wouldn't miss it.

5. The first day of rehearsal is always *chaotic*!

6. The sailors' work was *arduous*; it lasted from morning until night.

Learn About

IMAGERY

People learn about the world through their senses—sight, hearing, smell, taste, and touch. The poet is especially sensitive to sense impressions. To express an experience of a place, for example, the poet will depend greatly on sense impressions. These, added to thought and emotion, bring the scene alive for the reader.

Sense impression translated into words is called **imagery**. The poet will generally choose specific words rather than general ones to make the strongest statement. A *white-petaled daisy*, for example, is more specific than a *flower*. The more specific the poet is, the more vivid the imagery in the poem will be. The poet looks for fresh ways of expressing sense impressions, of course.

As you read the poem, ask yourself:

1. What sense impression did Whittier express in the poem?
2. Which sense did he call upon most for his imagery?

READING FOCUS

Understand Contrast To contrast is to look at differences. Seeing how one situation differs from another often provides important information. As you read "Song of Slaves in the Desert," think about how the lives of the people who have been captured will differ in quality from their lives in Africa. Look for places in the poem that contrast these two ways of life.

WRITING CONNECTION

Write *sight, sound, smell, taste, touch* on a piece of paper. Under each heading, write several phrases that create an image for that word. For example, *sound*: crashing, pounding waves.

Song of Slaves in the Desert

by John Greenleaf Whittier

Where are we going? where are we going,
Where are we going, Rubee?
Lord of peoples, lord of lands,
Look across these shining sands,
5   Through the furnace of the noon,
Through the white light of the moon.
Strong the Ghiblee wind is blowing,
Strange and large the world is growing!
Speak and tell us where we are going,
10   Where are we going, Rubee?

Bornou land was rich and good,
Wells of water, fields of food,
Dourra fields, and bloom of bean,
And the palm-tree cool and green:
15   Bornou land we see no longer,
Here we thirst and here we hunger,
Here the Moor-man smites in anger:
        Where are we going, Rubee?

When we went from Bornou land,
20   We were like the leaves and sand,
We were many, we are few;
Life has one, and death has two:
Whitened bones our path are showing,
Thou All-seeing, thou All-knowing!

Ghiblee (GIB lee) night wind that makes an eerie sound
Bornou land (BAWR noo) reference to homeland in Africa
Dourra (DUUR uh) (usually spelled durra) a kind of grain grown in Northern Africa
smites (SMYTS) inflicts a heavy blow; kills by striking
Moor (MUUR) referring to the African slave traders

25   Hear us, tell us, where are we going,
        Where are we going, Rubee?

    Moons of marches from our eyes
    Bornou land behind us lies;
    Stranger round us day by day
30   Bends the desert circle gray;
    Wild the waves of sand are flowing,
    Hot the winds above them blowing,—
    Lord of all things! where are we going?
        Where are we going, Rubee?

35   We are weak, but Thou art strong;
    Short our lives, but Thine is long;
    We are blind, but Thou hast eyes;
    We are fools, but Thou art wise!
    Thou, our morrow's pathway knowing
40   Through the strange world round us growing,
    Hear us, tell us where are we going,
        Where are we going, Rubee?

African Slave Trade, The Granger Collection

Review the Selection

UNDERSTAND THE SELECTION

Recall

1. About whom is this poem written?

2. Where did the Africans live?

3. Identify the speaker of the poem.

Infer

4. Explain the line, "Where are we going, . . . ?"

5. In your own words describe what "Bornou land" was like.

6. Interpret this line: "Here the Moorman smites in anger."

7. Which line did Whittier use to describe the passage of time?

Apply

8. Which line best describes what the song of the slaves was?

9. Suppose that you could answer the speaker in this poem. How would you respond?

10. The speaker states several times that the world is getting larger and growing. What does he or she mean by these words?

Respond to Literature

How does the "Song of Slaves in the Desert" reflect how writers of the 1800s were writing?

WRITE ABOUT THE SELECTION

John Greenleaf Whittier vividly described his feelings about slavery in "Song of Slaves in the Desert." In this poem, he made it very clear that he opposed slavery. Think about the question that the speaker repeats over and over again. "Where are we going? Where are we going? Where are we going, Rubee?" Write another stanza for this poem in which you answer that question. Describe what the speaker encounters after arriving at his or her destination.

Prewriting Before you start, reread the poem. Think about how Whittier used imagery. Then jot down some words or phrases you might want to use in the stanza you write. Visualize how it might look, feel, and sound to arrive in a new land.

Writing Use your notes to help you write a stanza in which you answer the question, "Where are we going?" Be sure to include several examples of imagery. You might want to compare the place from which the speaker came to the new place in which he or she arrives.

Revising When you revise, make sure that you have included two examples of imagery. If you have not, be sure to include them in your revision.

Proofreading Read over your paragraph to check for errors. Be sure each line of your poem begins with a capital letter.

THINK ABOUT IMAGERY

Imagery is the translation into words of sense impressions gained through sight, hearing, smell, taste, and touch, or feeling. No poem can be judged by its imagery alone, but imagery can vastly enhance the impact of the poem on the reader.

1. What senses does Whittier call on to tell how hot the march across the desert was?

2. What specific images do the African people in this poem have of their native Bornou land?

3. What specific images do they have of their desert environment?

4. What does Whittier mean when he says the Africans "were like the leaves and sand"? Why does he use the past tense?

5. The captured people repeatedly ask "Where are we going, Rubee?" To whom do you think the name *Rubee* refers? Explain your answer.

READING FOCUS

Understand Contrast What contrast does the poem make between the people's fate in an unknown land and their lives in Africa? Provide lines from the poem that illustrate the contrast.

DEVELOP YOUR VOCABULARY

Images that use specific words are more vivid than those that use general words. Specific words, however, can differ in their meaning. The most specific words in a language are those that refer to one-of-a-kind people, animals, places, or things: Michael Jackson, Lassie, Mount St. Helens, the *Mona Lisa*. It is not always necessary to be quite so specific as these, however. Somewhat more general terms would be *singer*, *dog*, *volcano*, and *painting*. Least specific of all would be *man*, *animal*, *mountain*, and *artwork*.

Rearrange these lists in order from most specific to most general.

1. shoe, footwear, cross-trainers, sneaker

2. publication, *Time*, periodical, magazine

3. male, Michael J. Fox, actor, TV star

4. literature, poetry, poem, "Song of Slaves in the Desert"

5. drum, percussion instrument, musical instrument, snare drum

WRITING APPLICATIONS

Write About Authors

Suppose that all the writers in the unit got together to discuss their work. What do you think they would say about their own and each other's writing? What criticisms or compliments would they offer to each other? Choose two authors from this unit and record their conversation.

Prewriting Before you begin to write, choose the two authors whose conversation you would like to think about. Then review their work. Emerson thought it was important that writers include what they believed in their writings. Examine how the work of the authors you have chosen might reflect Emerson's ideas so that you can include some interesting criticisms and compliments in the conversation. Jot down notes to help you write your conversation.

Writing Use your notes as a basis for your conversation. Be sure to include in the dialogue criticisms and compliments that each writer might have made about the other's work. When you write the dialogue be sure to set off the speaker's name with a colon (:) as in a drama.

Revising As you revise, be sure that you have included both criticisms and compliments. If you have not, be sure to include them in your revision.

Proofreading Reread your dialogue to check for errors in spelling and punctuation. Be sure you have put a colon (:) after each speaker's name.

Write About Poetry

In this unit, you have learned some of the different elements of poetry. Now you can use what you learned to analyze a poem. Choose a poem that you enjoyed reading. Then, using a list of the elements of poetry, prepare a paper in which you discuss how understanding these elements helped you to enjoy the poem.

Prewriting Review what the elements of poetry are. Then make a list of them, being sure to include rhythm, meter, and rhyme. At the top of your list, write the name of the poem you have chosen. Then check off which elements are used in the poem. You might also want to jot down specific kinds of figurative language that were used or how the poet used sound devices and imagery.

Writing Using your list and notes, write an analysis in which you tell how the elements of poetry increased your appreciation of the poem. Be sure to include specific examples.

Revising When you revise, make sure that you have made a reference to at least four different elements of poetry that increased your appreciation of the poem.

Proofreading Check your paper for errors in punctuation. Make sure that you have spelled all the words correctly.

Vocabulary

Onomatopoeia (AHN-uh-MAT-uh-PEE-uh) is the term used for words that imitate sounds. Some onomatopoeic words are *hiss*, *pop*, *whizz*, *buzz*, and *bang*. Onomatopoeia is a useful resource in the poet's—and the prose writer's—repertory of sound devices. It may be used openly, as in "Pop goes the weasel," or subtly, as in "The moan of doves in immemorial elms."

Write the following sentences. Then underline the onomatopoeic word in each one.

1. The chains in the back of the trunk clanked as we drove over the rough road.

2. The sleigh bells jingled merrily as the horse pulled us through the newly fallen snow.

3. A green snake slithered unnoticed through the tall grass.

4. Drops of water plopped into the puddles of water the rain had created.

5. High above us a skein of geese honked as they flew south.

6. A tiny locomotive chugged up the steep mountainside.

7. The ignition turned over, sputtered, and then died.

8. A whole sack of flour fell to the floor with a dull thud.

Grammar, Usage, and Mechanics

When you are writing a series of three or more items in a sentence, you should use commas to separate the items.

Example: Lisa bought lace, ribbons, pins, thread, and fabric.

Some authorities permit the omission of the comma before *and* if the meaning is clear without it. However this can sometimes lead to uncertainty of meaning.

Example: Alex bought Redbook, Sports Illustrated and Travel and Leisure.

If the comma is omitted before *and*, a reader might assume that *Travel and Leisure* is two magazines. A comma before *and* makes it clear that *Travel and Leisure* is a single magazine.

If you always put a comma before *and*, you will not have to stop and think whether the meaning is clear.

Add commas where they are needed in the following sentences.

1. Jack brought climbing boots walking boots sneakers and loafers with him.

2. Lee read Travels with Charley Twenty Thousand Leagues Under the Sea and Crime and Punishment last summer.

3. Larry subscribes to National Geographic Visions and Field and Stream.

4. Chris sent books magazines records tapes and newspapers to her brother in Ecuador.

SPEAKING AND LISTENING

One of the easiest and most effective ways to make a piece of literature interesting is to read it aloud. As a child, you loved hearing your favorite story. As an older student, you may find a difficult piece of literature more accessible if you hear someone read it aloud. Maybe that is because when you hear something, you allow your mind to visualize the words more easily than when you have to read the words yourself.

Before you choose a selection from this unit to read aloud, acquaint yourself with the following tips. They will help you to read aloud with more confidence and feeling.

1. Be selective. Choose something that you find interesting. This is important for two reasons. First of all, if you are bored when you read it, chances are your listeners will be bored and uninterested, too. Second, it's unfulfilling to read something you don't like.

2. Read the selection to yourself and become familiar with it. Get the feel for the language. This will help you to know what expression to use when you read aloud.

3. If the selection is perfect as it is, let it be, if not, do some editing. You might want to condense some of the dialogue or the longer sections, or you might want to paraphrase certain passages.

4. Your oral reading style should fit your personality. If it's not your style to use unique voices for each character, don't do it. If it makes you uncomfortable to read dramatically, then don't do it. Be natural and the words of the selection should grab the listeners without theatrics.

5. During your reading aloud, maintain good volume and expression in your voice. Make frequent eye contact with your listeners. This will involve them and make them feel that you are reading to them individually.

6. Practice so that you feel confident in your delivery. Choose a selection or part of a selection from this unit and prepare to read it aloud. Limit your presentation to about three minutes. Review the suggestions above to help you enjoy the experience.

CRITICAL THINKING

Classifying is the act of grouping things according to some principle. For example, when you rearrange your bookshelves, you may put all the fiction books on one shelf, the biographies on another shelf, and the hobby books on a third shelf. You have classified your books by their type.

When you classify things, you put them in **categories**. A category is a group of things that have some characteristic in common. In the bookshelf example, fiction is one category, biographies another, and hobby books are the third category. The principles that determine a category are many. You may classify by size, type, color, use, shape, purpose, and so on.

To determine a category, you must be able to see similarities and differences. Noting the similarities is called **comparing**. Noting the differences is called **contrasting**.

Authors often make use of classification and categorizing in order to make comparisons and contrasts. Choose a selection from this unit that classifies or categorizes some objects, ways of life, aspects of nature, characters, or ideas. Then answer the following questions.

1. What principle determines each category? Does the author explain the classification adequately?

2. What does the category enable the author to compare or contrast?

EFFECTIVE STUDYING

Following Directions Being able to follow directions is an important skill for school and the rest of your life. Throughout life, you may need to follow directions to get from one place to another or to do something or to make something.

Many directions must be followed in a precise sequence. In such directions, you may notice words such as *first, next, then,* and *last.* These words help you keep the sequence straight.

Here are some guidelines to help you.

1. To follow oral directions
   - Listen attentively.
   - If the instructions are detailed, you may wish to take notes.
   - If there are parts you do not understand, ask questions.
   - To double check your understanding, repeat the directions.

2. To follow written directions
   - Read them carefully.
   - Make sure you understand the sequence.
   - After each step, read the direction again to be sure that you followed it correctly.
   - If pictures accompany the directions, study them carefully.

Test Preparation

Be sure to follow test directions exactly. Reread the directions for each part of the test and circle the key words before you begin to answer the questions.

A Nation Expresses Itself

Dark hills at evening in the west,
Where sunset hovers like a sound
Of golden horns that sang to rest
Old bones of warriors under ground.
—Edwin Arlington Robinson

A Rest on the Ride, Albert Bierstadt. Three Lions/Superstock

1870 Bret Harte's
*The Luck of Roaring
Camp and Other
Sketches* appears.

1855 Walt Whitman
publishes *Leaves of Grass*.

1876 Mark Twain
publishes *Tom Sawyer*.

| 1850 | 1855 | 1860 | 1865 | 1870 | 1875 | 1880 | 18 |

1860 First transcontinental
telegraph line is completed.

1865 President Lincoln
is assassinated.

1876 The Battle of Little
Bighorn is fought.

1885 Statue of
Liberty is dedicated.

HISTORICAL HIGHLIGHTS

A Nation Expresses Itself

Before 1855, America consisted of farms and small towns. Between
1855 and 1915, however, there were many changes. The nation became
industrialized. Goods that used to be made mainly at home—everything
from clothes to furniture—could now be produced in greater quantity
and at lower cost in factories. Large cities grew up around the factories.
Many Americans and immigrants moved to a city during this period.

This was an age of great inventions. It was the invention of new
machinery that made it possible for goods to be mass produced. Beginning in the mid-nineteenth century, you could have sent a telegram. After
1876, you could have made a telephone call. You could have taken a train
across the continent in 1869, bought a car around the turn of the century,
or even—if you were daring enough—flown in an airplane after 1903.

■ ABOLITION AND THE CIVIL WAR

The most important change in America was the abolition of slavery.
This long-overdue measure finally became law with the Emancipation
Proclamation of 1863.

Unfortunately, it took a Civil War to bring it about. Eleven Southern
states seceded from the Union, many people were killed, and at the
war's end a great President was assassinated. Although the Civil War
ended with a Union victory in 1865, many years passed before the bitter
feelings between North and South were healed.

■ LITERATURE: FICTION AND POETRY

During this time, people turned more and more to reading for pleasure.
The most popular kinds of reading material between 1855 and 1915 were
fiction and poetry.

Walt Whitman was called the People's Poet. He loved to write about
America and the lives of everyday Americans. You will read three of his
poems. "I Hear America Singing" tells of ordinary people enjoying their

1891 Ambrose Bierce publishes *Tales of Soldiers and Civilians.*

1903 Jack London publishes *The Call of the Wild.*

1911 Edith Wharton publishes *Ethan Frome.*

1917 Pulitzer Prize awards are established.

90   1895   1900   1905   1910   1915   1920   1925

1903 Wright brothers pioneer air flight.

1894 Edison demonstrates first motion picture machine.

1908 Henry Ford builds Model T using mass production.

1917 U.S. enters World War I.

1914 World War I begins.

work, their country, and their lives in general. "When I Heard the Learn'd Astronomer" is about a student's reaction to a lecture about the stars. "O Captain! My Captain!" is a tribute to President Lincoln.

O. Henry, whose real name was William Sydney Porter, began writing short stories while serving time in prison for embezzlement. When you read "The Gift of the Magi," keep in mind that O. Henry's stories are known for their surprise endings.

Mark Twain's real name was Samuel Langhorne Clemens. He took his pen name from a term he learned while working on a steamboat. It refers to measuring the depth of the water. Twain became famous for creating such characters as Tom Sawyer and Huckleberry Finn. You will learn how he did this when you read his nonfiction article, "How to Tell a Story."

If you like adventure stories, you are sure to enjoy Jack London's "To Build a Fire," which is set in the Yukon of northern Canada during the Gold Rush. London was the first American author to become a millionaire, but he lost his money and died at the age of forty.

In 1922 Edwin Arlington Robinson received the first Pulitzer Prize for poetry. His poems have been described as short stories in verse. Like O. Henry, Robinson liked surprise endings, as you will see in "Richard Cory."

This period saw the emergence of more women writers. Three are highlighted in this unit. All were poets, but Mary E. Wilkins Freeman also wrote novels and short stories such as "The Revolt of Mother."

Sara Teasdale's first book of poems was published before she was twenty-five. Although her poetry generally stresses hope, she led a sad and lonely life. Do you think you can tell her true feelings from her poetry?

You have probably heard the first verse of "America the Beautiful" many times. However, Katharine Lee Bates wrote more than one stanza.

As you read these selections, try to notice differences from writings of earlier eras. Think about the differences you see.

SYMBOLISM

A **symbol** is something that represents, or stands for, something else. You will recognize some symbols from ordinary life: the scales of justice, the dove of peace, the donkey and elephant of the Democratic and Republican parties, the Stars and Stripes for the United States of America, the "*V* for Victory" sign. The meaning of all of these symbols is commonly agreed upon, but it is not always simple. The image behind a symbol may be a blend of many ideas and attitudes.

In literature, authors may not depend upon commonly agreed-upon symbols. Instead, they may devise their own from the context or substance of what they write about. The reader must make the connection between the literal image and the idea or the quality it stands for.

As you read these poems, ask yourself:
1. What symbol or symbols does Whitman use in each poem?
2. Why did he choose that symbol?

READING FOCUS

Compare and Contrast You compare things by looking at what they have in common, and you contrast them by looking at their differences. Three poems by the same person may have many things in common, but their differences can surprise you and teach you something about the poet. As you read the poems of Walt Whitman, think about their similarities and differences. How do you know that they were all written by the same person? What qualities tell you this?

WRITING CONNECTION

There are many symbols associated with the United States. Think of two such symbols and describe what they mean to you and why you associate them with this country.

I HEAR
AMERICA SINGING

by Walt Whitman

I hear America singing, the varied carols I hear,
Those of mechanics, each one singing his as it
    should be blithe and strong,
The carpenter singing his as he measures his
    plank or beam,
The mason singing his as he makes ready for
    work, or leaves off work,
5   The boatman singing what belongs to him in his
    boat, the deck-hand singing on the
    steamboat deck,
The shoemaker singing as he sits on his bench,
    the hatter singing as he stands,
The wood-cutter's song, the plowboy's on his way
    in the morning, or at noon intermission or at
    sundown,
The delicious singing of the mother, or of the
    young wife at work, or of the girl sewing or
    washing,
Each singing what belongs to him or her and to
    none else,
10   The day what belongs to the day—at night the
    party of young fellows, robust, friendly,
Singing with open mouths their strong melodious
    songs.

---

blithe (BLY*TH*) happy; cheerful
mason (MAY sun) stone worker
hatter (HAT ur) hat maker
robust (roh BUST) strong; healthy

The League Long Breakers Thundering on the Reef, William Trost Richards.
The Brooklyn Museum

O CAPTAIN! MY CAPTAIN!

by Walt Whitman

O Captain! my Captain! our fearful trip is done,
The ship has weather'd every rack, the prize we
    sought is won,
The port is near, the bells I hear, the people
    all exulting,
While follow eyes the steady keel, the vessel grim
    and daring;

5   But O heart! heart! heart!
       O the bleeding drops of red,
          Where on the deck my Captain lies,
            Fallen cold and dead.

---

weather (WE*TH* ur) last through; endure
rack (RAK) hardship; torture
exulting (ig ZULT ing) rejoicing; showing joy
keel (KEEL) "backbone" of a ship

O Captain! my Captain! rise up and hear the
    bells;

10   Rise up—for you the flag is flung—for you the
        bugle trills,

For you bouquets and ribbon'd wreaths—for you
    the shores a-crowding

For you they call, the swaying mass, their eager
    faces turning;

Here Captain! dear father!
    This arm beneath your head!

15   It is some dream that on the deck,
          You've fallen cold and dead.

My Captain does not answer, his lips are pale and
    still,

My father does not feel my arm, he has no pulse
    nor will,

The ship is anchor'd safe and sound, its voyage
    closed and done,

20   From fearful trip the victor ship comes in with
        object won;

    Exult O shores, and ring O bells!
      But I with mournful tread,
        Walk the deck my Captain lies,
          Fallen cold and dead.

---

trill (TRIL) play music with a quivering sound
will (WIL) wishes; desires
object (OB jekt) purpose; goal
tread (TRED) step; walk

WHEN I HEARD THE LEARN'D ASTRONOMER

by Walt Whitman

When I heard the learn'd astronomer,
When the proofs, the figures, were ranged in
   columns before me,
When I was shown the charts and diagrams, to
   add, divide, and measure them,
When I sitting heard the astronomer where he
   lectured with much applause in the lecture-
   room,
How soon unaccountable I became tired and sick,
Till rising and gliding out I wandered off by
   myself,
In the mystical moist night-air, and from time to
   time,
Looked up in perfect silence at the stars.

---

ranged (RAYNJD) set forth; arranged
unaccountable (un uh KOWN tuh bul) for no apparent reason
mystical (MIS tih kul) mysterious; having a hidden meaning

Walt Whitman (1819–1892)

"Wake up, America!" Walt Whitman's poetry seems to shout. "Wake up and look around. Wake up and listen. Wake up to a new life in a world that is wonder-full."

If any American deserves the title "People's Poet," it is Walt Whitman. He thought of himself as the poet of democracy. Everything inspired Whitman. Everything had meaning for him. His aim was to tell Americans about themselves in a way that would make them, too, feel fully alive.

Whitman was born into a farm family on Long Island, near New York City. At the age of eleven, he dropped out of school and went to work for a lawyer. In the years that followed, he worked as a carpenter, teacher, and newspaper writer and editor. These different trades and his travels around the United States gave him firsthand knowledge of the people he was later to celebrate in his poetry.

In 1850 Whitman suddenly quit a job as an editor and went back to live with his mother and father. Once a well-known figure in newspaper and political circles, he simply dropped out of sight. Then followed the five "dark years" in his life. Apparently he worked now and then as a carpenter, but most of the time he must have written poetry. In 1855 the "dark years" came to an end. In that year he gave the world *Leaves of Grass*, which, with its original poetic style, became perhaps the most important single collection of poems by an American poet. *Leaves of Grass* marks a turning point in American poetry, for it touches on all aspects of life, including subjects not previously found in verse. In 1856 an expanded edition appeared, after which Whitman continued to work on the volume, adding and dropping poems throughout most of his life.

Whitman was over 40 when the Civil War began, but he insisted on doing his part. He spent the war years nursing and comforting injured soldiers. By the end of the war, many wounded soldiers had met the big friendly man who usually dressed in a shabby wide-brimmed hat and an open shirt and jacket. The war service, however, affected Whitman's own health. In 1873, he suffered a stroke which made him an invalid for the last years of his life.

Why is Walt Whitman suited to the title "People's Poet"?

Review the Selection

UNDERSTAND THE SELECTION

Recall

1. Name four occupations Whitman mentions in "I Hear America Singing."

2. What is wrong with the Captain in "O Captain! My Captain!"?

3. What is "When I Heard the Learn'd Astronomer" about?

Infer

4. Identify a common element among the occupations mentioned in "I Hear America Singing."

5. In "O Captain! My Captain!," whom does the Captain symbolize?

6. What does the ship symbolize?

7. Describe the speaker in "When I Heard the Learn'd Astronomer."

Apply

8. In "I Hear America Singing," what does Whitman really hear?

9. Was "O Captain! My Captain!" written to sadden or cheer people?

10. What did the speaker learn from the "learn'd astronomer"? Explain.

Respond to Literature

Many changes in American life took place during this period. Identify a change implied in any of the poems.

WRITE ABOUT THE SELECTION

"O Captain! My Captain!" is full of symbolism. The two main symbols are the Captain and the ship. Reread the poem. You have already thought about who and what these symbols represent. What do you suppose was the cause of the Captain's death? What do you think will be the effect of his death upon the ship?

Prewriting Cause and effect are important elements of any logical thought process. For every effect, there must be a cause. Think about the Captain's death, in terms of its cause and its effect upon the fate of his ship. To help do this, make a chart with two columns. Write the headings *Cause* and *Effect* at the tops of the columns. In the first column, write down your ideas about possible causes. In the second column, write down what you think would be the effect resulting from each cause.

Writing Using your chart, write a paragraph about the cause and effects of the Captain's death. Be specific about who the Captain stands for and what the ship represents.

Revising In your discussion of effects, include additional symbolism to show how one effect can also become the cause of another effect.

Proofreading Review your paragraph to make sure that all sentences are complete sentences, with subject and verb.

THINK ABOUT SYMBOLISM

A **symbol** is something that represents, or stands for, something else. It does not always stand for an actual object, organization, or other concrete thing, however. It can also represent something intangible, such as an emotion or an idea.

1. In "I Hear America Singing," what do you think the various trades symbolize? Why do the tradespeople sing?

2. In "O Captain! My Captain!" Whitman uses the image of the ship symbolically. What does the ship symbolize?

3. What "fearful trip" has the Captain, who was Abraham Lincoln, been through?

4. In the same poem, what would you say was the "prize" that was sought and won?

5. What did the actual stars in "When I Heard the Learn'd Astronomer" symbolize and why was their meaning so important?

READING FOCUS

Compare and Contrast As you read the poetry of Walt Whitman, you probably noticed that the poems are similar in some ways but different in others. In what ways are the poems alike? What are some important differences?

DEVELOP YOUR VOCABULARY

English has been enriched by borrowing words from other languages such as Latin and Greek. Latin words entered English at several times in history. In ancient times, settlers from Roman-occupied areas brought Latin words with them wherever they traveled. Later, Roman missionaries brought words as well as religion to Britain. In the eleventh century, the French conquered England. Both Latin and Greek words entered English through French. The last great period of borrowing from Latin and Greek came in the sixteenth century. Interest in classical learning flourished, and English writers used many Latin and Greek words in their writing.

The following words all came from Latin or Greek. Look up each word in a dictionary that gives word histories and write whether the word is of Latin or Greek origin.

1. astronomer
2. port
3. mechanic
4. mystical
5. star
6. lecture

A character is a person in a narrative. In fiction, characters are made-up people. They may be patterned after real persons, or they may be figments of the author's imagination.

Authors determine when and how much to tell readers about the characters. They may give a great deal of detail about a character right away, or they may let the reader determine what the character is like through his or her words and actions as the story progresses. They may give a detailed physical description of a character, or they may let the reader create his or her own mental image. A character's personality traits, value system, or frame of mind may be well-defined from the beginning of the story or may be left to the reader to figure out as the plot unfolds.

As you read "The Gift of the Magi," ask yourself:

1. What do the characters look like?
2. What type of people are they?

READING FOCUS

Understand Imagery Imagery is language that appeals to your senses. Writers use imagery to try to make readers see sights, hear sounds, feel textures, smell scents, and taste flavors. Writers use only words to make you sense these things. As you read "The Gift of the Magi," look for images that make the settings and characters come alive for you. Note places in the text that make you see, hear, feel, smell, or taste something specific.

WRITING CONNECTION

If you were to write a short, fictional story, describe two characters that you would include. Give details of their physical appearance and personality.

THE GIFT OF THE MAGI

ADAPTED

by O. Henry

One dollar and eighty-seven cents. That was all. And sixty cents of it was in pennies. Pennies saved one and two at a time by bulldozing the grocer and the butcher until her cheeks burned with embarrassment. Three times Della counted it. One dollar and eighty-seven cents.[1] And the next day would be Christmas.

There was clearly nothing to do but flop down on the shabby little couch and howl. So Della did it. Which instigates the reflection that life is made up of three stages—sobs, sniffles, and smiles, with sniffles in the lead.

While the woman of the home is gradually coming down from the first stage to the second, take a look at the house. A furnished apartment at eight dollars per week. It did not exactly look like a *poor*house but it certainly brought that word to mind. Nothing worked exactly as it should. In the lobby below was a letter box into which no letter would go, and an electric button from which no mortal finger could tease a ring. And fixed to the box was a card with the name Mr. James Dillingham Young.

The "Dillingham" had been flung to the breeze during a former period of prosperity, when its owner was being paid thirty dollars per week. Now, when the income had shrunk to twenty dollars, the letters of Dillingham looked blurred, as though they were thinking seriously of contracting to a modest and unassuming little D. But whenever Mr. James Dillingham Young

---

Magi (MAY jy) the three wise men who, according to the biblical story, made the journey to Bethlehem to present gifts to the Christ child
bulldozing (BUL dohz ing) bullying; threatening
instigate (IN stuh gayt) bring about; stir up
reflection (rih FLEK shun) serious thought
contracting (kun TRAKT ing) growing smaller
unassuming (un uh SOOM ing) modest; quiet
[1]**One dollar and eighty-seven cents:** This story first appeared in 1905, when a dollar could buy much more than it can now. Think of all sums mentioned as multiplied by ten.

came home and reached his apartment above, he was called Jim and greatly hugged by Mrs. James Dillingham Young, already introduced to you as Della. Which is all very good.

Della finished her cry and powdered her cheeks. She stood by the window and looked out dully at a gray cat walking a gray fence in a gray backyard. Tomorrow would be Christmas Day, and she had only one dollar and eighty-seven cents with which to buy Jim a present. She had been saving every penny she could for months, with this result. Twenty dollars a week doesn't go far. Expenses had been greater than she had planned. They always are. Only one dollar and eighty-seven cents to buy a present for Jim. Her Jim. Many a happy hour she had spent planning for something nice for him. Something fine and rare and sterling—something just a little bit near to showing him the honor of being Mrs. James Dillingham Young.

There was a tall wall mirror between the windows of the room. Perhaps you have seen a wall mirror in an eight-dollar apartment. A very thin and very agile woman may, by seeing her reflection in a number of rapid steps, get a fairly good idea of her looks. Della, being slender, had mastered the art.

Suddenly she whirled from the window and stood before the glass. Her eyes were shining brightly, but her face lost its color within twenty seconds. Rapidly she pulled down her hair and let it fall to its full length.

Now, the James Dillingham Youngs owned just two things in which they both took a mighty pride. One was Jim's gold watch that had been his father's and his grandfather's. The other was Della's hair. Had the Queen of Sheba[2] lived in the apartment across the air shaft, Della would have let her hair hang out the window to dry some day just to make fun of her Majesty's jewels and gifts. Had King Solomon been the janitor, with all his treasures piled up in the basement, Jim would have pulled out his watch every time he passed, just to see him pull at his beard with envy.

So now Della's beautiful hair fell about her, rippling and shining like a cascade of brown waters. It reached below her knees and made almost a garment for her. And then she did it up again nervously and quickly. Once she faltered for a minute and stood still while a tear or two splashed on the worn red carpet.

On went her old brown jacket. On went her old brown hat. With a whirl of skirts and with the brilliant sparkle still in her eyes, she fluttered out the door and down the stairs to the street.

Where she stopped, the sign read: "Madame Sofronie. Wigs and Hair Goods of All Kinds." One flight up Della ran, and collected herself, panting. Madame was a

---

agile (AJ ul) nimble; well-coordinated
cascade (kas KAYD) waterfall
[2]**Queen of Sheba:** According to the Bible, the Queen of Sheba traveled from ancient Ethiopia to Israel to visit King Solomon. Amazed by the King's wisdom, she gave him much gold and other valuable gifts. (I Kings 10:1–13.)

large woman, chilly and much too white.

"Will you buy my hair?" asked Della.

"I buy hair," said Madame. "Take your hat off, and let's have a sight at the looks of it."

Down rippled the brown cascade.

"Twenty dollars," said Madame, lifting the hair with a practiced hand.

"Give it to me quick," said Della.

Oh, and the next two hours tripped by on rosy wings. Forget the hashed metaphor. Della was ransacking the stores for Jim's present.

She found it at last. It surely had been made for Jim and no one else. There was no other like it in any of the stores, and she had turned all of them inside out. It was a platinum watch chain, simple in design, free of silly and cheap decoration. It was even worthy of The Watch. As soon as she saw it, she knew it must be Jim's. It was like him. Quietness and value—the description applied to both. Twenty-one dollars they took from her for it, and she hurried home with the eighty-seven cents. With that chain on his watch, Jim might be properly anxious about the time in any company. Grand as the watch was, he sometimes looked at it on the sly because of the old leather strap that he used in place of a chain.

When Della reached home, her wild delight gave way a little to good common sense. She got out her hair curlers and lighted the gas stove. Then she went to work repairing the damage made by generosity added to love. Which is always a tremendous task, dear friends— a mammoth task.

Within forty minutes her head was covered with tiny, close-lying curls that made her look wonderfully like a playful schoolboy. She studied her reflection in the mirror long and carefully.

"If Jim doesn't kill me," she said to herself, "before he takes a second look at me, he'll say I look like a Coney Island chorus girl.[3] But what could I do? Oh, what could I do with a dollar and eighty-seven cents?"

At seven o'clock the coffee was made, and the frying pan was on the back of the stove, hot and ready to cook the chops.

Jim was never late. Della held the chain in her hand and sat on the corner of the table near the front door. Then she heard his step on the stair away down on the first flight, and she turned white for just a moment. She had a habit of saying little silent prayers about the simplest everyday things, and now she whispered: "Please, God, make him think I am still pretty."

The door opened, and Jim stepped in and closed it. He looked thin and very serious. Poor fellow—he was only twenty-two. He needed a new overcoat and he was without gloves.

Jim stopped inside the door. He froze suddenly, his eyes fixed upon Della.

---

trip (TRIP) run gracefully and lightly
hashed (HASHT) jumbled; all mixed up
metaphor (MET uh fur) figure of speech that makes a comparison
ransacking (RAN sak ing) searching furiously
[3]**Coney Island chorus girl:** A night-club dancer at Coney Island, once a busy amusement center on the edge of New York City.

ANGELO FRANÇOIS

There was an expression in them that she could not read, and it terrified her. It was not anger, nor disappointment, nor surprise, nor horror, nor any of the feelings she had been prepared for. He simply stood staring at her fixedly with that strange expression on his face.

Della wriggled off the table and went for him.

"Jim, darling!" she cried. "Don't look at me that way. I had my hair cut off and sold it, sure! But I did it because I couldn't live through Christmas without giving you a present. It'll grow out again. You won't mind, will you? I just had to do it. My hair grows awfully fast. Say "Merry Christmas," Jim, and let's be happy. You don't know what a nice—what a beautiful, nice gift I've got for you."

"You've cut off your hair?" he asked laboriously, with effort, as if he had not really noticed that fact yet, even after the hardest mental work.

"Cut it off and sold it," said Della. "Don't you like me just as well, anyhow? I'm *me* without my hair, aren't I?"

Jim looked about the room curiously.

"You say your hair is gone?" he said, speaking almost like an idiot.

"You needn't look for it," said Della. "It's sold, I tell you—sold and gone, too. It's Christmas Eve, Jim. Be good to me, because the hair went for you. Maybe the hairs of my head were numbered," she went on with a sudden serious sweetness, "but nobody could ever count my love for you. Shall I put the chops on, Jim?"

Out of his trance Jim seemed quickly to wake. He took Della in his arms. For ten seconds let us examine with discreet curiosity some unimportant object in the other direction. Eight dollars a week or a million a year—what is the difference? A mathematician would give you the wrong answer. The Magi brought valuable gifts, but this was not among them. That mysterious sentence will be illuminated later on.

Jim drew a package from his overcoat pocket and threw it on the table.

"Don't make any mistake, Dell," he said, "about me. I don't think there's anything in the way of a haircut or a shampoo that could make me like my girl any less. But if you'll unwrap that package, you may see why you had me going when I first walked in."

Nimble white fingers tore at the string and paper. And then an ecstatic scream of joy. And then—alas!—a rapid change to wild tears and heavy sobs.

For there lay The Combs—the set of combs, side and back, that Della had worshipped for long in a Broadway window. Beautiful combs, pure tortoiseshell with jeweled rims—just the shade to wear in the beautiful vanished hair. They were expensive combs, she knew. She had wanted them more than anything in the world, without the smallest hope of ever owning them. And now they were hers! But the waves of hair that should have held the combs were gone.

---

laboriously (luh BAWR ee us lee) with much labor and care
discreet (dih SKREET) wisely careful
illuminate (ih LOO muh nayt) make clear
nimble (NIM bul) quick and accurate; agile

Suddenly she hugged them to her throat, and before long she was able to look up with dim eyes and a smile. "My hair grows so fast, Jim," she said.

And then Della leaped up like a little singed cat and cried, "Oh, oh!"

Jim had not yet seen his beautiful present. She held it out to him eagerly upon her opened hand. The platinum seemed to flash with a reflection of her bright and ardent spirit.

"Isn't it something, Jim? I hunted all over town to find it. You'll have to look at the time a hundred times a day now. Give me your watch, I want to see how the chain looks on it."

Instead of obeying, Jim tumbled down on the couch and put his hands under the back of his head and smiled.

"Dell," said he, "let's put our Christmas presents away and keep them awhile. They're too nice to use just now. I sold the watch to get the money to buy your combs. And now, suppose you put the chops on."

The Magi, as you know, were wise men—wonderfully wise men—who brought gifts to the Babe in the manger. They invented the art of giving Christmas presents. Being wise, they no doubt gave wise gifts. And here I have lamely told you the sad little story of two foolish children who most unwisely sacrificed for each other the greatest treasures of their house. But in a last word to the wise of these days, let it be said that of all who gave gifts these two were the wisest. Of all who give and receive gifts, such as they are wisest. Everywhere they are wisest. They are the Magi.

---

ardent (AHR dunt) very eager; passionate

O. Henry (1862–1910)

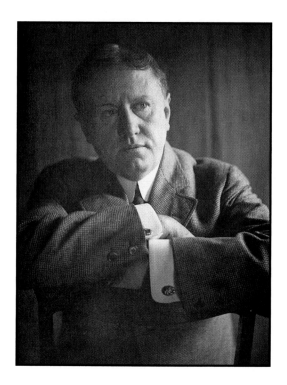

William Sydney Porter, or "O. Henry," was born in Greensboro, North Carolina. As a young man, he worked in Texas on a ranch, in a bank, and on a newspaper. Charged with stealing money from the bank, he fled to Central America. But news of his wife's illness brought him back, and he faced the bank robbery charges.

He practiced writing short stories while in prison. After his release, he moved to New York City and wrote a story a week for popular magazines. He made a lot of money but died before he was 50.

Today O. Henry is remembered as the master of the surprise ending. Among his best-known stories are "The Last Leaf," "The Furnished Room," and "The Gift of the Magi."

Review the Selection

UNDERSTAND THE SELECTION

Recall

1. How much money does Della have at the beginning of the story?

2. How much does she receive for selling her hair?

3. What gift does she buy for her husband?

Infer

4. Why does Jim use his middle name on his card?

5. How does Della feel while shopping for Jim's present?

6. Why does she buy the particular present that she does?

7. Why are these two "the wisest"?

Apply

8. How do you think Della feels about her poverty? Why do you think so?

9. What adjectives would you use to describe Della's feeling toward Jim?

10. Is your mental picture of one character clearer than the other? If so, explain why.

Respond to Literature

How do you think "The Gift of the Magi" reflects the material values of the early 1900s?

WRITE ABOUT THE SELECTION

An **analogy** compares two different things that share one element. This comparison can be between two concrete objects or between two abstract thoughts. Sometimes the easiest or clearest way to explain something unfamiliar is through an analogy with something that is familiar.

In this selection, although "the Magi" are part of the title, they are not mentioned until the end of the story. The plot does not involve them directly. The author uses them to draw an analogy. What is this analogy? How does it clarify the meaning of the story?

Prewriting To help understand the analogy, try "brainstorming." Use two lists. Under the heading *magi*, write ideas about the meaning of the Magi's gifts in the New Testament story of the Christ child. In a second list, under the heading *Della and Jim*, write ideas about the meaning of their gifts to each other.

Writing Compare the ideas in the two lists. Identify similarities between them. Then write a paragraph explaining the analogy upon which the title of the story is based.

Revising Rewrite the paragraph to include at least one example of the four types of sentences: declarative, interrogative, imperative, and exclamatory.

Proofreading Check the punctuation mark at the end of each sentence.

THINK ABOUT CHARACTER

Authors sometimes discuss the characteristics and traits of a character directly. In addition, they often give indirect clues from which the reader can surmise or guess other traits of the individual. Readers can watch for things the characters say, descriptions of what they think, and their actions.

1. How does O. Henry define Jim and Della's characters?

2. What indirect clues about their personalities can you find in the story?

3. Do you think that one character appreciates his or her Christmas present more than the other? Why?

4. What is your mental picture of Madame Sofronie?

5. What would you say the future holds for Della and Jim's marriage?

READING FOCUS

Understand Imagery As you read "The Gift of the Magi," you looked for imagery in the story. What are some images that helped the story come alive for you? To which of your five senses did these images appeal?

DEVELOP YOUR VOCABULARY

An **idiom** is an expression that has a meaning that is often different from the literal meaning of the words that form it. *With a high hand*, for example, has nothing to do with the location of a hand; it means "in a dictatorial manner."

Idioms are listed in your dictionary after the definitions of the entry word that is the main word in the phrase. Look up the italicized idioms in these quotations from "The Gift of the Magi." Then write an original sentence, using the idiom as it is used here.

1. ". . . life is *made up* of three stages, sobs, sniffles, and smiles."

2. "While the woman . . . is gradually *coming down* from the first stage to the second . . ."

3. "Della would have let her hair hang out the window . . . just *to make fun of* her Majesty's jewels and gifts."

4. "And then she *did* it *up* again . . ."

5. ". . . *before long* she was able to look up with . . . a smile."

Focus ON FICTION

*F*iction is any literary work that portrays imaginary characters and events. The basis of all fiction is the imagination of the author. Fiction is meant primarily to be entertaining. It may also be used for such purposes as teaching, influencing, or inspiring.

A work of fiction can take many forms. Chief among these are novels, short stories, plays, and poems. Several literary elements are associated with these various forms of fiction: setting, character, plot, theme, tone, imagery, and symbolism.

Setting   The setting of a story is the time and place in which it happens. The time may be the hour of the day, the season, the year, or a period in history. The place may include the general geographical location and environment as well as weather, scenery, terrain, sounds, and smells. It can also include specific places and objects such as buildings, furniture, clothing, windows, and animals. The clearer and more well-defined the setting, the more real and believable the story becomes.

Character   A character is a person in a story. There is often a great deal to find out about characters, particularly main characters. For example, values and frame of mind are two features to look for. Characters can be **flat**, one-dimensional stereotypes. These are usually secondary figures. Main characters should be **round**—individuals with personalities you get to know.

Plot   The plot consists of the events that happen in a story. It serves as a framework that establishes a relationship between episodes. Plot brings order by showing a few selected characters and incidents and uniting them into a whole. It organizes a story into a beginning, a middle, and an ending.

Sometimes, an author will give clues about what is going to happen in the plot. This is known as **foreshadowing**. Incidents build, through **rising action**, to a **climax**, or turning point. This may happen at the end of the story, or the climax may be followed by **falling action** and the **resolution** of the conflict.

The plot always centers on a **conflict**. This meeting of opposing forces may be internal (within the character) or external (between characters or between a character and some other force, such as nature). In the case of conflict between two characters, the main character is the **protagonist**; the other is the **antagonist**.

Theme   The theme is the meaning or message of a story. It is some central idea about life that the author is attempting to communicate. The theme may be stated clearly at any point in the story, or the author might leave it for the reader to determine.

Tone   Tone is the author's attitude toward either the subject matter or the reader. It may take many forms—serious or humorous, formal or informal, or direct or symbolic.

Imagery and Figurative Language   Imagery refers to the collection of images in a work of literature. Images are sensory in nature, meaning that they are designed to appeal to one of the five senses. Figures of speech, or figurative language, include simile and metaphor. **Similes** state a direct comparison between two unlike objects. They are often introduced with *like* or *as*. For example, *The house was like an empty cavern*. **Metaphors** suggest a comparison, giving one object the qualities of another. For example, *The house was an empty cavern*.

Symbolism   Symbolism is the use of one thing to represent another. Usually, the symbol is concrete and stands for some abstract idea, feeling, or quality.

The following is an annotated version of "The Revolt of Mother." **Annotated** means that notes have been added at various points in the story. The purpose of these annotations is to help you see and understand the function and interrelationships of literary elements in a work of fiction.

As you read, ask yourself:

1. How closely connected are the elements of character and plot? Is the concept of conflict involved with both of these?
2. What is the theme? What clues are given about the theme?

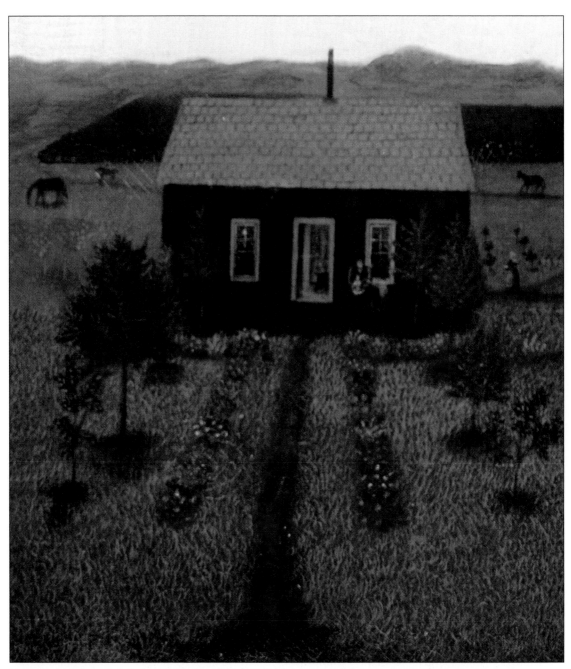

Homestead of Ellsworth Ball, detail, Sallie Cover. Private Collection

THE REVOLT OF MOTHER

ADAPTED

by Mary E. Wilkins Freeman

"**F**ather!"

"What is it?"

"What are them men diggin' over in the field for?"

There was a sudden dropping and enlarging of the lower part of the old man's face, as if some heavy weight had settled therein; he shut his mouth tight, and went on harnessing the great bay mare. He hustled the collar on to her neck with a jerk.

"Father!"

The old man slapped the saddle on the mare's back.

"Look here, Father, I want to know what them men are diggin' over in the field for, an' I'm goin' to know."

"I wish you'd go into the house, Mother, an' tend to your own affairs," the old man said then. He ran his words together, and his speech was almost as inarticulate as a growl.

But the woman understood; it was her most native tongue. "I ain't goin' into the house till you tell me what them men are doin' over there in the field," said she.

Then she stood waiting. She was a small woman, short and straight-waisted like a child in her brown cotton gown. Her forehead was mild and benevolent between the smooth curves of gray hair; there were meek downward lines about her nose and mouth; but her eyes, fixed upon the old man, looked as if the meekness had been the result of her own will, never of the will of another.

They were in the barn, standing before the wide-open doors. The spring air, full of the smell of growing grass and unseen blossoms,

FOCUS ON FICTION
STUDY HINTS

This is the first glimpse of the antagonist.

This is the first glimpse of the protagonist. It also foreshadows the conflict to come.

You are given a physical description of one character.

A good description of part of the setting is provided here.

came in their faces. The deep yard in front was littered with farm wagons and piles of wood; on the edges, close to the fence and the house, the grass was a vivid green, and there were some dandelions.

How is imagery used to describe the way Mother is standing?

The old man glanced doggedly at his wife as he tightened the last buckles on the harness. She looked as immovable to him as one of the rocks in his pasture land, bound to the earth with generations of blackberry vines. He slapped the reins over the horse, and started forth from the barn.

"*Father!*" said she.

The old man pulled up. "What is it?"

"I want to know what them men are diggin' over there in that field for."

"They're diggin' a cellar, I s'pose, if you've got to know."

"A cellar for what?"

"A barn."

"A barn? You ain't goin' to build a barn over there where we was goin' to have a house, Father?"

The old man said not another word. He hurried the horse into the farm wagon and clattered out of the yard, jouncing as sturdily on his seat as a boy.

The woman stood a moment looking after him, then she went out of the barn across a corner of the yard to the house. The house, standing at right angles with the great barn and a long reach of sheds and outbuildings, was infinitesimal compared with them. It was scarcely as commodious for people as the little boxes under the barn eaves were for doves.

Imagery is used to describe the girl's face.

A pretty girl's face, pink and delicate as a flower, was looking out of one of the house windows. She was watching three men who were digging over in the field which bounded the yard near the road line. She turned quietly when the woman entered.

"What are they diggin' for, Mother?" said she. "Did he tell you?"

"They're diggin' for—a cellar for a new barn."

"Oh, Mother, he ain't going to build another barn?"

---

doggedly (DAWG id lee) persistently; stubbornly
infinitesimal (in fin ih TES uh mul) too small to be measured
commodious (kuh MOH dee us) spacious; roomy

"That's what he says."

A boy stood before the kitchen glass combing his hair. He combed slowly and painstakingly, arranging his brown hair in a smooth hillock over his forehead. He did not seem to pay any attention to the conversation.

"Sammy, did you know Father was going to build a new barn?" asked the girl.

The boy combed assiduously.

"Sammy!"

He turned, and showed a face like his father's under his smooth crest of hair. "Yes, I s'pose I did," he said, reluctantly.

"How long have you known it?" asked his mother.

"Bout three months, I guess."

"Why didn't you tell of it?"

"Didn't think 'twould do no good."

"I don't see what Father wants another barn for," said the girl, in her sweet, slow voice. She turned again to the window and stared out at the digging men in the field. Her tender, sweet face was full of a gentle distress. Her forehead was as bald and innocent as a baby's, with the light hair strained from it in a row of curl papers. She was quite large, but her soft curves did not look as if they covered muscles.

Her mother looked sternly at the boy. "Is he goin' to buy more cows?" said she.

> How does the plot begin to develop?

The boy did not reply; he was tying his shoes.

"Sammy, I want you to tell me if he's goin' to buy more cows."

"I s'pose he is."

"How many?"

"Four, I guess."

His mother said nothing more. She went into the pantry, and there was a clatter of dishes. The boy got his cap from a nail behind the door, took an old arithmetic book from the shelf, and started for school. He was lightly built, but clumsy. He went out of the yard with a curious spring in his hips that made his loose home-made jacket tilt up in the rear.

The girl went to the sink and began to wash the dishes that were piled up there. Her mother came promptly out of the pantry

---

hillock (HIL uk) a small hill; mound

and shoved her aside. "You wipe 'em," said she. "I'll wash. There's a good many this mornin'."

The mother plunged her hands vigorously into the water; the girl wiped the plates slowly and dreamily. "Mother," said she, "don't you think it's too bad Father's going to build that new barn, much as we need a decent house to live in?"

This shows the author's attitude toward the two main characters.

Her mother scrubbed a dish fiercely. "You ain't found out yet, we're womenfolks, Nanny Penn," said she. "You ain't seen enough of menfolks yet to. One of these days you'll find it out, and then you'll know that we know only what menfolks think we do, so far as any use of it goes, an' how we'd ought to reckon menfolks in with Providence, an' not complain of what they do any more than we do of the weather."

"I don't care; I don't believe George is anything like that, anyhow," said Nanny. Her delicate face flushed pink; her lips pouted softly, as if she were going to cry.

"You wait an' see. I guess George Eastman ain't no better than other men. You hadn't ought to judge Father, though. He can't help it, 'cause he don't look at things jest the way we do. An' we've been pretty comfortable here, after all. The roof don't leak —ain't never but once—that's one thing. Father's kept it shingled right up."

"I do wish we had a parlor."

"I guess it won't hurt George Eastman any to come to see you in a nice clean kitchen. I guess a good many girls don't have as good a place as this. Nobody's ever heard me complain."

"I ain't complained either, Mother."

"Well, I don't think you'd better, a good father an' a good home as you've got. S'pose your father made you go out an' work for your livin'? Lots of girls have to that ain't no better able to than you be."

Can you find any theme clues here?

Sarah Penn washed the frying pan with a conclusive air. She scrubbed the outside of it as faithfully as the inside. She was a masterly keeper of her box of a house. Her one living room never seemed to have in it any of the dust which the friction of life with inanimate matter produces. She swept, and there seemed to be no dirt to go before the broom; she cleaned, and one could see no difference. She was like an artist so perfect that he has

---

inanimate (in AN uh mit) not living or moving

apparently no art. Today she got out a mixing bowl and a board, and rolled some pies, and there was no more flour upon her than upon her daughter who was doing finer work. Nanny was to be married in the fall, and she was sewing on some white cambric and embroidery. She sewed industriously while her mother cooked; her soft milk-white hands and wrists showed whiter than her delicate work

"We must have the stove moved out in the shed before long," said Mrs. Penn. "Talk about not havin' things, it's been a real blessin' to be able to put a stove up in that shed in hot weather. Father did one good thing when he fixed that stove pipe out there."

The literary elements of setting and character are interwoven here.

Sarah Penn's face as she rolled her pies had that expression of meek vigor which might have characterized one of the New Testament saints. She was making mince pies. Her husband, Adoniram Penn, liked them better than any other kind. She baked twice a week. Adoniram often liked a piece of pie between meals. She hurried this morning. It had been later than usual when she began, and she wanted to have a pie baked for dinner. However deep a resentment she might be forced to hold against her husband, she would never fail in sedulous attention to his wants.

Nobility of character manifests itself at loopholes when it is not provided with large doors, Sarah Penn's showed itself today in flaky dishes of pastry. She made the pies faithfully, while across the table she could see, when she glanced up from her work, the sight that rankled in her patient and steadfast soul—the digging of the cellar of the new barn in the place where Adoniram forty years ago had promised her their new house should stand.

What is the author's attitude toward Sarah?

The pies were done for dinner. Adoniram and Sammy were home a few minutes after twelve o'clock. The dinner was eaten with serious haste. There was never much conversation at the table in the Penn family. Adoniram asked a blessing, and they ate promptly, then rose up and went about their work.

Sammy went back to school, taking soft sly lopes out of the yard like a rabbit. He wanted a game of marbles before school, and feared his father would give him chores to do. Adoniram hastened to the door and called after him, but he was out of sight.

---

cambric (KAM brik) very fine, thin linen or cotton
sedulous (SEJ uh lus) hard-working; diligent; persistent

"I don't see what you let him go for, Mother," said he. "I wanted him to help me unload that wood."

Adoniram went to work out in the yard unloading wood from the wagon. Sarah put away the dinner dishes, while Nanny took down her curl papers and changed her dress. She was going down to the store to buy some more embroidery and thread.

When Nanny was gone, Mrs. Penn went to the door. "Father!" she called.

"Well, what is it!"

"I want to see you jest a minute, Father."

"I can't leave this wood nohow. I've got to git it unloaded and go for a load of gravel afore two o'clock. Sammy had ought to helped me. You hadn't ought to let him go to school so early."

"I want to see you jest a minute."

"I tell ye I can't, nohow, Mother."

Imagery is used to describe Sarah's movements.

"Father, you come here." Sarah Penn stood in the door like a queen; she held her head as if it bore a crown; there was the patience which makes authority in her voice. Adoniram went.

Mrs. Penn led the way into the kitchen, and pointed to a chair. "Sit down, Father," said she; "I've got somethin' I want to say to you."

He sat down heavily; his face was quite stolid, but he looked at her with restive eyes. "Well, what is it, Mother?"

"I want to know what you're buildin' that new barn for, Father?"

"I ain't got nothin' to say about it."

"It can't be you think you need another barn?"

"I tell ye I ain't got nothin' to say about it, Mother; an' I ain't goin' to say nothin'."

"Be you goin' to buy more cows?"

Adoniram did not reply; he shut his mouth tight.

"I know you be, as well as I want to. Now, Father, look here"— Sarah Penn had not sat down; she stood before her husband in the humble fashion of a Scripture woman—"I'm goin' to talk real plain to you; I never have sence I married you, but I'm goin' to now. I ain't never complained, an' I ain't goin' to complain now, but I'm goin' to talk plain. You see this room here, Father; you look at it well. You see there ain't no carpet on the floor, an' you see the paper is all dirty and droppin' off the walls. We ain't had no new paper on it for ten year, an' then I put it on myself, an' it didn't cost but nine cents a roll. You see this room, Father; it's all the one I've had to work in an' eat in an' sit in sence we was married. There ain't another woman in the whole town whose husband ain't got half the means you have but what's got better. It's all the room Nanny's got to have her company in; an' there ain't one of her mates but what's got better, an' their fathers not so able as hers is. It's all the room she'll have to be married in. What would you have thought, Father, if we had had our weddin' in a room no better than this? I was married in my mother's parlor, with a carpet on the floor, an' stuffed furniture, an' a mahogany card table. An' this is all the room my daughter will have to be married in. Look here, Father!"

Sarah Penn went across the room as though it were a tragic stage. She flung open a door and disclosed a tiny bedroom only large enough for a bed and bureau, with a path between. "There, Father," said she, "there's all the room I've had to sleep in

---

stolid (STOL id) expressing little emotion

in forty year. All my children were born there—the two that died an' the two that's livin'. I was sick with a fever, there."

She stepped to another door and opened it. It led into the small, ill-lighted pantry. "Here," said she, "is all the buttery I've got—every place I've got for my dishes, to set up my victuals in, an' to keep my milk pans in. Father, I've been takin' care of the milk of six cows in this place, an' now you're goin' to build a new barn, an' keep more cows, an' give me more to do in it."

She threw open another door. A narrow, crooked flight of stairs wound upward from it. "There, Father," said she, "I want you to look at the stairs that go up to them two unfinished chambers that are all the places our son and daughter have had to sleep in all their lives. There ain't a prettier girl in town nor a more ladylike one than Nanny, an' that's the place she has to sleep in. It ain't so good as your horse's stall; it ain't so warm an' tight."

Sarah Penn went back and stood before her husband. "Now, Father," said she, "I want to know if you think you're doin' right and accordin' to what you profess. Here, where we was married forty year ago, you promised me faithful that we should have a new house built in that lot over in the field before the year was out. You said you had money enough, an' you wouldn't ask me to live in no such place as this. It is forty year now, an' you've been makin' more money an' I've been savin' of it for you ever sence, an' you ain't built no house yet. You've built sheds an' cow houses an' one new barn, an' now you're goin' to build another. Father, I want to know if you think it's right. You're lodgin' your dumb beasts better than you are your own flesh and blood. I want to know if you think it's right."

"I ain't got nothin' to say."

"You can't say nothin' without ownin' it ain't right, Father. An' there's another thing—I ain't complained; I've got along forty year an' I s'pose I should forty more, if it wa'n't for that—if we don't have another house. Nanny she can't live with us after she's married. She'll have to go somewhere else to live away from us, an' it don't seem as if I could have it so, noways, Father. She wa'n't ever strong. She's got considerable color, but there wa'n't never any backbone to her. I've always took the heft of everything off her,

---

pantry (PAN tree) a small room or closet off the kitchen, where cooking ingredients and utensils, china, etc., are kept an' she ain't fit to keep house an' do everything herself. Think of her doin' all the washin' and ironin' and bakin' with them soft white hands and arms, an' sweepin'. I can't have it so, noways, Father."

Mrs. Penn's face was burning; her mild eyes gleamed. She had pleaded her little cause like a Webster; she had ranged from severity to pathos; but her opponent employed that obstinate silence which makes eloquence futile with mocking echoes. Adoniram arose clumsily.

"Father, ain't you got nothin' to say?" said Mrs. Penn.

"I've got to go off after that load of gravel. I can't stan' talkin' all day."

"Father, won't you think it over an' have a house built there instead of a barn?"

"I ain't got nothin' to say."

Adoniram shuffled out. Mrs. Penn went into her bedroom. When she came out, her eyes were red. She had a roll of un-bleached cotton cloth. She spread it out on the kitchen table, and began cutting out some shirts for her husband. The men over in the field had a team to help them this afternoon; she could hear their halloos. She had a scanty pattern for the shirts; she had to plan and piece the sleeves.

Nanny came home with her embroidery and sat down with her needlework. She had taken down her curl papers, and there was a soft roll of fair hair like an aureole over her forehead; her face was as delicately fine and clear as porcelain. Suddenly she looked up and the tender red flamed over her face and neck. "Mother," said she.

> How is imagery used to describe Nanny's face?

"What say?"

"I've been thinking—I don't see how we're goin' to have any wedding in this room. I'd be ashamed to have his folks come if we didn't have anybody else."

"Mebbe we can have some new paper before then; I can put it on. I guess you won't have no call to be ashamed of your belongin's."

---

pathos (PAY thos) an element in experience evoking pity
obstinate (OB stuh nut) stubborn
halloos (huh LOOZ) shouts; yells; calls
aureole (AWR ee ohl) a halo
porcelain (PAWR suh lin) china

Here is another example of foreshadowing. You are given a plot clue about what will happen later. Do you have any ideas?

"We might have the wedding in the new barn," said Nanny, with gentle pettishness. "Why, Mother, what makes you look so?"

Mrs. Penn had started and was staring at her with a curious expression. She turned again to her work, and spread out a pattern carefully on the cloth. "Nothin'," said she.

Presently Adoniram clattered out of the yard in his two-wheeled dump cart, standing as proudly upright as a Roman charioteer. Mrs. Penn opened the door and stood there a minute looking out; the halloos of the men sounded louder.

It seemed to her all through the spring months that she heard nothing but the halloos and the noises of saws and hammers. The new barn grew fast. It was a fine edifice for this little village. Men came on pleasant Sundays, in their meeting suits and clean shirt bosoms, and stood around it admiringly. Mrs. Penn did not speak of it and Adoniram did not mention it to her, although sometimes upon a return from inspecting it, he bore himself with injured dignity.

Does this give you a clue to the theme?

"It's a strange thing how your mother feels about the new barn," he said, confidentially, to Sammy one day.

Sammy only grunted after an odd fashion for a boy; he had learned it from his father.

The plot is about to take an unexpected twist.

The barn was all completed ready for use by the third week in July. Adoniram had planned to move his stock in on Wednesday; on Tuesday he received a letter which changed his plans. He came in with it early in the morning. "Sammy's been to the post office," said he, "an' I've got a letter from Hiram." Hiram was Mrs. Penn's brother who lived in Vermont.

"Well," said Mrs. Penn, "what does he say about the folks?"

The new plot event is revealed. What plot question does this raise?

"I guess they're all right. He says he thinks if I come up country right off there's a chance to buy jest the kind of a horse I want." He stared reflectively out of the window at the new barn.

Mrs. Penn was making pies. She went on clapping the rolling pin into the crust, although she was very pale, and her heart beat loudly.

"I dun' know but what I'd better go," said Adoniram. "I hate to go off jest now, right in the midst of hayin', but the ten-acre lot's cut,

---

edifice (ED uh fis) a large structure

an' I guess Rufus an' the others can git along without me three or four days. I can't get a horse round here to suit me, nohow, an' I've got to have another for all that wood haulin' in the fall. I told Hiram to watch out an' if he got wind of a good horse to let me know. I guess I'd better go."

"I'll get out your clean shirt an' collar," said Mrs. Penn calmly.

She laid out Adoniram's Sunday suit and his clean clothes on the bed in the little bedroom. She got his shaving water and razor ready. At last she buttoned on his collar and fastened his black cravat.

Adoniram never wore his collar and cravat except on extra occasions. He held his head high, with a rasped dignity. When he was all ready, with coat and hat brushed, and a lunch of pie and cheese in a paper bag, he hesitated on the threshold of the door. He looked at his wife and his manner was defiantly apologetic. "*If* them cows come today Sammy can drive them into the new barn," said he, "an' when they bring the hay up they can pitch it in there."

"Well," replied Mrs. Penn.

Adoniram set his shaven face ahead and started. When he had cleared the doorstep, he turned and looked back with a kind of nervous solemnity. "I shall be back by Saturday if nothin' happens," said he.

"Do be careful, Father," returned his wife.

She stood in the door with Nanny at her elbow and watched him out of sight. Her eyes had a strange, doubtful expression in them; her peaceful forehead was contracted. Nanny sat sewing. Her wedding day was drawing nearer and she was getting pale and thin with her steady sewing. Her mother kept glancing at her.

"Have you got that pain in your side this mornin'?" she asked.

"A little."

Mrs. Penn's face as she worked, changed; her perplexed forehead smoothed; her eyes were steady, her lips firmly set. She formed a maxim for herself, although incoherently with her

A new plot question: What does Sarah have in mind?

---

cravat (kruh VAT) a necktie; scarf
maxim (MAK sim) a statement of a general truth
incoherently (in koh HIR unt lee) not logically; disjointedly

unlettered thoughts. "Unsolicited opportunities are the guideposts of the Lord to the new roads of Life," she repeated in effect, and she made up her mind to her course of action.

"S'posin' I *had* wrote to Hiram," she muttered once, when she was in the pantry. "S'posin' I had wrote and asked him if he knew of any horse? But I didn't, an' Father's goin' wa'n't any of my doin'. It looks like a providence." Her mother's voice rang out quite loud at the last.

"What you talkin' about, Mother?" called Nanny.

"Nothin'."

Mrs. Penn hurried her baking; at eleven o'clock it was all done. The load of hay from the west field came slowly down the cart track and drew up at the new barn. Mrs. Penn ran out. "Stop!" she screamed, "stop!"

The men stopped and looked; Sammy upreared from the top of the load and stared at his mother.

"Stop!" she cried out again. "Don't you put the hay in that barn; put it in the old one."

This is a brief description of a stereotyped, secondary character. Would this character be considered round or flat?

"Why, he said to put it in here," returned one of the hay-makers wonderingly. He was a young man, a neighbor's son, whom Adoniram hired by the year to work on the farm.

"Don't you put the hay in the new barn; there's room enough in the old one, ain't there?" said Mrs. Penn.

"Room enough," returned the hired man, in his thick, rustic tones. "Didn't need the new barn, nohow, as far as room's concerned. Well, I s'pose he changed his mind." He took hold of the horses' bridles.

Mrs. Penn went back to the house. Soon the kitchen windows were darkened and a fragrance like warm honey came into the room.

Nanny laid down her work. "I thought Father wanted them to put the hay into the new barn?" she said, wonderingly.

"It's all right," replied her mother.

Sammy slid down from the load of hay and came in to see if dinner was ready.

"I ain't goin' to get a regular dinner today, as long as Father's

---

rustic (RUS tik) of or living in the country, rural; simple, plain; rough, awkward

Homestead of Ellsworth Ball, detail, Sallie Cover. Private Collection

gone," said his mother. "I've let the fire go out. You can have some bread an' milk an' pie. I thought we could get along." She set out some bowls of milk, some bread and a pie on the kitchen table. "You'd better eat your dinner now," said she. "You might jest as well get through with it. I want you to help me afterward."

Nanny and Sammy stared at each other. There was something strange in their mother's manner. Mrs. Penn did not eat anything herself. She went into the pantry and they heard her moving dishes while they ate. Presently she came out with a pile of plates. She got the clothes basket out of the shed and packed them in it. Nanny and Sammy watched. She brought out cups and saucers and put them in with the plates.

"What you goin' to do, Mother," inquired Nanny, in a timid voice. A sense of something unusual made her tremble, as if it were a ghost. Sammy rolled his eyes over his pie.

"You'll see what I'm goin' to do," replied Mrs. Penn. "If you're through, Nanny, I want you to go upstairs and pack your things; an' I want you, Sammy, to help me take down the bed in the bedroom."

"Oh, Mother, what for?" gasped Nanny.

"You'll see."

Some imagery that may be unfamiliar is explained.

During the next few hours a feat was performed by this simple pious New England mother which was equal in its way to Wolfe's storming of the Heights of Abraham. It took no more genius and audacity of bravery for Wolfe to cheer his wondering soldiers up those steep precipices, under the sleeping eyes of the enemy, than for Sarah Penn, at the head of her children, to move all their little household goods into the new barn while her husband was away.

Nanny and Sammy followed their mother's instructions without a murmur; indeed, they were overawed. There is a certain uncanny and super-human quality about all such purely original undertakings as their mother's was to them. Nanny went back and forth with her light loads and Sammy tugged with sober energy.

Do you think this is the climax of the plot?

At five o'clock in the afternoon the little house in which the Penns had lived for forty years had emptied itself into the new barn.

Every builder builds somewhat for unknown purposes, and is in a measure a prophet. The architect of Adoniram Penn's barn, while he designed it for the comfort of four-footed animals, had planned better than he knew for the comfort of humans. Sarah Penn saw at a glance its possibilities. Those great box stalls, with quilts hung before them, would make better bedrooms than the one she had occupied for forty years, and there was a tight carriage room. The harness room, with its chimney and shelves, would make a kitchen of her dreams. The great middle space would make a parlor, by-and-by, fit for a palace. Upstairs there was as much room as down, With partitions and windows, what a house there would be! Sarah looked at the row of stanchions before the allotted space for cows, and reflected she would have a front entry there.

---

precipices (PRES uh pis iz) steep cliffs; vertical or hanging rock faces
stanchions (STAN chunz) upright bars, beams or posts used as support

At six o'clock the stove was up in the harness room, the kettle was boiling, and the table set for tea. It looked almost as homelike as the abandoned house across the yard had ever done. The young hired man milked, and Sarah directed him calmly to bring the milk to the new barn. He came gasping, dropping little blots of foam from the brimming pails on the grass. Before the next morning he had spread the story of Adoniram Penn's wife moving into the new barn all over the little village. Men assembled in the store and talked it over; women with shawls over their heads scuttled into each other's houses before their work was done. Any deviation from the ordinary course of life in this quiet town was enough to stop all progress in it. Everybody paused to look at the staid, independent figure on the side track. There was a difference of opinion with regard to her. Some held her to be insane; some, of a lawless and rebellious spirit.

Friday the minister went to see her. It was in the forenoon, and she was at the barn door shelling peas for dinner. She looked up and returned his salutation with dignity; then she went on with her work. She did not invite him in. The saintly expression of her face remained fixed, but there was an angry flush over it.

The minister stood awkwardly before her, and talked. She handled the peas as if they were bullets. At last she looked up and her eyes showed a spirit that her meek front had covered for a lifetime.

"There ain't no use talkin', Mr. Hersey," said she. "I've thought it all over and over, an' I believe I'm doin' what's right. I've made it the subject of prayer, and it's betwixt me an' the Lord an' Adoniram. There ain't no call for nobody else to worry about it."

> Could this be another theme clue?

"Well, of course, if you have brought it to the Lord in prayer, and feel satisfied that you are doing right, Mrs. Penn," said the minister helplessly. His thin, gray-bearded face was pathetic. He was a sickly man; his youthful confidence had cooled; he had to scourge himself up to some of his pastoral duties, and then he was prostrated by the smart.

"I think it's right jest as much as I think it was right for our forefathers to come over from the old country 'cause they didn't have what belonged to 'em," said Mrs. Penn. She arose.

---

scourge (SKURJ) to whip; to chastise, punish
prostrated (PROS trayt id) laid low; completely overcome

Symbolism is used here. Plymouth Rock symbolizes the start of a new life in a new environment for the Penn family, just as it did for the Pilgrims.

The barn threshold might have been Plymouth Rock from her bearing. "I don't doubt you mean well, Mr. Hersey," said she, "but there are things people hadn't ought to interfere with. I've been a member of the church for over forty year. I've got my own mind an' my own feet, an' I'm goin' to think my own thoughts an' go my own ways, an' nobody but the Lord is goin' to dictate to me unless I've a mind to have him. Won't you come in an' set down? How is Mis' Hersey?"

"She is well, I thank you," replied the minister. He added some more perplexed, apologetic remarks; then he retreated.

He could expound the intricacies of every character study in the Scriptures; he was competent to grasp the Pilgrim Fathers and all historical innovators; but Sarah Penn was beyond him. He could deal with primal cases, but parallel ones worsted him. But, after all, although it was aside from his province, he wondered more how Adoniram Penn would deal with his wife than how the Lord would. Everybody shared the wonder. When Adoniram's four new cows arrived, Sarah ordered three put in the old barn, the other in the house where the cooking stove had stood. That added to the excitement. It was whispered that all four cows were domiciled in the house.

Toward sunset on Saturday, when Adoniram was expected home, there was a knot of men in the road near the new barn. The hired man had milked, but he still hung around the premises. There were brown bread and baked beans and a custard pie; it was the supper that Adoniram loved on a Saturday night. She had on a clean calico and she bore herself imperturbably. Nanny and Sammy kept close at her heels. Their eyes were large, and Nanny was full of nervous tremors. Still there was to them more pleasant excitement than anything else. An inborn confidence in their mother over their father asserted itself.

Is this rising action leading to the climax, or is it falling action headed toward resolution?

Sammy looked out of the harness-room window. "There he is," he announced, in an awed whisper. He and Nanny peeped around the casing. Mrs. Penn kept on about her work. The children

---

intricacies (IN trih kuh seez) complexities; complications
innovators (IN uh vayt urz) makers of changes; introducers of new methods
imperturbably (im pur TUR buh blee) in a manner that cannot be excited; impassively

watched Adoniram leave the new horse standing in the drive while he went to the house-door. It was fastened. Then he went around to the shed. That door was seldom locked, even when the family was away. The thought of how her father would be confronted by the cow flashed upon Nanny. There was a hysterical sob in her throat. Adoniram emerged from the shed and stood looking about in a dazed fashion. His lips moved; he was saying something, but they could not hear what it was. The hired man was peeping around a corner of the old barn but nobody saw him.

Adoniram took the new horse by the bridle and led him across the yard to the new barn. Nanny and Sammy slunk close to their mother. The barn doors rolled back and there stood Adoniram, with the long mild face of the great Canadian farm horse looking over his shoulder.

Nanny kept behind her mother, but Sammy stepped suddenly forward and stood in front of her.

Adoniram stared at the group, "What on airth you all down here for?" said he. "What's the matter over to the house?"

"We've come here to live, Father," said Sammy. His shrill voice quavered out bravely.

"What—" Adoniram sniffed—"what is it smells like cookin'?" said he. He stepped forward and looked in the open door of the harness room. Then he turned to his wife. His old bristling face was pale and frightened, "What on airth does this mean, Mother?"

Do you think this is a plot clue, a theme clue, or both?

"You come in here, Father," said Sarah. She led the way into the harness room and shut the door. "Now, Father," said she, "you needn't be scared. I ain't crazy. There ain't nothin' to be upset over. But we've come here to live an' we're goin' to live here. We've got jest as good a right here as new horses and cows. The house wa'n't fit for us to live in any longer, an' I made up my mind I wa'n't goin' to stay there. I've done my duty by you forty year an' I'm goin' to do it now, but I'm goin' to live here. You've got to put in some windows an' partitions, an' you'll have to buy some furniture."

"Why, Mother!" the old man gasped.

"You'd better take your coat off an' get washed—there's the wash basin—an' then we'll have supper."

"Why, Mother!"

From Arkansas, 1943, Georges Schreiber

Sammy went past the window, leading the new horse to the old barn. The old man saw him and shook his head speechlessly. He tried to take off his coat, but his arms seemed to lack the power. His wife helped him. She poured some water into the tin basin and put in a piece of soap. She got the comb and brush and smoothed his thin grey hair after he had washed. Then she put the beans, hot bread and tea on the table. Sammy came in and the family drew up. Adoniram sat looking dazedly at his plate and they waited.

"Ain't you goin' to ask a blessin', Father?" said Sarah.

And the old man bent his head and mumbled.

All through the meal he stopped eating at intervals and stared furtively at his wife, but he ate well. The home food tasted good to him and his old frame was too sturdily healthy to be affected by his mind. But after supper he went out and sat down on the step of the smaller door at the right of the barn, through which he had meant his Jerseys to pass in stately file, but which Sarah designed for her front house-door, and he leaned his head on his hands.

After the supper dishes were cleared away and the milk pans washed, Sarah went out to him. The twilight was deepening. There was a clear green glow in the sky. Before them stretched the smooth level of field; in the distance was a cluster of haystacks like the huts of a village; the air was very calm and sweet. The landscape might have been an ideal one of peace.

Sarah bent over and touched her husband on one of his thin, sinewy shoulders. "Father!"

The old man's shoulders heaved; he was weeping.

"Why, don't do so, Father," said Sarah.

"I'll—put up the—partitions, an'—everything you—want, Mother."

Sarah put her apron up to her face; she was overcome by her own triumph.

Adoniram was like a fortress whose walls had no active resistance, and went down the instant the right besieging tools were used. "Why, Mother," he said hoarsely, "I hadn't no idee you was so set on't it as all this comes to."

The last plot question is answered. The conflict has been resolved. Do you think this is the climax, the resolution, or both?

Finally, the theme is made clear. Imagery is added to enhance the meaning.

---

besieging (bih SEEJ ing) hemming in with armed forces; closing in; overwhelming

Review the Selection

UNDERSTAND THE SELECTION

Recall

1. In which season is the story set?

2. Why were the men digging?

3. How long had Sarah and Adoniram been married?

Infer

4. Why do you think Adoniram has never built a new house?

5. Discuss Sarah's attitude toward men.

6. Why do you think Sarah finally decides to act?

7. Why does Sarah not invite the minister in at first, and why does she later ask him in to sit down?

Apply

8. Give three examples to show why the old house was inadequate.

9. Select two setting descriptions that illustrate the type of housekeeper Sarah was.

10. What would have and have not happened if Adoniram did not receive the letter from Hiram when he did?

Respond to Literature

Do you think the lifestyle of the Penn family was unusual for that period in American history? Explain.

WRITE ABOUT THE SELECTION

An **epilogue** is writing added to the end of other writing. The dictionary defines *epilogue* as "a closing section added to a novel, play, etc., providing further comment, interpretation, or information."

At the end of "The Revolt of Mother," the new barn had become a new house. Suppose that you dropped by to visit the Penn family one year after the story ended. Write an epilogue to the story based on your observations.

Prewriting Think about the changes in character and setting you would observe. Write down ideas about what might have happened to the members of the Penn family and to their farm in the year since. Include ideas about Adoniram's feelings and state of mind, both at the end of the story and one year later.

Writing Bring these ideas together and write an epilogue to the story. Describe the changes, in terms of character and setting, that have taken place during the year since the story ended. Be sure to include sufficient details.

Revising Make the reader's mental picture clearer and more vivid by adding visual imagery to your description.

Proofreading Where a noun is described by more than one adjective, make sure the adjectives are separated by commas. Check that there is no comma between adjectives separated by *and*.

THINK ABOUT FICTION

It is the imagination of the author, rather than factual data, which forms the basis of any fictional work. This is not to say that fiction cannot include such things as historical events or the personal experiences of real people—including the author. These types of things can be woven into the story. However, the heart and soul of fictional literature remains the author's imagination.

1. Which element of setting—time or place—would you consider dominant in the story? Why?

2. Interpret the author's tone. What is her attitude toward the protagonist and antagonist?

3. Describe the type of conflict involved in the plot. Was there more than one type? Explain your answer.

4. What do you consider the climax or turning point of the plot? Is the resolution found in the climax or elsewhere? Explain your answer.

5. State in your own words what you consider to be the theme of the story.

DEVELOP YOUR VOCABULARY

A **dialect** is the form, or variety, of a spoken language used by members of a region, a community, or a social group. Each dialect has pronunciations, grammatical features, and vocabulary that are peculiar to it and different from those of other dialects.

In "The Revolt of Mother," the characters speak in dialect. The author shows that certain speech sounds are omitted by using an apostrophe in their place. She spells some words in the phonetic patterns used by the characters.

Rewrite each of these sentences from the story in standard English.

1. "You hadn't ought to judge Father, though."

2. "I ain't got nothin' to say about it, Mother; an' I ain't goin' to say nothin'."

3. "We ain't had no new paper on it for ten year."

4. "S'posin' I had wrote to Hiram."

5. "There ain't no call for nobody else to worry about it."

Samuel L. Clemens (Mark Twain) and His Memories,
1880. The Granger Collection

READING FOCUS

Compare and Contrast You have learned that comparing means finding similarities and contrasting means finding differences. By highlighting the common and unique qualities of different stories, you can learn more about each.

In "How to Tell a Story," Mark Twain states that there are three different kinds of stories. As you read, pay attention to how he compares and contrasts the three. Think about why he finds one kind of story much funnier than the other two.

EXPOSITION

Exposition, along with narration, description, and persuasion, is one of the four forms of discourse. The purpose of exposition is to explain. It is the kind of writing done, for example, to interpret facts and opinions, to explain the nature of freedom, to outline the structure of a government, or to account for events in history. In short, it is the kind of writing in which an author gives information about a subject.

Authors have several ways of explaining a subject. They may **define** it—tell what it is and demonstrate its purpose. They may **compare and contrast** it with something else—show its likenesses and differences. They may **classify** it—put it in its type or class. They may **analyze** it—focus on its elements and their significance.

As you read this selection, ask yourself:

1. Which way or ways of explaining does Twain use in this work?
2. Which form of discourse did Twain use in the examples he gives?

WRITING CONNECTION

Choose an object, such as a favorite possession, and write a paragraph defining its nature and use.

Old Barn in Field of Asters, Henry Poor. Corbis Bettmann

HOW TO
TELL A STORY

ADAPTED

by Mark Twain

I do not claim that I can tell a story as it ought to be told. I only claim to know how a story ought to be told, for I have been almost daily in the company of the most expert storytellers for many years.

There are several kinds of stories, but only one difficult kind—the humorous. I will talk mainly about that one. The humorous story is American; the comic story is English; the witty story is French. The humorous story depends for its effect upon the *manner* of the telling; the comic story and the witty story upon the *matter*.

The humorous story may be spun out to great length, and may wander around as much as it pleases, and arrive nowhere in particular; but the comic and witty stories must be brief and end with a point. The humorous story bubbles gently along; the others burst.

The humorous story is strictly a work of art—high and delicate art—and only an artist can tell it. But no art is necessary in telling the comic and the witty story; anybody can do it. The art of telling a humorous story—understand, I mean by word of mouth, not print—was created in America, and has remained at home.

The humorous story is told gravely. The teller does his best to conceal the fact that he even dimly suspects that there is anything funny about it. But the teller of the comic story tells you beforehand that it is one of the funniest things he has ever heard, then tells it with eager delight, and is the first person to laugh when he gets through. Sometimes, if he has had good success, he is so glad and happy that he will repeat the "nub" of it and glance around from face to face, collecting applause, and then repeat it again. It is a pathetic thing to see.

Very often, of course, the rambling humorous story also finishes with a nub, point, snapper, or whatever you like to call it. Then the listener must be alert, for in many cases, the teller will divert attention from that nub by dropping it in a carefully casual and indifferent way, as though he does not even know it is a nub.

But the teller of the comic story does not slur the nub; be shouts it at you—every time. And when he prints it, in England, France, Germany, and Italy, he *italicizes* it, puts some whooping exclamation points after it, and sometimes explains it in a parenthesis. All of which is very depressing, and makes one want to renounce joking and lead a better life.

Let me set down an instance of the comic method, using a story which has been popular all over the world for twelve or fifteen hundred years. The teller tells it in this way:

The Wounded Soldier

In a certain battle a soldier whose leg had been shot off appealed to another soldier who was hurrying by to carry him to the rear, informing him at the same time of the loss which he had sustained. The generous son of Mars,[1] shouldering the unfortunate, proceeded to carry out his desire. The bullets and cannonballs were flying in all directions, and presently one of the latter took the wounded man's head off— without, however, his deliverer being aware of it. In no long time he was hailed by an officer, who said:

"Where are you going with that carcass?"

"To the rear, sir—he's lost his leg!"

"His leg, really?" responded the astonished officer; "you mean his head, you fool."

At that the soldier relieved himself of his burden, and stood looking down upon it in great perplexity. At length he said:

"It is true, sir, just as you have said." Then after a pause he added, *"But he told me* IT WAS HIS LEG! ! ! !"

---

pathetic (puh THET ik) pitiful
divert (dih VURT) turn aside
indifferent (in DIF ur unt) not caring
slur (SLUR) make unclear; pass over carelessly
renounce (rih NOUNS) rejected; abandon with disgust
sustained (suh STAYND) experienced; suffered
carcass (KAHR kus) dead body, usually of an animal
perplexity (pur PLEK sih tee) confusion; uncertainty
[1]**Mars:** In ancient Roman mythology, Mars was the god of war.

Here the narrator bursts into explosion after explosion of horse-laughter, repeating that nub from time to time through his gaspings and shriekings and suffocatings.

It takes only a minute and a half to tell that in its comic story form, and isn't worth the telling after all. Put into the humorous story form, it takes ten minutes, and is about the funniest thing I have ever listened to—as James Whitcomb Riley[2] tells it.

He tells it in the character of a dull-witted old farmer who has just heard it for the first time, thinks it is unspeakably funny, and is trying to repeat it to a neighbor. But he can't remember it, so he gets all mixed up and wanders helplessly round and round, putting in tedious details that don't belong in the tale and only retard it; taking them out and putting in others that are just as useless; making minor mistakes now and then and stopping to correct them and explain how he came to make them; remembering things which he forgot to put in their proper place and going back to put them in there; stopping his narrative a good while in order to try to recall the name of the soldier that was hurt, and finally remembering that the soldier's name was not mentioned, and remarking thoughtfully that the name is of no real importance, anyway—better, of course, if one knew it, but not essential, after all—and so on, and so on, and so on.

To string incongruities and absurdities together in a wandering and sometimes purposeless way, and seem innocently unaware that they are absurdities, is the basis of the American art, if my position is correct. Another feature is the slurring of the point. A third is the dropping of a studied remark apparently without knowing it, as if one were thinking aloud. The fourth and last is the pause.

The pause is a very important feature in any kind of story, and a frequently recurring feature, too. It is a dainty thing, and delicate, and also uncertain and treacherous; for it must be exactly the right length—no more and no less—or it fails of its purpose and makes trouble.

On the platform I used to tell a story about a man who came to interview me once to get a sketch of my life. I consulted with a friend—a practical man—before he came, to know how I should treat him.

"Whenever you give the interviewer a fact," he said, "give him another fact that will contradict it. Then he'll go away with a jumble that he can't use at all. Be gentle, be sweet, smile like an idiot—just be natural." That's what my friend told me to do, and I did it:

An Encounter with an Interviewer

The nervous, dapper young man took the chair I offered him, and said he was connected with the *Daily Thunderstorm*, and added:

---

tedious (TEE dee us) boring; tiresome
incongruity (in kon GROO ih tee) something not fitting or not in harmony
absurdity (ab SUR duh tee) something absurd or ridiculous
recurring (rih KUR ing) occurring again and again
dapper (DAP ur) neat, trim
[2]**James Whitcomb Riley:** (1849–1916) a popular poet and speaker at the time

"Hoping it's no harm, I've come to interview you."

"Come to what?"

"*Interview* you."

"Ah! I see. Yes—yes. Um! Yes—yes."

I was not feeling bright that morning. Indeed, my powers seemed a bit under a cloud. However, I went to the bookcase, and when I had been looking six or seven minutes, I said:

"How do you spell it?"

"Spell what?"

"Interview."

"Oh, my goodness! What do you want to spell it for?"

"I don't want just to spell it; I want to spell it to see what it means."

"In, *in*, ter, *ter*, inter—"

"Then you spell it with an *I*?"

"Why, certainly!"

"Oh, that is what took me so long."

"Why, my *dear* sir, what did *you* propose to spell it with?"

"Well, I—I—hardly know. I had the Unabridged, and I was looking around in the back end, among the pictures. But it's a very old edition."

"Why, my friend, they wouldn't have a *picture* of it in even the latest e— My dear sir, I beg your pardon, I mean no harm in the world, but you do not look as—as—intelligent as I had expected you would. No harm—I mean no harm at all."

"Oh, don't mention it! It has often been said, and by people who would not flatter me, that I am quite remarkable in that way. Yes—yes; they always speak of it with pleasure."

"I can easily imagine it. But about this interview. You know it is the custom, now, to interview any man who has become famous."

"Indeed, I had not heard of it before. It must be very interesting. What do you do it with?"

"Ah, well—well—well—it *ought* to be done with a club in some cases. But usually the interviewer asks questions and the interviewed answers them. It is all the rage now. Will you let me ask you certain questions to bring out the salient points of your public and private history?"

"Oh, with pleasure—with pleasure. I have a very bad memory, but I hope you will not mind that. That is to say, it is an irregular memory—very irregular. Sometimes it goes in a gallop, and then again it will be as much as a week passing a given point. This is a great grief to me."

"Oh, it is no matter, so you will try to do the best you can."

"I will. I will put my whole mind on it."

"Thanks. Are you ready to begin?"

"Ready."

Q. How old are you?

A. Nineteen, in June.

Q. Indeed, I would have taken you to be thirty-five or -six. Where were you born?

A. In Missouri.

Q. When did you begin to write?

A. In 1836.

Q. Why, how could that be, if you are only nineteen now?

A. I don't know. It does seem curious, somehow.

---

salient (SAY lee unt) important; remarkable

Q. It does, indeed. Whom do you consider the most remarkable man you ever met?

A. Aaron Burr.[3]

Q. But you never could have met Aaron Burr, if you are only nineteen years—

A. Now, if you know more about me than I do, what do you ask me for?

Q. Well, it was only a suggestion; nothing more. How did you happen to meet Burr?

A. Well, I happened to be at his funeral one day, and he asked me to make less noise, and—

Q. But, good heavens! If you were at his funeral, he must have been dead, and if he was dead how could he care whether you made a noise or not?

A. I don't know. He was always a particular kind of man that way.

Q. Still, I don't understand it at all. You say he spoke to you, and that he was dead.

A. I didn't say he was dead.

Q. But wasn't he dead?

A. Well, some said he was, some said he wasn't.

Q. What did you think?

A. Oh, it was none of my business! It wasn't any of my funeral.

Q. Did you—However, we can never get this matter straight. Let me ask about something else. What was the date of your birth?

A. Monday. October 31, 1693.

Q. What! Impossible! That would make you a hundred and eighty years old. How do you account for that?

A. I don't account for it at all.

Q. But you said at first you were only nineteen, and now you make yourself out to be one hundred and eighty. It is an awful discrepancy.

A. Why, have you noticed that? (Shaking hands.) Many a time it has seemed to me like a discrepancy, but somehow I couldn't make up my mind. How quick you notice a thing!

Q. Thank you for the compliment, as far as it goes. Had you, or have you, any brothers or sisters?

A. Eh! I—I—I think so—yes—but I don't remember.

Q. Well, that is the most extraordinary statement I ever heard!

A. Why, what makes you think that?

Q. How could I think otherwise? Why, look here! Who is this a picture of on the wall? Isn't that a brother of yours?

A. Oh, yes, yes, yes! Now you remind me of it; that *was* a brother of mine, That's William—*Bill* we called him. Poor old Bill!

Q. Why? Is he dead, then?

A. Ah! Well, I suppose so. We never could tell. There was a great mystery about it.

Q. That is sad, very sad. He disappeared, then?

A. Well, yes, in a sort of general way. We buried him.

---

discrepancy (dih SKREP un see) difference; variation
[3]**Aaron Burr:** U.S. Vice President 1801–1805, died in 1836, the year after Twain was born.

Q. *Buried* him! *Buried* him, without knowing whether he was dead or not?

A. Oh, no! Not that. He was dead enough.

Q. Well, I confess that I can't understand this. If you buried him, and you knew he was dead—

A. No! no! We only thought he was.

Q. Oh, I see! He came to life again?

A. I bet he didn't.

Q. Well, I never heard anything like this. *Somebody* was dead, *Somebody* was buried. Now, where was the mystery?

A. Ah! That's just it! That's it exactly. You see, we were twins—defunct and I— and we got mixed in the bathtub when we were only two weeks old, and one of us was drowned. But we didn't know which. Some think it was Bill. Some think it was me.

Q. Well, that *is* remarkable. What do *you* think?

A. Goodness knows! I would give whole worlds to know. This solemn, this awful mystery has cast a gloom over my whole life. But I will tell you a secret now, which I never have revealed to any creature before. One of us had a peculiar mark—a large mole on the back of his left hand; that was *me*. *That child was the one that was drowned!*

Q. Very well, then, I don't see that there is any mystery about it, after all.

A. You don't? Well, *I* do. Anyway, I don't see how they could ever have been such a blundering lot as to go and bury the wrong child. But, 'sh!—don't mention it where the family can hear of it. Heaven knows they have heartbreaking troubles enough without adding this.

Q. Well, I believe I have got material enough for the present, and I am very much obliged to you for the pains you have taken. But I was a good deal interested in that account of Aaron Burr's funeral. Would you mind telling me what it was that made you think Burr was such a remarkable man?

A. Oh! It was a mere trifle! Not one man in fifty would have noticed it at all. When the sermon was over, and the procession all ready to start for the cemetery, and the body all arranged nice in the hearse, he said he wanted to take a last look at the scenery, and so he *got up and rode with the driver*.

Then the young man reverently withdrew. He was very pleasant company, and I was sorry to see him go.

---

defunct (dih FUNGKT) dead person
hearse (HURS) carriage for taking the dead to the grave

Mark Twain (1835–1910)

"The difference between the right word and the almost right word," wrote Mark Twain, "is the difference between lightning and the lightning bug." Finding that *just-right* word was Mark Twain's specialty.

America's favorite humorist was born Samuel Langhorne Clemens in 1835. He grew up in Hannibal, Missouri, on the west bank of the Mississippi River. His father died when he was 12, and "Sam'l" quit school to go to work for a printer. That was the first of his four careers. In the late 1850s he became a steamboat pilot, and in the 1860s he turned to newspaper work. Sketches and stories written for newspapers soon made him known across the country.

While working on his famous book *The Adventures of Tom Sawyer*, he often wrote fifty pages a day. After that book, he went on to write such classics as *Life on the Mississippi* and *The Adventures of Huckleberry Finn*.

Twain had many friends and was a concerned family man. He traveled often to many parts of the world. He made, lost, and then remade a fortune in business. But the shock of his wife's death in 1904 left him a troubled man, and his last years were not happy ones. His birth in 1835 had coincided with the appearance of Halley's comet. Knowing that the comet's next visit was due in 1910, Twain told his friends that he would "go out with it," too.

Twain was right about his death. This self-educated genius, this "Lincoln of our literature," died peacefully on the night of April 21, 1910.

Review the Selection

UNDERSTAND THE SELECTION

Recall

1. What three types of stories does Mark Twain talk about?

2. Which of these is most difficult?

3. What country does he say is associated with this most difficult type?

Infer

4. Whom does Mark Twain respect more, a storyteller or a story writer?

5. How does he feel about comic stories?

6. How does Twain feel about America as compared to other countries?

7. Why does Twain say that he is sorry to see the young man go?

Apply

8. Do you agree that this kind of story is more difficult to tell and therefore superior to the other kinds? Why?

9. How does Twain use pauses in "An Encounter with an Interviewer"?

10. What type of story is "An Encounter with an Interviewer"? Explain.

Respond to Literature

Do you think writers today are more concerned with storytelling than they were in Twain's time? Why?

WRITE ABOUT THE SELECTION

As an example of humorous story telling, Mark Twain writes about an interview he once had with a newspaper reporter. During the interview, Twain deliberately tried to confuse the interviewer by contradicting himself and making statements that were absurd or that made no sense.

Put yourself in the interviewer's position. Would you have realized what Twain was doing, or would you have thought he was crazy? How would you have written up the answers in a newspaper article?

Prewriting   When conducting an interview, note taking is very important. Assume you are the reporter in the story. Reread the interview and jot down notes from Twain's answers as you go along. Be sure to include some direct quotes. When you are finished, organize your notes in outline form, using dots or "bullets" in front of main ideas, and dashes for details that relate to each main idea.

Writing   On the basis of your notes, write a newspaper article reporting the results of your interview. Also include your perception of Twain and his responses. Decide on a particular tone to use in the article. State, at the end, what tone you have used.

Revising   Rewrite the article to the extent necessary to change the tone. Specify at the end what the new tone is.

Proofreading   Check for proper use of quotation marks and capitalization.

THINK ABOUT EXPOSITION

Defining, comparing and contrasting, classifying, and analyzing are techniques used in expository writing. **Exposition** is the form of discourse used to explain or inform. Expository works often begin with a **thesis statement**, a statement of what the author intends to explain in the work. Expository essays usually have a beginning, a middle, and an end.

1. Does Twain make a thesis statement? If so, what is it?

2. Which of the techniques of exposition do you see in Twain's essay? Support your ideas with examples.

3. What form of discourse other than exposition does Twain use?

4. For what purpose does he use this other form of discourse?

5. Does Twain's essay have a recognizable beginning, middle, and end?

READING FOCUS

Compare and Contrast Look at Twain's comparison and contrast of the three types of stories: comic, witty, and humorous. According to Twain, how are these three types of stories similar? How are they different?

DEVELOP YOUR VOCABULARY

A dictionary gives not only the correct spelling and definition of a word, but also shows how the word is divided into syllables. Consult a dictionary to review the meaning of the following words from the story. Also, rewrite each word in syllable form. Then identify the five words that contain four or more syllables. Show that you understand the meaning of these five words by using each of them in a short paragraph with a humorous tone.

1. pathetic
2. divert
3. indifferent
4. slur
5. renounce
6. sustained
7. carcass
8. perplexity
9. tedious
10. incongruity
11. absurdity
12. recurring
13. dapper
14. salient
15. discrepancy
16. defunct
17. hearse

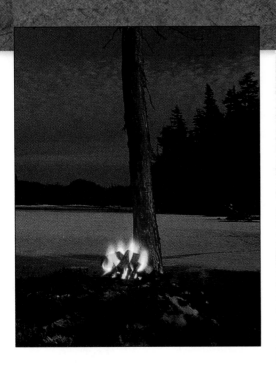

SETTING

Setting refers to where and when a story takes place, as well as to the general background of the action. Authors often describe the setting in detail. The more important the place of the action is to the plot, the more important it is for the author to describe it.

The location of a story may be very specific—a particular room in a particular house, a dungeon in a castle, or a shack in the woods. Behind the specific location there is always some general location—mountains, the desert, the seashore, a region, a city, or a country. The time of a story may specify day or night, a season of the year, or an historical era. Sometimes the location is the more important element in the setting; at other times, the time period is dominant.

As you read the story, ask yourself:

1. How important is the setting to this story?
2. Is time or place the more important element in the story?

WRITING CONNECTION

Think back to an enjoyable experience you have had recently. In four or five lines, describe the setting—time and place—of this experience.

READING FOCUS

Predict Outcomes To predict means to make an educated guess about what will happen next. When you read a story, you can use details, foreshadowing, and various clues to predict the story's outcome or ending. As you read "To Build a Fire," think about the importance of the title. Pay attention to the role of the fire in the story, to the man's character, and to the dog's concerns. Try to use these clues to predict the outcome of the story.

To Build a Fire

ADAPTED

by Jack London

Day had broken cold and gray, exceedingly cold and gray, when the man turned aside from the main Yukon trail and climbed the high earth-bank. Ahead of him, a dim and little-traveled trail led eastward through the fat spruce timberland. It was a steep bank, and he paused for breath at the top, excusing the act to himself by looking at his watch. It was nine o'clock. There was no sun nor hint of sun, though there was not a cloud in the sky. It was a clear day, and yet there seemed to be a subtle gloom over the face of things that made the day dark, and that was due to the absence of sun. This fact did not worry the man. He was used to the lack of sun. It had been days since he had seen the sun, and he knew that a few more days must pass before that cheerful orb would just peep above the hills and dip immediately from view.

The man flung a look back along the way he had come. The Yukon River lay a mile wide and hidden under three feet of ice. On top of this ice were as many feet of snow. It was all pure white, rolling in gentle undulations where the piles of ice had formed. North and south, as far as his eye could see, it was unbroken white, except for a small dark line that curved and twisted out of sight. This dark hairline was the trail—the main trail that led south five hundred miles to the Chilcoot Pass, Dyea, and salt water, and that led north seventy miles to Dawson, and still on to the north to St. Michael, on Bering Sea, a thousand miles and half a thousand more.

But all this—the mysterious, far-reaching hairline trail, the absence of sun, the tremendous cold, and the strangeness of it all—made no impression on the man.

---

subtle (SUT ul) faint and mysterious
orb (AWRB) round object
undulation (un juh LAY shun) wavy form or outline
hairline (HAIR lyn) very thin line

It was not because he was long used to it. He was a newcomer in the land, a *chechaquo*. This was his first winter. The trouble with him was that he was without imagination. He was quick and alert in the things of life, but only in the things, and not in their meanings. Fifty degrees below zero meant eighty-odd degrees of frost. Such fact impressed him as being cold and uncomfortable, and that was all. It did not lead him to meditate about his frailty as a creature of temperature. Neither did he think about the weakness of all people, able only to live within certain narrow limits of heat and cold. From there on it did not lead him to thoughts of immortality and man's place in the universe. Fifty degrees below zero stood for a bit of frost that hurt and that must be guarded against by the use of mittens, earflaps, warm boots, and thick socks. Fifty degrees below zero was to him just exactly fifty degrees below zero. That there should be anything more to it than that was a thought that never entered his head.

As he turned to go on, he spat speculatively. There was a sharp little explosion that startled him. He spat again. And again, in the air, before it could fall to the snow, the spittle popped. He knew that at fifty below spittle exploded on the snow, but this spittle had popped in the air. Undoubtedly it was colder than fifty below. How much colder he did not know. But the temperature did not matter. He was bound for the old claim on the left fork of Henderson Creek, where the men were already. They had come over mountains from the Indian Creek country, while he had come the other way. He had wanted to take a look at the possibilities of getting out logs in the spring from the islands in the Yukon. He would be in camp by six o'clock. That was a bit after dark, it was true, but the men would be there, a fire would be going, and a hot supper would be ready. As for lunch, he pressed his hand against the bundle under his jacket. It was also under his shirt, wrapped up in a handkerchief and lying against the naked skin. It was the only way to keep the biscuits from freezing. He smiled to himself as he thought of those biscuits, each cut open and sopped in bacon grease, and each enclosing a generous slice of fried bacon.

He plunged in among the big spruce trees. The trail was faint. A foot of snow had fallen since the last sled had passed, and he was glad he was without a sled, traveling light. In fact, he carried nothing but the lunch wrapped in the handkerchief. He was surprised, however, at the cold. It certainly was cold, he told himself. He rubbed his numb nose and cheekbones with his mittened hand. He was a warm-whiskered man, but the hair on his face

---

meditate (MED uh tayt) think deeply; ponder
immortality (im aw TAL ih tee) unending life
speculatively (SPEK yuh tiv lee) thinking about possibilities
spittle (SPIT ul) saliva; what one spits

did not protect the high cheekbones and the eager nose from the frosty air.

At the man's heels trotted a dog, a big husky. It was almost a wolf-dog, gray-coated and without any real difference from its brother, the wild wolf. The animal was saddened by the tremendous cold. It knew that this was no time for traveling. Its instinct told it a truer tale than was told to the man by the man's judgment. In truth, it was not just colder than fifty below zero. It was colder than sixty below, than seventy below. It was seventy-five below zero. Since the freezing point is thirty-two above zero, it meant that there were one hundred and seven degrees of frost. The dog did not know anything about thermometers. Possibly in its brain there was no sharp awareness of a condition of very cold such as was in the man's brain. But the beast had its instinct. It experienced a vague apprehension about the cold that made it sneak along at the man's heels. It questioned every movement of the man, as if expecting him to go into camp or to find shelter somewhere and build a fire. The dog had learned fire. Now it wanted fire, or else to dig under the snow and curl up away from the air.

The frozen moisture of the dog's breath had settled on its fur in a fine powder of frost, and its muzzle and eyelashes were whitened by its snowy breath. The man's red beard and mustache were likewise frosted, but more solidly. The ice on his face increased with every warm, moist breath he took. Also, the man was chewing tobacco, and the ice made his lips so stiff that he was unable to clear his chin when he spat out the juice. The result was that an icy brown beard was increasing its length on his chin. If he fell down it would shatter like glass into small pieces. But he did not mind it, really. It was the penalty all tobacco-chewers paid in that country. And he had been out before in two cold snaps. They had not been so cold as this, he knew. But by the thermometer at Sixty Mile he knew they had been fifty below and fifty-five.

He held on through the woods for several miles, crossed a wide flat place, and dropped down a bank to the frozen bed of a small stream. This was Henderson Creek, and he knew he was ten miles from the fork. He looked at his watch. It was ten o'clock. He was making four miles an hour, and he calculated that he would arrive at the fork at half-past twelve. He decided to celebrate that event by eating his lunch there.

The dog dropped behind again at his heels, with its tail drooping, as the man swung along the creekbed. The furrow of the old sled trail was plainly visible, but a dozen inches of snow covered the marks of the last runners. In a month no man had come up or down that silent creek. The man held steadily on. He was not much given to thinking, and just then he

---

apprehension (ap rih HEN shun) worry; fear of a coming event
muzzle (MUZ ul) mouth and nose of an animal

Trapper in the Wilderness, Sydney Laurence. The Shelburne Museum, Shelburne, VT

had nothing to think about. He knew that he would eat lunch at the fork and that at six o'clock he would be in camp with the men. There was nobody to talk to; and, had there been, speech would have been impossible because of the ice on his mouth. So he continued monotonously to chew tobacco and to increase the length of his brown beard.

Once in a while the thought reiterated itself that it was very cold and that he had never experienced such cold. As he walked along he rubbed his cheekbones and nose with the back of his mittened hand. He did this automatically, now and again changing hands. But rub as he would, the instant he stopped his cheekbones went numb, and the following instant the end of his nose went numb. He was sure to frost his cheeks; he knew that. He wished he had made a nose strap of the sort Bud wore in cold snaps. Such

---

reiterate (ree IT uh rayt) repeat tiresomely

a strap passed across the cheeks, as well, and saved them. But it didn't matter much, after all. What were frosted cheeks? A bit painful, that was all. They were never serious.

Empty as the man's mind was of thoughts, he was keenly observant. He noticed the changes in the creek, the curves and bends and logjams, and always he sharply noted where he placed his feet. Once, coming around a bend, he shied quickly, like a startled horse, curved away from the place where he had been walking, and took several steps back along the trail. The creek, he knew, was frozen clear to the bottom—but he knew also that there were springs that bubbled out from the hillsides and ran along under the snow and on top of the ice of the creek. He knew that the coldest snaps never froze these springs, and he knew likewise their danger. They were traps. They hid pools of water under the snow that might be three inches deep, or three feet. Sometimes a skin of ice half an inch thick covered them, and in turn was covered by the snow. So when one broke through he kept on breaking through, sometimes wetting himself to the waist.

That was why he had shied in such panic. He had felt the softness under his feet and heard the crack of a snow-hidden ice-skin. And to get his feet wet in such a temperature meant trouble and danger. At the very least it meant delay, for he would be forced to stop and build

a fire. Then he would have to bare his feet while he dried his socks and boots. He stood and studied the creek bed and its banks and decided that the flow of water seemed to come from the right. He reflected awhile, rubbing his nose and cheeks. Then he moved to the left, walking carefully and testing each step. Once clear of the danger, he took a fresh chew of tobacco and swung along at his four-mile gait.

In the next two hours he came upon several similar traps. Usually the snow above the hidden pools had a sunken, solid appearance that advertised the danger. Once again, however, he had a close call, and another time, suspecting danger, he made the dog go on in front. The dog did not want to go. It hung back until the man shoved it forward, and then it went quickly across the white, unbroken surface. Suddenly it broke through, floundered to one side, and got away to safety. It had wet its feet and legs, and almost immediately the water turned to ice. It made quick efforts to lick the ice off its legs, then dropped down in the snow and began to bite out the ice that had formed between the toes. This was a matter of instinct. To permit the ice to remain would mean sore feet. It did not know this. It just obeyed the mysterious orders that came from somewhere deep inside it. But the man knew, having made a judgment on the subject, and he removed the mitten from his right hand

---

shied (SHYD) drew back
reflect (rih FLEKT) think
gait (GAYT) manner of walking or running

and helped tear out the ice pieces. He did not uncover his fingers more than a minute, and was astonished at the swift numbness that hit them. It certainly was cold. He pulled on the mitten hastily, and beat the hand savagely across his chest.

At twelve o'clock the day was at its brightest. Yet the sun was too far south on its winter journey to appear in the sky. The man walked under a clear sky at noon and cast no shadow. At half-past twelve, to the minute, he arrived at the fork of the creek. He was pleased at the speed he had made. If he kept it up, he would certainly be with the men by six. He unbuttoned his jacket and shirt and drew forth his lunch. The action took no more than a quarter of a minute, yet in that brief time the numbness laid hold of the exposed fingers. He did not put the mitten on right away, but instead struck the fingers a dozen sharp smashes against his leg. Then he sat down on a snow-covered log to eat. The sting that followed the striking of his fingers against his leg stopped so quickly that he was startled. He had had no chance to take a bite of biscuit. He struck the fingers again and returned them to the mitten, baring the other hand for the purpose of eating. He tried to take a mouthful, but the ice on his face prevented it. He had forgotten to build a fire and thaw out. He chuckled at his foolishness, and as he chuckled he noted the numbness creeping into the bare fingers. Also, he noted that the stinging which had first come to his toes when he sat down was already passing away. He wondered whether the toes were warm or numb. He moved them inside the boots and decided that they were numb.

He pulled the mitten on hurriedly and stood up. He was a bit frightened. He stamped up and down until the stinging returned into the feet. It certainly was cold, was his thought. That man from Sulphur Creek had spoken the truth when telling how cold it sometimes got in this country. And he had laughed at him at the time! That showed one must not be too sure of things. There was no mistake about it—it was cold. He walked up and down, stamping his feet and swinging his arms, until he felt the returning warmth. Then he got out matches and proceeded to make a fire. From the bushes where high water of the spring had left a supply of twigs, he got his firewood. Working carefully from a small beginning, he soon had a roaring fire. He thawed the ice from his face, and in the protection of the fire he ate his biscuits. For the moment the cold was defeated. The dog took satisfaction in the fire, too, stretching out close enough for warmth and far enough away to escape being burned.

When the man had finished, he filled his pipe and took his comfortable time over a smoke. Then he pulled on his mittens. He settled the ear-flaps of his cap about his ears, and took the creek trail up the left fork. The dog was disappointed. It didn't want to leave the fire. This man did not know cold. Possibly all the man's ancestors had known nothing of cold, of real cold, of cold one hundred and seven degrees below the freezing point. But the dog knew. All its ancestors had known, and the knowledge had come down to it.

It knew that it was not good to walk abroad in such fearful cold. This was the time to lie snug in a hole in the snow and wait for better weather. There was no great intimacy between the dog and the man. The one was the slave of the other. The only caresses it ever received were the caresses of the whip. So the dog made no effort to communicate its apprehension to the man. It was not concerned about the safety of the man. It was for its own sake that it wanted to stay by the fire. But the man whistled, and spoke to it with the sound of a whip, and the dog swung in at the man's heel and followed after.

The man took a chew of tobacco and proceeded to start a new amber beard. Also, his moist breath quickly covered with white his mustache and eyebrows. There did not seem to be so many dangerous springs on the left fork of the Henderson, and for half an hour the man saw no signs of any. And then it happened. At a place where there were no signs, where the snow was soft and unbroken, the man broke through. It was not deep. He wet himself halfway to the knees before he floundered out.

He was angry, and cursed his luck aloud. He had hoped to get into camp with the men at six o'clock. This would delay him an hour, for he would have to build a fire and dry out his socks and boots. This was imperative at that low temperature—he knew that much.

He turned aside to the bank, which he climbed. On top, tangled in the bushes around the trunks of several small spruce trees, was some dry firewood. There were sticks and twigs, but also larger branches and fine, dry, last-year's grasses. He threw down several large pieces on top of the snow. This served for a foundation and prevented the young flame from drowning itself in the snow it otherwise would melt. The flame he got by touching a match to a small piece of birch bark that he took from his pocket. This burned even more easily than paper. Placing it on the foundation, he fed the young flame with dry grass and with the tiniest dry twigs. He worked slowly and carefully, keenly aware of his danger. Gradually, as the flame grew stronger, he increased the size of the twigs with which he fed it. He squatted in the snow, pulling the twigs out from the brush and feeding them directly to the flame. He knew there must be no failure. When it is seventy-five below zero, a man must not fail in his first attempt to build a fire—that is, if his feet are wet. If his feet are dry, and he fails, things are different. He can run along the trail for half a mile and regain his circulation. But the circulation of wet and freezing feet cannot be regained by running when it is seventy-five below. No matter how fast he runs, the wet feet will freeze harder and harder.

All this the man knew. The old-timer on Sulphur Creek had told him about it

---

intimacy (IN tuh muh see) very close friendship, even love
imperative (im PER uh tiv) really necessary; essential

in the fall, and now he was glad for the advice. Already all feeling had gone out of his feet. To build the fire he had been forced to remove his mittens, and the fingers had quickly gone numb. His walking speed of four miles an hour had kept his heart pumping blood to the surface of his body and to all the extremities. But the instant he stopped, the action of the pump slowed down. The cold of space had settled down on the unprotected tip of the planet. And he, being on that unprotected tip, received the full force of the blow. The blood of his body drew back before it. The blood was alive, like the dog, and like the dog it wanted to hide away and cover itself up from the fearful cold. So long as he walked four miles an hour, he pumped that blood to the surface. But now it ebbed away and sank down into the recesses of his body. The extremities were the first to feel its absence. His wet feet froze faster, and his bare fingers numbed faster, though they had not yet begun to freeze. Nose and cheeks were already freezing, while the skin of all his body chilled as it lost its blood.

But he was safe. Toes and nose and cheeks would be only touched by the frost, for the fire was now beginning to burn with strength. He was feeding it with twigs the size of his finger. In another minute he would be able to feed it with branches the size of his wrist. Then he could remove his wet boots and socks. While they dried, he could keep his naked feet warm by the fire, rubbing them at first, of course, with snow. The fire was a success. He was safe. He remembered the advice of the old-timer on Sulphur Creek, and smiled. The old-timer had been very serious in laying down the law that no man must travel alone in the Klondike[1] after fifty below. Well, here he was. He had had the accident. He was alone, and he had saved himself. Those old-timers were rather too fearful, some of them, he thought. All a man had to do was to keep his head, and he was all right. Any man who was a man could travel alone. But it was surprising, the speed with which his cheeks and nose were freezing. And he had not thought his fingers could go lifeless in so short a time. Lifeless they were, for he could hardly make them move together to grip a twig, and they seemed far from his body and from him. When he touched a twig, he had to look and see whether or not he had hold of it. The wires were pretty well down between him and his finger-ends.

All of which counted for little. There was the fire, snapping and growing and promising life with every dancing flame. He started to untie his boots. They were coated with ice. The thick German socks were like sheaths of iron halfway to the knees. The boot laces were like rods of

---

extremities (ik STREM ih teez) hands and feet; parts farthest away
ebb (EB) flow back or away
recess (rih SES) interior place
sheath (SHEETH) protective covering
[1]**The Klondike:** an area in northern Canada, next to Alaska.

steel all twisted and knotted as by some conflagration. For a moment he tugged with his numb fingers. Then, realizing the folly of his effort, he drew his knife.

But before he could cut the strings, it happened. It was his own fault or, rather, his mistake. He should not have built the fire under the spruce tree. He should have built it in the open. But it had been easier to pull the twigs from the brush and drop them directly on the fire. The tree under which he had done this carried a lot of snow on its branches. No wind had blown for weeks, and each branch was fully loaded. Now he had a growing fire, and he had been moving about under the tree. The heat and motion were not much, so far as he was concerned, but they were enough to bring about the disaster. High up in the tree one branch dumped its load of snow. This fell on the boughs beneath, making them dump their snow. This continued, spreading out over the whole tree. It grew like an avalanche, and it descended without warning upon the man and the fire. The fire was blotted out! Where it had burned was a mantle of fresh and disordered snow.

The man was shocked. It was as though he had just heard his own sentence of death. For a moment he sat and stared at the spot where the fire had been. Then he grew very calm. Perhaps the old-timer on Sulphur Creek was right. If he had only had a companion he would have been in no danger now. The other person could have built the fire. Well, it was up to him to build the fire over again, and this second time there must be no failure. Even if he succeeded, he would most likely lose some toes. His feet must be badly frozen by now, and there would be some time before the second fire was ready.

Such were his thoughts, but he did not sit and think them. He was busy all the time they were passing through his mind. He made a new foundation for a fire, this time in the open, where no treacherous tree could blot it out. Next, he gathered dry grasses and tiny twigs. He could not bring his fingers together to pull them out, but he was able to gather them by the handful. In this way he got many rotten twigs and bits of green moss that he didn't want, but it was the best he could do. He worked methodically, even collecting an armful of the larger branches to be used later when the fire gathered strength. And all the while the dog sat and watched him. There was a certain wishful look in its eyes, for it looked upon him to build a fire, and the fire was slow in coming.

When all was ready, the man reached in his pocket for a second piece of birch bark. He knew the bark was there. Though he could not feel it with his fingers, he could hear its crisp sound as he reached for it. Try as he would, he could not get hold of it. And all the time, in his mind, was the knowledge that each instant his feet were freezing. This

---

conflagration (kon fluh GRAY shun) huge fire
mantle (MAN tul) something that covers
methodically (muh THOD ik lee) orderly; systematically

thought might have put him in a panic, but he fought against it and kept calm. He pulled on his mittens with his teeth. He swung his arms back and forth, beating his hands with all his might against his sides. He did this sitting down, and he stood up to do it. All the while the dog sat in the snow, its tail curled around warmly over its feet, and its sharp wolfears pricked forward eagerly as it watched the man. And the man, as he beat his feet and waved his arms and hands, felt a great wave of envy. He knew that the dog was warm and safe in its natural covering.

After a time he was aware of the first far-away signals of feeling in his beaten fingers. The faint tingle grew stronger till it grew into a stinging ache that was excruciating, but the man greeted it with satisfaction. He stripped the mitten from his right hand and brought forth the birch bark. The bare fingers were quickly going numb again. Next he pulled out his bunch of matches. But the tremendous cold had already driven the life out of his fingers. In his effort to separate one match from the others, the whole bunch fell in the snow. He tried to pick it out of the snow, but failed, The dead fingers could neither touch nor grasp. He was very careful. He drove the thought of his freezing feet, and nose, and cheeks, out of his mind. He put his whole soul into getting the matches. He watched his hands, using the sense of vision in place of that of touch. When he saw his fingers on each side of the bunch, he closed them. That is, he tried to close them, for the wires were down, and the fingers did not obey. He pulled the mitten on the right hand, and beat it fiercely against his knee. Then, with both mittened hands, he scooped the bunch of matches, along with much snow, into his lap. Yet he was no better off.

After some trouble he managed to get the bunch between the heels of his mittened hands. In this way he carried it to his mouth. The ice snapped and broke when by a tremendous effort he opened his mouth. He drew the lower jaw in, and curled the upper lip out of the way. Then he scraped the bunch with his upper teeth in order to separate a match, He succeeded in getting one, which he dropped on his lap. He was no better off. He could not pick it up. Then he devised a way. He picked it up in his teeth and scratched it on his leg. Twenty times he scratched before he succeeded in lighting it. As it flamed he held it with his teeth to the birch bark. But the burning fumes went up his nostrils and into his lungs, causing him to cough spasmodically. The match fell into the snow and went out.

The old-timer on Sulphur Creek was right, he thought in the sad moment that followed. After fifty below, a man should travel with a partner. He beat his hands, but failed to regain any feeling. Suddenly he bared both hands, removing the mittens with his teeth. He caught the whole bunch of matches between the heels of his hands. His arm muscles

---

excruciating (ik SKROO shee ayt ing) very painful
spasmodically (spaz MOD ik lee) in sudden bursts

were not frozen, and he could press the hand-heels tightly against the matches. Then he scratched the bunch along his leg. It roared into flame, seventy matches at once! There was no wind to blow them out. He kept his head to one side to escape the fumes and held the blazing bunch to the birch bark. As he so held it, he became aware of feeling in his hand. His flesh was burning. He could smell it. Deep down below the surface he could feel it. The feeling turned into pain that grew and grew. And still he endured it, holding the flame of the matches clumsily to the bark that would not light easily because his own burning hands were in the way.

At last, when he could endure no more, he jerked his hands apart. The blazing matches fell sizzling into the snow, but the birch bark was on fire. He began laying dry grasses and the tiniest twigs on the flame. He could not pick and choose, for he had to lift the fuel between the heels of his hands. Small pieces of rotten wood and green moss clung to the twigs, and he bit these off as well as he could with his teeth. He cherished the flame carefully and awkwardly.

It meant life to him. The lack of blood on the surface of his body now made him begin to shiver, and he grew more awkward. A large piece of green moss fell directly on the little fire. He tried to poke it out with his fingers, but his shivering body made him poke too far, and he disturbed the center of the little fire. The burning grasses and tiny twigs separated

and scattered. He tried to poke them together again, but in spite of the effort, his shivering got away with him, and the twigs were hopelessly scattered. Each twig gave a puff of smoke and went out. The fire had failed. He had failed. As he looked apathetically about him, his eyes chanced on the dog. The animal was sitting across the ruins of the fire from him, in the snow, slightly lifting one front foot and then the other.

The sight of the dog put a wild idea into his head. He remembered the tale of

---

apathetically (ap uh THET ik lee) with little or no feeling the man, caught in a blizzard, who killed a steer and crawled inside the dead body, and so was saved. He would kill the dog now. He would bury his hands in the warm body until the numbness went out of them. Then he could build another fire. He spoke to the dog, calling it to him. But in his voice was a strange note of fear that frightened the animal, who had never known the man to speak in such a way before. Something was the matter. The dog felt the danger. It knew not what danger, but somewhere, somehow, in its brain there rose a distrust of the man. It flattened its ears down at the sound of the man's voice. It would not come to the man. He got on his hands and knees and crawled toward the dog. This unusual posture again made the dog suspicious, and the animal sidled away.

The man sat up in the snow for a moment and struggled for calmness. Then he pulled on his mittens, by using his teeth, and got to his feet. He glanced down, in order to make sure that he was really standing up, for the absence of feeling in his feet left him separated from the earth. His standing up in itself started to drive the webs of suspicion from the dog's mind. And when he spoke an order with the sound of a whip in his voice, the dog obeyed once again and came to him. As it came within reaching distance, the man lost his control. His arms flashed out to the dog. Then he discovered that his hands could not grasp, that there was neither bend nor feeling in the fingers. He had

forgotten for the moment that they were frozen and that they were freezing more and more. All this happened quickly. But before the animal could get away, he had its body in his arms. He sat down in the snow, and in this way held the dog, while it snarled and whined and struggled.

But it was all he could do, hold its body in his arms and sit there. He realized that he could not kill the dog. There was no way to do it. With his helpless hands he could neither draw nor hold his knife. Nor could he choke the animal. He let it go, and it plunged wildly away, with tail between legs, and still snarling. It stopped forty feet away and looked at him curiously, with ears sharply forward. The man looked down at his hands in order to locate them, and found them hanging on the ends of his arms. It struck him as curious that one should have to use his eyes in order to find out where his hands were. He began swinging his arms back and forth, beating the mittened hands against his sides. He did this for five minutes, very hard. His heart pumped enough blood up to the surface to put a stop to his shivering. But no feeling returned to the hands. They hung like weights on the ends of his arms.

A certain dull fear of death came to him now. This fear quickly became poignant as he realized that it was no longer a matter of just freezing his fingers and toes. It was no longer a matter of losing his hands and feet. No, it was a matter of life and death, with the chances against him. This threw

---

sidle (SYD ul) move sideways; edge along slyly
poignant (POIN yunt) sharp; keenly felt

him into a panic, and he turned and ran up the creek bed along the old, dim trail. The dog joined in behind and kept up with him. He ran blindly, without any real purpose in mind, filled with a fear such as he had never known in his life. Slowly, as he plowed and floundered through the snow, he began to see things again. The banks of the creek. The old logjams. The sky. The running made him feel better. He did not shiver. Maybe, if he ran on, his feet would thaw out. Anyway, if he ran far enough, he would reach camp and the men. Without doubt he would lose some fingers and toes and some of his face. But the men would take care of him, and save the rest of him when he got there. And at the same time there was another thought in his mind that said he would never get to the camp. It was too many miles away. The freezing had too great a start on him, and he would soon be stiff and dead. This second thought he tried to keep in the background. Sometimes it pushed itself forward and demanded to be heard, but he forced it back and tried to think of other things.

It struck him as curious that he could run at all. His feet were so frozen that he could not feel them when they struck the earth and took the weight of his body. He seemed to himself to glide along above the surface. He seemed to have no connection with the earth. Somewhere he had once seen a winged Mercury,[2] and he wondered

if Mercury felt as he felt when skimming over the earth.

His idea of running until he reached camp had one thing wrong with it: he lacked the endurance. Several times he stumbled, and finally he fell. When he tried to rise, he failed. He must sit and rest, he decided. The next time he would try only to walk and keep on going. As he sat and regained his breath, he noted that he was feeling quite warm and comfortable. He was not shivering, and it even seemed that a warm glow had come to his chest. And yet, when he touched his nose or cheeks, there was no feeling. Running would not thaw them out. Nor would it thaw out his hands and feet. Then the thought came to him that the frozen portions of his body must be growing larger. He tried to keep this thought down, to forget it, to think of something else. He was aware of the panicky feeling that it caused, and he was afraid of the panic. But the thought came again, and kept on coming, until he had a vision of his body totally frozen. This was too much. He made another wild run along the trail. Once he slowed down to a walk, but the thought of the freezing made him run again. And all the time the dog ran with him, at his heels. When he fell down a second time, it curled its tail over its front feet and sat facing him, curiously eager. The warmth and safety of the animal angered him, and he cursed it till it flattened down its ears appeasingly. This

---

appeasingly (uh PEEZ ing lee) in a manner to please or obey
[2]**Mercury:** the ancient Roman god who served as messenger of the gods and is often pictured with wings on his heels

time the shivering came more quickly upon the man. He was losing in his battle with the frost. It was creeping into his body from all sides. The thought of it drove him on, but he ran no more than a hundred feet, when he staggered and fell. It was his last panic. When he had recovered his breath and control, he sat up and thought about meeting death with dignity. However, the idea did not come to him in such terms. His idea of it was that he had been making a fool of himself. He had been running around like a chicken with its head cut off—such was the simile that occurred to him. Well, he was bound to freeze anyway, and he might as well take it with dignity. With this new-found peace of mind came the first drowsiness. A good idea, he thought, to sleep off to death. It was like taking an anesthetic. Freezing was not so bad as people thought. There were lots worse ways to die.

He pictured the men finding his body next day. Suddenly he found himself with them, coming along the trail and looking for himself. And, still with them, he came around a turn in the trail and found himself lying in the snow. He did not belong with himself anymore, for even then he was out of himself, standing with the men and looking at himself in the snow. It certainly was cold, was his thought. When he got back to the States he could tell the folks what real cold was. He drifted on from this to a vision of the old-timer on Sulphur Creek. He could see him quite clearly, warm and comfortable, and smoking a pipe.

"You were right, old hoss. You were right," the man mumbled to the old-timer of Sulphur Creek.

Then the man drowsed off into what seemed to him the most comfortable and satisfying sleep he had ever known. The dog sat facing him and waiting. The brief day drew to a close in a long, slow twilight. There were no signs of a fire to be made, and besides, never in the dog's experience had it known a man to sit like that in the snow and make no fire. As the twilight drew on, its need for the fire mastered it. It lifted its feet up and down. It whined softly, then flattened its ears down, expecting to be scolded by the man. But the man remained silent. Later, the dog whined loudly. And still later it crept close to the man and caught the scent of death. This made the animal bristle and back away. A little longer it delayed, howling under the stars that leaped and danced and shone brightly in the cold sky. Then it turned and trotted up the trail in the direction of the camp it knew, where were the other men, men with food and fire.

---

anesthetic (an is THET ik) substance that lessens pain

Jack London (1876–1916)

Jack London was born in San Francisco. He grew up there and in nearby Oakland. At fifteen he was a high-school dropout, a married man, and known as the "Prince of the Oyster Pirates." He worked in a canning factory and tramped around the United States. At seventeen he sailed the Pacific as a crew member on a sealing ship. At twenty-one he joined the gold rush in the Yukon, a region of northern Canada and the setting of "To Build a Fire." Like the characters in his stories and novels, London seemed always in motion.

However, London found the time to read a good deal. When he was about twenty, he decided to be a writer, and he thought a college education would be necessary. For three months he studied for hours every day to pass the entrance exams for the University of California. He succeeded—but then found college too slow for him. For the second time in his life he became a dropout.

London wrote about 150 short stories, selling his first one in 1899. In 1903, *The Call of the Wild*, a novel about a dog, made him famous. From then until his death, he averaged four books a year. He also served as a war reporter in the Far East and Mexico. He was the first American author to earn more than a million dollars from his writing, but he spent it quickly and finally suffered financial disaster while still a young man.

The brief biography you have just read gives several details about London's life before the age of twenty-one. In your opinion, in what way might these experiences have enriched his fiction?

Review the Selection

UNDERSTAND THE SELECTION

Recall

1. Where is "To Build a Fire" set?

2. What does the man eat for lunch?

3. Where is the man heading?

Infer

4. London writes that "he was without imagination." Why is this a problem?

5. Why does the dog think that "the man's ancestors had known nothing of cold"?

6. Explain the importance of the pieces of birch bark in the man's pocket.

7. Describe the relationship between the man and the dog.

Apply

8. How does London foreshadow the tragedy at the end of the story?

9. Predict what might have happened if the man had taken the advice of the old-timer from Sulphur Creek.

10. Would you have attempted what this man did? Why or why not?

Respond to Literature

Do you think the Gold Rush was the reason the man placed himself in this setting? Explain.

WRITE ABOUT THE SELECTION

Were you surprised at the ending or did you expect it? There are several other possible endings that the story could have if some of the elements of the story were changed: for example, the setting. What might have happened if there were no underground springs hidden beneath the snow? What might have happened if the temperature were only 50 degrees below zero, instead of 75 below? A change in the setting could affect the outcome of the story.

Think of some changes to the setting and some different endings to the story that may have resulted from these changes. Then write a new ending.

Prewriting Think about these changes and list them. Think about different endings that would result from these changes.

Writing Write a new ending to the story. Explain how the changes in the setting have contributed to this.

Revising Make one more change to the setting that reinforces the new ending. Does the new ending reflect the changes you have made in the setting?

Proofreading Read your revised paragraph over. Make sure that all your sentences are complete. Remember, complete sentences include a subject (a person, place, or thing) and a predicate that shows an action or a state of being.

THINK ABOUT SETTING

Setting deals primarily with place and time. It also includes everything in the environment, such as objects that are important to the story.

1. How important is the setting to this story?

2. Which aspect of setting—time or place—is dominant in this story? Explain why.

3. Pick three sentences from the story that describe the different elements of nature that contribute to the setting. Explain their significance to the plot.

4. Do you consider the dog to be part of the setting or a character? Why?

5. The author does not give the man's name or any details of his background. Does this work? Explain.

READING FOCUS

Predict Outcomes As you read "To Build a Fire," you made predictions about the outcome of the story. Did you predict the outcome of the story correctly? If so, identify the clues in the story that helped you make your prediction. If not, identify the clues that suggested the ending you predicted.

DEVELOP YOUR VOCABULARY

The Inuit people of the far north, where "To Build a Fire" takes place, have contributed several words to English. *Inuit* is the preferred term for the people we used to call Eskimos. These people live near the Arctic Circle, where it is very cold. They have learned over generations how to keep warm in such a frozen climate.

Look in a dictionary that has word histories for the meaning of each of the following words. Then use each word in a sentence of your own. Tell how each object named might or might not have helped save the life of the main character of "To Build a Fire."

1. anorak
2. husky
3. igloo
4. malamute
5. mukluk
6. umiak

Rhyme is the recurrence of the same or similar sounds at regular intervals in one or more lines of poetry. The sameness in rhyme is based on the sounds of the vowel and the consonant that follows it. For example, *fit* and *sit* have the same vowel sound followed by the same consonant sound. Only the consonant before the vowel is different. This kind of rhyme is called **perfect rhyme**.

The rhyme must also involve the accented syllable. For example, two words ending in *-ing* do not necessarily rhyme because the *-ing* syllable does not have the emphasis, or accent. Thus, *saying* and *playing* rhyme, but *looking* and *seeing* do not.

Most rhymes are **end rhymes**; that is, the words with the same sounds are at the end of the lines. However, poems may also have **internal rhymes**—two rhyming words within the same line.

As you read the selection, ask yourself:
1. Which are the rhyming words in the poem?
2. Does the author use end rhymes, internal rhymes, or both?

READING FOCUS

Support an Opinion It is important to support an opinion. Giving reasons for an opinion makes the opinion more convincing. As you read this poem, look for how the writer supports her opinion that America is beautiful.

WRITING CONNECTION

Write two lines that have end rhymes. Write two lines that have internal rhymes.

Mount Katahdin, Maine, 1853, Frederick Edwin Church. The Granger Collection

AMERICA THE BEAUTIFUL

by Katherine Lee Bates

O beautiful for spacious skies,
For amber waves of grain,
For purple mountain majesties
Above the fruited plain!

Wheatfield Watercolor, Emil Nolde. Corbis Bettmann

5   America! America!
       God shed His grace on thee
And crown thy good with brotherhood
      From sea to shining sea!

    O beautiful for pilgrim feet,
10   Whose stern, impassioned stress
    A thoroughfare for freedom beat
      Across the wilderness!
      America! America!
      God mend thine every flaw,
15   Confirm thy soul in self-control,
      Thy liberty in law!

    O beautiful for heroes proved
      In liberating strife,
Who more than self their country loved,
20   And mercy more than life!
      America! America!
      May God thy gold refine,
Till all success be nobleness
      And every gain divine!

25   O beautiful for patriot dream
      That sees beyond the years
Thine alabaster cities gleam
      Undimmed by human tears!
      America! America!
30   God shed His grace on thee
And crown thy good with brotherhood
      From sea to shining sea!

---

impassioned (im PASH und) determined; filled with
  passionate feeling
thoroughfare (THUR oh fair) passage; way through

Review the Selection

UNDERSTAND THE SELECTION

Recall

1. How many stanzas are there all together in "America the Beautiful"?

2. What colors are mentioned?

3. Is any part of the poem repeated? If so, which part?

Infer

4. What does "fruited plain" mean?

5. To what do you think "Confirm thy soul in self-control" refers?

6. To what does the reference "from sea to shining sea" refer?

7. What is "liberating strife"?

Apply

8. Would you say that "America the Beautiful" is a poem or a song—or both? Explain.

9. Do you see any relationship between stanzas in poetry and paragraphs in prose? Explain.

10. What kind of rhyming scheme can you notice? Is more than one pattern used? Explain.

Respond to Literature

Does the imagery in this poem apply to America today in the same way as when Katherine Lee Bates wrote it? Explain.

WRITE ABOUT THE SELECTION

There are many great things in America to be seen and experienced. When you think about our country, what other images come to your mind? Write another stanza to "America the Beautiful."

Prewriting   One good way to organize descriptive thoughts and details is the "cluster" method. Start by writing the name of your subject, in this case "America, " in the middle of a page and draw a circle around it. Next, think of at least four things in and about America. Write these down around the subject word; circle them and draw a line between each of these and "America." Finally, think of at least two descriptive terms for each of these things. Write these down around the word they describe; circle them and draw lines between each and the term being described. You will now have a cluster of at least eight adjectives connected to four nouns, connected to the subject.

Writing   Using the nouns and adjectives from your cluster, write a description of America. Put this in the form of an additional stanza to "America the Beautiful."

Revising   Enhance your imagery by adding one more adjective to each description you have used. Are your adjectives and details concrete? Do they appeal to the reader's senses?

Proofreading   Make sure you have used commas to separate adjectives used in a series to describe the same noun.

THINK ABOUT RHYME

Rhyme adds greatly to the beauty of much poetry, but have you thought about why this is so? One reason is that rhyme has a musical quality; the repetition of sounds has an echo-like quality that is pleasing to the ear. Rhyme also has a rhythmic function; it is a kind of "time-beater" since the rhyming words note the end of a **verse**, or line of poetry. It also helps to delineate divisions of the poem.

1. Which words in the first four lines of each stanza rhyme?

2. What are rhymes of this kind called?

3. What end rhymes are there in the second four lines of each stanza?

4. Are there any other rhymes in the second four lines of each stanza? If so, what are they called?

5. Are there imperfect rhymes in the poem? If so, what are they?

> ## READING FOCUS
> **Support an Opinion** How did Katherine Lee Bates support her opinion that America is beautiful in these areas?
> • its physical beauty
> • its history in becoming a country
> • its struggles

DEVELOP YOUR VOCABULARY

Adjectives are words that describe. They are used to limit, or modify, the meaning of nouns. In her poem, Bates uses strong, vivid adjectives to create images for the reader. Some of these are *spacious*, *amber*, *purple*, *fruited*, *impassioned*, *liberating*, and *alabaster*. Notice that her choices include not only adjectives but participles used as adjectives.

Read the following sentences. Then change the italicized weak adjective in each for a more vivid one. You can use two or more adjectives for the italicized one, if you wish.

1. An *awful* rain fell all day.

2. The doorbell made a *funny* noise.

3. I had a *great* time at the picnic.

4. The day of our hike was *nice*.

5. We moved the *old* bed up to the attic.

Learn About

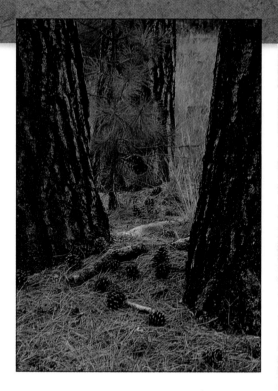

RHYME SCHEME

Rhymes usually occur in the same places throughout a poem. This regularity is known as the **rhyme pattern** or **rhyme scheme**. You can detect a rhyme scheme by assigning letters to designate the words at the end of the lines. The same letter is used for words having the same sounds. Thus, a simple rhyme scheme would be *abcb*. This pattern shows that the words at the end of lines two and four rhyme, but that the words at the end of lines one and three do not.

There are many different kinds of rhyme schemes. They depend on the number of lines per stanza and on which lines rhyme. It is not necessary that every line rhyme with some other line.

As you read the poems by Teasdale, ask yourself:

1. Which are the rhyming words in each poem?
2. What is the rhyme scheme of each poem?

WRITING CONNECTION

Think of a four-line stanza of a poem that you know. If you can't think of a poem, think of a song or nursery rhyme. Write it down. Then, using the form shown above, write the rhyme scheme.

READING FOCUS

Recognize Figures of Speech A figure of speech is an imaginative statement rather than a statement of fact. Instead of saying "The sun was setting," a writer might say "The red sun was pasted in the sky like a wafer." The statement is not literally true; it is an imaginative way to make the reader see the sunset.

Look for figures of speech in Teasdale's poems. Examine the suggested meaning of the words in each figure of speech to help determine the picture the poet is trying to create.

BARTER

by Sara Teasdale

Life has loveliness to sell,
    All beautiful and splendid things,
Blue waves whitened on a cliff,
    Soaring fire that sways and sings,
5   And children's faces looking up
Holding wonder like a cup.

Life has loveliness to sell,
    Music like a curve of gold,
Scent of pine trees in the rain,
10   Eyes that love you, arms that hold,
And for your spirit's still delight,
Holy thoughts that star the night.

Spend all you have for loveliness,
    Buy it and never count the cost;
15 For one white singing hour of peace
    Count many a year of strife well lost,
And for a breath of ecstasy
Give all you have been, or could be.

---

barter (BAHRT ur) trade; exchanging one thing for another
soaring (SAWR ing) rising or gliding high into the air
wonder (WUN dur) feeling of surprise, admiration, awe, caused by something strange, unexpected, or incredible
star (STAHR) to mark or set with stars, as a decoration
strife (STRYF) troublesome conflict; quarreling
ecstasy (EK stuh see) a feeling of overpowering joy; great delight

The Northern Lights, Sydney Laurence. Shelburne Museum, Shelburne, VT

THE FALLING STAR

by Sara Teasdale

I saw a star slide down the sky,
Blinding the north as it went by,
Too burning and too quick to hold,
Too lovely to be bought or sold,
Good only to make wishes on
And then forever to be gone.

THE LONG HILL

by Sara Teasdale

I must have passed the crest a while ago
    And now I am going down—
Strange to have crossed the crest and not to know,
    But the brambles were always catching the hem of my gown.

5   All the morning I thought how proud I should be
    To stand there straight as a queen,
Wrapped in the wind and the sun with the world under me—
    But the air was dull, there was little I could have seen.

It was nearly level along the beaten track
10   And the brambles caught in my gown—
But it's no use now to think of turning back,
    The rest of the way will be only going down.

Southwest Wind, Childe Hassam. Corbis Bettmann

---

crest (KREST) the top of anything; summit; ridge
brambles (BRAM bulz) prickly shrubs

I SHALL NOT CARE

by Sara Teasdale

When I am dead and over me bright April
    Shakes out her rain-drenched hair,
Tho' you should lean above me broken-hearted,
    I shall not care,

I shall have peace, as leafy trees are peaceful
    When rain bends down the bough,
And I shall be more silent and cold-hearted
    Than you are now.

A Summer Night, 1890, Winslow Homer. The Granger Collection

---

drenched (DRENCHT) soaked; wet all over
bough (BOU) a large branch of a tree

Sara Teasdale (1884–1933)

Readers of the hopeful poems of Sara Teasdale are tempted to see her as the happiest of human beings. Such readers forget to separate the *speaker* in a poem from the *poet*. Her life was often a troubled one. As she herself put it in a poem called "The Long Hill," after one has achieved a certain height in life, "The rest of the way will be only going down."

Born in St. Louis, Missouri, Sara Teasdale won early success as a poet. She published her first poems as a girl and her first book before she was twenty-five. For years she was in and out of love with a well-known poet named Vachel Lindsay. But she could not bring herself to accept the second-place role of a famous man's wife in the America of the time. Finally, Lindsay married someone else, and Teasdale rushed into a bad marriage with a businessman named Filsinger. In 1929 she divorced Filsinger and turned again to Lindsay. But it was too late. Lindsay killed himself in 1931, leaving her a lonely, disappointed woman. In 1933 Teasdale, too, committed suicide.

These sad facts help to make the point, once again, that the speaker in a poem is not to be confused with the poet. We can safely say, however, that Sara Teasdale must have known moments of great beauty. Perhaps she valued these moments all the more because of the numerous disappointments and tragedies in her life.

How did Sara Teasdale's life differ from the kind of life suggested by many of her poems?

Review the Selection

UNDERSTAND THE SELECTION

Recall

1. Which word in each stanza summarizes the theme of "Barter"?

2. In "The Falling Star," why can't you buy or sell a falling star?

3. In "The Long Hill," what has the speaker "passed" and "crossed"?

Infer

4. Of these four poems, which is the most positive or optimistic? Why?

5. What could "The Falling Star" symbolize?

6. What do the "hill" and the "crest" represent in "The Long Hill"?

7. In "I Shall Not Care," explain who "you" might be.

Apply

8. Select three things described in "Barter." Of what experiences does each remind you?

9. Is the mood of "The Falling Star" positive or negative? Explain.

10. Predict what the speaker is heading toward at the end of "The Long Hill."

Respond to Literature

By reading Teasdale's poems, could you tell when they were written? Explain.

WRITE ABOUT THE SELECTION

The last line of "The Long Hill" speaks of "the rest of the way . . . only going down." What do you think "the rest of the way" refers to? What does "only going down" mean? Think about what the hill represents and the kind of journey the speaker is making. Consider what might happen to the speaker from this point onward, Add a fourth stanza to "The Long Hill."

Prewriting Write down different ideas about what lies ahead for the speaker. Think about what kinds of things might happen and how the speaker might react.

Writing Transform these ideas into a fourth stanza of the poem. Make the new stanza four lines long, and try to match the rhythm of the rest of the poem. Do not be concerned about rhyme at this stage. Try to continue the thought process set forth in the poem, and bring the plot to an ultimate conclusion.

Revising Keeping the same thought content, revise the new stanza to follow either the rhyme scheme that has been established or a new pattern. At least two of the lines should rhyme. Using the "a-b . . ." method, indicate at the end what rhyme scheme you have used.

Proofreading Make sure that at least two of the four lines end in "perfect" rhymes. Check that the rhyme scheme is accurate and that your stanza has the right sound by reading it aloud.

THINK ABOUT RHYME SCHEME

Once a rhyme scheme has been established in the first stanza, it is usually followed in all subsequent stanzas. The pattern of the rhymes helps to give a certain form to each stanza and to the poem as a whole.

1. What is the rhyme scheme of "Barter"? What do you notice about the first and third lines of each stanza?

2. What is the rhyme scheme in "The Falling Star"?

3. What is the rhyme scheme of "The Long Hill"?

4. What is the rhyme scheme in "I Shall Not Care"? Does the poem contain internal rhymes as well as end rhymes?

5. Find three instances in these poems in which the rhyming words have different numbers of syllables.

READING FOCUS

Recognize Figures of Speech Choose one figure of speech from any of the four poems in this selection. Paraphrase it as a plain statement of fact and compare the two versions. Why do you think Teasdale chose to use the figure of speech rather than the literal statement? What does it contribute to the poem that the literal statement does not?

DEVELOP YOUR VOCABULARY

A noun names a person, a place, or a thing. A verb names an action or a state of being. Some words can be used as both nouns and verbs. Their part of speech depends on how they are used in a sentence. For example: Joe and Emma have to *look* for the book, You should have seen the *look* on his face. In these sentences, *look* is used first as a verb, then as a noun. The way in which any word is classified as a part of speech depends on the way it is used in a sentence.

Review the meaning of the following words in a dictionary. State which way each is used in the context of the poem. Then write two sentences for each of the words, using the word as a noun in one sentence and as a verb in the other. At the end of each sentence, tell how the word has been used.

1. barter
2. waves
3. wonder
4. star
5. cost
6. crest

Irony occurs when the intent or tone of the words used is exactly opposite of what the actual meaning of the words say. For example, if someone asks you if you mind having a flu shot, you may reply, "I can hardly wait!" Are you really eager to have the shot, or are you dreading it? Your words say you are eager, but your tone of voice expresses a feeling that is the opposite of eager. This example explains one kind of irony.

Another kind is called **irony of situation**. This term refers to events that turn out to be the opposite of what you expect or consider appropriate. Suppose, for example, that someone taunts you for some misfortune. If that person, without knowing it, is at that moment suffering the same misfortune, that is irony of situation.

As you read the poem, ask yourself:
1. Which type of irony does the poem tell about?
2. Does the author offer any comment about the events?

WRITING CONNECTION

Assume that a friend has just broken a favorite possession of yours. Write what you would say that would show a contrast between what your words are and what you mean.

READING FOCUS

Make Inferences From Connotations
Connotations suggest connections beyond a word's literal meaning. For example, you might describe a man's profile as "carved from flint." The phrase suggests a quality of hardness and harshness that the word *strong* does not convey. As you read "Richard Cory," think about the connotations of each word used to describe him. What inferences can you make about Richard Cory from these connotations?

RICHARD CORY

by Edwin Arlington Robinson

Whenever Richard Cory went down town,
We people on the pavement looked at him:
He was a gentleman from sole to crown,
Clean favored, and imperially slim.

5   And he was always quietly arrayed,
And he was always human when he talked;
But still he fluttered pulses when he said,
"Good-morning," and he glittered when he
        walked.

And he was rich—yes, richer than a king—
10 And admirably schooled in every grace:
In fine, we thought that he was everything
To make us wish that we were in his place.

So on we worked, and waited for the light,
And went without the meat, and cursed the
        bread;
15 And Richard Cory, one calm summer night,
Went home and put a bullet through his head.

---

favored (FAY vurd) featured
imperially (im PIR ee ul ee) supremely
arrayed (uh RAYD) dressed
admirably (AD mur uh blee) excellently
fine (FYN) summary; conclusion

Review the Selection

Recall

1. What type of physical build did Richard Cory have?

2. What are the only words he is quoted as saying in the poem?

3. In what season did he kill himself?

Infer

4. How do you think Richard Cory traveled about? Explain why you have this impression.

5. Paraphrase the expression "from sole to crown."

6. Why do you think he "fluttered pulses" when he spoke to people?

7. Why do you think people "cursed the bread"?

Apply

8. How do you think Cory would have treated you if you met? Why?

9. Select three adjectives to describe this man.

10. Why do you think Richard Cory killed himself?

Respond to Literature

Suppose that Richard Cory had lived in a country that had royalty. What do you think his position would have been?

WRITE ABOUT THE SELECTION

"Richard Cory" not only has a surprise ending, but a shocking and violent one. The last line stands out in stark contrast to everything that has preceded it. It changes the meaning and impact of the poem.

The image we are given of this man through the first fifteen lines of the poem gives us no reason to suspect the outcome or climax.

Have you ever heard the saying "All that glitters is not gold"? Think about its meaning as it applies to the poem. Write a fifth stanza to "Richard Cory" that uses the idea of that saying. Expand on the idea and explain it as best you can.

Prewriting Think about how this saying can be applied to the plot of the poem. Jot down your thoughts in note form.

Writing Arrange your notes and write a fifth stanza to the poem. This will be the resolution—following the climax—of the plot. In this resolution stanza, describe how the saying relates to the climax. Write four lines. Have at least two of them end in rhyming words.

Revising Follow the same rhyming scheme by having the last words of the first and third lines rhyme as well as those of the second and fourth lines.

Proofreading Check your stanza for spelling errors. Also make sure that you followed the *abab* rhyme scheme.

THINK ABOUT IRONY

Irony is a common form of expression in literature—as in life. It is an effective way of contrasting the literal meaning of words with the opposite meaning behind those words. Irony of situation refers to events that are contrary to what the reader or characters in the literary work expect or believe to be appropriate.

1. Which sort of irony does Robinson use in his poem?

2. What characteristics of Richard Cory made him someone with whom people would like to change places?

3. Does the author have any comments to make about the ending of the poem? If so, what is his message?

4. What does Robinson mean when he says that Richard Cory "glittered when he walked"?

5. Does the poem suggest to you any general lessons about life? If so, what are they?

READING FOCUS

Make Inferences From Connotations List some of the words and phrases used to describe Richard Cory. Identify what these words and phrases connote beyond their literal definitions. Then explain what you infer about Cory from the language used to describe him.

DEVELOP YOUR VOCABULARY

Robinson creates some memorable images in "Richard Cory." Note particularly his choice of verbs. Cory wasn't merely *dressed*; he was *arrayed*. He didn't *make pulses skip a beat*; he *fluttered pulses*. Other people didn't *complain* about their lot; they *cursed* the bread.

Verbs are important in writing. Since they carry the action, strong, vivid verbs can make your writing lively.

Choose the most vivid verbs from the list in parentheses:

1. The thief (*walked, slunk, crept, went*) away in the night.

2. Alfonso (*tiptoed, moved, walked*) across the library.

3. My brother (*devoured, gobbled, ate*) the snacks eagerly.

4. The fire (*flamed, burned, blazed*) hotly in the fireplace.

5. The child (*pleaded, asked, requested*) not to be punished.

WRITING APPLICATIONS

Write About Character

The Civil War brought about a change in the American economy. America switched from a predominantly agricultural economy to a manufacturing one. The literature of the age, however, reflected both city and country life.

Select three characters from the selections in this unit. Discuss how each of them reflects life in the city or country, whichever is appropriate during this period.

Prewriting Select the three characters. With each name as the heading, make a list of words and phrases that describe their qualities (as opposed to physical characteristics). Make a list for each character, circling the qualities the three have in common, and checking off the ones they do not share with the others.

Writing Using your lists of descriptions, write a paragraph comparing the similarities of these three characters. Explain how they are alike, despite the different settings in which they are found. Include at least two descriptive words or phrases from the text for each one.

Revising Check to see that you have accurately described the characters. Change vague adjectives and verbs to vivid ones.

Proofreading Since you have used quotes from the text, check that your usage of commas, quotation marks, and capitalization is correct.

Write About Elements in Fiction

In the section entitled "Focus on Fiction," six literary skills were discussed. Choose any of the selections in this unit, except the annotated one, and write a critical analysis of its four basic elements: setting, character, plot, and theme.

Prewriting Organize the facts about these elements by making a three-column chart. First, list the "5 Ws": *who, what, when, where, why*. Next to each of these, write which of the four literary elements is associated with it. Then, in the third column, write down the appropriate information you have chosen.

Writing Use your "5 Ws" chart to relate each element to the selection. Include the following points in your analysis:

Setting—What is the time and place?

Character—Identify the protagonist and antagonist. Are they *round* or *flat*?

Plot—What is the nature of the conflict? What is the climax?

Theme—What is the meaning, or message? Why do you think this?

Revising Expand the "5 Ws" by analyzing the climax. Tell at what point it occurs and whether it is followed by falling action leading to a resolution.

Proofreading Read over your analysis. Make sure that all sentences are complete and that your page is divided properly into paragraphs.

Vocabulary

A **contraction** is a shortened form of one or two words. Two words may be combined by replacing one or more letters with an apostrophe.

> *Examples:* you're = you are
> that's = that is
> I'd = I had
> how's = how is
> he'll = he will
> isn't = is not
> won't = will not

In the annotated story in this unit, it was noted that the language used by the characters was a dialect. A dialect was used to provide regional, social, and character clues.

The following words from passages in the story are contractions. Copy the list. Next to each, write the word or words that the contraction stands for and indicate whether it is standard English or colloquial.

1. s'pose	**11.** 'cause
2. you've	**12.** don't
3. didn't	**13.** an'
4. 'twould	**14.** we've
5. I'll	**15.** I'm
6. there's	**16.** ain't
7. you'll	**17.** what's
8. we'd	**18.** it's
9. hadn't	**19.** she'll
10. can't	**20.** I've

Grammar, Usage, and Mechanics

When you are writing or quoting, you should know when to use capital letters. If the sentence contains a direct quotation, capitalize the first word of the quotation. Do not capitalize the first word of an indirect quotation.

> *Examples:* All at once, I heard Chuck say, "The circus is in town."
>
> All at once, I heard Chuck say that the circus is in town.

In writing lines of poetry, capitalize the first word of each line, unless the poet does not follow this procedure.

> *Example:*
> I measure every grief I meet
> With analytic eyes,
> I wonder if it weighs like mine
> Or has an easier size.
> —Emily Dickinson

Capitalize these sentences and quotations correctly.

1. "nevertheless, i will go," Andy said.

2. soon Lois said that the mail had come.

3. my friend said, "this book is good."

4. there was water in the pool.

UNIT 4 *Review*

In an earlier lesson you were asked to read aloud. In that lesson, it was suggested that you choose something to read aloud that you especially liked. In this lesson that is also one of the suggestions. However, since this time you will be asked to read a poem aloud, there are additional ideas that will make the experience an enjoyable one for you and for your audience.

1. Start with the basics—select a poem that you *like*!

2. Read the poem at least three times: the first time to get acquainted with it, the second time to identify any words that may be difficult, and the third time to grasp the meaning of the poem.

3. Decide what the mood of the poem is. This is important because you want your voice to convey the feeling of the poem. Decide if the poem has different moods. If so, you will want to adapt your voice to fit those moods.

4. Practice reading the poem aloud until your voice perfectly reflects the mood(s) of the poem. You want to find the right voice; so ask someone to listen to you while you read. Ask for their suggestions on how you might improve your reading.

5. If possible, tape-record yourself reading the poem. Listen to your voice as you say the words of the poem. Pay attention to the pauses you make. Ask yourself if your voice sounds natural and whether or not the emotion of the poem is coming through.

6. Once you have prepared your poem for reading aloud, practice it several times. You don't need to memorize it, but you want to be thoroughly familiar with it.

7. When you present your poem to your class, be sure you can see your audience and that you maintain some eye contact. This will involve your listener and it will help you pay attention to your body language.

Now, look back at the poems in this unit and choose one of them to present orally. With your teacher's permission, you may select a poem from another source if you prefer. At any rate, follow the guidelines above to help you prepare for reading a poem aloud, The important thing is to choose a poem whose meaning is special to you. Select a poem you really like and share it.

CRITICAL THINKING

Part-Whole Relationships   A **whole** is all of something. A whole is made up of **parts**. Look at a piano, for example. It is made up of keys, pedals, strings, hammers, felts, and a wooden case. It takes all of these parts working together to make up the whole that is a piano.

Understanding the relationship of part to whole is the key to understanding anything—a poem, an idea, a jet engine, a way of doing something, an organization, a clock mechanism, a football team, the plot of a story, a car, the recipe for a cake, a family, an insect, or a flower.

Literature often deals with part-whole relationships. Consider Walt Whitman's "I Hear America Singing," for example. In this poem, Whitman lists the songs of various American workers. Each song, as he sees it, is a part that contributes to the whole of America—to the varied carols he hears.

To understand a piece of literature, you must see how all the parts work together as a whole. Choose any selection in this unit. List as many of the elements that contribute to it as you can. Then answer the following questions.

1. Which are major elements of the whole and which are minor elements?

2. If any element were changed, how would the other elements be affected? Would the nature of the work change?

EFFECTIVE STUDYING

Summarizing   You will often need to prepare a summary of your work. A **summary** is a brief digest of the main ideas in a lecture, a performance, or a piece of writing. Do not confuse summarizing with rewording; a summary condenses the ideas, it does not simply restate them.

Here is how to write a summary:

1. Before writing:
   - Read the material carefully.
   - Look for the main idea or ideas.
   - Topic sentences and key words in the material may be of help.

2. Writing:
   - Write down the main idea or ideas in your own words, but be exact.
   - Be brief; remember, you are trying "to make a long story short."
   - Omit unimportant ideas.
   - Combine ideas when doing so will make the summary shorter or clearer.

3. After writing:
   - Review your summary to be sure that all the necessary information has been included.
   - Clarify any ideas that have not been expressed clearly.

Test Preparation

Summarizing your class notes is a good way to prepare for a test. You might also summarize a piece of writing to answer an essay question.

The Modern View

When all our hopes are sown on stony ground,
And we have yielded up the thought of gain,
Long after our last songs have lost their sound
We may come back, we may come back again.
—Arna Bontemps

Janitor's Holiday, Paul Sample. The Metropolitan Museum of Art,
Arthur Hoppock Hearn Fund

LITERARY HIGHLIGHTS

1916 Carl Sandburg
publishes *Chicago Poems*.

1926 Langston Hughes's
first poetry is published.

1913 Robert
Frost's first volume
of poetry, *A Boy's
Will*, appears.

1918 Willa Cather's novel,
My Antonia, is published.

1910   1915   1920   1925

1918 World War I
armistice is signed.

1920 Nineteenth Amendment
gives women the right to vote.

1927 Charles Lindbergh flies
nonstop from New York to Paris.

HISTORICAL HIGHLIGHTS

The Modern View

You probably know people who lived in America between 1915 and
1946. Have you ever asked them what their lives were like during
those years? In those three decades, Americans went through two
world wars, a period of great prosperity, and a period of terrible
economic hardship.

■ WORLD WAR I AND THE 1920s

In 1914, World War I erupted and spread quickly across Europe. Three
years later the United States was swept into the conflict. Americans'
struggles and sacrifices at home, in factories, and on distant battlefields
helped to win the war in 1918. After World War I, many people wanted
a better life. They dedicated themselves to making money and having
fun. The decade became known as the Roaring Twenties.

■ THE LOST GENERATION

What is your feeling about this new attitude in the United States in the
1920s? Some U.S. writers were impatient with it. They believed that the
war had forever altered their lives. They felt alienated, or cut off, from
a country whose values they no longer shared. These writers became
known as the Lost Generation. Some of them chose to leave the United
States and live in Europe.

■ POETRY IN THE 1920s

In the 1920s, some American poets became dissatisfied with traditional
poetry. Robert Frost and Carl Sandburg developed new kinds of poetry
using repetition and colloquial, or everyday, speech. They stopped using
nature as a kind of romantic inspiration. Nature, they believed, was
simply a powerful force, neither good nor bad. They helped to create
modern poetry.

1929 William Faulkner publishes *The Sound and the Fury.*

1932 Pearl Buck receives Pulitzer Prize for *The Good Earth.*

1939 John Steinbeck's *The Grapes of Wrath* appears.

1940 Richard Wright publishes *Native Son.*

1945 Gwendolyn Brooks's first book of poems is published.

1930   **1935**   **1940**   **1945**

1929 Stock market crash begins world-wide depression.

1939 Germany invades Poland; World War II begins.

1941 Japan's attack on Pearl Harbor brings U.S. into World War II.

1945 Two atomic bombs dropped on Japan end war.

■ SOCIAL CHANGE

In the 1920s, a group of African American writers decided to use literature as a peaceful instrument of social change. Many joined a New York City movement that became known as the Harlem Renaissance. In an explosion of creativity, African American writers and poets like Langston Hughes transferred the sounds and rhythms of music, especially jazz, to their own work. Their writing not only protested social injustice and racial discrimination; it also expressed pride in African American achievements and culture.

In 1920, women were finally recognized as United States citizens and given the right to vote. The growing awareness of women's rights produced important new literature by women writers, including Gwendolyn Brooks in Chicago; Eudora Welty in the South; and Edna St. Vincent Millay in New York City. Yet each of these writers was able to generalize her experiences and express essential truths about all people.

■ DEPRESSION AND WAR

On October 29, 1929, the stock market crashed, triggering the Great Depression. For the next 12 years, millions of Americans lived in poverty. Popular entertainment provided some relief. People flocked to movie theaters to witness the "talking picture."

By 1930, one out of three American homes had a radio. In 1937 millions of Americans heard President Roosevelt denounce the dictators in Europe and Japan. The threat of another world war was growing, and people were anxious. Listening to a realistic radio drama, *The War of the Worlds*, in 1938, thousands of people thought Martians had landed.

Unfortunately, Americans did not have to wait very long for real war to break out. In 1941, the United States was propelled into World War II, which lasted until 1945 and cost millions of lives.

As you read the selections, ask how they relate to your own life.

Learn About

CHARACTER

A **character** in literature is the representation in words of a person, or in some instances, an animal. Writers reveal the traits, or personality, of a character through description, dialogue, actions, and commentary. Often, writers present direct information about a character. This may include a description of a character's physical appearance. The words a character uses may clearly tell what he or she is thinking and feeling.

Writers also present less obvious, indirect information, called **character clues**. You can look closely at what a character does, says, feels, and thinks, and how other characters talk about and act toward that character, to make intelligent guesses about that character's personality.

As you read "A Day's Wait," ask yourself:

1. What kind of character is Schatz?
2. What actions does he take that reveal his character?

READING FOCUS

Identify Imagery Imagery consists of words that describe what you might feel, hear, see, taste, or smell if you were in the scene. Writers use imagery to make the readers feel as though they are experiencing the story or poem first-hand. Look for imagery as you read the story.

WRITING CONNECTION

Write a paragraph that reveals a strong character trait of a person you know well. Be sure to include enough specific information to help your reader decide what this person is really like.

A DAY'S WAIT

by Ernest Hemingway

He came into the room to shut the windows while we were still in bed and I saw he looked ill. He was shivering, his face was white, and he walked slowly as though it ached to move.

"What's the matter, Schatz?"

"I've got a headache."

"You better go back to bed."

"No. I'm all right."

"You go to bed. I'll see you when I'm dressed."

But when I came downstairs he was dressed, sitting by the fire, looking a very sick and miserable boy of nine years. When I put my hand on his forehead I knew he had a fever.

"You go up to bed," I said, "you're sick."

"I'm all right," he said.

When the doctor came he took the boy's temperature.

"What is it?" I asked him.

"One hundred and two."

Downstairs, the doctor left three different medicines in different colored capsules with instructions for giving them. One was to bring down the fever, another a purgative, the third to overcome an acid condition. The germs of influenza can only exist in an acid condition, he explained. He seemed to know all about influenza and said there was nothing to worry about if the fever did not go above one hundred and four degrees. This was a light epidemic of flu and there was no danger if you avoided pneumonia.

Back in the room I wrote the boy's temperature down and made a note of the time to give the various capsules.

---

purgative (PUR guh tiv) strong laxative
influenza (in floo EN zuh) disease usually called "flu"

"Do you want me to read to you?"

"All right. If you want to," said the boy. His face was very white and there were dark areas under his eyes. He lay still in the bed and seemed very detached from what was going on.

I read aloud from Howard Pyle's *Book of Pirates*; but I could see he was not following what I was reading.

"How do you feel, Schatz?" I asked him.

"Just the same, so far," he said.

I sat at the foot of the bed and read to myself while I waited for it to be time to give another capsule. It would have been natural for him to go to sleep, but when I looked up he was looking at the foot of the bed, looking very strangely.

"Why don't you try to go to sleep? I'll wake you up for the medicine."

"I'd rather stay awake."

After a while he said to me, "You don't have to stay in here with me, Papa, if it bothers you."

"It doesn't bother me."

"No, I mean you don't have to stay if it's going to bother you."

I thought perhaps he was a little lightheaded and after giving him the prescribed capsules at eleven o'clock I went out for a while.

It was a bright, cold day, the ground covered with a sleet that had frozen so that it seemed as if all the bare trees, the bushes, the cut brush and all the grass and the bare ground had been varnished with ice. I took the young Irish setter for a little walk up the road and along a frozen creek, but it was difficult to stand or walk on the glassy surface and the red dog slipped and slithered and I fell twice, hard, once dropping my gun and having it slide away over the ice.

We flushed a covey of quail under a high clay bank with overhanging brush and I killed two as they went out of sight over the top of the bank. Some of the covey lit in trees, but most of them scattered into brush piles and it was necessary to jump on the ice-coated mounds of brush several times before they would flush. Coming out while you were poised unsteadily on the icy, springy

---

slither (SLITH ur) slip and slide
flush (FLUSH) drive birds or animals from hiding place
covey (KUV ee) flock of birds

Adirondacks, Winslow Homer. Corbis Bettmann

brush they made difficult shooting and I killed two, missed five, and started back pleased to have found a covey close to the house and happy there were so many left to find on another day.

At the house they said the boy had refused to let anyone come into the room.

"You can't come in," he said. "You mustn't get what I have."

I went up to him and found him in exactly the position I had left him, white-faced, but with the tops of his cheeks flushed by the fever, staring still, as he had stared, at the foot of the bed.

I took his temperature.

"What is it?"

"Something like a hundred," I said. It was one hundred and two and four tenths.

"It was a hundred and two," he said.

"Who said so?"

"The doctor."

"Your temperature is all right," I said. "It's nothing to worry about."

"I don't worry," he said, "but I can't keep from thinking."

"Don't think," I said. "Just take it easy."

"I'm taking it easy," he said and looked straight ahead. He was evidently holding tight onto himself about something.

"Take this with water."

"Do you think it will do any good?"

"Of course it will."

I sat down and opened the *Pirate* book and commenced to read, but I could see he was not following, so I stopped.

"About what time do you think I'm going to die?" he asked.

"What?"

"About how long will it be before I die?"

"You aren't going to die. What's the matter with you?"

"Oh, yes, I am. I heard him say a hundred and two."

"People don't die with a fever of one hundred and two. That's a silly way to talk."

"I know they do. At school in France the boys told me you can't live with forty-four degrees. I've got a hundred and two."

He had been waiting to die all day, ever since nine o'clock in the morning.

"You poor Schatz," I said. "Poor old Schatz. It's like miles and kilometers. You aren't going to die. That's a different thermometer. On that thermometer thirty-seven is normal. On this kind it's ninety-eight."

"Are you sure?"

"Absolutely," I said. "It's like miles and kilometers. You know, like how many kilometers we make when we do seventy miles in the car?"

"Oh," he said.

But his gaze at the foot of the bed relaxed slowly. The hold over himself relaxed too, finally, and the next day it was very slack and he cried very easily at little things that were of no importance.

---

commence (kuh MENS) begin

Ernest Hemingway (1899–1961)

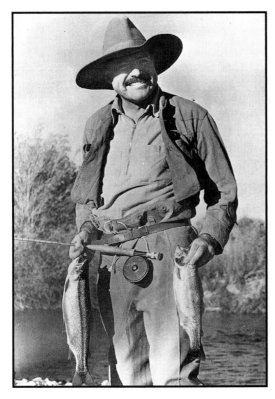

Quick! List three facts about a famous living American writer.

Could you do it? Maybe. But if you'd lived during the time of Ernest Hemingway, you probably could have done it easily. Wherever he went and whatever he did, Hemingway was always big news. His name was often in the headlines:

HEMINGWAY BREAKS NOSE IN BOXING RING
PLANE CRASH KILLS HEMINGWAY IN AFRICA
GOOD NEWS: HEMINGWAY ALIVE!
HEMINGWAY MARRIES FOR FOURTH TIME
HEMINGWAY YACHT IN U-BOAT CHASE
GUN ACCIDENT INJURES HEMINGWAY

A bear of a man, Hemingway photographed well. All America knew what he looked like. He seemed always in action: skiing in Switzerland, hunting in Africa, fishing from his private yacht, risking his life as a reporter on distant war fronts. Yet, somehow during his active life, he took the time to write the stories and novels that won him the highest honor a writer can earn, the Nobel Prize.

"All you have to do is, write one true sentence," Hemingway discovered when he was starting out. "Write the truest sentence you know." That one sentence, he found, would lead to another, to a paragraph, to a story. He disliked fancy writing; he wanted it pure and simple, lifelike and honest. Do you think any other author of our century has had a greater influence upon modern American writers than Ernest Hemingway?

How did Hemingway differ from the stereotype you may have in mind of a "famous author"?

Review the Selection

UNDERSTAND THE SELECTION

Recall

1. Between what times of day does "A Day's Wait" take place?

2. At what object in his room does Schatz constantly gaze?

3. What is Schatz's temperature the second time it is taken?

Infer

4. What is the first clue that Schatz is worried about more than his fever?

5. Why does Schatz suggest to his father that he may leave the room?

6. How does the reader know when Schatz has stopped worrying?

7. Why does Schatz cry very easily the next day?

Apply

8. If you were Schatz, what thoughts would run through your mind?

9. What might have happened if Schatz had heard what the doctor really said?

10. Choose two other appropriate titles for "A Day's Wait."

Respond to Literature

What events in the early twentieth century might have prompted Hemingway to write this story of courage?

WRITE ABOUT THE SELECTION

"A Day's Wait" is about a boy's courage in the face of what he thinks is overwhelming danger. The author implies that a person's true character is revealed only when he or she is facing ultimate peril. This would still hold true if the danger were only in the person's mind. Do you agree with this idea? Are there other circumstances in which a person's true character can be revealed? Think of other circumstances in which someone's true character is revealed and write a short paragraph that explains your views.

Prewriting   Freewrite an informal list of situations, such as an argument, a sports competition, or a date, in which people are apt to reveal their true characters. The incident could be something ordinary that happens every day. Then, freewrite specific character traits that may surface in the particular situation you choose to write about.

Writing   Use your freewriting lists to write a paragraph that explains one situation, other than danger, in which a person's true character is revealed.

Revising   Reread your paragraph and decide whether any specific information can be added to make your explanation clearer to a reader. Have you made clear the reasons behind people's actions?

Proofreading   Read over your paragraph and check for errors.

THINK ABOUT CHARACTER

A **character** is a person or animal in a story, poem, or drama. Readers infer what a character's words, actions, feelings, and thoughts really show about his or her personality. Readers may also learn about a character through the things other characters say about him or her.

1. What kind of a person is Schatz?

2. Writers usually describe a character's physical appearance. Yet, in the story, Hemingway only describes Schatz's face, and then, briefly. What other character clues help you to determine what Schatz is really like?

3. Select three of Schatz's statements and explain how each contributes to your understanding of his character. Explain what each statement revealed about him.

4. Understanding a character's personality allows you to predict how he or she may react to other events. When he is older, how might Schatz react to a physically dangerous fire or storm? Explain your answer.

READING FOCUS

Identify Imagery As you read, you were able to identify words that described sights, sounds, smells, tastes, and feelings of touch. Choose an example of imagery from the story that particularly appealed to you. Explain why you chose it.

DEVELOP YOUR VOCABULARY

A **synonym** is a word that has the same or nearly the same meaning as another word. For instance, Schatz is described as being *detached*—not really involved with what is going on in his room. The author might have used the words *distracted* or *preoccupied* as synonyms for *detached*.

Read the sentences below and choose the best synonym for the *italicized* word.

1. He could fall and *slither* across the frozen pond.
   - **a.** pause
   - **b.** glide
   - **c.** relax
   - **d.** listen
   - **e.** stumble

2. Hunters often use dogs to *flush* their prey from hiding places.
   - **a.** dislodge
   - **b.** smell
   - **c.** force
   - **d.** recover
   - **e.** convince

3. We were startled by a *covey* of pigeons . . .
   - **a.** handful
   - **b.** group
   - **c.** feather
   - **d.** line
   - **e.** regiment

4. Each time that his father *commenced* reading, Schatz would turn away.
   - **a.** halted
   - **b.** interrupted
   - **c.** started
   - **d.** paused
   - **e.** ended

Learn About

LYRIC POETRY

Of the many types of poetry written, the lyric is perhaps the most varied in structure, subject matter, and mood. Some characteristics that **lyric poems** have in common, however, are these: they are brief and imaginative; they have "melody;" they express the personal, emotional feelings and thoughts of a single speaker.

Lyric poems make use of many poetic techniques to achieve their musical quality. Two such techniques are repetition and alliteration. **Repetition**, using the same or similar words over again, may occur at regular or irregular places in the poem. Alliteration is also a device of repetition. In **alliteration**, it is the initial consonant (or sometimes vowel) sounds of nearby words that are repeated, as in "*Bend* the *bow*; let the *bolt burst* the *bubble* apart."

As you read the poems, ask yourself:

1. What unified emotional impression does each poem make?
2. What poetic devices are used in each poem?

WRITING CONNECTION

Using alliteration, write a four-line stanza in which at least two words in each line begin with the same sound.

READING FOCUS

Evaluate the Writer's Purpose Evaluating the writer's purpose means figuring out why the author wrote something. This will give you insight into the deeper meanings of the work. Also, as a reader you can evaluate whether you agree or disagree with the author's attitude toward the subject. As you read each of these poems, decide what the poet's purpose is and whether you agree with it.

Lament

by Edna St. Vincent Millay

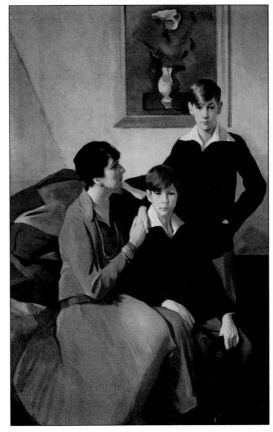

Listen, children:
Your father is dead.
From his old coats
I'll make you little jackets;
5   I'll make you little trousers
From his old pants.
There'll be in his pockets
Things he used to put there,
Keys and pennies
10   Covered with tobacco;
Dan shall have the pennies
To save in his bank;
Anne shall have the keys
To make a pretty noise with.
15   Life must go on,
And the dead be forgotten;
Life must go on,
Though good men die;
Anne, eat your breakfast;
20   Dan, take your medicine;
Life must go on;
I forget just why.

My Family, Leopold Seyffert. The Brooklyn Museum

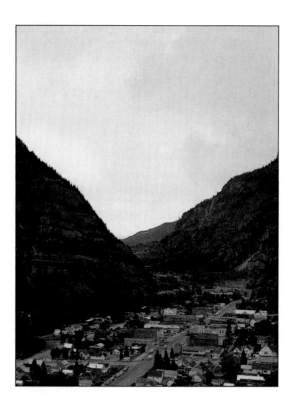

Afternoon on a Hill

by Edna St. Vincent Millay

I will be the gladdest thing
    Under the sun!
I will touch a hundred flowers
    And not pick one.
5 I will look at cliffs and clouds
    With quiet eyes,
Watch the wind bow down the grass,
    And the grass rise.
10 And when lights begin to show
    Up from the town,
I will mark which must be mine,
    And then start down!

Edna St. Vincent Millay (1892–1950)

Edna St. Vincent Millay was a writer who wanted to tell the truth about life and love from a woman's point of view. In the 1920s, Millay became a symbol of life, love, and a newfound freedom. She would start a poem:

> What lips my lips have kissed, and
> where, and why,
> I have forgotten . . .

In the 1920s, this was scandalous, but for many people delightfully so. Curious poetry lovers flocked to her poetry readings across the country. There they found a small, attractive young woman with golden red hair, a sensitive voice, and a dignified manner. They also found that Millay's reputation as a symbol of bright, adventurous youth was only part of the picture. Most of her best poems did not concern love at all, and she often spoke of sorrow, hardship, and loss. It is upon this reputation that her fame rests.

Hardship and loss were hardly strangers to the young poet. Her early life on the coast of Maine had been generally happy but far from easy. Her parents were divorced when she was a young girl, and for years her mother supported the family on what she could earn as a nurse. Although Millay was an active, prize-winning student in high school, there was no money for college. Accepting this loss as a fact of life, she continued to work at her poetry. A long poem called "Renascence," written when she was nineteen, brought her early fame. Then came college, success, years of travel, and a good marriage. Much of her later work reveals an inner anguish caused by what she saw as human injustice and stupidity. Her greatest regret was that even a perfect poem can do little to remake an imperfect world.

Why do you think Millay's poems were so shocking in the 1920s?

Review the Selection

UNDERSTAND THE SELECTION

Recall

1. What is the subject of "Lament"?

2. What items does the wife retrieve from her husband's pockets?

3. Identify the elements of nature mentioned in "Afternoon on a Hill."

Infer

4. How old do you think the two children in "Lament" are? Why?

5. Has the speaker in "Lament" accepted her husband's death? Explain.

6. Why is "Afternoon on a Hill" written in the future tense?

7. In "Afternoon on a Hill," what do you think "quiet eyes" means?

Apply

8. How would you characterize the mother in "Lament"?

9. On one level, "Afternoon on a Hill" is about someone thinking about spending an afternoon on a hill. What is another meaning of the poem?

10. Why will the speaker in "Lament" remember that life must go on?

Respond to Literature

How does the subject matter of "Lament" reflect the changing roles of women in U.S. society during the 1920s?

WRITE ABOUT THE SELECTION

From reading "Afternoon on a Hill," you have seen that a poem need not be about an extraordinary event or experience. What makes an ordinary event come alive however, is the arrangement of vivid, descriptive words. Almost any event or experience can be made significant through the use of interpretation and creativity. Write a short poem about an incident in your own life this week, that at first seemed unimportant or insignificant.

Prewriting Brainstorm an event you experienced this week. It could be one of the following: a small act of kindness; the joy of watching a sports team win; or perhaps discovering a new side to a friend's personality. Then decide what rhythm or flow you think will best communicate the experience in a poem.

Writing Now, write a short poem that shows the true importance of something that happened to you this week. In it, try to have the poem's rhythm match the rhythm of the event. Use Millay's poems as models if you wish.

Revising When you revise your poem, read it out loud to determine if the way the words flow contributes to how you feel about the event. Your words should capture the mood of the event.

Proofreading Read your poem and check for errors. Use the correct line format for poetry.

THINK ABOUT LYRIC POETRY

Lyric poems may have any of a number of rhythmic patterns and may be either rhymed or unrhymed. Sometimes rhythms can be varied by the kinds of consonants the poet chooses. For instance, consonants like *l*, *m*, *n*, and *r* can be drawn out to produce a smooth rhythm when spoken aloud. Consonants like *b*, *d*, *k*, *p*, and *t*, however, create a quickened or staccato rhythm.

1. What rhythmic devices can you find in the first poem you read, "Lament"?

2. What rhythmic devices do you find in the second poem "Afternoon on a Hill"?

3. How does the repetition of the sentence "Life must go on" in "Lament" contribute to the meaning of the poem?

4. Explain the sequence of events in "Afternoon on a Hill."

5. Who is the speaker in each poem?

READING FOCUS

Evaluate the Writer's Purpose What do you think the poet's purpose is in "Lament"? What is the poet's purpose in writing "Afternoon on a Hill"? Provide details from each poem to support your responses.

DEVELOP YOUR VOCABULARY

Figurative language is a way of putting words and phrases together to create a meaning that is different from the dictionary meaning of the individual words. For instance, in "The reader *jumped* to the wrong conclusion," the word *jump* is used figuratively to suggest that the reader assumed something too quickly.

Words or phrases that mean exactly what they say are called **literal language**. In "The track runner *jumped* the hurdles successfully," the words mean exactly, or literally, what they say.

For each pair of sentences below, determine which sentence uses figurative and which sentence uses literal language.

1. The substitute teacher *saddled* us with too much homework.

2. The cowboy *saddled* his spotted pony and began his journey.

3. The pianist *struck the right notes*.

4. The politician *struck the right notes* in her reelection speech.

Learn About

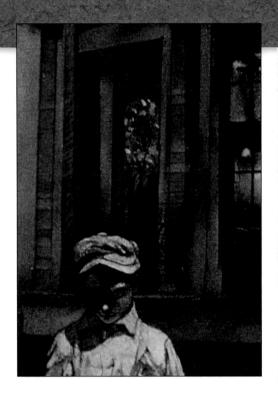

SETTING

Setting is the time and place in which fiction, such as a short story, poem, or play, occurs. You can think of setting as the total environment, or the created world, in which a work of literature happens.

To determine setting, look for word clues that tell *where* and *when* the story takes place. For example, look for specific words and phrases that describe the location and scenery of the story. To understand the *when* of a story—its time frame—read for details that show the historical time period, season of year, and time of day. Remember, too, that story settings can change over time.

Setting is crucial because it can affect people and events in a story. Setting can force a character to act or feel in certain ways. For example, you would expect a person who is caught in a terrible snowstorm to behave differently than one who is relaxing on a warm, sunny beach.

As you read "home" ask yourself:

1. What is the setting of the story?
2. How does the setting affect the character's behavior?

READING FOCUS

Recognize Implied Theme A theme is the message that a story is written to convey. An implied theme is one that you must infer from the work as a whole. As you read "home," think about the larger message the author may be sending.

WRITING CONNECTION

Writers use details to help the reader visualize a setting. Write a brief description of a favorite place and include vivid and specific details.

home

ADAPTED

by Gwendolyn Brooks

What had been wanted was this always, this always to last, the talking softly on this porch, with the snake plant in the jardiniere in the southwest corner, and the obstinate slip from Aunt Eppie's magnificent Michigan fern at the left side of the friendly door. Mama, Maud Martha, and Helen rocked slowly in their rocking chairs, and looked at the late afternoon light on the lawn, and at the emphatic iron of the fence and at the poplar tree. These things might soon be theirs no longer. Those shafts and pools of light, the tree, the graceful iron, might soon be viewed possessively by different eyes.

Papa was to have gone that noon, during his lunch hour, to the office of the Home Owners' Loan. If he had not succeeded in getting another extension, they would be leaving this house in which they had lived for more than 14 years. There was little hope. The Home Owners' Loan was hard. They sat, making their plans.

"We'll be moving into a nice flat somewhere," said Mama. "Somewhere on South Park, or Michigan, or in Washington Park Court." Those flats, as the girls and Mama knew well, were burdens on wages twice the size of Papa's. This was not mentioned now.

"They're much prettier than this old house," said Helen. "I have friends that wouldn't come down this far for anything, unless they were in a taxi."

Yesterday, Maud Martha would have attacked her. Tomorrow she might. Today she said nothing. She merely gazed at a little hopping robin in the tree, her tree, and tried to keep her eyes dry.

---

jardiniere (jahr duh NIR) a decorative flower pot or stand
obstinate (OB stuh nut) stubborn
emphatic (em FAT ik) very striking; definite
flat (FLAT) an apartment with rooms on one floor

"Well, I do know," said Mama, turning her hands over and over, "that I've been getting tireder and tireder of doing that firing. From October to April, there's firing to be done."

"But lately we've been helping, Harry and I," said Maud Martha. "And sometimes in March and April and in October, and even in November, we could build a little fire in the fireplace. Sometimes the weather was just right for that."

She knew, from the way they looked at her, that this had been a mistake. They did not want to cry.

But she felt that the little line of white, somewhat ridged with smoked purple, and all that cream-shot saffron, would never drift across any western sky except that in back of this house. The rain would drum with as sweet a dullness nowhere but here. The birds on South Park were mechanical birds, no better than the poor caught canaries in those "rich" women's sun parlors.

"It's just going to kill Papa!" burst out Maud Martha. "He loves this house! He *lives* for this house!"

"He lives for us," said Helen. "It's us he loves. He wouldn't want the house, except for us."

"And he'll have us," added Mama, "wherever."

"You know," Helen sighed, "if you want to know the truth, this is a relief. If this hadn't come up, we would have gone on, just dragged on, hanging out here forever."

"It might," allowed Mama, "be an act of God. God may just have reached down, and picked up the reins."

"Yes," Maud Martha cracked in, "that's what you always say —that God knows best."

Her mother looked at her quickly, decided the statement was not suspect, looked away.

Helen saw Papa coming. "There's Papa," said Helen.

They could not tell a thing from the way Papa was walking. It was that same dear little staccato walk, one shoulder down, then the other, then repeat, and repeat. They watched his progress. He passed the Kennedy's, he passed the vacant lot, he passed Mrs. Blakesmore's. They wanted to hurl themselves over the fence, into the street, and shake the truth out of his collar. He opened his gate—

---

firing (FYR ing) to light a fire in a boiler
saffron (SAF run) bright, orange-yellow color
staccato (stuh KAHT oh) short, distinct movement

Oil Sketch for *American Gothic*, Grant Wood. Rinard Collection, Estate of Grant Wood/Licensed by VAGA, New York, NY

the gate—and still his stride and face told them nothing.

"Hello," he said.

Mama got up and followed him through the front door. The girls knew better than to go in too.

Presently Mama's head emerged. Her eyes were lamps turned on.

"It's all right," she exclaimed. "He got it. It's all over. Everything is all right."

The door slammed shut. Mama's footsteps hurried away.

"I haven't given a party since I was eleven. I'd like some of my friends to just casually see that we're homeowners."

---

presently (PREZ unt lee) in a little while

Review the Selection

UNDERSTAND THE SELECTION

Recall

1. Where does "home" take place?

2. For whom are the women waiting?

3. Would it cost the family the same, more, or less money to live in a flat?

Infer

4. Do you think the family could move into a nice flat? Why?

5. Do you think Helen is stating her real feelings about moving away?

6. Why does Maud Martha fear that her comment about "a little fire in the fireplace" will make the others cry?

7. Why does Helen decide to give a party at the conclusion of the story?

Apply

8. Defend or refute: "Characters always believe they have complete control over their lives."

9. Contrast Mama's attitude about leaving with Maud Martha's. Would you expect a mother to act this way?

10. Brooks tries to show people coping with disappointment. Is she successful? Explain.

Respond to Literature

How does "home" reflect the experience of many American families?

WRITE ABOUT THE SELECTION

Suppose that Papa's homeowners' loan extension has not been approved, and the family has to move into an apartment. How would the characters feel about their new home? Would they adjust in time? Which character would have the most difficult time? How would they get along with the neighbors? Write a brief passage that describes one aspect of their new neighborhood or apartment.

Prewriting   Write an informal outline describing what this new location might look like. Think about the scenery, the outside of the building, and the neighborhood as well as the apartment's individual rooms. include the time of day or particular season in your outline.

Writing   Use your informal outline to write a passage that describes one aspect of the family's new home. In it, create a mood appropriate to the way the family members might really feel. Try to make the characters' reactions consistent with their personalities and their attitudes.

Revising   When you revise your passage, consider whether the descriptive words or phrases you used reflect the mood or atmosphere of the setting.

Proofreading   Read over your passage to check for errors. Be sure that all your sentences end with periods, question marks, or exclamation marks. Check your internal punctuation as well. Review the correct use of commas.

THINK ABOUT SETTING

Setting often contributes to a particular mood or atmosphere in a story, poem, or play. A large, comfortable front porch establishes one set of feelings, while a small, cramped apartment creates quite different feelings. Characters in a story are usually influenced by the setting.

1. Describe the setting that Gwendolyn Brooks created in "home."

2. What time of day does "home" take place?

3. How does the setting contribute to the mood or atmosphere of "home"?

4. Find two descriptions of the setting of "home" that you feel are especially powerful or vivid. What words does the author use to help you picture the setting?

5. The setting of "home" is perhaps the dominant element in the story. Should setting always be this important? Explain.

READING FOCUS

Recognize Implied Theme What was the implied theme in "home"? What clues in the story helped you to determine this?

DEVELOP YOUR VOCABULARY

You can often figure out the meaning of an unfamiliar word by looking closely at its **context**, that is, the words that surround it. For example, you may be unfamiliar with the meaning of *recluse* in "The old *recluse* lived alone, cut off from the rest of the world." By examining the words surrounding *recluse*, you should be able to guess that it means, "someone who lives alone, away from others."

Use context clues to determine the meaning of the italicized words below. Then, use all the italicized words in original sentences.

1. The *obstinate* teenager refused her parents' repeated requests to clean her room.

2. The grasshopper made short *staccato* hops across the corn field.

3. Her responsibility was *firing* the cold, unlit stove . . .

4. The vocabulary test would begin *presently*; I had about five minutes.

Learn About

Self Portrait, Marvin Gray Johnson.
National Museum of American Art

READING FOCUS

Evaluate the Poet's Style A poet's style is how the poet conveys a message. Does the poet use a particular poetry form, such as lyric or free verse? Does the poet use a particular type of speech—formal or informal? The style a poet chooses often greatly affects the meaning of his or her work. As you read these poems, look for a common style that would define the poetry of Langston Hughes.

CONFLICT

In literature, **conflict** is the struggle that occurs between opposite forces in a plot. As you know, there are two types of conflict. The first, **external conflict**, involves a person's struggle against an outside force, such as another person, nature, or even the society in which he or she lives.

Internal conflict, as you may suspect, involves an emotional or psychological struggle within a person's mind. In this type of conflict, an individual is divided by two opposing ideas or feelings.

It may help you to think of conflict as a battle, the fighting of which produces a certain tension. This tension excites our interest. We read further to see who wins a particular struggle and how the tension is released.

As you read the following poems by Langston Hughes, ask yourself:

1. What external and internal conflicts occur in the poems?
2. How, if ever, are these conflicts resolved?

WRITING CONNECTION

Write a short paragraph, or a four-line stanza, about an important conflict in your own life. Describe whether the struggle is external, internal, or both.

DREAM VARIATIONS

by Langston Hughes

To fling my arms wide
In some place of the sun,
To whirl and to dance
Till the white day is done.
5 Then rest at cool evening
Beneath a tall tree
While night comes on gently,
    Dark like me—
That is my dream!

10 To fling my arms wide
In the face of the sun,
Dance! Whirl! Whirl!
Till the quick day is done,
Rest at pale evening . . .
15 A tall, slim tree . . .
Night coming tenderly
    Black like me.

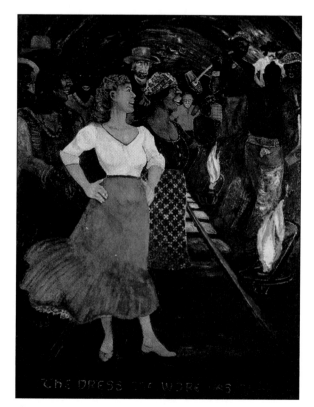

The Dress She Wore Was Blue, John Henry series
by Palmer Hayden. Museum of African American Art,
Palmer C. Hayden Collection

THEME FOR ENGLISH B

by Langston Hughes

The instructor said,

> *Go home and write*
> *a page tonight.*
> *And let that page come out of you—*
5 > *Then, it will be true.*

I wonder if it's that simple?

I am twenty-two, colored, born in Winston-Salem.[1]
I went to school there, then Durham,[2] then here
to this college on the hill above Harlem.[3]
10 I am the only colored student in my class.
The steps from the hill lead down into Harlem,
through a park, then I cross St. Nicholas,
Eighth Avenue, Seventh, and I come to the Y,
the Harlem Branch Y, where I take the elevator
15 up to my room, sit down, and write this page:

It's not easy to know what is true for you or me
at twenty-two, my age. But I guess I'm what
I feel and see and hear, Harlem, I hear you:
hear you, hear me—we two—you, me talk on this page.
20 (I hear New York, too.) Me—who?
Well, I like to eat, sleep, drink, and be in love.
I like to work, read, learn, and understand life.
I like a pipe for a Christmas present,
or records—Bessie,[4] bop, or Bach.

---

[1]**Winston Salem:** city in North Carolina
[2]**Durham:** city in North Carolina
[3]**Harlem:** a section of New York City that mostly lies between the East and Hudson Rivers and north of Central Park
[4]**Bessie Smith:** a famous jazz singer

25 I guess being colored doesn't make me *not* like
the same things other folks like who are other races.
So will my page be colored that I write?
Being me, it will not be white.
But it will be
30 a part of you, instructor.
You are white—
yet a part of me, as I am a part of you.
That's American.
Sometimes perhaps you don't want to be a part of me.
35 Nor do I often want to be a part of you.
But we are, that's true!
As I learn from you,
I guess you learn from me—
although you're older—and white—
40 and somewhat more free.

This is my page for English B.

from
Montage of a Dream Deferred

ADAPTED

by Langston Hughes

Dream Boogie

Good morning, daddy!¹
Ain't you heard
The boogie-woogie rumble
Of a dream deferred?

5 Listen closely:
You'll hear their feet
Beating out and beating out a—

*You think
It's a happy beat?*

10 Listen to it closely:
ain't you heard
something underneath
like a—

What did I say?

15 Sure,
I'm happy!
Take it away!

*Hey, pop!
Re-bop!*
20 *Mop!*

Y-e-a-h!

---

montage (mon TAHZH) picture made up of a number of separate pictures
deferred (dih FURD) put off
¹**daddy:** here slang for "friend" or "brother"

Warning

Daddy,
don't let your dog
curb you!

Tell Me

Why should it be *my* loneliness,
Why should it be *my* song,
Why should it be *my* dream
    deferred
      overlong?

Request

Gimme $25.00
and the change.
I'm going
where the morning
and the evening
won't bother me.

Argument

White is right,
Yellow mellow,
Black, get back!

    Do you believe that, Jack?

5   Sure do!

    Then you're a dope
    for which there ain't no hope.
    Black is fine!
    And, God knows,
10   *It's mine!*

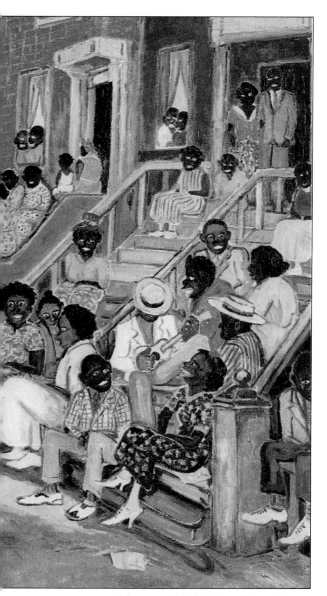

Midsummer Night in Harlem, Palmer Hayden.
Museum of African American Art

Blues at Dawn

I don't dare start thinking in the morning.
I don't dare start thinking in the morning.
    If I thought thoughts in bed,
    Them thoughts would bust my head—
5   So I don't dare start thinking in the morning.

I don't dare remember in the morning.
Don't dare remember in the morning.
    If I recall the day before,
    I wouldn't get up no more—
10   So I don't dare remember in the morning.

Harlem

What happens to a dream deferred?

Does it dry up
like a raisin in the sun?
Or fester like a sore—
5   And then run?
Does it stink like rotten meat?
Or crust and sugar over—
like a syrupy sweet?

Maybe it just sags
10   like a heavy load.

Or does it explode?

Island

Between two rivers,
North of the park,
Like darker rivers
The streets are dark.

5   Black and white,
Gold and brown—
Chocolate-custard
Pie of a town.

Dream within a dream
10   *Our dream deferred.*

Good morning, daddy!

Ain't you heard?

Langston Hughes (1902–1967)

Who are you, Langston Hughes? What do you stand for? Let's let the poet himself tell us:

> I play it cool
> And dig all jive.
> That's the reason
> I stay alive.
>
> My motto,
> As I live and learn,
>   is:
> *Dig and Be Dug*
> *In Return.*

The American people have "dug" the poetry of Langston Hughes for over seventy years. His language is direct and uncomplicated. He catches the rhythms of jazz and the soulful sounds of the blues. In his own words, he gives us the "music of a community."

Langston Hughes was born in Joplin, Missouri, in 1902. After high school he traveled, worked at odd jobs, and polished his writing in his spare time. His first book, *The Weary Blues*, came out in 1926. Soon after graduating from Lincoln University, in Pennsylvania in 1929, he settled down in the Harlem section of New York City. In addition to poetry, Hughes wrote stories, novels, plays, articles for magazines and newspapers, and even an autobiography. During his life his name appeared on the covers of about thirty books.

The short poem on the left is entitled "Motto." What do the last two lines mean? How is that meaning related to Langston Hughes's life and career?

Review the Selection

UNDERSTAND THE SELECTION

Recall

1. In "Theme for English B," where does the speaker live?

2. Identify three musical elements in *Montage*.

3. In "Harlem," what is compared to "a raisin in the sun" and "rotten meat"?

Infer

4. What is the "dream deferred"?

5. "Warning," is an example of figurative language. Explain what it means.

6. Why does the poet call his poem a "montage"? Explain.

7. In "Dream Variations," what is the speaker's real hope?

Apply

8. How would you characterize the speaker in "Theme for English B"?

9. What might Hughes have done if he hadn't become a poet?

10. In "Theme for English B," how might the instructor grade the poet's theme?

Respond to Literature
How are the themes of Hughes's poems consistent with developments in America during the early 20th century?

WRITE ABOUT THE SELECTION

In the 1920s, Langston Hughes wrote poems that challenged racial inequality in the United States. If he were living today, would the poet find these same conditions? What has changed? What has remained the same? Write a brief, persuasive paragraph that explains whether or not Langston Hughes would encounter similar societal conflicts today.

Prewriting Make a web to organize your thoughts. Note your central opinion in the middle of the diagram. Next, list the main reasons that support your opinion. Then, note important details about each reason.

Writing Use your web to write a brief, persuasive paragraph. In it, explain whether Langston Hughes would find in our society the same conflicts that existed during his lifetime. Remember to list your reasons in the order of their importance. Discuss similarities and differences between conditions in the 1920s and those today.

Revising When you revise your paragraph, check to see if you have used convincing words and phrases that emphasize your views. Reread your last sentence to make sure it leaves the reader with a vivid impression.

Proofreading Read over your paragraph to check for errors. Be sure that you have used persuasive words accurately, and that you have spelled them correctly.

THINK ABOUT CONFLICT

External conflict always involves a struggle between a person and an opposing force, such as another person, nature, or society. **Internal conflict**, however, concerns a struggle within a person's own mind. Conflict is not only an element in a plot, it can also become the theme—the central, or dominating, idea in an author's work.

1. What external or internal conflict does the speaker of "Blues at Dawn" experience?

2. What opposing thoughts or feelings does the speaker of "Theme for English B" reveal?

3. In "Argument," part of the speaker's ordeal involves an external or outside force. What is that force?

4. How is the tension that is expressed throughout "Dream Boogie," finally released?

5. A conflict is resolved when one side wins the "battle." Does "Montage" seem to end with any resolution? What gives you the feeling that the conflict will continue?

READING FOCUS

Evaluate the Poet's Style How would you describe Langston Hughes's style? How does his style of writing affect the meaning of the poems?

DEVELOP YOUR VOCABULARY

A **simile** is a direct comparison in which one thing is said to be similar to, or like, something else. The words *like* or *as* are used in a simile. In "He's as skinny as a rail," a person is compared to a rail to show how thin he is.

A **metaphor** is a comparison in which one thing is said to *be* something else. A metaphor often uses the words *is*, *are*, *was*, or *were*. In "A blanket of snow covered our village," snow is compared to a blanket to create a visual picture of the spreading snow.

Read the sentences below and tell which contain a simile and which contain a metaphor. What is being compared?

1. The professional wrestler's body was as solid as a rock.

2. Their escape plan was a shining jewel, perfect in every way.

3. The tears from her eyes fell like tiny raindrops.

4. Pace yourself, for life is a long and winding road.

5. Always courageous, the comic book hero had nerves of steel.

Learn About

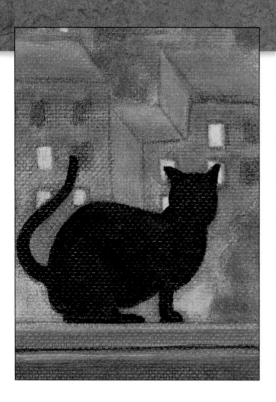

MOOD

Whether reading a letter from a friend or listening to a favorite song, you are constantly responding to feelings suggested by words and phrases.

Works of literature, too, summon emotional responses. The feelings that a poem, play, or short story conveys are called its **mood**. The mood may be peaceful, gloomy, joyous, or mysterious. In other words, mood is the total atmosphere that a writer creates through his or her imaginative use of language.

Mood is suggested through setting, imagery, action, and the words of characters. For example, an autumn afternoon setting may establish an atmosphere of serenity. Conversely, startled deer, fleeing from a thunderstorm, can suggest a mood of uncertainty and fear.

When reading, look at how the descriptive words create a mood.

As you read "Fog," ask yourself:
1. What mood, or feeling, does this poem give you?
2. What sensory details contribute to this mood?

READING FOCUS

Recognize Figurative Language Figurative language is often used to compare things in literature and poetry. The comparison can be a metaphor in which one thing stands for something else. For example, "The star was a beacon." Read "Fog" to discover what metaphor Sandburg uses for fog.

WRITING CONNECTION

Write a four-sentence passage that describes the room in which you are sitting. Using sensory details, suggest the mood of the room.

FOG

by Carl Sandburg

The fog comes
on little cat feet.

It sits looking
over harbor and city
on silent haunches
and then moves on.

Savannah Nocturne, Eliot Clark

Review the Selection

UNDERSTAND THE SELECTION

Recall

1. What is the poem's subject?

2. To what object does the poet compare this subject?

3. What is the setting of the poem?

Infer

4. To which sense does the poem most appeal?

5. Is the fog an invited guest?

6. What do you know about the sound of fog from this poem?

7. What do the phrases "comes on" and "moves on" suggest about the fog's visits?

Apply

8. The poet compares the fog to just one thing throughout the poem. Is this effective? Explain.

9. To what other animal might you compare fog? Explain.

10. Why do you think Sandburg chose to write a *poem* about fog, instead of a short story or nonfiction article?

Respond to Literature

Compare "Fog" to other poems you have read in this unit. What elements does it have in common with them? What elements differ?

WRITE ABOUT THE SELECTION

Many students consider "Fog" one of their favorite poems. Perhaps this is because comparison between an element of nature and an animal is a visually appealing way of thinking about these two subjects. Write a six-line poem in which you compare a natural event, such as a winter snowstorm, an earthquake, or a cooling summer rain, to an animal. Make sure that you can think of similarities between the event and the animal.

Prewriting After choosing the subjects you want to compare, make a list of the character traits of the animal and a list of vivid details about the natural event. Decide how you will show similarities between the two.

Writing Use your informal outline to write a six-line poem that compares the natural event to the animal. In it, try to match the characteristics of the animal with those of the natural event. Think carefully about the characteristics of each as you write.

Revising When you revise your poem, be sure that the details you use are consistent with the physical qualities of both the natural event and the animal.

Proofreading Read over your poem to check for errors. Make sure you use a consistent method of capitalizing and punctuating the poem. Remember to start a new line of text for each new line of the poem.

THINK ABOUT MOOD

Mood is the feeling that a work of literature expresses to the reader. Mood is created through the author's choice of sensory words, setting details, actions, and words that characters speak. It also results from an author's use of such techniques as meter, rhyme (or no rhyme), alliteration, repetition, imagery, and symbolism. In short, mood is created by combinations and variations in the poetic and literary devices available to the writer.

1. Describe the mood of "Fog."

2. What descriptive words or phrases does the poet use to create this feeling?

3. What other words might you use to add to this particular mood?

4. The poet purposely selects certain traits of a cat and leaves out others. How would the mood of the poem change if the poet had compared the fog to a kitten? Would the poem be as successful?

5. The poet uses alliteration in the poem. What two sounds does he particularly repeat?

READING FOCUS

Recognize Figurative Language What metaphor is used for fog in this poem? Why do you think the poet uses this metaphor?

DEVELOP YOUR VOCABULARY

The **denotation** of a word is its usual meaning, or "dictionary definition." The **connotation** of a word is the feeling or thought that the word suggests. For instance, *beckon*, *invite*, and *summon* have similar denotations, or definitions, but their connotations are different. The word *beckon*, is somehow more mysterious or tantalizing than the more conventional word *invite*.

For each sentence below, choose the word with the more vivid connotation and explain your reasoning.

1. The stallion (*jumped*, *bounded*) over the wooden fence in one easy motion.

2. The (*musty*, *stale*) odor of the attic reminded me of a damp shoe.

3. A few crumbling bricks were all that was left of the (*old*, *ancient*) Greek temple.

4. Which soldier dared to follow the enemy down the dark (*cavity*, *hole*)?

5. This particular robbery case (*confused*, *baffled*) the detective.

6. The (*hungry*, *famished*) hikers frantically searched for something to eat.

Learn About

SYMBOLISM

A **symbol** is something that stands for, or represents, something else. In literature, a symbol is a person, place, object, or event that represents a particular idea or concept. For example, the Statue of Liberty is more than just a large object that stands in New York City's harbor. For people all over the world, the Statue of Liberty represents (or symbolizes) the freedom and justice that is found in the United States.

Writers use symbols to convey a deeper meaning than could be expressed by the **literal**, or exact meaning, of the words. If, for instance, the Statue of Liberty were mentioned several times in a poem about immigrants journeying to the United States, you might conclude that the poem was about freedom and justice.

As you read the following poems by Robert Frost, ask yourself:

1. What symbols does the poet use in his poems?
2. What ideas or concepts do these symbols represent?

READING FOCUS

Make Inferences Making inferences means making logical guesses about information not stated directly in a story or poem. You can do this by paying attention to clues the author provides, or by applying your own knowledge and experiences. You can make inferences to connect ideas, to figure out a mystery, or to predict what might happen next. As you read these poems, make inferences about the situations presented.

WRITING CONNECTION

Many sports teams use animals or objects in their names. Think of the Chicago Bears and the Oakland Raiders. What is the name of your school's sports team? Explain briefly the idea symbolized by that name.

The Pasture

by Robert Frost

I'm going out to clean the pasture spring;
I'll only stop to rake the leaves away
(And wait to watch the water clear, I may):
I shan't be gone long.—You come too.

I'm going out to fetch the little calf
That's standing by the mother. It's so young
It totters when she licks it with her tongue.
I shan't be gone long.—You come too.

Evening Glow, The Old Red Cow, Albert Pinkham Ryder.
The Brooklyn Museum

---

fetch (FECH) get and bring back

The Road Not Taken

by Robert Frost

Two roads diverged in a yellow wood,
And sorry I could not travel both
And be one traveler, long I stood
And looked down one as far as I could
5   To where it bent in the undergrowth;

Then took the other, as just as fair,
And having perhaps the better claim,
Because it was grassy and wanted wear;
Though as for that, the passing there
10   Had worn them really about the same,

And both that morning equally lay
In leaves no step had trodden black.
Oh, I kept the first for another day!
Yet knowing how way leads on to way,
15   I doubted if I should ever come back.

I shall be telling this with a sigh
Somewhere ages and ages hence:
Two roads diverged in a wood, and I—
I took the one less traveled by,
20   And that has made all the difference.

---

diverge (dih VURJ) spread apart

Landscape, Ernest Lawson. The Brooklyn Museum

Woodland Repose, John F. Carlson. Toledo Museum of Art

Stopping by Woods on a Snowy Evening

by Robert Frost

Whose woods these are I think I know.
His house is in the village though;
He will not see me stopping here
To watch his woods fill up with snow.

5 My little horse must think it queer
To stop without a farmhouse near
Between the woods and frozen lake
The darkest evening of the year.

He gives his harness bells a shake
10 To ask if there is some mistake.
The only other sound's the sweep
Of easy wind and downy flake.

The woods are lovely, dark and deep.
But I have promises to keep,
15 And miles to go before I sleep,
And miles to go before I sleep.

Robert Frost (1874–1963)

One day in 1909 the State Superintendent of Schools in New Hampshire dropped into a small high school. His inspection included an English classroom—and a happy surprise. "A class of boys and girls were listening open-mouthed to the teacher," he wrote later. "Slumped down behind a desk at the front of the room was a young man who was talking to the students as he might talk to a group of friends around his own fireside." The inspector had discovered "the best teacher in New Hampshire."

Inspector Charles Silver couldn't have known, of course, that he had also discovered a talented young poet named Robert Frost. His visit was to mark a turning point in Frost's life. Up to that time, Frost had thought of himself as a failure. He had failed at college, dropping out after two years. He had failed as a chicken farmer. And most important to him, he had failed to get many of his poems printed.

Then the turning point arrived. With Silver's help, Frost found a job teaching in a New Hampshire school. He still wanted to write, however, and in 1912, he sold his farm and moved his family to England, an attempt to "get away from it all." In 1913, his first book of poems was accepted by a London publisher. At the age of 39, Frost was finally on his way. He decided to return to the United States after the beginning of WW I.

Before long, Robert Frost was able to live the life he wanted. He bought a small farm in New Hampshire. He taught and traveled a little. He published book after book and collected prize after prize. His hair slowly turned gray with age, and white with wisdom. "America's beloved poet" lived to be nearly 90.

Frost is often called a "nature poet," but he never liked the term. "I guess I'm just not a nature poet," he once said. "I have only written two poems without a human being in them." He might have added that his real subject was *human* nature.

Review the Selection

UNDERSTAND THE SELECTION

Recall

1. In "The Pasture" what two actions does the speaker plan to accomplish?

2. Where does "The Road Not Taken" take place?

3. What happens in "Stopping by Woods on a Snowy Evening"?

Infer

4. In which season does "The Road Not Taken" take place?

5. Why do you think the speaker in "The Road Not Taken" chooses the road that he or she does?

6. Do you think the horse in "Stopping by Woods on a Snowy Evening" shares the speaker's thoughts?

7. What does the speaker of "Stopping by Woods" feel?

Apply

8. Why might Frost have often begun his poetry readings with "The Pasture"?

9. Would the speaker of "The Road Not Taken" now choose the other road?

10. Where do you think the speaker in "Stopping by Woods" is going?

Respond to Literature

How does the poet's use of nature reflect one aspect of modern poetry?

WRITE ABOUT THE SELECTION

The speaker of "The Road Not Taken" seems to feel that his or her choice of the proper road in life has produced favorable results. Have you made difficult choices in life, too? How have these decisions worked out? Write a two-stanza poem about a difficult choice you have made, and describe the results.

Prewriting Create a cause-and-effect chart. In it, list an important situation you once faced in your life. Then, draw arrows from this situation, linking the choices available to you at the time, the decision you eventually made, and the results of that specific decision.

Writing Use your informal cause-and-effect chart to write a two-stanza poem that describes the particularly difficult choice you made, and the effects of that choice on your life today. You may choose to follow one of Robert Frost's rhyme schemes.

Revising When you revise your poem, make sure you have described the original situation, your decision, and the effects of that decision. Read closely to see whether any symbols you used clearly represent your ideas or feelings about that important decision.

Proofreading When you proofread your poem, you may find it necessary to change the order of certain words or letters. Use this proofreading mark [∾] to make those changes. This is called transposing (tr.).

THINK ABOUT SYMBOLISM

Writers use symbols to deepen and enrich the meaning of a work of literature. Symbols may or may not be simple, however. The image behind the symbol may consist of many ideas and attitudes. You might find it helpful to think of a **symbol** as something visible used to represent something invisible, such as an idea, concept, or hidden truth.

1. What symbols does the poet use in "The Road Not Taken"?

2. What do you think the two roads in "The Road Not Taken" represent? Explain your thinking.

3. In "Stopping by Woods on a Snowy Evening," what is the literal meaning of the word *miles*?

4. What idea or concept is conveyed by the poet's use of the word *miles*?

5. In the work of Robert Frost and many other poets water is a symbol of truth. Explain how this symbol contributes to your understanding of "The Pasture."

READING FOCUS

Make Inferences What inferences did you make about the farm and the two woods described in these poems? What personal experiences did you draw from to make these inferences?

DEVELOP YOUR VOCABULARY

The development of the English language falls into three historical periods. The oldest, the Old English (or Anglo-Saxon) period, began around A.D. 440, when northern European tribes invaded the British Isles. The blending of their languages produced what we now call Old English.

Over the centuries, Old English gave way to Middle English and then to Modern English. Many changes occurred. In addition, English acquired hundreds of thousands of words from other languages.

Robert Frost's poetic vocabulary is made up almost exclusively of words that trace back to Old English. Look up the following words in a dictionary that has word histories. Which words do not come from Old English. From what languages do they come?

1. rake	9. doubt
2. watch	10. sigh
3. tongue	11. hence
4. pasture	12. house
5. yellow	13. stop
6. both	14. snow
7. morning	15. farm
8. black	16. wind

Summer at Campobello, New Brunswick, detail,
Edward W.D. Hamilton. Museum of Fine Arts, Boston

READING FOCUS

Interpret Dialogue Dialogue is the
words that characters speak in a story.
As in real life, what the characters say
may not be what they really feel or
believe. You must use the context and
tone of their words to interpret their
real meanings. As you read this story,
think about what the ladies mean
when they speak, rather than concentrating on the actual words they say.

CHARACTER

You know from previous selections
that writers create characters through
description, dialogue, action, and the
comments made about them by other
characters in the story.

In literature, a character can be either
flat or round. A **flat character** shows you
only one side of his or her personality and
is therefore not very true to life. A flat
character usually represents a single idea
or attitude. Many fairy tale characters
are flat since they have only one of their
personality traits exposed. An example
would be a wicked stepmother.

A **round character** is someone you
come to know from the inside out. A
round character has many sides and is
much more complex and lifelike. He or
she is capable of responding to certain
problems and situations in ways that
may surprise you.

As you read "Lily Daw and the Three
Ladies," ask yourself:
1. Which characters are uncomplicated,
   or flat?
2. Which characters do or say things
   that surprise you?

WRITING CONNECTION

Write a description of your favorite
person. Include those specific qualities
that make him or her a special, unique
human being.

LILY DAW AND THE THREE LADIES

ADAPTED

by Eudora Welty

Mrs. Watts and Mrs. Carson were both in the post office in Victory when the letter came from the Ellisville Institute for the Feeble-minded of Mississippi. Aimee Slocum, with her hand still full of mail, ran out in front and handed it straight to Mrs. Watts and they all three read it together. Mrs. Watts held it taut between her pink hands and Mrs. Carson underscored each line slowly with her thimbled finger. Everybody else in the post office wondered what was up now.

"What will Lily say," beamed Mrs. Carson at last, "when we tell her we're sending her to Ellisville!"

"She'll be tickled to death," said Mrs. Watts, and added in a gutteral voice to a deaf lady, "Lily Daw's getting in at Ellisville!"

"Don't you-all dare go off and tell Lily without me!" called Aimee Slocum, trotting back to finish putting up the mail.

"Do you suppose they'll look after her down there?" Mrs. Carson began to carry on a conversation with a group of Baptist ladies waiting in the post office. She was the Baptist preacher's wife.

"I've always heard it was lovely down there, but crowded," said one.

"Lily lets people walk over her so," said another.

"Last night at the tent show—" said another, and then popped her hand over her mouth.

"Don't mind me; I know there are such things in the world," said Mrs. Carson, looking down and fingering the tape-measure which hung over her bosom.

"Oh, Mrs. Carson. Well, anyway, last night at the tent show, why, the man was just before making Lily buy a ticket to get in."

"A ticket!"

"Till my husband went up and explained she wasn't bright, and so did everybody else."

---

feeble-minded (FEE buhl MIN dihd) an out-of-date expression for a person with a weak or slow mind
taut (TAWT) stretched tightly
underscored (UN dur skawrd) underlined
thimbled (THIM buld) wearing a small, protective cap used in sewing
gutteral (GUT ur ul) harsh or growling sound

Summer at Campobello, New Brunswick, Edward W.D. Hamilton. Museum of Fine Arts, Boston

The ladies all clicked their tongues.

"Oh, it was a very nice show," said the lady who had gone. "And Lily acted very nice. She was a perfect lady—she just set in her seat and stared."

"Oh, she can be, she can be," said Mrs. Carson, shaking her head and turning her eyes up.

"Yes'm, she kept her eyes on what's that thing makes all the commotion? The xylophone," said the lady. "Didn't turn her head to the right or left the whole

---

commotion (kuh MOH shun) noisy confusion

time. Sat in front of me."

"The point is, what did she do after the show?" asked Mrs. Watts practically. "Lily has gotten so she is very mature for her age."

"Oh, Hermine!" protested Mrs. Carson, looking at her wildly for a moment.

"And that's how come we are sending her to Ellisville," finished Mrs. Watts.

"I'm ready, you-all," said Aimee Slocum, running out with white powder all over her face. "Mail's up."

"Well, of course, I do hope it's for the best," said several of the other ladies. They did not go at once to take their mail out of their boxes; they felt a little left out.

The three women stood at the foot of the water tank.

"To find Lily is a different thing," said Aimee Slocum. "Where in the wide world do you suppose she'd be?"

"I don't see a sign of her either on this side of the street or on the other side," said Mrs. Carson as they walked along.

Ed Newton was stringing Redbird school tablets on the wire across the store.

"If you're looking for Lily, she come in here an' tole me she was goin' to git married, while ago," he said.

"Ed Newton!" cried the ladies, clutching one another. Mrs. Watts began to fan herself at once with the letter from Ellisville. She wore widow's black and the least thing made her hot.

"Why, she's not, she's going to Ellisville, Ed," said Mrs. Carson gently.

"Mrs. Watts and I and Aimee Slocum are sending her, out of our own pockets. Besides, the boys of Victory are on their honor—Lily's not going to get married, that's just an idea she's got in her head."

"More power to you, ladies," said Ed Newton, spanking himself with a tablet.

They saw Estelle Mabers sitting on the rail of the bridge over the railroad track, slowly drinking a Ne-Hi orange drink. "Have you seen Lily?" they asked her.

"I'm supposed to be out here watching for her now," said the Mabers girl, as though she weren't there yet. "For Jewel. Jewel says Lily come in the store while ago and took a two-ninety-eight hat and wore it off. Jewel wants to swap her something else for it."

"Oh, Estelle, Lily says she's going to get married!" cried Aimee Slocum.

"Well, I declare," said Estelle; she never understood anything.

Loralee Adkins came riding by in her Willys-Knight[1], blowing the horn to find out what they were talking about.

Aimee ran waving out into the street and yelled: "Loralee, you got to ride us up to Lily Daw's. She's up yonder fixing to git married!"

"Well, that just shows you right now," said Mrs. Watts, groaning as she was helped into the back seat. "What we've got to do is persuade Lily it will be nicer to go to Ellisville."

"Just to think." While they rode around the corner Mrs. Carson was going

---

tablet (TAB lit) pad of writing paper
[1]**Willys-Knight:** type of car made in this period

on in her sad voice, like soft noises in the henhouse at twilight. "We buried Lily's poor defenseless mother. We gave Lily all her food and kindling and every stitch she had on. Sent her to Sunday school to learn the Lord's teachings, had her baptized a Baptist. And when her old father commenced beating her and tried to cut her head off with the butcher-knife, why, we took her away from him and gave her a place to stay."

The paintless frame house was three stories high in places and had red and green stained-glass windows in front and gingerbread around the porch. It leaned steeply to one side and the front steps were gone. The car drew up under the cedar tree.

"Now Lily's almost grown up," Mrs. Carson continued; "in fact, she's grown," she concluded, getting out.

"Talking about getting married," said Mrs. Watts disgustedly. "Thanks, Loralee, you run on home."

They climbed over the dusty zinnias onto the porch and walked through the open door without knocking.

Lily was there, in the empty dark center hall, kneeling on the floor beside a small open trunk. ("There certainly is always a funny smell in this house. I say it every time I come," said Aimee Slocum.)

When Lily saw them she put a zinnia in her mouth.

"Hello, Lily," said Mrs. Carson reproachfully.

"Hello," said Lily, and gave a suck on the zinnia stem that sounded exactly like a jay-bird. She was wearing a petticoat for a dress, one of the things Mrs. Carson kept after her about. Her milky-yellow hair streamed freely down from under a new hat. You could see the wavy scar on her throat if you knew it was there.

Mrs. Carson and Mrs. Watts, the two fattest, sat in the double rocker. Aimee Slocum sat on the wire chair donated from the drugstore that burned.

"Well, what are you doing, Lily?" asked Mrs. Watts.

Lily smiled.

The trunk was old and lined with yellow and brown paper with an asterisk pattern showing in darker circles and rings. The ladies indicated mutely that they did not know where in the world it had come from. It was empty except for two bars of soap and a green washcloth, which Lily was trying to arrange in the bottom.

"Go on and tell us what you're doing, Lily," said Aimee Slocum.

"Packing, silly," said Lily.

"Where are you going?"

"Going to get married, and I bet you wish you was me now," said Lily. But shyness overcame her suddenly and she popped the zinnia back in her mouth.

"Talk to me, dear," said Mrs. Carson.

---

kindling (KIND ling) small pieces of dry firewood
stitch (STICH) slang for clothing
reproachfully (rih PROHCH fuh lee) scolding; blaming
petticoat (PET ee koht) type of woman's underskirt
asterisk (AS tur isk) star-shaped sign or symbol
mutely (MYOOT lee) silently

"Tell old Mrs. Carson why you want to get married."

"No," said Lily, after a moment's hesitation.

"Well, we've thought of something that will be so much nicer," said Mrs. Carson. "You can go to Ellisville."

"Won't that be lovely?" said Mrs. Watts. "Why, yes."

"It's a lovely place," said Aimee Slocum uncertainly.

"You've got bumps on your face," said Lily.

"Aimee, dear, you stay out of this if you don't mind," said Mrs. Carson anxiously. "I don't know what it is coming over Lily when you come around her."

Lily stared at Aimee Slocum meditatively.

"There—wouldn't you like to go to Ellisville now?" asked Mrs. Carson.

"No'm," said Lily.

"Why not?" All the ladies looked down at her in impressive astonishment.

"'Cause I'm goin' to git married," said Lily.

"Well, and who are you going to marry, dear?" said Mrs. Watts. She knew how to pin people down and make them deny what they'd already said.

Lily bit her lip and began to smile. She reached into the trunk and held up both cakes of soap and wagged them.

"Tell us," said Mrs. Watts, "who you're going to marry, now?"

"A man last night."

There was a gasp from each lady. The possible reality of a lover descended suddenly like a summer hail over their heads. Mrs. Watts stood up.

"One of those show fellows! A musician!" she cried.

Lily looked up in admiration.

"Did he—did he do anything to you?" It was still only Mrs. Watts who could take charge.

"Oh, yes'm," said Lily. She patted the cakes of soap fastidiously with the tips of her small fingers and tucked them in with the washcloth.

"What?" demanded Aimee Slocum, tottering before her scream.

"Don't ask her what," said Mrs. Carson. "Tell me, Lily, are you the same as you were?"

"He had a red coat, too," said Lily graciously. "He took little sticks and went ping-pong! ding-dong!"

"Oh, I think I'm going to faint," said Aimee Slocum.

"The xylophone!" cried Mrs. Watts. "The xylophone player they talked about! Why, the coward, he ought to be run out of town on a rail."

"Oh, he is out of town by now," cried Aimee. "Don't you know—the sign in the cafe—Victory on the ninth and Como on the tenth? He's in Como! Como!"

"Then we'll bring him back!" cried Mrs. Watts. "He can't get away from me!"

"Hush," said Mrs. Carson. I don't think it's any use following that line of

---

meditatively (MED uh tayt iv lee) thinking quietly
reality (ree AL uh tee) truth; fact
fastidiously (fa STID ee us lee) very sensitive; dainty

reasoning at all. It's better in the long run for him to be gone out of our lives for good and all. That kind of a man. He wanted Lily's body alone. He wouldn't make the poor little thing happy, even if we was to force him to marry her like he ought, at the point of a gun."

"Still," began Aimee.

"Shut up," said Mrs. Watts. "Mrs. Carson, you're right, I suppose."

"This is my hope chest², see?" said Lily. "You haven't looked at it. I've already got soap and a washrag. And I have my hat—on. What are you-all going to give me?"

"Lily," said Mrs. Watts, starting over, "we'll give you lots of gorgeous things if you'll only go to Ellisville instead of getting married."

"What will you give me?" asked Lily.

"I'll give you a pair of hem-stitched pillowcases," said Mrs. Carson.

"I'll give you a big caramel cake," said Mrs. Watts.

"I'll give you a souvenir from Jackson, a little toy bank," said Aimee Slocum. "Now will you go?"

"No'm," said Lily.

"I'll give you a pretty little Bible with your name on it in real gold," said Mrs. Carson.

"What if I was to give you a pink crepe-de-chine brassiere with adjustable shoulder straps?" asked Mrs. Watts grimly.

"Oh, Hermine."

"Well, she needs it," said Mrs. Watts. "Unless she'll wear dresses in Ellisville."

"I wish *I* could go to Ellisville!" said Aimee Slocum luringly.

"What will they have for me down there?" asked Lily softly.

"Oh! Lots of things. You'll weave baskets, I expect . . ." Mrs. Carson looked vaguely at the others.

"Oh, yes, they'll let you make all sorts of baskets," said Mrs. Watts; then her voiced too trailed off.

"No'm, I'd rather git married," said Lily.

"Lily Daw! Now that's just plain stubbornness!" cried Mrs. Watts. "You almost said you'd go and then took it back."

"We've all asked God, Lily," said Mrs. Carson finally, "and God seemed to tell us—Mr. Carson too—that the place where you ought to be, so as to be happy, was Ellisville."

"We've really just got to get her there—now!" screamed Aimee Slocum suddenly. "Suppose—! She can't stay here! *You know—you* know!"

"Oh, no, no, no," said Mrs. Carson hurriedly. "We mustn't think that."

"Could I take my hope chest—for Ellisville?" asked Lily shyly, looking at them sidewise.

"Why, yes," said Mrs. Carson blankly.

"If I could just take my hope chest!"

"All the time it was just her hope chest!" cried Aimee Slocum.

---

²**hope chest:** box in which a woman collects linen and clothing before being married
luringly (LUUR ing lee) to tempt or attract

Lady in a Black Hat, J. Alden Weir. The Brooklyn Museum

"It's settled!" Mrs. Watts struck her palms together.

"Praise the fathers," murmured Mrs. Carson.

"O.K.—Toots!" said Lily, her eyes gleaming with the triumph of a quotation.

The ladies were backing away to the door. "I think I'd better stay," said Mrs. Carson, stopping in her tracks. "Where—where could she have learned that terrible expression?"

"Pack her things," said Mrs. Watts. "Make the 12:35."

In the station the train was puffing. Nearly everyone in Victory was hanging around waiting for it to leave. The Victory Civic Band was scattered through the crowd. Ed Newton gave false signals to

start on his bass horn. Everybody wanted to see Lily all dressed up, but Mrs. Carson and Mrs. Watts had sneaked her into the train from the other side of the tracks. The two ladies were going to travel as far as Jackson to help Lily change trains.

Lily sat between them with her hair combed and pinned up into a figure-eight knot under a small blue hat without flowers. She wore a thin made-over black dress from Mrs. Watts's last summer's mourning. Pink straps glowed through. She had a purse and a Bible and a cake in a tin box, all in her lap.

Aimee Slocum had been getting the outgoing mail stamped and bundled. She stood in the aisle of the coach now, tears shaking from her eyes. "Good-bye, Lily," she said. She was the one who felt things.

"Good-bye, silly," said Lily.

"Oh, dear, I hope they get our telegram to meet her in Ellisville!" Aimee cried suddenly, as she thought how far away it was. "And it was so hard to get it all in ten words, too."

"Get off, Aimee," said Mrs. Watts, all settled and waving her dressy fan from the funeral parlor. "I declare I'm so hot, as soon as we get a few miles out of town I'm going to slip my corset down."

"Oh, Lily, be good down there, weave baskets and do anything else they tell you—it's all because they love you." Aimee drew her mouth down and backed down the aisle.

Lily laughed. She pointed across Mrs. Carson out the window toward a man who had stepped off the train and stood there in the dust. He was a stranger and wore a cap. "Look," she said, laughing softly through her fingers.

"Don't look," said Mrs. Carson, very distinctly, as if to impress these two column words out of all she had ever spoken upon Lily's soft little brain. "Just don't look at anything till you get to Ellisville."

Outside, Aimee Slocum was crying and almost ran into the stranger. He wore a cap and was short and seemed to have on perfume.

"Could you tell me, lady," he said, "where a little lady lives in this burg³ name of Miss Lily Daw?" He lifted his cap; he had red hair.

"What do you want to know for?" asked Aimee.

"Talk louder," said the stranger. He almost whispered, himself.

"She's gone away—she's gone to Ellisville!"

"Gone?"

"Gone to Ellisville!"

"Well, I like that!" breathed the man.

"What business did you have with the lady?" cried Aimee suddenly.

"We was only going to get married, that's all," said the man. He laid the cap back on his hair and gave an agitated pat to the plaid-covered button.

Aimee Slocum started to scream in front of all those people. She almost pointed to the long black box she saw lying on the ground at the man's feet. Then she jumped back in fright. "The xylophone! The xylophone!" she cried, looking back and forth from the man to the hissing train. The bell began to ring hollowly and the man was talking.

"Did you say Ellisville—that in the state of Mississippi?" He was writing in a red notebook entitled *Permanent Facts & Data*. "I don't hear well."

Aimee nodded her head up and down.

Under "Ellis-Ville Miss" he was drawing a line; now he was flicking it with two little marks. "Maybe she didn't say she would. Maybe she said she wouldn't." He suddenly laughed very loudly, after the way he had whispered. Aimee cringed. "Women!—Well, if we play anywheres near Ellisville, Miss., in the future, I may look her up, and I may not," he said.

The bass horn sounded the true signal for the band to begin.

"Wait!" Aimee Slocum did scream. "Wait, Mister! I can get her for you!"

Then there she was back on the train screaming in Mrs. Carson's and Mrs. Watts's faces. "The xylophone player! He meant it! He wants to marry her! There he is!"

"Nonsense," murmured Mrs. Watts, peering over the others to look where Aimee pointed. "If he's there I don't see him. Where is he? You're looking at One-Eye Beasley."

"That little man with the cap—no, with the red hair! Hurry—the train—"

"Is that really him?" Mrs. Carson asked Mrs. Watts in wonder. "Mercy! He's small, isn't he?"

"Never saw him before in my life," cried Mrs. Watts.

---

³**burg:** slang for small town

The Coming Train, Edward Lamson Henry. Toledo Museum of Art

"Come on!" cried Aimee Slocum. Her nerves were all unstrung.

"All right. Hold your horses, girl," said Mrs. Watts. "Come on," she cried thickly to Mrs. Carson.

"Where are we going now?" asked Lily as they struggled down the aisle.

"We're taking you to get married," said Mrs. Watts. "Mrs. Carson, you'd better call up your husband from the station."

"But I don't want to git married," said Lily, beginning to whimper. "I'm going to Ellisville."

"Hush, and we'll all have some ice cream cones later," whispered Mrs. Carson.

Just as they appeared on the steps of the train the band went into the "Independence March."

The xylophone player was still there. He came up and said, "Hello, Toots. What's up—tricks?" and kissed Lily with a smack, after which she hung her head.

"So you're the young man we've heard so much about," said Mrs. Watts. Her smile was brilliant. "Here's your little Lily."

"What say?" asked the xylophone player.

"My husband happens to be the Baptist preacher of Victory," said Mrs. Carson, in a louder voice. "Isn't that lucky? I can get him here in five minutes."

They were in a circle around the xylophone player, all going into the white waiting-room.

"Oh, I feel just like crying, at a time like this," said Aimee Slocum. She looked back and saw the train moving slowly away, going under the bridge at Main Street. Then it disappeared around the curve.

"And whom have we the pleasure of addressing?" Mrs. Watts was shouting.

The band went on playing. Some of the people thought Lily was on the train, and some swore she wasn't. Everybody cheered, though, and a straw hat was thrown into the telephone wires.

Review the Selection

UNDERSTAND THE SELECTION

Recall

1. Where does the story take place?

2. How have the three ladies helped Lily Daw in the past?

3. Where do they want to send her?

Infer

4. Who, among the three ladies, is employed? What is her job?

5. Who is the leader? Explain.

6. Would Lily have been happy at Ellisville? Explain.

7. Why are the three ladies so anxious to get Lily Daw on the first train?

Apply

8. Select a passage that shows Lily is not as "feeble-minded" as the ladies want to believe.

9. Were the three ladies acting in Lily's best interest when they decided not to send her to Ellisville?

10. If you were the xylophone player, would you be surprised by the end of the story?

Respond to Literature

Discuss which changes in U.S. society during the 1920s and 1930s gave Eudora Welty the opportunity to explore women's characters.

WRITE ABOUT THE SELECTION

At the conclusion of the story, Lily Daw is taken from the train against her will to be married to a man she doesn't really know. Based on your understanding of Lily's character, and the character of the xylophone player, write two paragraphs that explain whether you think Lily's marriage is a good idea. Include reasons to support your opinions.

Prewriting Write an informal list of each character's qualities, or personality traits. It may help to reread those sections of the story, including dialogue and comments, that vividly illustrate both Lily's and the xylophone player's characters.

Writing Use your lists to write two paragraphs that express your opinion of Lily's upcoming marriage. In it, use specific examples from the story to support your opinion.

Revising When you revise your work, make sure the first sentence of each paragraph begins with a clear, convincing statement. Check to see if you have included enough comments and dialogue from the story to support this statement. Finally, make sure your final paragraph closes with a sentence that reinforces your original opinion.

Proofreading Find and correct punctuation errors in your two paragraphs. Where necessary, add commas, quotation marks, and periods. Check your spelling to be sure it is correct.

THINK ABOUT CHARACTER

Although flat characters are usually less complex and lifelike than round characters, they still serve an important purpose. Often, writers create a variety of simple, or flat, characters to give you a vivid impression about the different kinds of people who live in a particular place.

1. What kind of characters are Ed Newton, Estelle Mabers, and Loralee Adkins? How do you know?

2. Briefly characterize Aimee Slocum.

3. What does their last-minute decision to make Lily marry the xylophone player reveal about the three ladies?

4. Describe what the author thinks about Mrs. Carson in the sentence, "Mrs. Carson was going on in her sad voice, like soft noises in the henhouse at twilight."

5. What does Lily Daw do or say in the story that surprises you?

READING FOCUS

Interpret Dialogue In the story, whose dialogue was the easiest to interpret? Why do you think this is so?

DEVELOP YOUR VOCABULARY

Adjectives are words that modify nouns and pronouns. For instance, *talented* writer, *several* typewriters, *plastic* cup. **Adverbs** are words that modify adjectives, verbs, and other adverbs. For instance, spoke *loudly*, *reasonably* correct, ran *quickly*.

You can often form adverbs from adjectives by adding the suffix *-ly* to the adjective. For instance, "The children's problem was most *unfortunate*." "*Unfortunately*, the children's problem was never solved."

Copy the adjectives below on a separate sheet of paper and write an original sentence for each. Then add *-ly* to each adjective and write a sentence that shows your understanding of the newly formed adverb.

1. mute
2. fastidious
3. anxious
4. eager
5. hesitant
6. dangerous
7. serious
8. bright

HUMOR

In literature, humor is any writing that produces an amused response. As you explore humor, you will develop the ability to distinguish between the different techniques that writers use to make you laugh.

Much of what we find funny, or humorous, comes from the comic reactions of characters to a particular problem or situation. When a character makes sharp, clever remarks about a situation, we may laugh at his wit. When someone behaves in a way that is entirely unexpected, or "out of character," we often find that person's actions amusing.

Humor often comes from the difference between what you think will happen in a situation, and what actually occurs. An example of this **irony of situation**, is when a tragic or seemingly dangerous event turns out to be quite funny.

As you read *The Still Alarm*, ask yourself:
1. Which dialogue or actions in the play are humorous?
2. What makes them humorous?

READING FOCUS

Understand Cause and Effect In many works of literature an author first creates an event—the cause. Then the author shows a logical effect to demonstrate that the events are related. However, sometimes the effect is unexpected, and that makes the story or play funny. Look for unexpected effects as you read *The Still Alarm*. Think about how these unexpected events add humor to the play.

WRITING CONNECTION

Think about the last time you laughed, and write a brief paragraph that explains what made you think the statement, action, or event to which you reacted was funny.

THE STILL ALARM

by George S. Kaufman

(Vital Note: It is important that the entire play be acted calmly and politely, in the manner of an English drawing-room[1] comedy. No actor ever raises his voice; every line must be read as though it were an invitation to a cup of tea. If this direction is disregarded, the play has no point at all.)

The scene is a hotel bedroom. Two windows are in the rear wall with a bed between them. A telephone stand is at one end of the bed and a dresser is near the other. In the right wall is a door leading to the hall with a chair nearby. In the left wall is a door to another room; near it is a small table and two chairs. ED *and* BOB *are on the stage.* ED *is getting into his overcoat as the curtain rises. Both are at the hall door.*

ED: Well, Bob, it's certainly been nice to see you again.

BOB: It was nice to see *you*.

ED: You come to town so seldom, I hardly ever get the chance to—

BOB: Well, you know how it is. A business trip is always more or less of a bore.

ED: Next time you've got to come out to the house.

BOB: I want to come out. I just had to stick around the hotel this trip.

ED: Oh, I understand. Well, give my best to Edith.

BOB (*remembering something*): Oh, I say, Ed. Wait a minute.

ED: What's the matter?

BOB: I knew I wanted to show you something. (*Crosses to table. Gets roll of blueprints from drawer.*) Did you know I'm going to build?

---

[1] **drawing room:** formal living room or parlor. A "drawing room comedy" is a humorous play acted out in a dignified, serious manner.

ED (*follows to table*): A house?

BOB: You bet it's a house! (*Knock on hall door.*) Come in! (*Spreads plans.*) I just got these yesterday.

ED (*sits*): Well, that's fine! (*The knock is repeated—louder. Both men now give full attention to the door.*)

BOB: Come! Come in!

BELLBOY (*enters*): Mr. Barclay?

BOB: Well?

BELLBOY: I've a message from the clerk, sir. For Mr. Barclay personally.

BOB (*crosses to* BOY): I'm Mr. Barclay. What is the message?

BELLBOY: The hotel is on fire, sir.

BOB: What's that?

BELLBOY: The hotel is on fire.

ED: This hotel?

BELLBOY: Yes, sir.

BOB: Well—is it bad?

BELLBOY: It looks pretty bad, sir.

ED: You mean it's going to burn down?

BELLBOY: We think so—yes, sir.

BOB (*a low whistle of surprise*): Well! We'd better leave.

BELLBOY: Yes, sir.

BOB: Going to burn down, huh?

BELLBOY: Yes, sir. If you'll step to the window you'll see. (BOB *goes to a window.*)

BOB: Yes, that is pretty bad. H'm (*to* ED). I say, you really ought to see this—

ED (*crosses to window, peers out*): It's reached the floor right underneath.

BELLBOY: Yes, sir. The lower part of the hotel is about gone, sir.

BOB (*still looking out—looks up*): Still all right up above, though. (*Turns to* BOY.) Have they notified the Fire Department?

BELLBOY: I wouldn't know, sir. I'm only the bellboy.

BOB: Well, that's the thing to do, obviously—(*Nods head to each one as if the previous line was a bright idea.*)—notify the Fire Department. Just call them up, give them the name of the hotel—

ED: Wait a minute. I can do better than that for you. (*To the* BOY.) Ring through to the Chief, and tell him that Ed Jamison told you to telephone him. (*To* BOB.) We went to school together, you know.

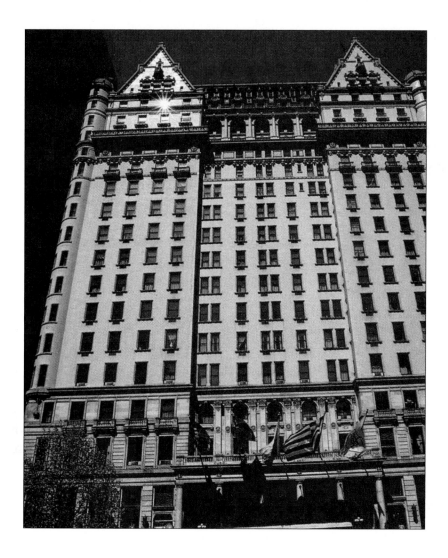

BOB: That's fine. (*To the* BOY) Now, get that right. Tell the Chief that Mr. Jamison said to ring him.

ED: *Ed* Jamison.

BOB: Yes, *Ed* Jamison.

BELLBOY: Yes, sir. (*Turns to go.*)

BOB: Oh! Boy! (*Pulls out handful of change; picks out a coin.*) Here you are.

BELLBOY: Thank you, sir. (*Exit* BELLBOY.)

(ED *sits at table, lights cigarette, and throws match on floor, then steps on it. There is a moment's pause.*)

BOB: Well! (*Crosses and looks out window.*) Say, we'll have to get out of here pretty soon.

ED (*going to window*): How is it—no better?

BOB: Worse, if anything. It'll be up here in a few moments.

ED: What floor *is* this?

BOB: Eleventh.

ED: Eleven. We couldn't jump, then.

BOB: Oh, no. You never could jump. (*Comes away from window to dresser.*) Well, I've got to get my things together. (*Pulls out suitcase.*)

ED (*smoothing out the plans*): Who made these for you?

BOB: A fellow here—Rawlins. (*Turns a shirt in his hand.*) I ought to call one of the other hotels for a room.

ED: Oh, you can get in.

BOB: They're pretty crowded. (*Feels something on the sole of his foot; inspects it.*) Say, the floor's getting hot.

ED: I know it. It's getting stuffy in the room, too. Phew! (*He looks around, then goes to the phone.*) Hello. Ice water in eleven eighteen. (*Crosses to table.*)

BOB (*at bed*): That's the stuff. (*Packs.*) You know, if I move to another hotel I'll never get my mail. Everybody thinks I'm stopping here.

ED (*studying the plans*): Say, this isn't bad.

BOB (*eagerly*): Do you like it? (*Remembers his plight.*) Suppose I go to another hotel and there's a fire there, too!

ED: You've got to take *some* chance.

BOB: I know, but here I'm sure. (*Phone rings.*) Oh, answer that, will you, Ed? (*To dresser and back.*)

ED (*crosses to phone*): Sure. (*At phone.*) Hello— Oh, that's good. Fine. What? Oh! Well, wait a minute. (*To* BOB.) The firemen are downstairs and some of them want to come up to this room.

BOB: Tell them, of course.

ED (*at phone*): All right. Come right up. (*Hangs up, crosses, and sits at table.*) Now we'll get some action.

BOB (*looks out of window*): Say, there's an awful crowd of people on the street.

ED (*absently, as he pores over the plans*): Maybe there's been some kind of accident.

---

plight (PLYT) bad condition or problem
absently (AB sunt lee) with attention elsewhere
pore over (PAWR OH vur) study carefully

BOB (*peering out, suitcase in hand*)**:** No. More likely they heard about the fire. (*A knock at the door.*) Come in.

BELLBOY (*enters*)**:** I beg pardon, Mr. Barclay, the firemen have arrived.

BOB: Show them in. (*Crosses to door.*)

(*The door opens. In the doorway appear two* FIREMAN *in full regalia. The* FIRST FIREMAN *carries a hose and rubber coat; the* SECOND *has a violin case.*)

FIRST FIREMAN (*very apologetically*)**:** Mr. Barclay.

BOB: I'm Mr. Barclay.

FIRST FIREMAN: We're the firemen, Mr. Barclay. (*They remove their hats.*)

BOB: How de do?

ED: How de do?

BOB: A great pleasure, I assure you. Really must apologize for the condition of this room, but—

FIRST FIREMAN: Oh, that's all right. I know how it is at home.

BOB: May I present a friend of mine, Mr. Ed Jamison—

FIRST FIREMAN: How are you?

ED: How are you, boys? (SECOND FIREMAN *nods.*) I know your Chief.

FIRST FIREMAN: Oh, is that so? He knows the Chief—dear old Chiefie. (SECOND FIREMAN *giggles.*)

BOB (*embarrassed*)**:** Well, I guess you boys want to get to work, don't you?

FIRST FIREMAN: Well, if you don't mind. We would like to spray around a little bit.

BOB: May I help you?

FIRST FIREMAN: Yes, if you please. (BOB *helps him into his rubber coat. At the same time the* SECOND FIREMAN, *without a word, lays the violin case on the bed, opens it, takes out the violin, and begins tuning it.*)

BOB (*watching him*)**:** I don't think I understand.

FIRST FIREMAN: Well, you see, Sid doesn't get much chance to practice at home. Sometimes, at a fire, while we're waiting for a wall to fall or something, why, a fireman doesn't really have anything to do, and personally I like to see him improve himself symphonically. I hope you don't resent it. You're not antisymphonic?

---

regalia (rih GAYL yuh) signs of royalty, such as special dress (here used ironically)
antisymphonic (an tih sim FON ik) against music

BOB: Of course not—(BOB *and* ED *nod understandingly; the* SECOND FIREMAN *is now waxing the bow.*)

FIRST FIREMAN: Well, if you'll excuse me—(*To window. Turns with decision toward the window. You feel that he is about to get down to business.*)

BOB: Charming personalities.

ED (*follows over to the window*): How is the fire?

FIRST FIREMAN (*feels the wall*): It's pretty bad right now. This wall will go pretty soon now, but it'll fall out that way, so it's all right. (*Peers out.*) That next room is the place to fight it from. (*Crosses to door in left wall.* BOB *shows ties as* ED *crosses.*)

ED (*sees ties*): Oh! Aren't those gorgeous!

FIRST FIREMAN (*to* BOB): Have you the key for this room?

BOB: Why, no. I've nothing to do with that room. I've just got this one. (*Folding a shirt as he talks.*)

ED: Oh, it's very comfortable.

FIRST FIREMAN: That's too bad. I had something up my sleeve, if I could have gotten in there. Oh, well, may I use your phone?

BOB: Please do. (*To* ED) Do you think you might hold this? (*Indicates the hose.*)

ED: How?

FIRST FIREMAN: Just crawl under it. (*As he does that.*) Thanks. (*At phone.*) Hello. Let me have the clerk, please. (*To* SECOND FIREMAN.) Give us that little thing you played the night the Equitable Building burned down. (*Back to phone.*) Are you there? This is one of the firemen. Oh, *you* know. I'm in room—ah—(*Looks at* BOB.)

BOB: Eleven-eighteen.

FIRST FIREMAN: Eleven-eighteen, and I want to get into the next room—Oh, goody. Will you send someone up with the key? There's no one in there? Oh, super-goody! Right away. (*Hangs up.*)

BOB: That's fine. (*To* FIREMEN.) Won't you sit down?

FIRST FIREMAN: Thanks.

ED: Have a cigar?

FIRST FIREMAN (*takes it*): Much obliged.

BOB: A light?

FIRST FIREMAN: If you please.

ED (*failing to find a match*): Bob, have you a match?

BOB (*crosses to table*): I thought there were some here. (*Hands in pockets.*)

FIRST FIREMAN: Oh, never mind. (*He goes to a window, leans out, and emerges with cigar lighted.* BOB *crosses to dresser, slams drawer. The* SECOND FIREMAN *taps violin with bow.*)

FIRST FIREMAN: Mr. Barclay, I think he's ready now.

BOB: Pardon me.

(*They all sit. The* SECOND FIREMAN *takes center of stage, with all the manner of a concert violinist. He goes into "Keep the Home Fires Burning."* BOB, ED, *and* FIRST FIREMAN *wipe brow as lights dim to red on closing eight bars.*)

---

emerge (ih MURJ) come out into view

Review the Selection

UNDERSTAND THE SELECTION

Recall

1. On which floor of the hotel does the play take place?

2. What instrument does the Second Fireman play?

3. What song is played at the end?

Infer

4. How do you know that Bob is from out of town?

5. What is the name of Bob's wife? How do you know?

6. How does the First Fireman light his cigar?

7. Why is Ed's reaction to the crowd in the street so unusual?

Apply

8. Compare and contrast the behavior of the firemen in *The Still Alarm* to the actions of real firefighters.

9. If you were in the hotel, what would you do?

10. Discuss why the blueprints for Bob's new house make an excellent subject for conversation in this play.

Respond to Literature

Explain why an American audience in the 1930s might be entertained by *The Still Alarm*.

WRITE ABOUT THE SELECTION

Much of what is humorous about *The Still Alarm* comes from the way each character calmly ignores the danger of the fire, even as the hotel is literally burning down. Add an episode, or scene, to the play that shows Bob trying to reserve a room in another hotel.

Prewriting Write a list of questions that will help you imagine the kind of conversation that Bob might have with the hotel manager, and how Ed might react to it. Think about the tone of voice Bob might use, the reasons he might tell for wanting to move to another hotel, and the pointless comments that Ed would probably make.

Writing Use your list of questions to add a short, humorous scene to the play. In it, write dialogue that shows Bob attempting to reserve a room at a hotel across town. When you write the dialogue for Bob and Ed, have them speak the way they do in the play.

Revising When you revise your scene, read it aloud to see whether you have captured the proper mood. Check to see that your stage directions describe the emotions and gestures of each character in an accurate way.

Proofreading Reread your scene and correct any punctuation errors. Make sure that your written script resembles the format of *The Still Alarm*.

Sometimes an author will share with you an important secret that the characters in the play, poem, or short story don't know. This technique, called **dramatic irony**, can help you appreciate the humorous aspects of a problem or situation that the characters do not even know is funny.

1. How do Bob and Ed react when they first learn of the fire?

2. What do you know that the two characters fail to understand?

3. Playing a violin during a fire is an allusion, or reference, to a famous historical event. The Roman Emperor Nero was said to have played the violin while he watched Rome burn. How does this allusion contribute to the humor of the play?

4. Why is it essential that *The Still Alarm* be acted in a dignified, serious manner?

READING FOCUS

Understand Cause and Effect Identify a cause and effect relationship in the play. Is it humorous? Explain why or why not.

Nouns are words that name people, places, objects, or ideas. In the sentence, "The committee met secretly," *committee* is the noun. **Verbs** are words that express action or a state of being. In the sentence, "He sprinted for the bus," *sprinted* is the verb.

Read each of the sentences below and decide whether the italicized word is used as a noun or a verb. You may consult a dictionary to learn how each word is used in the sentence.

1. The batter slammed the *pitch* against the outfield wall.
   Pitch in and we'll finish the job today.

2. This inflatable bag will *cushion* the stuntwoman's fall.
   I sat down on the soft *cushion*.

3. Our new quarterback just may *spark* this team to victory.
   We need a small *spark* to light this fire.

4. A small *shudder* passed through him.
   I *shudder* to think of the hard work ahead.

Focus on Drama

A drama, or play, is a work of literature intended to be spoken or acted out. While drama shares many elements (or essential parts) with poetry, fiction, and nonfiction, it also has qualities which make it unique. Studying how the elements of drama work together can help you better understand a particular play.

Character   In literature a character is the representation of a person or animal. A playwright—the author—creates action and personalities through the dialogue spoken between characters. These characters reveal themselves by the way they speak.

Sometimes a character will speak directly to the audience. During this **soliloquy**, the character tells us directly about his or her hopes, fears, dreams, and intentions.

In a play, many of the minor, or less important characters, are flat, and the major, or main, characters are round. **Flat characters** show only one side, or aspect, of their personality, and usually represent a single idea or attitude. **Round characters** are more complete human beings whose reactions to certain problems and events may surprise you.

Setting   Setting is the time and place in which a play, poem, or story occurs. Stage plays are usually limited to three or four **sets**, or locations, while radio, television, and movie plays can take place in an unlimited number of settings.

To determine the *when* of a setting, you should look for clues that tell the historical time period, time of day, season of year, or passage of time. The *where* of a play is its location, scenery, even natural events, such as the weather.

While reading a play, you should pay attention to the **stage directions**. These are instructions that tell how characters should talk and move, and help you visualize the setting.

Plot   In literature, plot is the sequence of related events that make up a story. In drama, plot is established through connected **scenes**, or incidents, that usually take place in one location, and focus on a single conversation or event.

Plot begins with exposition, which gives you the background information you need to understand the action. Exposition is followed by complication. As the plot becomes more complicated, you approach the climax, or turning point, of the play. After the climax, you know how the drama will end. In the final part of the play, called the resolution, the conflict is resolved.

The plot of a drama may be moved along by a narrator, or announcer. You may think of this character as a storyteller who provides you with information not spoken by the characters.

Plot does not have to flow in chronological order. Sometimes, a writer will use **foreshadowing** to give you hints about events that are going to happen. Writers also use **flashbacks** to go back in time and tell you about something important that happened.

Conflict   To figure out the plot, you should think about the *conflicts* that the characters experience. **External conflict** is a struggle with an outside force, such as another person, nature, or society. **Internal conflict** is the emotional or psychological battle that takes place within a character.

Symbolism and Allegory   Often, a writer may use a person, place, object, or event that represents, or **symbolizes** a special idea, concept, or hidden truth. When an entire play or story is symbolic, we call it an **allegory**. Allegories are often used for explaining moral principles.

Theme   The central message, or main point, of a play, poem, or story is called its theme. Understanding the relationship between characters, events, and their outcomes, helps you figure out the basic idea about human experience, or theme.

As you read *Invasion from Mars*, ask yourself:

1. What characters are introduced?
2. When does the play take place? How many different settings are described?
3. What are the conflicts? How is the main conflict resolved?
4. Does the play have a theme? What is it?

Invasion from Mars

ADAPTED   *by Howard Koch*

CHARACTERS
THREE ANNOUNCERS
ORSON WELLES
CARL PHILLIPS, *radio commentator*
PROFESSOR RICHARD PIERSON, *astronomer*
A POLICEMAN
MR. WILMUTH, *a farmer*
BRIGADIER GENERAL MONTGOMERY SMITH
HARRY McDONALD
CAPTAIN LANSING
SECRETARY OF THE INTERIOR
SOLDIERS OF THE 22ND FIELD ARTILLERY: *An officer, a gunner, and an observer*
LIEUTENANT VOGHT, *commander of an Army bomber plane*
FIVE RADIO OPERATORS
A STRANGER

COLUMBIA BROADCASTING SYSTEM
ORSON WELLES AND MERCURY THEATRE
ON THE AIR
SUNDAY, OCTOBER 30, 1938
8:00 TO 9:00 P.M.

ANNOUNCER: The Columbia Broadcasting System and its associated stations present Orson Welles and the Mercury Theatre on the Air in a radio play by Howard Koch suggested by the H. G. Wells novel *The War of the Worlds*. (*Mercury Theatre Musical Theme*)

ANNOUNCER: Ladies and gentlemen: the director of the Mercury Theatre and star of these broadcasts, Orson Welles . . .

ORSON WELLES: We know now that in the early years of the twentieth century this world was being watched closely by

FOCUS ON DRAMA
STUDY HINTS

Notice the foreshadowing here. What event are you being prepared for?

intelligences greater than man's and yet as mortal as his own. We know now that as human beings busied themselves about their various concerns they were examined, perhaps almost as narrowly as a man with a microscope might scrutinize the transient creatures that swarm and multiply in a drop of water. With infinite contentment people went to and fro over the earth about their little affairs, serene in the assurance of their rule over this small spinning fragment of solar driftwood which by chance or design man has inherited out of the dark mystery of Time and Space. Yet across an immense ethereal gulf, minds that are to our minds as ours are to the beasts in the jungle, intellects vast, cool and unsympathetic, regarded this earth with envious eyes and slowly and surely drew their plans against us. In the thirty-eighth year of the twentieth century came the great disappointment.

It was near the end of October. Business was better. The war was over. More men were back at work. Sales were picking up. On this particular evening, October 30, the Crossley service[1] estimated that thirty-two million people were listening in on radios.

ANNOUNCER: . . . for the next twenty-four hours not much change in temperature. A slight atmospheric disturbance of undetermined origin is reported over Nova Scotia,[2] causing a low pressure area to move down rather rapidly over the northeastern states, bringing a forecast of rain, accompanied by winds of light gale force. Maximum temperature 66; minimum 48. This weather report comes to you from the Government Weather Bureau.

. . . We now take you to the Meridian Room in the Hotel Park Plaza in downtown New York, where you will be entertained by the music of Ramon Raquello and his orchestra.

(*Spanish theme song . . . fades.*)

---

mortal (MAWR tul) subject to death
transient (TRAN shunt) not permanent; passing quickly
ethereal (ih THIR ee uhl) of the upper regions of space
[1]**Crossley service:** a service that estimated the size of radio audiences as the Nielsen rating service estimates the size of television audiences today
[2]**Nova Scotia:** a southeastern province of Canada

Note the new setting. Observe how frequently the setting begins to change.

ANNOUNCER THREE: Good evening, ladies and gentlemen. From the Meridian Room in the Park Plaza in New York City, we bring you the music of Ramon Raquello and his orchestra. With a touch of the Spanish, Ramon Raquello leads off with "La Cumparsita."

(*Piece starts playing.*)

Here is the first hint of the problem, or conflict.

ANNOUNCER TWO: Ladies and gentlemen, we interrupt our program of dance music to bring you a special bulletin from the Intercontinental Radio News. At twenty minutes before eight, central time, Professor Farrell of the Mount Jennings Observatory, Chicago, Illinois, reports observing several explosions of flaming gas, occurring at regular intervals on the planet Mars.

The spectroscope indicates the gas to be hydrogen and moving toward the earth with enormous speed. Professor Pierson of the observatory at Princeton[3] confirms Farrell's observation, and describes the phenomenon as (quote) like a jet of blue flame shot from a gun (unquote). We now return you to the music of Ramon Raquello, playing for you in the Meridian Room of the Park Plaza Hotel, situated in downtown New York.

(*Music plays for a few moments until piece ends . . . sound of applause*)

Now a tune that never loses favor, the ever-popular "Stardust." Ramon Raquello and his orchestra . . .

(*Music*)

ANNOUNCER TWO: Ladies and gentlemen, following on the news given in our bulletin a moment ago, the Government Meteorological Bureau has requested the large observatories of the country to keep an astronomical watch on any further disturbances occurring on the planet Mars. Due to the unusual nature of this occurrence, we have arranged an interview with the noted astronomer, Professor Pierson, who will give us his

---

spectroscope (SPEK truh skohp) a scientific instrument used to identify substances
phenomenon (fih NOM uh non) a fact or event that can be described in a scientific way
[3]**Princeton:** a university in New Jersey

views on this event. In a few moments we will take you to the Princeton Observatory at Princeton, New Jersey. We return you until then to the music of Ramon Raquello and his orchestra.

(*music . . .*)

ANNOUNCER TWO: We are ready now to take you to the Princeton Observatory at Princeton where Carl Phillips, our commentator, will interview Professor Richard Pierson, famous astronomer. We take you now to Princeton, New Jersey.

The main character or protagonist, is introduced.

(*Echo chamber*)

PHILLIPS: Good evening, ladies and gentlemen. This is Carl Phillips, speaking to you from the observatory at Princeton. I am standing in a large semi-circular room, pitch black except for an oblong split in the ceiling. Through this opening I can see a sprinkling of stars that cast a kind of frosty glow over the complex mechanism of the huge telescope. The ticking sound you hear is the vibration of the clockwork. Professor Pierson stands directly above me on a small platform, peering through the giant lens. I ask you to be patient, ladies and gentlemen, during any delay that may arise during our interview. Beside his ceaseless watch of the heavens, Professor Pierson may be interrupted by telephone or other communications. During this period he is in constant touch with the astronomical centers of the world . . . Professor, may I begin our questions?

PIERSON: At any time, Mr. Phillips.

PHILLIPS: Professor, would you please tell our radio audience exactly what you see as you observe the planet Mars through your telescope?

PIERSON: Nothing unusual at the moment, Mr. Phillips. A red disk swimming in a blue sea. Transverse stripes across the disk. Quite distinct now because Mars happens to be at the point nearest the earth . . . in opposition, as we call it.

Why is this information important to the plot development?

PHILLIPS: In your opinion, what do these transverse stripes signify, Professor Pierson?

PIERSON: Not canals, I can assure you, Mr. Phillips, although

---

oblong (OB lawng) rectangle shaped
transverse (trans VURS) crossing from side to side

that's the popular conjecture of those who imagine Mars to be inhabited. From a scientific viewpoint the stripes are merely the result of the planet's atmospheric conditions.

PHILLIPS: Then you're quite convinced as a scientist that living intelligence as we know it does not exist on Mars?

PIERSON: I should say the chances against it are a thousand to one.

PHILLIPS: And yet how do you account for these gas eruptions occurring on the surface of the planet at regular intervals?

PIERSON: Mr. Phillips, I cannot account for it.

PHILLIPS: By the way, Professor, for the benefit of our listeners, how far is Mars from the earth?

PIERSON: Approximately forty million miles.

PHILLIPS: Well, that seems a safe enough distance.

PHILLIPS: Just a moment, ladies and gentlemen, someone has just handed Professor Pierson a message. While he reads it, let me remind you that we are speaking to you from the observatory in Princeton, New Jersey, where we are interviewing the world-famous astronomer, Professor Pierson . . . One moment, please. Professor Pierson has passed me a message which he has just received . . . Professor, may I read the message to the listening audience?

PIERSON: Certainly, Mr. Phillips.

PHILLIPS: Ladies and gentlemen, I shall read you a wire addressed to Professor Pierson from Dr. Gray of the National History Museum, New York. "9:15 P.M. Eastern Standard Time. Seismograph registered shock of almost earthquake intensity occurring within a radius of twenty miles of Princeton. Please investigate. Signed, Lloyd Gray, Chief of Astronomical Division." . . . Professor Pierson, could this occurrence possibly have something to do with the disturbances observed on the planet Mars?

PIERSON: Hardly, Mr. Phillips. This is probably a meteorite of unusual size and its arrival at this particular time is merely a

Here, the plot begins to build. Does Professor Pierson see any relationship between the disturbances on Mars and these earthquake shocks?

---

conjecture (kun JEK chur) an opinion formed without facts but based on pertinent knowledge or experience; guess

seismograph (SYZ muh graf) an instrument that records the intensity and duration of earthquakes

intensity (in TEN suh tee) strength; force

meteorite (MEET ee uh ryt) part of a heavenly body that passes through the atmosphere and falls to the earth's surface as a piece of matter coincidence. However, we shall conduct a search, as soon as daylight permits.

PHILLIPS: Thank you, Professor. Ladies and gentlemen, for the past ten minutes we've been speaking to you from the observatory at Princeton, bringing you a special interview with Professor Pierson, noted astronomer. This is Carl Phillips speaking. We now return you to our New York studio.

(*Fade in piano playing*)

ANNOUNCER TWO: Ladies and gentlemen, here is the latest bulletin from the Intercontinental Radio News. Montreal, Canada: Professor Morse of McGill University reports observing a total of three explosions on the planet Mars, between the hours of 7:45 P.M. and 9:20 P.M., Eastern Standard Time. This confirms earlier reports received from American observatories. Now, nearer home, comes a special announcement from Trenton,[4] New Jersey. It is reported that at 8:50 P.M. a huge, flaming object, believed to be a meteorite, fell on a farm in the neighborhood of Grovers Mill, New Jersey, twenty-two miles from Trenton. The flash in the sky was visible for several hundred miles and the noise of the impact was heard as far north as Elizabeth.

We have sent a special mobile unit to the scene, and will have our commentator, Mr. Phillips, give you a word description as soon as he can reach there from Princeton. In the meantime, we take you to the Hotel Martinet in Brooklyn, where Bobby Millette and his orchestra are offering a program of dance music.

(*Swing band for twenty seconds . . . then cut*)

ANNOUNCER TWO: We take you now to Grovers Mill, New Jersey. (*Crowd noises . . . police sirens*)

PHILLIPS: Ladies and gentlemen, this is Carl Phillips again, at the Wilmuth farm, Grovers Mill, New Jersey. Professor Pierson and myself made the eleven miles from Princeton in ten minutes. Well, I . . . I hardly know where to begin, to paint for you a word picture of the strange scene before my eyes, like

Note how the change of setting adds a certain reality, or truth, to the broadcast.

---

[4]**Trenton:** the capital of New Jersey

Notice the descriptive words that help you visualize this new setting.

something out of a modern *Arabian Nights*.[5] Well, I just got here. I haven't had a chance to look around yet. I guess that's it. Yes, I guess that's the . . . thing, directly in front of me, half buried in a vast pit. Must have struck with terrific force. The ground is covered with splinters of a tree it must have struck on its way down. What I can see of the . . . object itself doesn't look very much like a meteor, at least not the meteors I've seen. It looks more like a huge cylinder. It has a diameter of . . . what would you say, Professor Pierson?

PIERSON (*off*): About thirty yards.

PHILLIPS: About thirty yards . . . The metal on the sheath is . . . well, I've never seen anything like it. The color is sort of yellowish-white. Curious spectators now are pressing close to the object in spite of the efforts of the police to keep them back. They're getting in front of my line of vision. Would you mind standing on one side, please?

POLICEMAN: One side, there, one side.

PHILLIPS: While the policemen are pushing the crowd back, here's Mr. Wilmuth, owner of the farm here. He may have

---

sheath (SHEETH) a case or covering
[5]***Arabian Nights:*** a collection of tales from Arabia, India, and Persia.

some interesting facts to add . . . . Mr. Wilmuth, would you please tell the radio audience as much as you remember of this rather unusual visitor that dropped in your backyard? Step closer, please. Ladies and gentlemen, this is Mr. Wilmuth.

WILMUTH: I was listenin' to the radio.

PHILLIPS: Closer and louder, please.

WILMUTH: Pardon me!

PHILLIPS: Louder, please, and closer.

WILMUTH: Yes, sir—while I was listening to the radio and kinda drowsin', that Professor fellow was talkin' about Mars, so I was half dozin' and half . . .

PHILLIPS: Yes, Mr. Wilmuth. Then what happened?

WILMUTH: As I was sayin', I was listenin' to the radio kinda halfways . . .

PHILLIPS: Yes, Mr. Wilmuth, and then you saw something?

WILMUTH: Not first off. I heard something.

PHILLIPS: And what did you hear?

WILMUTH: A hissing sound. Like this: sssssss . . . kinda like a Fourt'-of-July rocket.

PHILLIPS: Then what?

> Notice that Mr. Wilmuth says he was listening to the radio program. Why does the writer have him make this remark?

Tell briefly whether Mr. Wilmuth is a flat or round character.

WILMUTH: Turned my head out the window and would have swore I was asleep and dreamin'.

PHILLIPS: Yes?

WILMUTH: I seen a kinda greenish streak and then zingo! Somethin' smacked the ground. Knocked me clear out of my chair!

PHILLIPS: Well, were you frightened, Mr. Wilmuth?

WILMUTH: Well, I—I ain't quite sure. I reckon I—I was kinda riled.

PHILLIPS: Thank you, Mr. Wilmuth. Thank you.

WILMUTH: Want me to tell you some more?

PHILLIPS: No . . . That's quite all right, that's plenty.

Here Mr. Phillips helps you picture the setting in your mind.

PHILLIPS: Ladies and gentlemen, you've just heard Mr. Wilmuth, owner of the farm where this thing has fallen. I wish I could convey the atmosphere . . . the background of this . . . fantastic scene. Hundreds of cars are parked in a field in back of us. Police are trying to rope off the roadway leading into the farm. But it's no use. They're breaking right through. Their headlights throw an enormous spot on the pit where the object's half buried. Some of the more daring souls are venturing near the edge. Their silhouettes stand out against the metal sheen.

(*Faint humming sound*)

To what sense does Mr. Phillips' description appeal?

One man wants to touch the thing . . . he's having an argument with a policeman. The policeman wins . . . Now, ladies and gentlemen, there's something I haven't mentioned in all this excitement, but it's becoming more distinct. Perhaps you've caught it already on your radio. Listen: (*Long pause*) . . . Do you hear it? It is a curious humming sound that seems to come from inside the object. I'll move the microphone nearer. Here. (*Pause*) Now we're not more than twenty-five feet away. Can you hear it now? Oh, Professor Pierson!

PIERSON: Yes, Mr. Phillips?

PHILLIPS: Can you tell us the meaning of that scraping noise inside the thing?

PIERSON: Possibly the unequal cooling of its surface.

PHILLIPS: Do you still think it's a meteor, Professor?

---

riled (RYLD) irritated; angered
silhouettes (sil oo ETS) dark shapes, or outlines, seen against a light background

PIERSON: I don't know what to think. The metal casing is definitely extraterrestrial . . . not found on this earth. Friction with the earth's atmosphere usually tears holes in a meteor. This thing is smooth and, as you can see, shaped like a cylinder.

How has Professor Pierson's attitude changed?

PHILLIPS: Just a minute! Something's happening! Ladies and gentlemen, this is terrific! This end of the thing is beginning to flake off! The top is beginning to rotate like a screw! The thing must be hollow!

Here the plot begins to build faster.

VOICES: She's a movin'!

Look, the darn thing's unscrewing!

Keep back, there! Keep back, I tell you!

Maybe there's men in it trying to escape!

It's red hot, they'll burn to a cinder!

Keep back there. Keep those idiots back!

What feelings do the shouting background voices convey?

(*Suddenly the clanking sound of a huge piece of falling metal*)

VOICES: She's off! The top's loose!

Look out there! Stand back!

PHILLIPS: Ladies and gentlemen, this is the most terrifying thing I have ever witnessed . . . Wait a minute! *Someone's crawling out of the hollow top.* Someone or . . . something. I can see peering out of that black hole two glowing disks . . . are they eyes? It might be a face. It might be . . .

(*Shout of awe from the crowd*)

PHILLIPS: Good heavens, something's wriggling out of the shadow like a gray snake. Now it's another one, and another. They look like tentacles to me. There, I can see the thing's body. It's large as a bear and it glistens like wet leather. But that face. It . . . it's indescribable. I can hardly force myself to keep looking at it. The eyes are black and gleam like a serpent. The mouth is V-shaped with saliva dripping from its rimless lips that seem to quiver and pulsate. The monster or whatever it is can hardly move. It seems weighed down by . . . possibly gravity or something. The thing's raising up. The crowd falls back. They've seen enough. This is the most extraordinary experience. I can't find words . . . I'm pulling this

Here, an alien character is introduced. What do Mr. Phillips's sensory words suggest about the visitor?

---

friction (FRIK shun) resistance
pulsate (PUL sayt) throb in a regular rhythm

microphone with me as I talk. I'll have to stop the description until I've taken a new position. Hold on, will you please, I'll be back in a minute.

(*Fade into piano*)

ANNOUNCER TWO: We are bringing you an eyewitness account of what's happening on the Wilmuth farm, Grovers Mill, New Jersey. (*More piano*) We now return you to Carl Phillips at Grovers Mill.

PHILLIPS: Ladies and gentlemen (Am I on?). Ladies and gentlemen, here I am, in back of a stone wall that adjoins Mr. Wilmuth's garden. From here I get a sweep of the whole scene. I'll give you every detail as long as I can talk. As long as I can see. More state police have arrived. They're drawing up a cordon in front of the pit, about thirty of them. No need to push the crowd back now. They're willing to keep their distance. The captain is speaking with someone. We can't quite see who. Oh yes, I believe it's Professor Pierson. Yes, it is. Now they've parted. The professor moves around one side, studying the object, while the captain and two policemen advance with something in their hands. I can see it now. It's a white handkerchief tied to a pole . . . a flag of truce. If those creatures know what that means . . . what anything means! . . . *Wait!* Something's happening!

(*Hissing sound followed by a humming that increases in intensity.*)

A humped shape is rising out of the pit. I can make out a small beam of light against a mirror. What's that? There's a jet of flame springing from that mirror, and it leaps right at the advancing men. It strikes them head on! Good Lord, they're turning into flame!

(*Screams and unearthly shrieks*)

Now the whole field's caught fire. (*Explosion*) The woods . . . the barns . . . the gas tanks of automobiles . . . it's spreading everywhere. It's coming this way. About twenty yards to my right . . .

---

cordon (KAWR dun) a line or circle of police stationed around an area to guard it

Notice the continuing use of foreshadowing.

Would you expect visitors from another planet to understand our symbol for peace?

Is the conflict external or internal?

(Crash of microphone . . . then dead silence)

ANNOUNCER TWO: Ladies and gentlemen, due to circumstances beyond our control, we are unable to continue the broadcast from Grovers Mill. Evidently there's some difficulty with our field transmission. However, we will return to that point at the earliest opportunity. In the meantime, we have a late bulletin from San Diego, California. Professor Indellkoffer, speaking at a dinner of the California Astronomical Society, expressed the opinion that the explosions on Mars are undoubtedly nothing more than severe volcanic disturbances on

What do the explosions on the surface of Mars really represent?

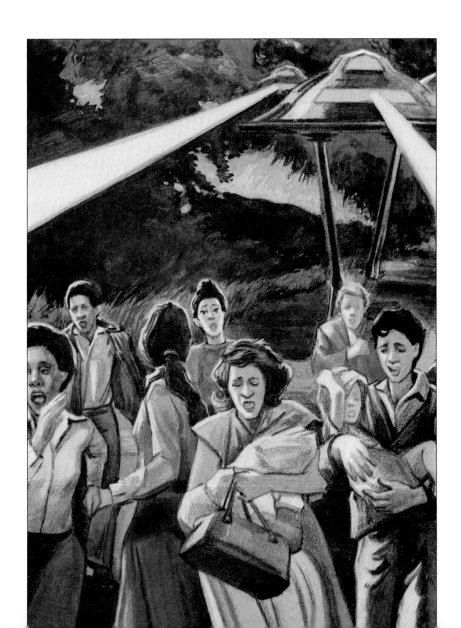

the surface of the planet. We continue now with our piano interlude.

(*Piano . . . then cut*)

Ladies and gentlemen, I have just been handed a message that came in from Grovers Mill by telephone. Just a moment. At least forty people, including six state troopers lie dead in a field east of the village of Grovers Mill, their bodies burned and twisted beyond all possible recognition. The next voice you hear will be that of Brigadier General Montgomery Smith, commander of the state militia at Trenton, New Jersey.

SMITH: I have been requested by the governor of New Jersey to place the counties of Mercer and Middlesex as far west as Princeton, and east to Jamesburg, under martial law. No one will be permitted to enter this area except by special pass issued by state or military authorities. Four companies of state militia are proceeding from Trenton to Grovers Mill, and will aid in the evacuation of homes within the range of military operations. Thank you.

Notice how the tension *appears* to be resolved. Do you think the Martians will decide to seek peace?

ANNOUNCER: You have just been listening to General Montgomery Smith, commanding the state militia at Trenton. In the meantime, further details of the disaster at Grovers Mill are coming in. The strange creatures, after making their deadly assault, crawled back in their pit and made no attempt to prevent the efforts of the firemen to recover the bodies and extinguish the fire. Combined fire departments of Mercer County are fighting the flames which threaten the entire countryside.

We have been unable to establish any contact with our mobile unit at Grovers Mill, but we hope to be able to return you there at the earliest possible moment. In the meantime we take you—uh, just one moment please.

(*Long pause*)

Notice that the Announcer has lowered his voice. Why does he do this?

(*Whisper*) Ladies and gentlemen, I have just been informed that we have finally established communication with an

---

interlude (IN tur lood) musical performance between the acts of a play
martial law (MAHR shul LAW) temporary rule by the military authorities
militia (muh LISH uh) an army of citizens rather than professional soldiers, called out in time of emergency

eyewitness of the tragedy. Professor Pierson has been located at a farmhouse near Grovers Mill where he has established an emergency observation post. As a scientist, he will give you his explanation of these terrible events. The next voice you hear will be that of Professor Pierson, brought to you by direct wire. Professor Pierson.

PIERSON: Of the creatures in the rocket cylinder at Grovers Mill, I can give you no reliable information—either as to their nature, their origin, or their purposes here on earth. Of their destructive instrument I might venture some conjectural explanation. For want of a better term, I shall refer to the mysterious weapon as a heat ray. It's all too evident that these creatures have scientific knowledge far in advance of our own. It is my guess that in some way they are able to generate an intense heat in a chamber of practically absolute nonconductivity. This intense heat they project in a parallel beam against any object they choose, by means of a polished parabolic mirror of unknown composition, much as the mirror of a lighthouse projects a beam of light. That is my conjecture of the origin of the heat ray . . .

> How do the words that Professor Pierson uses make him sound like a scientist?

ANNOUNCER TWO: Thank you, Professor Pierson. Ladies and gentlemen, here is a bulletin from Trenton. It is a brief statement informing us that the burnt body of Carl Phillips has been identified in a Trenton hospital. Now here's another bulletin from Washington, D.C.

Office of the director of the National Red Cross reports ten units of Red Cross emergency workers have been assigned to the headquarters of the state militia stationed outside of Grovers Mill, New Jersey. Here's a bulletin from state police, Princeton Junction: The fires at Grovers Mill and vicinity are now under control. Scouts report all quiet in the pit, and no sign of life appearing from the mouth of the cylinder . . . And now, ladies and gentlemen, we have a special statement from Mr. Harry McDonald, vice-president in charge of operations.

McDONALD: We have received a request from the militia at Trenton

---

eyewitness (EYE wit nis) person who actually saw something happen
nonconductivity (non kon duk TIV uh tee) the ability to contain and not transmit heat
parabolic (par uh BOL ik) bowl shaped

to place at their use our entire broadcasting facilities. In view of the seriousness of the situation, and believing that radio has a definite responsibility to serve in the public interest at all times, we are turning over our facilities to the state militia at Trenton.

ANNOUNCER: We take you now to the field headquarters of the state militia near Grovers Mill, New Jersey.

CAPTAIN: This is Captain Lansing of the signal corps,[6] attached to the state militia now engaged in military operations in the vicinity of Grovers Mill. Situation arising from the reported presence of certain individuals of unidentified nature is now under complete control.

The cylindrical object which lies in a pit directly below our position is surrounded on all sides by eight battalions of infantry, without heavy fieldpieces, but adequately armed with rifles and machine guns. All cause for alarm, if such cause ever existed, is now entirely unjustified. The things, whatever they are, do not even venture to poke their heads above the pit. I can see their hiding place plainly in the glare of the searchlights here. With all their reported resources, these creatures can scarcely stand up against heavy machine-gun fire. Anyway, it's an interesting outing for the troops. I can make out their khaki uniforms, crossing back and forth in front of the lights. It looks almost like a real war. There appears to be some slight smoke in the woods bordering the Millstone River. Probably fire started by campers. Well, we ought to see some action soon. One of the companies is deploying on the left side. A quick thrust and it will all be over. Now wait a minute! I see something on top of the cylinder. No, it's nothing but a shadow. Now the troops are on the edge of the Wilmuth farm. Seven thousand armed men closing in on an old metal tube. Wait, that wasn't a shadow! It's something moving . . . solid metal . . . kind of a shieldlike affair rising up out of the cylinder . . . It's going higher and higher. Why, it's standing on legs . . . actually rearing up on a sort of metal framework. Now it's reaching above the trees and the searchlights are on it! Hold on!

Do you think the conflict has been resolved?

What do the Captain's words suggest about his abilities as a commander?

---

fieldpieces (FEELD pees iz) mobile artillery
deploying (dih PLOI ing) spreading out
[6]**signal corps:** the part of the army in charge of communications

ANNOUNCER: Ladies and gentlemen, I have a grave announcement to make. Incredible as it may seem, both the observations of science and the evidence of our eyes lead to the inescapable assumption that those strange beings who landed in the Jersey farmlands tonight are the vanguard of an invading army from the planet Mars. The battle which took place tonight at Grovers Mill has ended in one of the most startling defeats ever suffered by an army in modern times; seven thousand men armed with rifles and machine guns set against a single fighting machine of the invaders from Mars. One hundred and twenty known survivors. The rest are scattered over the battle area from Grovers Mill to Plainsboro crushed and trampled to death under the metal feet of the monster, or burned to cinders by its heat ray. The monster is now in control of the middle section of New Jersey and has effectively cut the state through its center. Communication lines are down from Pennsylvania to the Atlantic Ocean. Railroad tracks are torn and service from New York to Philadelphia discontinued except routing some of the trains through Allentown and Phoenixville.[7] Highways to the north, south, and west are clogged with frantic human traffic. Police and army reserves are unable to control the mad rush. By morning the fugitives will have swelled Philadelphia, Camden and Trenton, it is estimated, to twice their normal population.

At this time, martial law prevails throughout New Jersey and eastern Pennsylvania. We take you now to Washington for a special broadcast on the National Emergency . . . the Secretary of the Interior . . .

SECRETARY: Citizens of the nation: I shall not try to conceal the gravity of the situation that confronts the country, nor the concern of your government in protecting the lives and property of its people. However, I wish to impress upon you— private citizens and public officials, all of you—the urgent need of calm and resourceful action. Fortunately, this powerful enemy is still confined to a comparatively small area, and we

---

Note the outcome of the battle between the Martians and the army. Predict what the Martians will do next.

Describe the reactions of people in New Jersey and Pennsylvania.

What is the Secretary of Interior really feeling? Is he optimistic?

---

assumption (uh SUMP shun) idea accepted as true without proof
vanguard (VAN gahrd) the part of an army that goes ahead of the main
   body in an advance
[7]**Allentown and Phoenixville:** cities in eastern Pennsylvania

may place our faith in the military forces to keep them there. In the meantime, placing our faith in God, we must continue the performance of our duties each and every one of us, so that we may confront this destructive enemy with a nation united, courageous, and consecrated to the preservation of human supremacy on this earth. I thank you.

ANNOUNCER: You have just heard the Secretary of the Interior speaking from Washington. Bulletins too numerous to read are piling up in the studio here. We are informed that the central portion of New Jersey is blacked out from radio communication due to the effect of the heat ray upon power lines and electrical equipment. Here is a special bulletin from New York. Cables received from English, French, German scientific organizations offering assistance. Astronomers report continued gas outbursts at regular intervals on planet Mars. Majority voice opinion that enemy will be reinforced by additional rocket machines. Attempts made to locate Professor Pierson of Princeton, who has observed Martians at close range. It is feared he was lost in recent battle. Langham Field, Virginia: Scouting planes report three Martian machines visible above treetops, moving north toward Somerville with population fleeing ahead of them. Heat ray not in use; although advancing at express-train speed, invaders pick their way carefully. They seem to be making conscious effort to avoid destruction of cities and countryside. However, they stop to destroy power lines, bridges, and railroad tracks. Their apparent objective is to crush resistance, paralyze communication, and disorganize human society.

Here is a bulletin from Basking Ridge, New Jersey: Raccoon hunters have stumbled on a second cylinder similar to the first lying in the great swamp twenty miles south of Morristown. U.S. army fieldpieces are proceeding from Newark to blow up second invading unit before cylinder can be opened and the fighting machine rigged. They are taking up position in the foothills of Watchung Mountains.[8] Another bulletin from Langham Field, Virginia: Scouting planes report enemy machines, now three in number, increasing speed northward

How do you know that so far, the Martians have only landed in the United States?

Notice the increasing number of bulletins. How do they contribute to the growing tension in the drama?

---

consecrated (KON sih krayt id) dedicated
[8]**Watchung Mountains:** a range of low mountains in New Jersey

kicking over houses and trees in their evident haste to unite with their allies south of Morristown. Machines also sighted by telephone operator east of Middlesex within ten miles of Plainfield. Here's a bulletin from Winston Field, Long Island. Fleet of army bombers carrying heavy explosives flying north in pursuit of enemy. Scouting planes act as guides. They keep speeding enemy in sight. Just a moment please. Ladies and gentlemen, we've run special wires to the artillery line in adjacent villages to give you direct reports in the zone of the advancing enemy. First we take you to the battery of the 22nd Field Artillery, located in the Watchung Mountains.

OFFICER: Range, thirty-two meters.

GUNNER: Thirty-two meters.

OFFICER: Projection, thirty-nine degrees.

GUNNER: Thirty-nine degrees.

OFFICER: Fire! (*Boom of heavy gun . . . pause*)

OBSERVER: One hundred and forty yards to the right, sir.

OFFICER: Shift range . . . thirty-one meters.

GUNNER: Thirty-one meters.

OFFICER: Projection . . . thirty-seven degrees.

GUNNER: Thirty-seven degrees.

OFFICER: Fire! (*Boom of heavy gun . . . pause*)

OBSERVER: A hit, sir! We got the tripod of one of them. They've stopped. The others are trying to repair it.

OFFICER: Quick, get the range! Shift thirty meters.

GUNNER: Thirty meters.

OFFICER: Projection . . . twenty-seven degrees.

GUNNER: Twenty-seven degrees.

OFFICER: Fire! (*Boom of heavy gun . . . pause*)

OBSERVER: Can't see the shell land, sir. They're letting off a smoke.

OFFICER: What is it?

OBSERVER: A black smoke, sir. Moving this way. Lying close to the ground. It's moving fast.

OFFICER: Put on gas masks. (*Pause*) Get ready to fire. Shift to twenty-four meters.

GUNNER: Twenty-four meters.

Is this new development a genuine cause for hope?

Describe the conflict in this scene.

---

adjacent (uh JAY sunt) near or next to
tripod (TRY pod) three legged support

Invasion from Mars ■ 425

OFFICER: Fire! (*Boom*)

GUNNER: Still can't see, sir. The smoke's coming nearer.

OFFICER: Get the range. (*Coughs*)

OBSERVER: Twenty-three meters. (*Coughs*)

OFFICER: Twenty-three meters. (*Coughs*)

GUNNER: Twenty-three meters. (*Coughs*)

OBSERVER: Projection, twenty-two degrees. (*Coughing*)

OFFICER: Twenty-two degrees. (*Fade in coughing*)

(*Fading in . . . sound of airplane motor*)

COMMANDER: Army bombing plane, V-8-43, off Bayonne, New Jersey, Lieutenant Voght, commanding eight bombers. Reporting to Commander Fairfax, Langham Field . . . This is Voght, reporting to Commander Fairfax, Langham Field . . . Enemy tripod machines now in sight. Reinforced by three machines from the Morristown cylinder . . . six altogether. One machine partially crippled. Believed hit by shell from army gun in Watchung Mountains. Guns now appear silent. A heavy black fog hanging close to the earth . . . of extreme density, nature unknown. No sign of heat ray. Enemy now turns east, crossing Passaic River into the Jersey marshes. Another straddles the Pulaski Skyway.[9] Evident objective is New York City. They're pushing down a high tension power station. The machines are close together now, and we're ready to attack. Planes circling, ready to strike. A thousand yards and we'll be over the first—eight hundred yards . . . six hundred . . . four hundred . . . two hundred . . . There they go! The giant arm raised . . . Green flash! They're spraying us with flame! Two thousand feet. Engines are giving out. No chance to release bombs. Only one thing left . . . drop on them, plane and all. We're diving on the first one. Now the engine's gone! Eight . . .

OPERATOR ONE: This is Bayonne, New Jersey, calling Langham Field . . .

This is Bayonne, New Jersey, calling Langham Field.

Come in, please . . . Come in, please. . .

OPERATOR TWO: This is Langham Field . . . go ahead . . .

OPERATOR ONE: Eight army bombers in battle with enemy tripod

What happens to the soldiers?

Where are the Martians now heading?

Notice the rising level of tension in the Commander's voice. What does his final action tell about the Commander's character?

---

density (DEN suh tee) thickness
9**Pulaski Skyway:** an elevated highway in eastern New Jersey

machines over Jersey marshlands. Engines disabled by heat ray. All crashed. One enemy machine destroyed. Enemy now discharging heavy black smoke in direction of—

OPERATOR THREE: This is Newark, New Jersey . . .

This is Newark, New Jersey . . .

Warning! Poisonous black smoke pouring in from Jersey marshes. Reaches South Street. Gas masks useless. Urge population to move into open spaces . . . automobiles use Routes 7, 23, 24 . . . Avoid congested areas. Smoke now spreading over Raymond Boulevard . . .

OPERATOR FOUR: 2X2L . . . calling CQ . . .

2X2L . . . calling CQ . . .   2X2L . . . calling 8X3R . . .

Come in, please . . .

OPERATOR FIVE: This is 8X3R . . . coming back at 2X2L.

OPERATOR FOUR: How's reception? How's reception? K, please. Where are you, 8X3R?

What's the matter? Where are you?

(Bells ringing over city gradually diminishing)

ANNOUNCER: I'm speaking from the roof of Broadcasting Building, New York City. The bells you hear are ringing to warn the people to evacuate the city as the Martians approach. Estimated in last two hours three million people have moved out along the roads to the north. Hutchison River Parkway still kept open for motor traffic. Avoid bridges to Long Island . . . hopelessly jammed. All communication with Jersey shore closed ten minutes ago. No more defenses. Our army wiped out . . . artillery, air force, everything wiped out. This may be the last broadcast. We'll stay here to the end . . . People are holding service below us . . . in the church.

(Voices singing hymn)

Now I look down the harbor. All manner of boats, overloaded with fleeing population, pulling out from docks.

(Sound of boat whistles)

Streets are all jammed. Noise in crowds is like New Year's Eve in the city. Wait a minute . . . Enemy now in sight above

> How powerful is the Martian's poison gas?

---

congested (kun JEST id) clogged, overcrowded

What words or phrases help you determine the size of the Martian machines?

the Palisades.[10] Five great machines. First one is crossing river. I can see it from here, wading the Hudson like a man wading through a brook . . . A bulletin's handed me . . . Martian cylinders are falling all over the country. One outside Buffalo, one in Chicago, St. Louis . . . seem to be timed and spaced . . . Now the first machine reaches the shore. He stands watching, looking over the city. His steel, cowlish head is even with the skyscrapers. He waits for the others. They rise like a line of new towers on the city's west side . . . Now they're lifting their metal hands. This is the end now. Smoke comes out . . . black smoke, drifting over the city. People in the streets see it now. They're running toward the East River . . . thousands of them, dropping in like rats. Now the smoke's spreading faster.

Notice the comparison of people to rats. What attitude does this comparison suggest?

It's reached Times Square. People trying to run away from it, but it's no use. They're falling like flies. Now the smoke's crossing Sixth Avenue . . . Fifth Avenue . . . one hundred yards away . . . it's fifty feet . . .

OPERATOR FOUR: 2X2L calling CQ . . .
2X2L calling CQ . . .
2X2L calling CQ . . . New York.
Isn't there anyone on the air?
Isn't there anyone . . .
2X2L—

Notice that the original announcer interrupts the radio drama to tell the audience something important.

ANNOUNCER: You are listening to a CBS presentation of Orson Welles and the Mercury Theatre on the Air in a original dramatization of *The War of the Worlds* by H. G. Wells. The performance will continue after a brief intermission.
This is the Columbia . . . Broadcasting System.

(*Music*)

Explain the meaning of the figurative expression, "small island of daylight."

PIERSON: As I set down these notes on paper, I'm consumed by the thought that I may be the last living man on earth. I have been hiding in this empty house near Grovers Mill—a small island of daylight cut off by the black smoke from the rest of the world. All that happened before the arrival of these monstrous creatures in the world now seems part of another life

---

cowlish (KOUL ish) hood shaped
[10]**Palisades:** the line of steep cliffs in northeastern New Jersey and southeastern New York on the west shore of the Hudson River

. . . a life that has no relation to the present, furtive existence of the lonely derelict who pencils these words on the back of some astronomical notes bearing the signature of Richard Pierson. I look down, at my blackened hands, my torn shoes, my tattered clothes, and I try to connect them with a professor who lives at Princeton, and who on the night of October 30, glimpsed through his telescope an orange splash of light on a distant planet. My wife, my fellow professors, my students, my books, my observatory, my . . . my world . . . where are they? Did they ever exist? Am I Richard Pierson? What day is it? Do days exist without calendars? Does time pass when there are no human hands left to wind the clocks? . . . In writing down my daily life I tell myself I shall preserve human history between the dark covers of this little book that was meant to record the movements of the stars . . . But to write I must live, and to live I must eat . . . I find moldy bread in the kitchen, and an orange not too spoiled to swallow. I keep watch at the window. From time to time I catch sight of a Martian above the black smoke.

The smoke still holds the house in its black coil . . . But at length there is a hissing sound and suddenly I see a Martian mounted on his machine, spraying the air with a jet of steam, as if to clear away the smoke. I watch in a corner as his huge metal legs nearly brush against the house. Exhausted by terror, I fall asleep . . . It's morning. Sun streams in the window. The black cloud of gas has lifted, and the scorched meadows to the north look as though a black snowstorm has passed over them. I venture from the house. I make my way to a road. No traffic. Here and there a wrecked car, baggage overturned, a blackened skeleton. I push on north. For some reason I feel safer trailing these monsters than running away from them. And I keep a careful watch. I have seen the Martians feed. Should one of their machines appear over the top of trees, I am ready to fling myself flat on the earth. I come to a chestnut tree. October, chestnuts are ripe. I fill my pockets. I must keep alive. Two days I wander in a vague northerly direction through a barren world. Finally I notice a living creature . . . a small red squirrel in a beech tree. I stare at him, and wonder. He stares back at me.

Notice the plot development. Can Professor Pierson believe what has happened to him?

What does Professor Pierson seem to be questioning?

Imagine what it might be like to think you were the last person on Earth. How would you feel?

---

furtive (FUR tiv) sneaky, secretive

I believe at that moment the animal and I shared the same emotion . . . the joy of finding another living being . . . I push on north. I find dead cows in a brackish field. Beyond, the charred ruins of a dairy. The silo remains standing guard over the wasteland like a lighthouse deserted by the sea. Astride the silo perches a weathervane. The arrow points north.

Notice Professor Pierson's use of flash-back. What might this suggest about the outcome of his story?

Next day I came to a city vaguely familiar in its contours, yet its buildings strangely dwarfed and leveled off, as if a giant had sliced off its highest towers with a capricious sweep of his hand. I reached the outskirts. I found Newark, unde-molished, but humbled by some whim of the advancing Martians. Presently, with an odd feeling of being watched, I caught sight of something crouching in a doorway. I made a step toward it, and it rose up and became a man—a man, armed with a large knife.

Here, a new conflict begins to develop.

STRANGER: Stop . . . Where did you come from?

PIERSON: I come from . . . many places. A long time ago from Princeton.

STRANGER: Princeton, huh? That's near Grovers Mill!

PIERSON: Yes.

What do his comments suggest about the Stranger's character?

STRANGER: Grovers Mill . . . (*Laughs as at a great joke*) There's no food here. This is my country . . . all this end of town down to the river. There's only food for me . . . Which way are you going?

PIERSON: I don't know. I guess I'm looking for—for people.

STRANGER: (*nervously*) What was that? Did you hear something just then?

PIERSON: Only a bird (*marvels*) . . . A live bird!

STRANGER: You get to know that birds have shadows these days . . . Say, we're in the open here. Let's crawl into this doorway and talk.

PIERSON: Have you seen any Martians?

STRANGER: They've gone over to New York. At night the sky is alive with their lights. Just as if people were still living in it. By daylight you can't see them. Five days ago a couple of them carried something big across the flats from the airport. I believe they're learning how to fly.

---

brackish (BRAK ish) salty and marshy
capricious (kuh PRISH us) without apparent reason

PIERSON: Fly!

STRANGER: Yeah, fly.

PIERSON: Then it's all over with humanity. Stranger, there's still you and I. Two of us left.

STRANGER: They got themselves in solid; they wrecked the greatest country in the world. Those green stars, they're probably falling somewhere every night. They've only lost one machine. There isn't anything to do. We're done. We're licked.

If you were listening to this radio drama in 1938, would this statement have caused you to jump up and look outside your windows?

PIERSON: Where were you? You're in a uniform.

STRANGER: What's left of it. I was in the militia—National Guard . . . That's good! Wasn't any war any more than there is between men and ants.

Does the Stranger feel the participants in the war were evenly matched?

PIERSON: And we're edible ants. I found that out . . . What will they do to us?

STRANGER: I've thought it all out. Right now we're caught as we're wanted. The Martian only has to go a few miles to get a crowd on the run. But they won't keep doing that. They'll begin catching us systematic like—keeping the best and storing us in cages and things. They haven't begun on us yet!

PIERSON: Not begun!

STRANGER: Not begun. All that's happened so far is because we don't have sense enough to keep quiet . . . bothering them with guns and such stuff and losing our heads and rushing off in crowds. Now instead of our rushing around blind we've got to fix ourselves up according to the way things are now. Cities, nations, civilization, progress . . . done.

PIERSON: But if that's so, what is there to live for?

STRANGER: There won't be any more concerts for a million years or so, and no nice little dinners at restaurants. If it's amusement you're after, I guess the game's up.

PIERSON: And what is there left?

STRANGER: Life . . . that's what! I want to live. And so do you! We're not going to be exterminated. And I don't mean to be caught, either, and tamed, and fattened like an ox.

PIERSON: What are you going to do?

STRANGER: I'm going on . . . right under their feet. I gotta plan. We humans as humans are finished. We don't know enough. We gotta learn plenty before we've got a chance. And we've got to live and keep free while we learn. I've thought it all out, see.

Does the Stranger see the Martian invasion the same way as Professor Pierson?

PIERSON: Tell me the rest.

What does the Stranger think about the way that most people used to live?

STRANGER: Well, it isn't all of us that are made for wild beasts, and that's what it's got to be. That's why I watched you. All these little office workers that used to live in these houses—they'd be no good. They haven't any stuff to 'em. They just used to run off to work. I've seen hundreds of 'em, running wild to catch their commuters' train in the morning for fear that they'd get canned if they didn't; running back at night afraid they won't be in time for dinner. Lives insured and a little invested in case of accidents. And on Sundays, worried about the hereafter. The Martians will be a blessing for those guys. Nice roomy cages, good food, no worries. After a week or so chasing about the fields on empty stomachs they'll come and be glad to be caught.

PIERSON: You've thought it all out, haven't you?

What is the Stranger's view of human beings?

STRANGER: You bet I have! And that isn't all. These Martians will make pets of some of them, train 'em to do tricks. Who knows? Get sentimental over the pet boy who grew up and had to be killed. And some, maybe, they'll train to hunt us.

PIERSON: No, that's impossible. No human being . . .

STRANGER: Yes, they will. There's people who'll do it gladly. If one of them ever comes after me . . .

Do Professor Pierson and the Stranger seek the same human qualities in each other?

PIERSON: In the meantime, you and I and others like us . . . where are we to live when the Martians own the Earth?

STRANGER: I've got it all figured out. We'll live underground. I've been thinking about the sewers. Under New York are miles and miles of 'em. The main ones are big enough for anybody. Then there's cellars, vaults, underground storerooms, railway tunnels, subways. You begin to see, eh? And we'll get a bunch of strong people together. No weak ones, that garbage, out.

PIERSON: And you meant me to go?

STRANGER: Well, I gave you a chance, didn't I?

PIERSON: We won't quarrel about that. Go on.

STRANGER: And we've got to make safe places for us to stay in, see, and get all the books we can—science books. That's where people like you come in, see? We'll raid the museums, we'll even spy on the Martians. It may not be so much we have to learn before—just imagine this: four or five of their own fighting machines suddenly start off—heat rays right and left and not a Martian in 'em. Not a Martian in 'em. But humans—humans who have learned the way how. It may even be in our time. Gee! Imagine having one of them lovely things with its heat ray wide and free! We'd turn it on Martians, we'd turn it on people. We'd bring everybody down to their knees.

PIERSON: That's your plan?

STRANGER: You and me and a few more of us we'd own the world.

PIERSON: I see.

STRANGER: Say, what's the matter? Where are you going?

PIERSON: Not to your world . . . Good-bye, stranger . . .

PIERSON: After parting with the artilleryman, I came at last to the Holland Tunnel.[11] I entered that silent tube anxious to know the fate of the great city on the other side of the Hudson. Cautiously I came out of the tunnel and made my way up Canal Street.

I reached Fourteenth Street, and there again were black powder and several bodies, and an evil ominous smell from the gratings of the cellars of some of the houses. I wandered up through the Thirties and Forties;[12] I stood alone on Times Square.[13] I caught sight of a lean dog running down Seventh Avenue with a piece of dark brown meat in his jaws, and a pack of starving mongrels at his heels. He made a wide circle around me, as though he feared I might prove a fresh competitor. I walked up Broadway in the direction of that strange powder—past silent shop windows, displaying their quiet wares to empty sidewalks—past the Capitol Theater, silent, dark—past a shooting gallery, where a row of empty guns faced a halted line of wooden ducks. Near Columbus Circle I noticed models of 1939 motorcars in the showrooms facing empty streets. From over the top of the General Motors Building, I watched a flock of black birds circling in the sky. I hurried on. Suddenly I caught sight of the hood of a Martian machine, standing somewhere in Central Park, gleaming in the late afternoon sun. An insane idea! I rushed recklessly across

What is the Stranger's goal?

What does "world" mean in this phrase?

What sensory words does the author use to help you visualize the remains of New York City?

Note the foreshadowing; when do birds usually "circle in the sky"?

---

ominous (OM uh nus) threatening; sinister
[11]**Holland Tunnel:** a tunnel under the Hudson River between New York and New Jersey
[12]**Thirties and Forties:** numbered streets across Manhattan
[13]**Times Square:** the center of the theater district in New York City

Columbus Circle and into the Park. I climbed a small hill above the pond at Sixtieth Street. From there I could see, standing in a silent row along the mall, nineteen of those great metal Titans, their cowls empty, their steel arms hanging limp by their sides. I looked in vain for the monsters that inhabit those machines.

What conflict is finally resolved in this climax?

Suddenly, my eyes were attracted to the immense flock of black birds that hovered directly below me. They circled to the ground, and there before my eyes, stark and silent, lay the Martians, with the hungry birds pecking and tearing brown shreds of flesh from their dead bodies. Later when their bodies were examined in laboratories, it was found that they were killed by the putrefactive and disease bacteria against which their systems were unprepared . . . slain, after all man's defenses had failed, by the humblest thing that God in His wisdom put upon this earth.

Before the cylinder fell there was a general belief that through all the deep of space no life existed beyond the petty

---

Titans (TYT unz) giants
putrefactive (pyoo truh FAK tiv) rotting; decomposing

surface of our tiny planet. Now we see further. Dim and wonderful is the vision I have pictured in my mind of life spreading slowly from this little seedbed of the solar system throughout the inanimate vastness of space. But that is a remote dream. It may be that the destruction of the Martians is only a reprieve. To them, and not to us, is the future ordained perhaps.

Here, the author gives you a hint about the theme of the radio drama.

Strange it now seems to sit in my peaceful study at Princeton writing down this last chapter of the record begun at a deserted farm in Grovers Mill. Strange to see from my window the university spires dim and blue through an April haze. Strange to watch children playing in the streets. Strange to see young people strolling on the green, where the new spring grass heals the last black scars of a bruised earth. Strange to watch the sightseers enter the museum where the disassembled parts of a Martian machine are kept on public view. Strange when I recall the time when I first saw it, bright and clean-cut, hard and silent, under the dawn of that last great day.

Notice that the action has shifted to the present time.

(*Music*)

This is Orson Welles, ladies and gentlemen, out of character to assure you that *The War of the Worlds* has no further significance than as the holiday offering it was intended to be. The Mercury Theatre's own radio version of dressing up in a sheet and jumping out of a bush and saying Boo! Starting now, we couldn't soap all your windows and steal all your garden gates, by tomorrow night . . . so we did the next best thing. We destroyed the world before your very ears, and utterly ruined the Columbia Broadcasting System. You will be relieved, I hope, to learn that we didn't mean it, and that both institutions are still open for business. So good-bye everybody, and remember, please, for the next day or so, the terrible lesson you learned tonight. That grinning, glowing, globular invader of your living room is an inhabitant of the pumpkin patch, and if your doorbell rings and nobody's there, that was no Martian . . . it's Hallowe'en.

To what event does the narrator compare the radio drama, "Invasion from Mars"?

Who is this invader?

---

inanimate (in AN uh mit) without life
reprieve (rih PREEV) postponement
globular (GLOB yuh lur) rounded

Review the Selection

Recall

1. Where do the Martians first land?

2. Where does Pierson work?

3. Identify the Martians' primary objective.

Infer

4. Describe the reactions of most New Yorkers to the Martian invasion.

5. Why is the Martians' final defeat ironic? Explain your answer.

6. Why does the original announcer interrupt the radio play?

7. Why do you think Professor Pierson decides not to join the Stranger?

Apply

8. Briefly characterize the Martians. Support your answer with specific words and phrases from the play.

9. Compare and contrast the play with a real emergency broadcast.

10. Imagine you were listening to the radio in New Jersey on the night of October 30, 1938. How would you have responded?

Respond to Literature

What technological changes in the United States during the 1930s gave *Invasion from Mars* such a large audience?

WRITE ABOUT THE SELECTION

When Howard Koch was thinking about the setting for his drama, he opened a map, closed his eyes, and dropped his pencil directly on a town called Grovers Mill. Then he began to develop characters, think about dialogue, and create conflicts that would make his audience sit at the edge of their seats.

Imagine you have just encountered an army of aliens marching on your town or city. Write a short radio drama in which you try to tell a friend, a member of your family, or a teacher, about the very real danger they face.

Prewriting   Make an informal list of the elements of drama that you will include in your scene. Include details of setting, dialogue that reveals both your own and your listener's character, and of course, a conflict (perhaps this person refuses to believe your story).

Writing   Use your informal list to write a brief radio drama in which you attempt to convince someone you know, of an alien invasion. In it, include as many elements of drama as you can.

Revising   When you revise your scene, reread it to discover if listeners can understand it without having to see it.

Proofreading   When you proofread your scene, check to see if the commas, periods, and exclamation points are properly placed.

THINK ABOUT DRAMA

Once a drama is written, the finished **script** is performed by actors, who make the printed words come alive.

The **characters** include the people, animals, or even Martians in a drama. Their personalities are revealed by actions and **dialogue**. Characters are often affected by their **setting**, the time and place in which their stories take place. The sequence of actions, events, and conflicts that characters experience is called the **plot**. The principal, or main, message of a play is called its **theme**.

1. Describe in detail two settings from *Invasion from Mars*.

2. Reread the dialogue on pages 411 through 413. What kind of man is Professor Pierson?

3. What is the central conflict?

4. What kind of conflict does Pierson face? What choice does he make?

5. What is the theme of the drama?

DEVELOP YOUR VOCABULARY

Jargon refers to the particular words and phrases, or special language, used by a group of people who share the same job, profession, hobby, or interest. When musicians talk about playing a *gig*, or hiring *roadies*, for example, they are using jargon to talk about their next concert or performance, and the people who handle their musical equipment when they are touring on the road.

Jargon is usually understood by people who are part of the group. Those outside the group however, may be unfamiliar with the unusual words and terms.

Use a dictionary or encyclopedia to determine the meaning of each of the following "space" jargon words, and write original sentences using six of them. If you choose, you may suggest additional space jargon words.

1. booster
2. G-suit
3. pitch
4. dry run
5. Mach
6. touchdown
7. glitch
8. LEM

Learn About

READING FOCUS

Evaluate the Poet's Purpose Knowing the writer's purpose, or reason for writing a piece, helps the reader know how to react to it. Think about the poet's purpose as you read "Futility."

TONE

In literature, **tone** is a writer's emotional attitude toward his or her subject. Tone is expressed through a writer's choice of words and details, and the way that he or she describes characters and events.

You may find it helpful to think of tone as a writer's way of "speaking." If, for example, a writer feels pleasantly amused or happy about a particular subject, he or she might "speak" with descriptive words, such as *gleeful*, *delighted*, or *thrilled*.

As you read, pay close attention to the words and phrases that a writer uses to reveal his or her particular attitude. Ask yourself whether these words suggest a tone of anger, sadness, joy, amazement, or some other emotion.

As you read "Futility," ask yourself:
1. What is the tone, or author's attitude, in this poem?
2. What words or phrases help you to determine this attitude?

WRITING CONNECTION

On a piece of paper, write the words "Nice outfit." Say the words out loud. What attitude do they suggest? Now, write the various meanings you might achieve if you pronounced this phrase in different tones of voice.

FUTILITY

by Mary S. Hawling

I try to capture rhythm with
The make-shift words that limit me:
The wind has more success than I
By simply bending down a tree.

5   I seek for color, and must be
Content with some cold, distant name:
Yet swiftly, as the night walks near,
The sky is surging bronze and flame.

I struggle for a single line
10   To measure an emotion by:
A wild bird, effortless, takes wing
And writes a poem across the sky.

---

futility (fyoo TIL ih tee) lack of success; uselessness
make-shift or **makeshift** (MAYK shift) substitute; temporary

Review the Selection

Recall

1. What has more success than the speaker at capturing rhythm?

2. According to the speaker, what colors light the night sky?

3. To what does the speaker compare a wild bird?

Infer

4. Do you think the speaker of the poem finds writing difficult? Explain.

5. Explain the meaning of *name* in "Content with some cold distant name."

6. What do the last two lines of the poem mean to you?

7. What do you think the speaker is saying about writing a poem?

Apply

8. Compare and contrast the poet's efforts with the efforts of nature.

9. Do you think the author is successful in communicating beauty?

10. Choose two new titles for the poem.

Respond to Literature

Do you think "Futility" is an appropriate choice to conclude this unit? What events in the early 20th century might be characterized as futile?

WRITE ABOUT THE SELECTION

Have you ever tried to communicate a special feeling about a person, idea, or event, but were unable to find the proper combination of words and phrases that expressed your attitude? Mary S. Hawling expresses that situation in her poem, "Futility." Write a brief letter to a friend in which you explain exactly why you admire a particular person.

Prewriting   Think of a person you know well, or have read about. What qualities about him or her do you find admirable? What is special about the person? Make an informal list of descriptive words that might convey this specific attitude.

Writing   Use your informal list to write a brief letter to a friend. In it, express your admiration about an acquaintance or historical figure.

Revising   When you revise your letter, imagine you are the person to whom it is addressed. Think whether you could determine the writer's tone of admiration. Then, make sure that you have included enough specific details and descriptive words that consistently express a tone of admiration.

Proofreading   Read over your completed letter to check for spelling errors. If you are unsure about the correct spelling of a particular word, consult the dictionary. Spelling mistakes can distract your reader and make it hard for him or her to understand what you are trying to say.

THINK ABOUT TONE

When we talk about the sarcastic tone of a cutting remark or the friendly tone of a personal letter, we mean the specific attitude that is expressed by the speaker or writer. Another way to understand a writer's **tone**, is to think of it as his or her tone of voice. Just as you speak harshly when you are angry, an angry writer will use descriptive words that convey that feeling. A writer who is trying to convey a sympathetic tone will use words that express sympathy.

1. Does the title of the poem suggest that it will have a certain tone?

2. Does your reading of the poem support the view?

3. What word details help you to determine the tone of the poem?

4. What words would you use to change this tone?

5. The author says that writing a poem is an exercise in futility. Do you agree with her attitude? Explain the reasons for your opinion.

READING FOCUS

Evaluate the Poet's Purpose What do you think the poet's purpose was in writing "Futility"? Why do you think she expressed these thoughts in a poem? How did you react, knowing her purpose?

DEVELOP YOUR VOCABULARY

Antonyms are words that have opposite, or nearly opposite, meanings. For example, *reprimand* means "to scold harshly." An antonym for *reprimand* is *praise*. Understanding antonyms helps you to figure out contrasting ideas or statements.

Read each sentence below and choose the correct antonym for each italicized word. You may consult a dictionary.

1. The teacher *deferred* our test until next week.
   - **a.** postponed
   - **b.** delayed
   - **c.** rushed
   - **d.** moved

2. Preparing for the debate had put him in a *pensive* mood.
   - **a.** thoughtful
   - **b.** silly
   - **c.** tired
   - **d.** cultured

3. The *tumult* from the cheering crowd drowned out the announcer's voice.
   - **a.** disturbance
   - **b.** uproar
   - **c.** silence
   - **d.** screaming

4. Lost in a pleasant *reverie*, she didn't hear the doorbell ring.
   - **a.** distraction
   - **b.** concentration
   - **c.** daydream
   - **d.** diversion

UNIT 5 *Review*

Write About Conflict

If there is a single element that links the different selections in this unit, it is the conflict between tradition and social change. Do you think the changes that are expressed in these stories, poems, and dramas are limited only to their specific time period? Or, do some have a more timeless meaning? Choose one selection in this unit and explain whether it would have the same impact if it had been written today.

Prewriting   Before you begin to write your essay, think of a selection in this unit that you feel has a timeless message, or theme. Ask yourself whether the events, situations, or conflicts in it, have any significance for the social changes happening in the United States today. Then freewrite your response.

Writing   Use your freewriting to write a two-paragraph essay that explains which selection might have a large impact on a modern audience.

Revising   When you revise your essay, make sure that you have included specific details from the selection to support your argument.

Proofreading   If you have used compound sentences in your essay, make sure that a comma separates the two distinct thoughts in that sentence. Be alert for errors in capitalization. Remember that proper names and story titles are always capitalized.

Write About Literary Elements

One of a writer's chief responsibilities is to make you, the reader, familiar with the unfamiliar. Think about the literary elements—character, dialogue, setting, plot, symbolism, and theme—that you have studied in this unit. Choose one selection and write a paragraph that explains which elements helped you feel "at home" in the writer's created world.

Prewriting   Before you begin to write, review your responses to the questions in the "Think About . . ." sections in this unit. Then, make an informal list of the literary elements that appeared in your chosen selection, and think about how the author successfully combined these elements in the story, poem, or drama.

Writing   Use your informal list to write a brief essay that describes which combination of literary elements effectively drew you into the writer's imaginary world. In it, make specific references to descriptions, dialogue, events, and situations.

Revising   When you revise your essay, check to see if the sentences vary in length. Mixing long and short sentences can help you capture and maintain your reader's interest.

Proofreading   When you proofread your essay, make sure that you have used quotation marks to indicate an author's exact words. Check to see that all commas, and periods have been placed inside quotation marks.

BUILD LANGUAGE SKILLS

Vocabulary

Context often provides clues that help you figure out the meaning of an unfamiliar word. You can also use context clues to determine the proper meaning of a word that has several definitions.

For example, *house* can mean: a dwelling; a royal family; a building where animals are kept; or a legislative assembly. In the sentence, "We saw the lizards in the zoo's reptile *house*," only the third meaning of *house* fits the context.

Read each sentence below and choose the meaning that best fits the context.

1. Besides being a true artist, Hemingway was a great historical *figure*.
   a. outline or shape
   b. illustration or diagram
   c. special person

2. The news reporter traveled to every *corner* of our state to cover the story.
   a. secret place
   b. particular region
   c. awkward position

3. Taking math and history will help me achieve a *broad* education.
   a. long
   b. varied
   c. easy to understand

4. The first draft of the escape plan was *rough*, but we could always revise it.
   a. not level
   b. violent or stormy
   c. unfinished

Grammar, Usage, and Mechanics

A well-written sentence should contain enough words to achieve your intended effect. Too few words might not provide your reader with enough information and too many words can distract your reader.

Repetition is a common cause of unclear sentences. Often, you can make a sentence more concise by eliminating repeated words and redundant phrases, different groups of words that mean exactly the same thing.

Read the sentences below. Underline the repeated words or redundant phrases. Then make each sentence more concise.

1. We toured the old ancient war museum.

2. Our principal gave a long speech that was lengthy and put us to sleep.

3. At first his initial look didn't reveal anything unusual about the setting.

4. Robert Frost became the most famous and well-known poet in America.

5. The homework the teacher gave was the tenth assignment she had given this week.

6. She saw some prehistoric tools that had been used before history was written.

7. They had played a practical joke on Sam deliberately on purpose.

SPEAKING AND LISTENING

Improvised dialogue is a kind of reader's theatre. It is a form of oral presentation that has an emphasis on devising and reading dialogue rather than on memorizing lines that are already written. Improvised dialogue is less structured than a scripted play or the dialogue in a story because it is composed and performed without much preparation. It can be used to tell a folk tale, to play a scene from a story, to convey the message of a poem, or to show the relationship between characters. In short, improvised dialogue has a wide range of uses. In fact, there is no limit to its possibilities as long as you use your imagination.

There are a few guidelines that you should be familiar with if you are to be successful. Read these before you try your hand at improvised dialogue.

1. Since improvised dialogue is an activity that gives little time for preparation, it is important that each participant be familiar with the material used for the dialogue. It should be understood by all those involved.

2. Once the selection has been read and discussed, choose the cast of characters. The participants should decide how the scene they will improvise will be set up. One way to arrange the characters is to have them sit in a row in order of their appearance. Then they can move in and out of the scene as needed.

3. Practice and replay the scene. Since this is improvised—using more or less spur-of-the-moment dialogue—your words may change, but the idea of the scene will remain the same. Practicing and replaying the scene will work out the rough spots.

4. Cooperation is a key to successful improvised dialogue. Each character will have to listen and be attentive to catch their own cues.

Now that you have some basic guidelines, choose a selection from this unit and try your hand at improvised dialogue. Devise dialogue where none previously existed and replay the scene before an audience. Limit your dialogue to about three minutes. Remember, you need a pretty good idea of the sequence of the events and the characters, so get to know them.

CRITICAL THINKING

Make Inferences An **inference** is a conclusion drawn from known facts or evidence. Look at this example:

If the motor is broken, the machine will not run. The motor is broken.

What can you infer, or conclude, from these statements of fact? The logical conclusion, or inference, is that the machine will not run.

Authors often make the reader supply inferences about a character or an event. They may choose not to state certain information. Using information that *is* supplied, the reader may infer the missing information. The evidence to support the inference may come from the expressions and gestures of characters, action and details in the plot, sensory words, descriptions, and dialogue.

Choose a selection and study it to discover what new inferences you can make about character, setting, conflict, theme, or the author's purpose. As you study, answer the following questions:

1. What evidence is available on which to base an inference? Explain.

2. What evidence is missing? Do I know of similar people or situations like the one in the literary work?

EFFECTIVE STUDYING

Read Effectively Not everything you read deserves the same amount of attention. If you read something for fun, you probably find the reading easy. You are using **rapid reading** skills for such material.

Some things, like looking over a page to find a specific piece of information—a telephone number, a particular date, a statistic—requires a kind of reading called **skimming**. For skimming, you merely run your eyes down the page, stopping when you find the information you want.

Careful reading is needed when you want to remember details. Careful reading is used for reading textbooks or for taking tests.

Critical reading is reading in which you need to stop to examine and weigh ideas, understand them, and form opinions about them.

Here are some guidelines for reading effectively:

- Pace your reading according to the purpose for which you are reading.
- Try to increase the number of words your eyes focus on at any given time.
- Read a lot to increase your vocabulary.

Test Preparation

In a test situation, read the directions carefully to be sure you understand them. If the test requires that you respond to a reading selection, use your critical reading skills.

The Contemporary Perspective

Wish for nothing larger
Than your own small heart
Or greater than a star.
—Alice Walker

Christina's World, Andrew Wyeth, 1948. Tempera on gessoed panel, 32¼" × 47¾" (81.9 × 121.3 cm). Collection, The Museum of Modern Art, New York. Purchase. Photograph ©2000 The Museum of Modern Art, New York

1949 Arthur Miller's play, *Death of a Salesman*, wins acclaim.

1952 Ernest Hemingway's *The Old Man and the Sea* appears.

1959 Lorraine Hansberry's *A Raisin in the Sun* is produced.

1962 Rachel Carson's *Silent Spring* is published.

1967 Joyce Carol Oates publishes *A Garden of Earthly Delights*.

1950	1955	1960	1965	1970

1950 President Truman orders U.S. troops to Korea.

1955 Martin Luther King, Jr., leads a boycott of buses in Montgomery, Alabama.

1954 Supreme Court bans segregation in public schools.

1963 President Kennedy is assassinated.

1969 Two American astronauts are first to walk on the moon.

1967 Thurgood Marshall is first African-American Supreme Court Justice.

HISTORICAL HIGHLIGHTS

The Contemporary Perspective

At the beginning of this book, you supposed that you were a visitor from colonial America. Now think about being a time traveler from fifty years ago. Think of the changes you would see in the United States today.

Are you surprised at how much time people spend watching TV? Fifty years ago, television was a new medium. Do you wonder at all the tasks computers perform? Fifty years ago, computers were just beginning to come into use. Are you amazed by the space program? In your time, space exploration was only an idea.

Now think about the opportunities available to people in this country. They may surprise you, too.

■ CIVIL RIGHTS MOVEMENTS

How would you feel if you were not allowed to sit at a lunch counter or go to a school of your choice because of your race? Martin Luther King, Jr., and other great African American leaders led civil rights workers in peaceful protests against these and other injustices. Their efforts were responsible for such laws as the Civil Rights Act of 1964, which banned discrimination in education, employment, voting, and public facilities.

During this time too, women demanded equal rights. The women's rights movement has succeeded in making more types of jobs available to women and in reducing other discrimination against women.

These and similar movements have helped make people in the United States aware of the need to respect all people's rights.

■ NEW VOICES IN LITERATURE

Fifty years ago, you might not have had the chance to read some of the selections in this book. The writers may have been ignored because of their race or their gender, or both. Today, all have a chance to be

| 1975 E.J. Doctorow publishes *Ragtime*. | 1983 Alice Walker wins Pulitzer for *The Color Purple*. | 1987 August Wilson wins Pulitzer for *Fences*. | 1993 Toni Morrison wins Nobel Prize for literature. | 1994–8 John Grisham's legal thrillers topped the best seller fiction list from 1994–1998. |

1977 Toni Morrison's novel *Song of Solomon* appears.

1993 The movie *The Joy Luck Club* is released.

1975   1980   1985   1990   1995   2000

1979 U.S. resumes diplomatic relations with China.

1981 Sandra Day O'Connor is first female Supreme Court justice.

1991 U.S. defeats Iraq in Persian Gulf War.

1992 World Wide Web system and software are released.

1986 *Challenger* space shuttle explodes killing 6 astronauts and a teacher.

1999 People around the world celebrated the dawn of a new century.

heard. In this unit, you will read the works of a variety of writers— men and women, African American, white, and Hispanic. They tell about their values and opinions. Readers learn their points of view.

Characters in literature often search for a meaning to their lives, just as real people do. Has your reading ever helped you discover something you have always wondered about? In "The Secret," two young girls discover the secret of life in a single line of a poem.

Do you always agree with your friends? Today we know that it is all right to see things differently. The second selection in this unit consists of three poems that present unusual ways of looking at the world.

The characters in "Two Kinds" and "The World Is Not a Pleasant Place to Be" illustrate a common need: to love and be loved. They realize that people depend on others for many things. What things do you depend on from your family and friends?

It is a common experience to make a decision that turns out differently than expected. If this has ever happened to you, you will enjoy the story "Journey." It describes a choice and its results.

Two aspects of the terrible impact of racism are shown in *Black Boy* and "Little Things Are Big." In the first, a poor young boy learns to survive in a tough world. In the second, a young man personally experiences the effects of racism. How do these stories help you to understand how racism affects people?

What aspects of your heritage are you especially proud of? "Everyday Use" and *The Woman Warrior*, celebrate two different cultures.

The final selections, "This Is Just to Say" and "The Term," describe everyday experiences in new ways.

Literature today reflects a variety of ideas. What values and ideas are important to you? Which can you find in these selections?

Learn About

POETIC FORM

A poem can be written in many different ways. A poem can read like a speech or like someone talking to you. How a poem affects you as you read it depends partly on its form, the way the poem is organized. Nothing about a poem is accidental; its words and the way they are organized are carefully considered.

There are different ways a poem can be organized; one basic way is by stanza. A **stanza** is simply two or more lines of poetry grouped together. A stanza may consist of one thought, action, image, or emotion, or more than one. Stanzas can be arranged by the passage of time, by subject, or as part of a series, one leading to the next. A stanza may have meaning by itself; some stanzas must be read together to have meaning.

As you read "The Secret," ask yourself:

1. How does one stanza lead to another?
2. How could the poem be organized differently?

WRITING CONNECTION

The form of a poem can make its meaning clearer or more difficult. Rewrite the poem in sentence form to see if the effect is different.

READING FOCUS

Summarize Text When you summarize text, you condense it to its most important points. Even a short poem can be summarized in a sentence or two that express the main idea or ideas of the poem. After you read the next selection, reread it and try writing a summary of its meaning. Notice how doing this improves your understanding of the main idea.

THE SECRET

by Denise Levertov

Two girls discover
the secret of life
in a sudden line of
poetry.

5   I who don't know the
secret wrote
the line. They
told me

(through a third person)
10   they had found it
but not what it was
not even

what line it was. No doubt
by now, more than a week
15   later, they have forgotten
the secret,

the line, the name of
the poem. I love them
for finding what
20   I can't find,

and for loving me
for the line I wrote,
and for forgetting it
so that

25   a thousand times, till death
finds them, they may
discover it again, in other
lines

in other
30   happenings. And for
wanting to know it,
for

assuming there is
such a secret, yes,
35   for that
most of all.

Ruby Green Singing, James Chapin.
Norton Museum of Art, West Palm Beach, FL.
Bequest of R.H. Norton

Review the Selection

Recall

1. Where is the secret of "The Secret" discovered?

2. Why does the poet love the two girls "most of all"?

3. Explain how the poet knew the girls discovered the secret.

Infer

4. How did the two girls discover the secret?

5. The girls forgot the secret—why isn't that important?

6. Name several other places the secret might be found.

7. Why is the line of poetry described as sudden?

Apply

8. Imagine you discovered the secret of life. What do you think it is? How would you know when you found it? What might make you forget it?

9. Where would you look for the secret of life?

10. Write another title for the poem.

Respond to Literature

This poem says that the secret of life is ours to discover. Why is it important that we do?

WRITE ABOUT THE SELECTION

In "The Secret," the poet describes her own reaction to the girls' discovery. Think about what happens from the two girls' point of view. They read a poem, discover a secret, tell someone about it, and then forget both the poem and the secret. Write a conversation you might have with the girls in which you remind them of and question them about the poem and their discovery.

Prewriting Outline a list of five questions you would like to ask the two girls and what you think their answers would be. Think about how you would try to find out about the secret.

Writing Use your informal outline to write a conversation between yourself and the girls, based on the questions you've thought up.

Revising When you revise what you wrote, make sure the questions are specific. If necessary, reword the questions to make them clearer.

Proofreading Read over your conversation to check for errors. Periods and commas are always placed inside quotation marks. Exclamation points, question marks, and dashes are placed inside quotation marks when they are part of the quotation and outside quotation marks if they are not part of the quotation. Check your writing to see if the quotation marks are placed correctly.

THINK ABOUT POETIC FORM

The division of a poem into stanzas is only one aspect of poetic form. Each aspect, or element, of the poem except the **substance**—what the poem is about—contributes to the form. Rhythms fall into forms, as do meters. Rhyme scheme, if there is one, is a matter of form. So are length of line, length of poem, each individual image, and the relationship of one image to another. In short, **form** concerns the pattern, or structure, that is used to give expression to what the author wishes to say—to the content, or substance, of the poem.

1. Describe the form of the stanzas in "The Secret."

2. Where is the most important thought of the poem located?

3. Does each stanza contain a single thought or emotion?

4. What is the poet explaining in lines 21 to 35?

5. How would the effect of the poem be changed if the lines were grouped into one long stanza?

READING FOCUS

Summarize Text After you read "The Secret," you summarized it. In one sentence, state the main idea. How did summarizing the poem help you understand its meaning?

DEVELOP YOUR VOCABULARY

What do the words *foreign* and *alien* have in common? They are **synonyms**, meaning that they share the same, or almost the same, meaning.

In daily usage, however, synonyms can carry meanings that are quite different. Consider the noun *speech*, meaning "a talk or address given in public." Synonyms for *speech* include *address*, *oration*, *lecture*, *talk*, and *sermon*. Each of these synonyms means more than the general definition of *speech*. You would expect to hear a lecture in a classroom or a speech at a political meeting, but not in a church, where a sermon might be expected instead.

1. Which of the following are synonyms for *happening*?
   a. schedule   c. location
   b. occurrence   d. event

2. Which of the following words are synonyms for *beautiful*?
   a. pretty   c. wealthy
   b. lovely   d. abundant

FIGURATIVE LANGUAGE

Figurative language is language that departs from the original, exact, or literal meaning of words in order to achieve a fresh way of expressing an idea or image. Some types of figurative language are listed below.

Personification is a figure of speech in which inanimate things or abstract ideas are given human qualities or sensibilities.

Onomatopoeia is the use of words whose sounds suggest their meaning. Some examples are *buzz*, *jingle*, *bang*, and *pop*.

Simile is a figure of speech in which one thing is specifically likened to a dissimilar thing; the words *like* or *as* are used in the comparison.

Metaphor is a figure of speech in which two dissimilar things are likened to each other directly, as if one were the other.

As you read the poems, ask yourself:
1. What figures of speech are used in the poems?
2. What fresh impressions do you get from reading the poems?

READING FOCUS

Paraphrase Poetry When you paraphrase, you restate the speaker's experiences and feelings in your own words. Restating the lines or stanzas of a poem will help you to clarify their meanings. As you read the next three poems, practice paraphrasing the lines of each one.

WRITING CONNECTION

Write four sentences, using a different figure of speech in each.

SNOW

by Dorothy Aldis

The fenceposts wear marshmallow hats
On a snowy day;
Bushes in their night gowns
Are kneeling down to pray—
And all the trees have silver skirts
And want to dance away.

December Snow, C.E. Burchfield. Kennedy Galleries, Inc.

UMBILICAL

by Eve Merriam

Still Life Radio Tube, Stuart Davis.
The Bettmann Archive

You can take away my mother,
you can take away my sister,
but don't take away
my little transistor.

5   I can do without sunshine,
I can do without Spring,
but I can't do without
my ear to that thing.

I can live without water,
10 in a hole in the ground,
but I can't live without
that sound that sound that sound that sOWnd.

---

transistor (tran ZIS tur) here, it means a transistor radio
umbilical (um BIL ih kul) here, necessary for life; from "umbilical cord,"
  which keeps an unborn baby alive

Cloud World, Dixon. Arizona West Galleries

Cumulus Clouds

by Sheryl Nelms

a gallon of
rich
country cream

hand-whipped
5   into stiff
peaks

flung
from the beater

into dollops
10   across a blue oilcloth

---

cumulus (KYOO myuh lus) a type of rounded, fluffy cloud
dollops (DOL ups) mounds
oilcloth (OIL klawth) waterproofed cloth

Review the Selection

UNDERSTAND THE SELECTION

Recall

1. What is described in "Snow"?

2. How is the sky described in "Cumulus Clouds"?

3. What is most important to the person in "Umbilical"?

Infer

4. What general image does Dorothy Aldis use for snow?

5. What color are the clouds?

6. Why are the bushes described as kneeling?

7. Why do you think the last word in "Umbilical" is spelled "sOWnd"?

Apply

8. Imagine a snow-covered field. What is an everyday household object to which you could compare it?

9. Write another title for "Umbilical." Be sure it expresses the poem's meaning.

10. Why do you think the speaker of "Umbilical" says "you can take away my mother" and "sister"?

Respond to Literature

We live in a high-tech society; what does the poem "Umbilical" say about the effect of technology in our lives?

WRITE ABOUT THE SELECTION

To which of your five senses does the imagery in "Cumulus Clouds" appeal? Write a paragraph that describes a day like the one in "Cumulus Clouds." The paragraph should appeal to all five senses.

Prewriting   Think about the rest of the scene in the poem—the place, the time of day, the season, the weather—and how it would appeal to each of your five senses. Make a chart with each sense used as a heading. On the left hand side, write down several elements of the setting. Next to the element, under the appropriate heading, write a word which describes the element as it relates to one of the five senses.

Writing   Using the words in your chart, write a paragraph–long description of the entire scene as you imagine it.

Revising   Try to include as many adjectives in your description as you can to make the scene more vivid. For example, instead of saying "a tree," revise your writing to tell what kind of tree it is.

Proofreading   Read over your description to check for errors. Be sure that your adjectives modify nouns and that your adverbs modify verbs, adjectives or other adverbs.

THINK ABOUT FIGURES OF SPEECH

Figures of speech help to clarify and illustrate ideas. They make writing more vivid and give life to inanimate objects. They aid readers in making new associations. A figure of speech is sometimes so essential to a poem that to remove it would destroy the poem.

1. When Aldis says that fenceposts wear hats she is using what figure of speech? Name two other examples of this figure of speech in her poem.

2. The title "Umbilical" is an example of which figure of speech? What comparison is implied in the title?

3. Why does the poet spell the last *sound* in "Umbilical" as *sOWnd*?

4. The entire third poem is an extended metaphor for what two things?

5. Are there any similes in the three poems? If so, where are they?

READING FOCUS

Paraphrase Poetry You have paraphrased the poems you just read. In your own words, state how paraphrasing helped to clarify the poems' meanings for you.

DEVELOP YOUR VOCABULARY

There are many ways in which the vocabulary of English has expanded. One way is by the addition of new words to the language. Another is by adding new meanings to existing words. Many words have gained new meanings by way of **metaphor**. The process is simple: a word used in one context is applied, by its similarity, to an object in another context. This is how names of parts of the body came to be applied to so many other things. Examples are the *arms* and *legs* of a chair, the *hands* and *face* of a clock, or the *eye* of a potato.

In the following sentences, all of the items *except one* are correct. Which item in each sentence is the incorrect one?

1. *Saws*, *rakes*, *gears*, and *rivers* have teeth.

2. A *drum*, *beet*, *hammer*, and a *pin* have a head.

3. A *bottle*, *violin*, *bale of hay*, and a *person* have a neck.

4. A *laundry bag*, *bed*, *book page*, and a *hill* have a foot.

Learn About

CHARACTERS' MOTIVES

A **motive** is an emotion or reason that causes a character to behave in a certain way. A motive may also cause an action to occur. There may even be more than one motive behind a character's actions.

The motive may come about as a result of outside forces. It may be a deep impulse within a person.

An author does not always clearly state characters' motive. Often you must read between the lines to identify it.

As you read this selection, ask yourself:

1. Why is the character behaving as she does?
2. Are the causes of her behavior internal or external?

WRITING CONNECTION

Write a short paragraph describing how you behaved in a specific social situation. What external or internal motives caused your behavior?

READING FOCUS

Use Word Identification What do you do when you encounter a word you do not understand? A dictionary may not always be close at hand. Therefore, it is helpful to know how to figure out word meanings. To do this, break the word down into prefixes, suffixes, roots, and other words with which you are familiar. As you encounter unfamiliar words, ask yourself:

1. Which parts of this word look familiar?
2. What are the meanings of the recognizable word parts?
3. What can I infer is the meaning of the whole word?

TWO KINDS
from The Joy Luck Club

by Amy Tan

My mother believed you could be anything you wanted to be in America. You could open a restaurant. You could work for the government and get good retirement. You could buy a house with almost no money down. You could become rich. You could become instantly famous.

"Of course you can be prodigy, too," my mother told me when I was nine. "You can be best anything. What does Auntie Lindo know? Her daughter, she is only best tricky."

America was where all my mother's hopes lay. She had come here in 1949 after losing everything in China: her mother and father, her family home, her first husband, and two daughters, twin baby girls. But she never looked back with regret. There were so many ways for things to get better.

We didn't immediately pick the right kind of prodigy. At first my mother thought I could be a Chinese Shirley Temple. We'd watch Shirley's old movies on TV as though they were training films. My mother would poke my arm and say, *"Ni kan"* — You watch. And I would see Shirley tapping her feet, or singing a sailor song, or pursing her lips into a very round O while saying, "Oh my goodness."

"Ni kan," said my mother as Shirley's eyes flooded with tears. "You already know how. Don't need talent for crying!"

Soon after my mother got this idea about Shirley Temple, she took me to a beauty training school in the Mission district and put me in the hands of a student who could barely hold the scissors without shaking. Instead of getting big fat curls, I emerged with an uneven mass of crinkly black fuzz. My mother dragged me off to the bathroom and tried to wet down my hair.

"You look like Negro Chinese," she lamented, as if I had done this on purpose.

The instructor of the beauty training school had to lop off these soggy clumps to make my hair even again. "Peter Pan is very popular these days," the instructor assured my mother. I now had hair the length of a boy's, with straight-across bangs that hung at a slant two inches above my eyebrows. I liked the haircut and it made me actually look forward to my future fame.

In fact, in the beginning, I was just as excited as my mother, maybe even more so.

---

prodigy (PRAHD uh jee) a child remarkably bright in some way

I pictured this prodigy part of me as many different images, trying each one on for size. I was a dainty ballerina girl standing by the curtains waiting to hear the right music that would send me floating on my tiptoes. I was like the Christ child lifted out of the straw manger, crying with holy indignity. I was Cinderella stepping from her pumpkin carriage with sparkly cartoon music filling the air.

In all of my imaginings, I was filled with a sense that I would soon become *perfect*. My mother and father would adore me. I would be beyond reproach. I would never feel the need to sulk for anything.

But sometimes the prodigy in me became impatient. "If you don't hurry up and get me out here, I'm disappearing for good," it warned. "And then you'll always be nothing."

Every night after dinner, my mother and I would sit at the Formica kitchen table. She would present new tests, taking her examples from stories of amazing children she had read in *Ripley's Believe It or Not*, or *Good Housekeeping*, *Reader's Digest*, and a dozen other magazines she kept in a pile in our bathroom. My mother got these magazines from people whose houses she cleaned. And since she cleaned many houses each week, we had a great assortment. She would look through them all, searching for stories about remarkable children.

The first night she brought out a story about a three-year-old boy who knew the capitals of all the states and even most of the European countries. A teacher was quoted as saying the little boy could also pronounce the names of the foreign cities correctly.

"What's the capital of Finland?" my mother asked me, looking at the magazine story.

All I knew was the capital of California, because Sacramento was the name of the street we lived on in Chinatown. "Nairobi!" I guessed, saying the most foreign word I could think of. She checked to see if that was possibly one way to pronounce "Helsinki" before showing me the answer.

The tests got harder—multiplying numbers in my head, finding the queen of hearts in a deck of cards, trying to stand on my head without using my hands, predicting the daily temperatures in Los Angeles, New York, and London.

One night I had to look at a page from the Bible for three minutes and then report everything I could remember. "Now Jehoshaphat had riches and honor in abundance and . . . that's all I remember, Ma," I said.

And after seeing my mother's disappointed face once again, something inside of me began to die. I hated the tests, the raised hopes and failed expectations. Before going to bed that night, I looked in the mirror above the bathroom sink and when I saw only my face staring back—and that it would always be this ordinary face—I began to cry. Such a sad, ugly girl! I made high-pitched noises like a crazed animal, trying to scratch out the face in the mirror.

Formica (for MY kuh) trade name for heat-resistant plastic

And then I saw what seemed to be the prodigy side of me—because I had never seen that face before. I looked at my reflection, blinking so I could see more clearly. The girl staring back at me was angry, powerful. This girl and I were the same. I had new thoughts, willful thoughts, or rather thoughts filled with lots of won'ts. I won't let her change me, I promised myself. I won't be what I'm not.

So now on nights when my mother presented her tests, I performed listlessly, my head propped on one arm. I pretended to be bored. And I was. I got so bored I started counting bellows of the foghorns out on the bay while my mother drilled me in other areas. The sound was comforting and reminded me of the cow jumping over the moon. And the next day, I played a game with myself, seeing if my mother would give up on me before eight bellows. After a while I usually counted only one, maybe two bellows at most. At last she was beginning to give up hope.

Two or three months had gone by without any mention of my being a prodigy again. And then one day my mother was watching *The Ed Sullivan Show* on TV. The TV was old and the sound kept shorting out. Every time my mother got halfway up from the sofa to adjust the set, the sound would go back on and Ed would be talking. As soon as she sat down, Ed would go silent again. She got up, the TV broke into loud piano music. She sat down. Silence. Up and down, back and forth, quiet and loud. It was like a stiff embraceless dance between her and the TV set. Finally she stood by the set with her hand on the sound dial.

She seemed entranced by the music, a little frenzied piano piece with this mesmerizing quality, sort of quick passages and then teasing lilting ones before it returned to the quick playful parts.

"Ni kan," my mother said, calling me over with hurried hand gestures, "Look here."

I could see why my mother was fascinated by the music. It was being pounded out by a little Chinese girl, about nine years old, with a Peter Pan haircut. The girl had the sauciness of Shirley Temple. She was proudly modest like a proper Chinese child. And she also did this fancy sweep of a curtsy, so that the fluffy skirt of her white dress cascaded slowly to the floor like the petals of a large carnation.

In spite of these warning signs, I wasn't worried. Our family had no piano and we couldn't afford to buy one, let alone reams of sheet music and piano lessons. So I could be generous in my comments when my mother bad-mouthed the little girl on TV.

"Play note right, but doesn't sound good! No singing sound," complained my mother.

"What are you picking on her for?" I said carelessly. "She's pretty good. Maybe she's not the best, but she's trying hard." I knew almost immediately I would be sorry I said that.

---

bellows (BEHL ohz) roars; loud noises
mesmerizing (MEHZ muh ry zing) hypotizing; casting a spell
sauciness (SAH see nuhs) state of being bold or rude
cascaded (kas KAY dihd) flowed down like a small waterfall

"Just like you," she said. "Not the best. Because you not trying." She gave a little huff as she let go of the sound dial and sat down on the sofa.

The little Chinese girl sat down also to play an encore of "Anitra's Dance" by Grieg. I remember the song, because later on I had to learn how to play it.

Three days after watching *The Ed Sullivan Show*, my mother told me what my schedule would be for piano lessons and piano practice. She had talked to Mr. Chong, who lived on the first floor of our apartment building. Mr. Chong was a retired piano teacher and my mother had traded housecleaning services for weekly lessons and a piano for me to practice on every day, two hours a day, from four to six.

When my mother told me this, I felt as though I had been sent to hell. I whined and then kicked my foot a little when I couldn't stand it anymore.

"Why don't you like me the way I am? I'm *not* a genius! I can't play the piano. And even if I could, I wouldn't go on TV if you paid me a million dollars!" I cried.

My mother slapped me. "Who ask you be genius?" she shouted. "Only ask you be your best. For your sake. You think I want you be genius? Hnnh! What for! Who ask you!"

"So ungrateful," I heard her mutter in Chinese. "If she had as much talent as she has temper, she would be famous now."

Mr. Chong, whom I secretly nicknamed Old Chong, was very strange, always tapping his fingers to the silent music of an invisible orchestra. He looked ancient in my eyes. He had lost most of his hair on top of his head and he wore thick glasses and had eyes that always looked tired and sleepy. But he must have been younger than I thought, since he lived with his mother and was not yet married.

I met Old Lady Chong once and that was enough. She had this peculiar smell like a baby that had done something in its pants. And her fingers felt like a dead person's, like an old peach I once found in the back of the refrigerator; the skin just slid off the meat when I picked it up.

I soon found out why Old Chong had retired from teaching piano. He was deaf. "Like Beethoven!" he shouted to me. "We're both listening only in our head!" And he would start to conduct his frantic silent sonatas.

Our lessons went like this. He would open the book and point to the different things, explaining their purpose: "Key! Treble! Bass! No sharps or flats! So this is C major! Listen now and play after me!"

And then he would play the C scale a few times, a simple chord, and then, as if inspired by an old, unreachable itch, he gradually added more notes and running trills and a pounding bass until the music was really something quite grand.

I would play after him, the simple scale, the simple chord, and then I played some nonsense that sounded like a cat running up and down on top of garbage cans.

---

sonatas (suh NAH tuhs) compositions for one or two musical instruments

Old Chong smiled and applauded and then said, "Very good! But now you must learn to keep time!"

So that's how I discovered that Old Chong's eyes were too slow to keep up with the wrong notes I was playing. He went through the motions in half-time. To help me keep rhythm, he stood behind me, pushing down on my right shoulder for every beat. He balanced pennies on top of my wrists so I would keep them still as I slowly played scales and arpeggios. He had me curve my hand around an apple and keep that shape when playing chords. He marched stiffly to show me how to make each finger dance up and down, staccato like an obedient little soldier.

He taught me all of these things, and that was how I also learned I could be lazy and get away with mistakes, lots of mistakes. If I hit the wrong notes because I hadn't practiced enough, I never corrected myself. I just kept playing in rhythm. And Old Chong kept conducting his own private reverie.

So maybe I never really gave myself a fair chance. I did pick up the basics pretty quickly, and I might have become a good pianist at that young age. But I was so determined not to try, not to be anybody different that I learned to play only the most ear-splitting preludes, the most discordant hymns.

Over the next year, I practiced like this, dutifully in my own way. And then one day I heard my mother and her friend Lindo Jong both talking in a loud bragging tone of voice so others could hear. It was after church, and I was leaning against the brick wall wearing a dress with stiff white petticoats. Auntie Lindo's daughter, Waverly, who was about my age, was standing farther down the wall about five feet away. We had grown up together and shared all the closeness of two sisters squabbling over crayons and dolls. In other words, for the most part, we hated each other. I thought she was snotty. Waverly Jong had gained a certain amount of fame as "Chinatown's little Chinese Chess Champion."

"She bring home too many trophy," lamented Auntie Lindo that Sunday. "All day she play chess. All day I have no time do nothing but dust off her winnings." She threw a scolding look at Waverly, who pretended not to see her.

"You lucky you don't have this problem," said Aunt Lindo with a sigh to my mother.

And my mother squared her shoulders and bragged: "Our problem worser than yours. If we ask Jing-mei wash dish, she hear nothing but music. It's like you can't stop this natural talent."

And right then, I was determined to put a stop to her foolish pride.

A few weeks later, Old Chong and my mother conspired to have me play in a talent show which would be held in the

---

arpeggios (ahr PEHJ ee ohz) notes in a chord played in quick succession
staccato (stuh KAHT oh) music played with distinct breaks between notes
reverie (REHV uh ree) dreamy thoughts of pleasant things
petticoats (PEHT ee kohts) lace or ruffles on the bottom of a skirt
spinet (SPIHN it) small piano

church hall. By then, my parents had saved up enough to buy me a secondhand piano, a black Wurlitzer spinet with a scarred bench. It was the showpiece of our living room.

For the talent show, I was to play a piece called "Pleading Child" from Schumann's *Scenes from Childhood*. It was a simple, moody piece that sounded more difficult than it was. I was supposed to memorize the whole thing, playing the repeat parts twice to make the piece sound longer. But I dawdled over it, playing a few bars and then cheating, looking up to see what notes followed. I never really listened to what I was playing. I daydreamed about being somewhere else, about being someone else.

The part I liked to practice best was the fancy curtsy: right foot out, touch the rose on the carpet with a pointed foot, sweep to the side, left leg bends, look up and smile.

My parents invited all the couples from the Joy Luck Club to witness my debut. Auntie Lindo and Uncle Tin were there. Waverly and her two older brothers had also come. The first two rows were filled with children both younger and older than I was. The littlest ones got to go first. They recited simple nursery rhymes, squawked out tunes on miniature violins, twirled Hula Hoops, pranced in pink ballet tutus, and when they bowed or curtsied, the audience would sigh in unison, "Awww," and then clap enthusiastically.

When my turn came, I was very confident. I remember my childish excitement.

It was as if I knew, without a doubt, that the prodigy side of me really did exist. I had no fear whatsoever, no nervousness. I remember thinking to myself, This is it! This is it! I looked out over the audience, at my mother's blank face, my father's yawn, Auntie Lindo's stiff-lipped smile, Waverly's sulky expression. I had on a white dress layered with sheets of lace, and a pink bow in my Peter Pan haircut. As I sat down I envisioned people jumping to their feet and Ed Sullivan rushing up to introduce me to everyone on TV.

And I started to play. It was so beautiful. I was so caught up in how lovely I looked at first I didn't worry how I would sound. So it was a surprise to me when I hit the first wrong note and I realized something didn't sound quite right. And then I hit another and another followed that. A chill started at the top of my head and began to trickle down. Yet I couldn't stop playing, as though my hands were bewitched. I kept thinking my fingers would adjust themselves back, like a train switching to the right track. I played this strange jumble through two repeats, the sour notes staying with me all the way to the end.

When I stood up, I discovered my legs were shaking. Maybe I had just been nervous and the audience, like Old Chong, had seen me go through the right motions and had not heard anything wrong at all. I swept my foot out, went down on my knee, looked up and smiled. The room was quiet, except for Old Chong, who was beaming and shouting,

---

Joy Luck Club (JOY LUK KLUB) a group of women who met to play games and tell stories

"Bravo! Bravo! Well done!" But then I saw my mother's face, her stricken face. The audience clapped weakly, and as I walked back to my chair, with my whole face quivering as I tried not to cry, I heard a little boy whisper loudly to his mother, "That was awful," and the mother whispered back, "Well, she certainly tried."

And now I realized how many people were in the audience, the whole world it seemed. I was aware of eyes burning into my back. I felt the shame of my mother and father as they sat stiffly throughout the rest of the show.

We could have escaped during intermission. Pride and some strange sense of honor must have anchored my parents to their chairs. And so we watched it all: the eighteen-year-old boy with a fake mustache who did a magic show and juggled flaming hoops while riding a unicycle. The breasted girl with white makeup who sang from *Madama Butterfly* and got honorable mention. And the eleven-year-old boy who won first prize playing a tricky violin song that sounded like a busy bee.

After the show, the Hsus, the Jongs, and the St. Clairs from the Joy Luck Club came up to my mother and father.

"Lots of talented kids," Auntie Lindo said vaguely, smiling broadly.

"That was somethin' else," said my father, and I wondered if he was referring to me in a humorous way, or whether he even remembered what I had done.

Waverly looked at me and shrugged her shoulders. "You aren't a genius like me," she said matter-of-factly. And if I hadn't felt so bad, I would have pulled her braids and punched her stomach.

But my mother's expression was what devastated me: a quiet, blank look that said she had lost everything. I felt the same way, and it seemed as if everybody were now coming up, like gawkers at the scene of an accident, to see what parts were actually missing. When we got on the bus to go home, my father was humming the busy-bee tune and my mother was silent. I kept thinking she wanted to wait until we got home before shouting at me. But when my father unlocked the door to our apartment, my mother walked in and then went to the back, into the bedroom. No accusations. No blame. And in a way, I felt disappointed, I had been waiting for her to start shouting, so I could shout back and cry and blame her for all my misery.

I assumed the talent-show fiasco meant I never had to play the piano again. But two days later, after school, my mother came out of the kitchen and saw me watching TV.

"Four clock," she reminded me as if it were any other day. I was stunned, as though she were asking me to go through the talent-show torture again. I wedged myself more tightly in front of the TV.

"Turn off TV," she called from the kitchen five minutes later.

I didn't budge. And then I decided. I didn't have to do what my mother said

---

accusations (AK yoo ZAY shuhnz) charges of wrongdoing
fiasco (fee AS koh) a humiliating failure

anymore. I wasn't her slave. This wasn't China. I had listened to her before and look what happened. She was the stupid one.

She came out of the kitchen and stood in the arched entryway of the living room. "Four clock," she said once again, louder.

"I'm not going to play anymore," I said nonchalantly. "Why should I? I'm not a genius."

She walked over and stood in front of the TV. I saw her chest was heaving up and down in an angry way.

"No!" I said, and I now felt stronger, as if my true self had finally emerged. So this was what had been inside me all along.

"No! I won't!" I screamed.

She yanked me by the arm, pulled me off the floor, snapped off the TV. She was frighteningly strong, half pulling, half carrying me toward the piano as I kicked the throw rugs under my feet. She lifted me up onto the hard bench. I was sobbing now, looking at her bitterly. Her chest was heaving even more and her mouth was open, smiling crazily as if she were pleased I was crying.

"You want me to be someone that I'm not!" I sobbed. "I'll never be the kind of daughter you want me to be!"

"Only two kinds of daughters," she shouted in Chinese. "Those who are obedient and those who follow their own mind! Only one kind of daughter can live in this house. Obedient daughter!"

"Then I wish I wasn't your daughter. I wish you weren't my mother," I shouted. As I said these things I got scared. It felt like worms and toads and slimy things crawling out of my chest, but it also felt

good, as if this awful side of me had surfaced, at last.

"Too late change this," said my mother shrilly.

And I could sense her anger rising to its breaking point. I wanted to see it spill over. And that's when I remembered the babies she had lost in China, the ones we never talked about. "Then I wish I'd never been born!" I shouted. "I wish I were dead! Like them."

It was as if I had said the magic words. Alakazam!—and her face went blank, her mouth closed, her arms went slack, and she backed out of the room, stunned, as if she were blowing away like a small brown leaf, thin, brittle, lifeless.

It was not the only disappointment my mother felt in me. In the years that followed, I failed her so many times, each time asserting my own will, my right to fall short of expectations. I didn't get straight A's. I didn't become class president. I didn't get into Stanford. I dropped out of college.

For unlike my mother, I did not believe I could be anything I wanted to be. I could only be me.

And for all those years, we never talked about the disaster at the recital or my terrible accusations afterward at the piano bench. All that remained unchecked, like a betrayal that was now unspeakable. So I never found a way to ask her why she had hoped for something so large that failure was inevitable.

And even worse, I never asked her what frightened me the most: Why had she given up hope?

For after our struggle at the piano, she never mentioned my playing again. The lessons stopped. The lid to the piano was closed, shutting out the dust, my misery, and her dreams.

So she surprised me. A few years ago, she offered to give me the piano, for my thirtieth birthday. I had not played in all those years. I saw the offer as a sign of forgiveness, a tremendous burden removed.

"Are you sure?" I asked shyly. "I mean, won't you and Dad miss it?"

"No, this is your piano," she said firmly. "Always your piano. You only one can play."

"Well, I probably can't play anymore," I said. "It's been years."

"You pick up fast," said my mother, as if she knew this was certain. "You have a natural talent. You could be genius if you want to."

"No I couldn't."

"You just not trying," said my mother. And she was neither angry nor sad. She said it as to announce a fact that could never be disproved. "Take it," she said.

But I didn't at first. It was enough that she offered it to me. And after that, every time I saw it in my parents' living room, standing in front of the bay windows, it made me feel proud, as if it were a shiny trophy I had won back.

Last week I sent a tuner over to my parents' apartment and had the piano reconditioned, for purely sentimental reasons. My mother had died a few months before and I had been getting things in order for my father, a little bit at a time. I put the jewelry in special silk pouches. The sweaters she had knitted in yellow, pink, bright orange—all the colors I hated—I put those in moth-proof boxes. I found some old Chinese silk dresses, the kind with little slits up the sides. I rubbed the old silk against my skin, then wrapped them in tissue and decided to take them home with me.

After I had the piano tuned, I opened the lid and touched the keys. It sounded even richer than I remembered. Really, it was a very good piano. Inside the bench were the same exercise notes with handwritten scales, the same secondhand music books with their covers held together with yellow tape.

I opened up the Schumann book to the dark little piece I had played at the recital. It was on the left-hand side of the page, "Pleading Child." It looked more difficult than I remembered. I played a few bars, surprised at how easily the notes came back to me.

And for the first time, or so it seemed, I noticed the piece on the right-hand side. It was called "Perfectly Contented." I tried to play this one as well. It had a lighter melody but the same flowing rhythm and turned out to be quite easy. "Pleading Child" was shorter but slower; "Perfectly Contented" was longer, but faster. And after I played them both a few times, I realized they were two halves of the same song.

---

disproved (dis PROOVD) shown to be incorrect or false

Review the Selection

Recall

1. How did the mother pay for her daughter's piano lessons?

2. What did the narrator call her piano teacher?

3. Describe the mother's reaction to her daughter's performance.

Infer

4. How are the mother's hopes for her daughter a reflection of her attitude toward the United States?

5. What is the narrator's attitude toward Mr. Chong? How do you know?

6. In the mother's opinion, what kind of daughter is the narrator?

7. Was the father involved in his daughter's life? Explain.

Apply

8. When someone has high expectations for you, are you motivated to do your best or to give up?

9. What are some common conflicts that arise between young people and their parents or guardians?

10. What are two qualities of a good mother? A good daughter?

Respond to Literature

What causes tension between the mother and daughter in "Two Kinds"?

WRITE ABOUT THE SELECTION

The mother in "Two Kinds" has lived in China and the United States. She is an eyewitness to the differences—cultural, physical, and economic—between these countries.

For this assignment you are to be a newspaper reporter assigned to interview the mother for a story. Newspaper stories usually include information that answers these questions: *Who? What? Where? When? Why? How?* Write a brief newspaper article about an interview with the mother.

Prewriting   Think of as many questions as you can that you would like to ask the mother. Be sure that you address the six questions mentioned above. Choose the ten most important questions and number them. Then, answer them as you think the mother would.

Writing   In a brief article, write an account of your interview with the mother, based on the ten questions. Use prewriting questions, and write what you think the mother's answers would be.

Revising   One way to make your interview subject seem more like a real person is to tell your reader what the subject looks like and how she acts. Add a description of the mother to your article.

Proofreading   Read over your article to check for errors. Remember that quotation marks enclose direct quotations. Indirect quotations do not require quotation marks.

THINK ABOUT MOTIVE

Writers reveal characters' motives as a means of creating round, more complete characters. Identifying and analyzing these motives help the reader gain insight into the character's personality.

1. What are the mother's motives for wanting her daughter to be a prodigy?

2. What do these motives reveal about the mother's personality?

3. What is the narrator's motive for refusing to master the piano?

4. What does her refusal to play the piano reveal about her personality?

5. Is the daughter driven by outside forces, or does a deeper impulse explain her behavior? Explain.

READING FOCUS

Use Word Identification Choose two words from the selection that were unfamiliar to you. List and define the word parts. Then define the complete word. Next, use each word in a sentence about the story.

DEVELOP YOUR VOCABULARY

A suffix is a word part added to the end of a base word to make a new word. By adding a suffix to a root, or base, word, you can change the meaning. For example, the word *care* means "to feel an interest or worry." When you add the suffix *–less* to the root word to make *careless*, the meaning is the opposite, or "done without care." More than one suffix can be added to the same word, such as *care*, *careless*, *carelessly*.

The words below came from the story. Identify and define each root word within the longer word. Then identify the suffix or suffixes and meaning of the longer word. Use the longer word in an original sentence.

Suffixes	Meaning
-ful	full of
-ly	in a certain way
-ness	the condition that is

1. carelessly
2. enthusiastically
3. nervousness

4. frighteningly
5. instantly
6. powerful

Learn About

TONE

No matter what its subject is, every work of literature carries with it its own, individual **tone**. Tone can be defined as the author's attitude toward the subject of his or her work. Tone is also defined as the author's attitude toward the audience reading his or her work.

As you read a poem ask yourself how the poet feels about his or her subject. Tone can be any number of different attitudes toward the subject of the work: formal, serious, informal, playful, intimate, sarcastic or doubtful, to name a few. A subject important to the writer may be treated solemnly or seriously. The writer will treat the subject seriously if he or she wants you to take it seriously.

As you read the poem, ask yourself:

1. How does the poet feel about her subject?
2. How does the poet want the reader to feel about the subject?

WRITING CONNECTION

Writers use tone to reveal their attitude toward a subject. Think of an activity you like and one that you do not like. Write a paragraph about each, telling your reader why you like or do not like the activity. Compare the tone of each paragraph with that of the other.

READING FOCUS

Understand Levels of Meaning Many writers—and especially poets—write on more than one level of meaning. You can take their words literally, but there is also a deeper meaning. For example, the story of the three little pigs can be enjoyed just as it is told, but may also be taken as a lesson about the results of acting foolishly. In the poem on the next page, the first three stanzas have two levels of meaning. After reading the poem a few times, write down the deeper meaning that you find.

The World Is Not a Pleasant Place to Be

by Nikki Giovanni

the world is not a pleasant place
to be without
someone to hold and be held by

5 a river would stop
its flow if only
a stream were there
to receive it

an ocean would never laugh
if clouds weren't there
10 to kiss her tears

the world is not
a pleasant place to be without
someone

Honeymooners, William H. Johnson. The Aaron Douglas Collection of The Amistad Research Center, Tulane University

Review the Selection

UNDERSTAND THE SELECTION

Recall

1. How often is the title repeated?

2. What do we need to make the world a pleasant place?

3. What elements of nature are mentioned in the poem?

Infer

4. Why do you think the river in this poem would stop by a stream?

5. How do you think the ocean feels?

6. Would you describe this poem as a question? an answer? a statement?

7. What natural event could be represented by the image of a cloud kissing the ocean's tears?

Apply

8. How else could you define "someone to hold and be held by"?

9. What do the images of nature all have in common?

10. What other moment in nature can illustrate the theme of this poem?

Respond to Literature

In this poem, Giovanni describes a need that all people share. What must people have in order to survive? What is most important to you? Explain.

WRITE ABOUT THE SELECTION

"The World Is Not a Pleasant Place to Be" is a poem which considers a single idea—the need for love that all human beings share. It is this feeling which makes the world, according to the poet, a pleasant place to live. Think of something in your life which makes your world pleasant. Can you think of a concrete example to illustrate it? Write a paragraph to persuade people that your concept is important.

Prewriting   Think of a simple concept whose presence in your life is important. The concept could be something such as "freedom," "nature," or "art," for example. Make two lists—the first a list of key words which define the concept; the second, a list of reasons that explain why you think the concept is important.

Writing   Write a persuasive paragraph to convince the reader of the concept's importance. First, define the concept, using the key words in your first list. Then present your argument by writing about the reasons in your second list.

Revising   To make sure the reader understands the importance of the concept in your life, add to your paragraph an actual example that illustrates it.

Proofreading   Read over your paragraph to check for errors. When you write about your life, or something that happened to you, you should write from the first-person point of view.

THINK ABOUT TONE

Tone may be described as a common ground between the author and the reader, reached when both understand what the author is trying to create. If the reader misunderstands a writer's tone, he or she will miss a great deal of the meaning of the work.

1. The poem "The World Is Not a Pleasant Place to Be" gives two examples illustrating its main idea. Where are they?

2. How did you feel after you read the poem?

3. What emotions are expressed in the poem?

4. Characterize the tone of the poem.

5. What does the image of "to kiss her tears" suggest to you?

READING FOCUS

Understand Levels of Meaning As you read "The World Is Not a Pleasant Place to Be," you thought about the levels of meaning in the poem. What deeper meaning beyond the literal did you find in the first three stanzas? Write down the literal meaning and the deeper meaning of each stanza.

DEVELOP YOUR VOCABULARY

Homophones are words that sound alike but are different in spelling, meaning, and origin. Read this sentence, for example: The Smiths' party was a *boar, accept* for *there* food. The writer has incorrectly used homophones for the three italicized words in the sentence. Corrected, the sentence would read: The Smiths' party was a *bore, except* for *their* food.

Using a homophone in place of the correct word in a sentence can confuse the reader and make nonsense of your writing. If you are not sure of which homophone to use, check in a dictionary.

Look at the poem to find a homophone for each of these words.

1. floe
2. wood
3. knot
4. plaice
5. bee
6. two
7. buy
8. tiers

Nichols Canyon Road, David Hockney. Art Resource

READING FOCUS

Make Inferences When you make an inference, you come to your own conclusion based on information you have received. For example, a detective who knows that a criminal is heading to the airport with a bag of stolen money infers that the crook is about to leave town. Active readers are like detectives. They use information from the text to infer something that is not directly stated. As you read the next selection, ask yourself questions that begin with *Why* or *How*. Then, use clues in the selection to infer the answers.

POINT OF VIEW

Point of view refers to the vantage point from which an author views the events of a fictional story. Sometimes an author takes the position of an all-knowing observer who can describe the events and thoughts of all characters in the story. This point of view, called the **omniscient point of view**, is written in the third person. An author may write in the third person but present the story as seen by only one character. This is called the **limited point of view**.

At other times a single character tells the story as he or she experienced it. Such a character may be the main character, a minor one, or a mere bystander. In any case, the character, called a **first-person narrator**, tells the story in the first person.

It is very rare that any story is told in the second person. Second-person point of view means the author places you, the reader, as the character experiencing the events.

As you read the story, ask yourself:
1. Who is telling the story?
2. In what person is the story told?

WRITING CONNECTION

Write a paragraph in the first person, telling a brief story. Rewrite the paragraph, using the third person. Compare the two.

JOURNEY

by Joyce Carol Oates

You begin your journey on so high an elevation that your destination is already in sight—a city that you have visited many times and that, moreover, is indicated on a traveler's map you have carefully folded up to take along with you. You are a lover of maps, and you have already committed this map to memory, but you bring it with you just the same.

The highway down from the mountains is broad and handsome, constructed after many years of ingenious blasting and leveling and paving. Engineers from all over the country aided in the construction of this famous highway. Its cost is so excessive that many rumors have circulated about it—you take no interest in such things, sensing that you will never learn the true cost anyway, and that this will make no difference to your journey.

After several hours on this excellent highway, where the sun shines ceaselessly and where there is a moderate amount of traffic, cars like your own at a safe distance from you, as if to assure you that there are other people in the world, you become sleepy from the monotony and wonder if perhaps there is another, less

---

elevation (el uh VAY shun) a high place
ingenious (in JEEN yus) clever, resourceful
excessive (ik SES iv) going beyond what's right or usual
moderate (MOD ur it) within reasonable limits; not excessive
monotony (muh NOT un ee) tiresome sameness

perfect road parallel to this. You discover on the map a smaller road, not exactly parallel to the highway and not as direct, but one that leads to the same city.

You turn onto this road, which winds among foothills and forests and goes through several small villages. You sense by the attitude of the villagers that traffic on this road is infrequent but nothing to draw special attention. At some curves the road shrinks, but you are fortunate enough to meet no oncoming traffic.

The road leads deep into a forest, always descending in small cramped turns. Your turning from left to right and from right to left, in a slow hypnotic passage, makes it impossible for you to look out at the forest. You discover that for some time you have not been able to see the city you are headed for, though you know it is still somewhere ahead of you.

By mid-afternoon you are tired of this road, though it has served you well, and you come upon a smaller, unpaved road that evidently leads to your city, though in a convoluted way. After only a moment's pause you turn onto this road, and immediately your automobile registers the change—the chassis bounces, something begins to vibrate, something begins to rattle. This noise is disturbing, but after a while you forget about it in your interest in the beautiful countryside. Here the trees are enormous. There are no villages or houses. For a while the dirt road runs alongside a small river, dangerously close to the river's steep bank, and you begin to feel apprehension. It is necessary for you to drive very slowly. At times your speedometer registers less than five miles an hour. You will not get to the city before dark.

The road narrows until it is hardly more than a lane. Grass has begun to grow in its center. As the river twists and turns, so does the road twist and turn, curving around hills that consist of enormous boulders, bare of all trees and plants, covered only in patches by a dull, brown lichen that is unfamiliar to you. Along one stretch, rocks of varying sizes have fallen down onto the road, so that you are forced to drive around them with great caution.

---

hypnotic (hip NOT ik) causing sleep
convoluted (KON vuh loot id) twisting; indirect
chassis (CHAS ee) a car's frame
apprehension (ap rih HEN shun) fear; dread
lichen (LY kun) a mosslike plant which grows on rocks and trees

Stone City, Iowa, Grant Wood. Joslyn Art Museum, Omaha, Nebraska. Estate of Grant Wood/Licensed by VAGA, New York, NY

Navigating these blind turns, you tap your horn to give warning in case someone should be approaching. But it is all unnecessary, since you come upon no other travelers.

Late in the afternoon, your foot numb from its constant pressure on the accelerator, your body jolted by the constant bumps and vibrations of the car, you decide to make the rest of your journey on foot, since you must be close to your destination by now.

A faint path leads through a tumble of rocks and bushes and trees, and you follow it enthusiastically. You descend a hill, slipping a little, so that a small rockslide is released; but you are able to keep your balance. At the back of your head is the precise location of your parked car, and behind that the curving dirt road,

---

navigating (NAV uh gayt ing) steering
enthusiastically (en thoo zee AS tik lee) eagerly

and behind that the other road, and then the magnificent highway itself: you understand that it would be no difficult feat to make your way back to any of these roads, should you decide that going by foot is unwise. But the path, though overgrown, is through a lovely forest, and then through a meadow in which yellow flowers are blooming, and you feel no inclination to turn back.

By evening you are still in the wilderness and you wonder if perhaps you have made a mistake. You are exhausted, your body aches, your eyes are seared by the need to stare so intently at everything around you. Now that the sun has nearly set, it is getting cold; evenings here in the mountains are always chilly.

You find yourself standing at the edge of a forest, staring ahead into the dark. Is that a field ahead, or a forest of small trees? Your path has long since given way to wild grass. Clouds obscure the moon, which should give you some light by which to make your way, and you wonder if you dare continue without this light.

Suddenly you remember the map you left back in the car, but you remember it as a blank sheet of paper.

You resist telling yourself you are lost. In fact, though you are exhausted and it is almost night, you are not lost. You have begun to shiver, but it is only with cold, not with fear. You are really satisfied with yourself. You are not lost. Though you can remember your map only as a blank sheet of paper, which can tell you nothing, you are not really lost.

If you had the day to begin again, on that highway which was so wide and clear, you would not have varied your journey in any way: in this is your triumph.

---

feat (FEET) accomplishment
inclination (in kluh NAY shun) preference
seared (SIRD) scorched; burned
obscure (ub SKYOOR) darken; dim; hide from sight

Joyce Carol Oates (1938–)

"If you are a writer, you locate yourself behind a wall of silence, and no matter what you are doing, driving a car or walking or doing housework, which I love, you can still be writing, because you have that space."

This remark by Joyce Carol Oates may explain why she is one of the most productive and versatile writers today. To her, writing is mostly daydreaming. When the idea is all set in her mind, she just sits down and writes it.

Oates has been creating fictional worlds all her life, which began in Lockport, New York, and continued in a rural area of Erie County. She submitted her first novel to a publisher at the age of fifteen. It was rejected for being too depressing, but this slight did not stop her. She entered Syracuse University in 1956, and she wrote a novel each semester. She went on to become co-winner of the *Mademoiselle* college fiction award in 1959 for her short story "In the Old World." In addition to writing, upon graduation in 1960, she was elected to the Phi Beta Kappa honor society and was valedictorian of her class.

Joyce Carol Oates does not spend all of her time writing. In addition to her one to four volumes a year, she involves herself in a parallel career in teaching. From 1962 to 1967, she taught at the University of Detroit and from 1967 to 1978 at the University of Windsor in Ontario. In 1978, she joined the faculty of Princeton University. Her books have won many awards, and her talent seems to continue to grow. She has earned a reputation as one of America's finest and best-known writers.

Oates says that she locates herself behind a "wall of silence" to write her stories. Why do you suppose that such a "wall of silence" is necessary for a writer?

Review the Selection

UNDERSTAND THE SELECTION

Recall

1. How much traffic is on the highway?

2. What is the destination?

3. When does the journey end?

Infer

4. Why do you think the broad highway is famous?

5. Why do you think you turn off onto a smaller road?

6. Why do you think your destination must be close as you start walking on the path?

7. Why does the day end in triumph?

Apply

8. Predict what might have happened if you had not turned off the broad highway.

9. What might have happened if you had not left the map in the car?

10. What do you think this journey represents?

Respond to Literature

Think about the freedom you have to make important decisions in your life. Different people choose different roads to follow. Why do you think it is important that choices and the freedom to choose are available to everyone?

WRITE ABOUT THE SELECTION

"Journey" ends in the forest, with night falling and you on foot. You have made a number of choices during the day. What would have happened if you had not decided to drive down smaller and smaller roads? How long would it take to reach the city? What would you do there? Write a paragraph that describes an alternate journey in which you made other choices and followed other roads.

Prewriting Write an informal outline of the sequence of events that would occur if you had stayed on the main highway. Use your imagination to create a different set of circumstances and a different ending.

Writing Use your informal outline to write a five-sentence paragraph describing the alternate journey. Be sure to include a description of how you feel during this journey.

Revising When you revise your paragraph, add specific details about the weather, the scenery, and the highway to create your own setting. The language you use should create a vivid mental image in your readers' minds.

Proofreading Read over your paragraph to check for errors. If you use compound adjectives, use a hyphen between them. For example: the tree-lined highway, the sun-splashed beach, the cloud-flecked sky. Check to see that you have used commas correctly as well.

THINK ABOUT POINT OF VIEW

Point of view is very important in fiction because it governs how the writer tells the story. If, for example, the first-person narrator tells the story, only his or her thoughts can be recorded, and only actions that he or she views can be told.

1. The grammatical person used in this story is unusual. Who is it?

2. Some people would think that "you" in the story is not really "the person being spoken to" but a substitute for "I." Do you agree? Why or why not?

3. How did the author's use of *you* make you feel as you read the story?

4. Do you think "you" should have been more concerned about "your" plight as the way became more and more difficult? Why or why not?

5. Do you think the end of the strange journey was indeed a triumph for "you"?

> ### READING FOCUS
> **Make Inferences** Write a few of the *Why* and *How* questions you asked yourself as you read "Journey." For each question, state the inferences you made and provide details from the story that helped you make it.

DEVELOP YOUR VOCABULARY

An **antonym** is a word whose meaning is the opposite of that of another word. *Happy* and *sad* are common examples.

Words are sometimes antonyms in one context but not in another. The adjectives *fast* and *slow* are usually antonyms. In the sentence "The carrots are *fast* in the ground," however, *fast* means "firmly fixed." The opposite of *fast* in this sentence is not *slow*, but *loose*.

The *italicized* words below are from "Journey." Choose the word that is the better antonym in the context given.

1. an *excessive* explanation:
   a. moderate   **b.** insufficient

2. *ingenious* blasting:
   a. stupid   **b.** unskillful

3. *convoluted* roadway:
   a. straight   **b.** simple

4. follow the path *enthusiastically*:
   a. unwillingly   **b.** soberly

Learn About

Slum Child, Margaret Burroughs. Collection of the artist

READING FOCUS

Understand Meaning Through Context
When you come upon an unfamiliar word as you read, you might be able to figure out what the word means by looking at the rest of the sentence or the paragraph it is in. As you read the excerpt from *Black Boy*, jot down each unfamiliar word. Then write what you think it means, based on the context of the sentence or sentences around it.

PURPOSE

Authors write to inform, to describe, to entertain or amuse, or to persuade. Any one or more of these may serve as an author's reason for giving readers a unified impression of his or her character, personality, and thoughts.

Autobiography can be defined as a narrative of an author's life written by him- or herself. What might motivate a person to write his or her own life story? Perhaps the author was a part of historical events or movements that would make his or her life inherently interesting.

An author may know, too, that his or her life experience and philosophy are so special that they may help or inspire others. The mere process of exploring one's own personality may result in insights that the author knows will interest the reader.

As you read the incident from Wright's boyhood, ask yourself:
1. Why did Wright tell the incident?
2. What did he want to accomplish by telling it?

WRITING CONNECTION

Write a short paragraph telling of an incident from your life. Then write another telling why you chose that incident.

from

BLACK BOY

by Richard Wright

Hunger stole upon me so slowly that at first I was not aware of what hunger really meant. Hunger had always been more or less at my elbow when I played, but now I began to wake up at night to find hunger standing at my bedside, staring at me gauntly. The hunger I had known before this had been no grim, hostile stranger; it had been a normal hunger that had made me beg constantly for bread, and when I ate a crust or two I was satisfied. But this new hunger baffled me, scared me, made me angry and insistent. Whenever I begged for food now my mother would pour me a cup of tea which would still the clamor in my stomach for a moment or two; but a little later I would feel hunger nudging my ribs, twisting my empty guts until they ached. I would grow dizzy and my vision would dim. I became less active in my play, and for the first time in my life I had to pause and think of what was happening to me.

"Mama, I'm hungry," I complained one afternoon.

"Jump up and catch a kungry," she said, trying to make me laugh and forget.

"What's a *kungry*?"

"It's what little boys eat when they get hungry," she said.

"What does it taste like?"

---

gauntly (GAWNT lee) in the manner of a thin bony person
grim (GRIM) very serious
still (STIL) make calm and quiet
clamor (KLAM ur) noise; excitement

"I don't know."

"Then why do you tell me to catch one?"

"Because you said that you were hungry," she said, smiling.

I sensed that she was teasing me and it made me angry.

"But I'm hungry. I want to eat."

"You'll have to wait."

"But I want to eat now."

"But there's nothing to eat," she told me.

"Why?"

"Just because there's none," she explained.

"But I want to eat," I said, beginning to cry.

"You'll just have to wait," she said again.

"But why?"

"For God to send some food."

"When is He going to send it?"

"I don't know."

"But I'm hungry!"

She was ironing and she paused and looked at me with tears in her eyes.

"Where's your father?" she asked me.

I stared in bewilderment. Yes, it was true that my father had not come home to sleep for many days now and I could make as much noise as I wanted. Though I had not known why he was absent, I had been glad that he was not there to shout his restrictions at me. But it had never occurred to me that his absence would mean that there would be no food.

"I don't know," I said.

"Who brings food into the house?" my mother asked me.

"Papa," I said. "He always brought food."

"Well, your father isn't here now," she said.

"Where is he?"

"I don't know," she said.

"But I'm hungry," I whimpered, stomping my feet.

"You'll have to wait until I get a job and buy food," she said.

As the days slid past the image of my father became associated with my pangs of hunger, and whenever I felt hunger I thought of him with a deep biological bitterness.

---

image (IM ij) mental picture
pangs (PANGZ) sharp pains

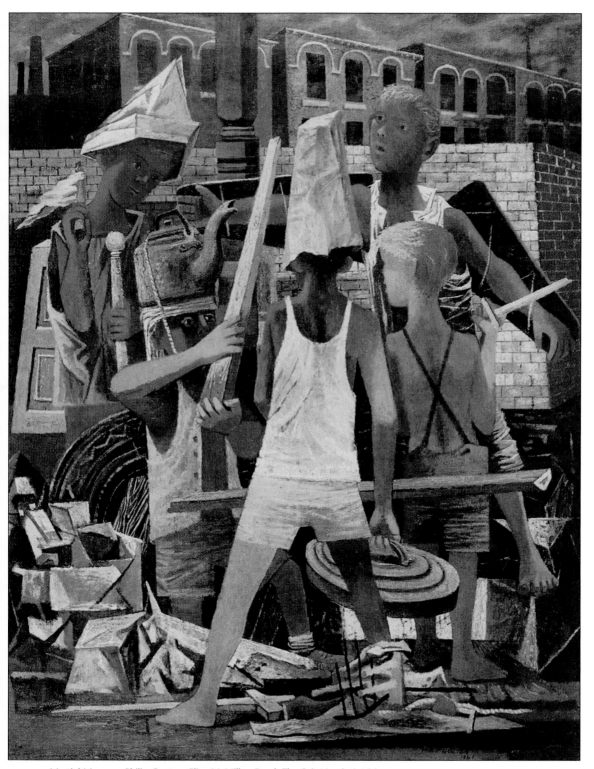

Martial Memory, Philip Guston. Eliza McMillan Fund, The Saint Louis Art Museum

My mother finally went to work as a cook and left me and my brother alone in the flat each day with a loaf of bread and a pot of tea. When she returned at evening she would be tired and dispirited and would cry a lot. Sometimes, when she was in despair, she would call us to her and talk to us for hours, telling us that we now had no father, that our lives would be different from those of other children, that we must learn as soon as possible to take care of ourselves, to dress ourselves, to prepare our own food; that we must take upon ourselves the responsibility of the flat while she worked. Half frightened, we would promise solemnly. We did not understand what had happened between our father and our mother and the most that these long talks did to us was to make us feel a vague dread. Whenever we asked why father had left, she would tell us that we were too young to know.

One evening my mother told me that thereafter I would have to do the shopping for food. She took me to the corner store to show me the way. I was proud; I felt like a grownup. The next afternoon I looped the basket over my arm and went down the pavement toward the store. When I reached the corner, a gang of boys grabbed me, knocked me down, snatched the basket, took the money, and sent me running home in panic. That evening I told my mother what had happened, but she made no comment; she sat down at once, wrote another note, gave me more money, and sent me out to the grocery again. I crept down the steps and saw the same gang of boys playing down the street. I ran back into the house.

"What's the matter?" my mother asked.

"It's those same boys," I said. "They'll beat me."

"You've got to get over that," she said. "Now, go on."

"I'm scared," I said.

"Go on and don't pay any attention to them," she said.

I went out of the door and walked briskly down the sidewalk, praying that the gang would not molest me. But when I came abreast of them someone shouted.

"There he is!"

They came toward me and I broke into a wild run toward home. They overtook me and flung me to the pavement. I yelled,

---

flat (FLAT) apartment
dispirited (dih SPIR it id) discouraged; low in spirits
molest (muh LEST) bother, annoy

pleaded, kicked, but they wrenched the money out of my hand. They yanked me to my feet, gave me a few slaps, and sent me home sobbing. My mother met me at the door.

"They b-beat m-me," I gasped. "They t-t-took the m-money."

I started up the steps, seeking the shelter of the house.

"Don't you come in here," my mother warned me.

I froze in my tracks and stared at her.

"But they're coming after me," I said.

"You just stay right where you are," she said in a deadly tone. "I'm going to teach you this night to stand up and fight for yourself."

She went into the house and I waited, terrified, wondering what she was about. Presently she returned with more money and another note; she also had a long heavy stick.

"Take this money, this note, and this stick," she said. "Go to the store and buy those groceries. If those boys bother you, then fight."

I was baffled. My mother was telling me to fight, a thing that she had never done before.

"But I'm scared," I said.

"Don't you come into this house until you've gotten those groceries," she said.

"They'll beat me; they'll beat me," I said.

"Then stay in the streets; don't come back here!"

I ran up the steps and tried to force my way past her into the house. A stinging slap came on my jaw. I stood on the side-walk, crying.

"Please, let me wait until tomorrow," I begged.

"No," she said. "Go now! If you come back into this house without those groceries, I'll whip you!"

She slammed the door and I heard the key turn in the lock. I shook with fright. I was alone upon the dark, hostile streets and gangs were after me. I had the choice of being beaten at home or away from home. I clutched the stick, crying, trying to reason. If I were beaten at home, there was absolutely nothing that I could do about it; but if I were beaten in the streets, I had a chance to fight and defend myself. I walked slowly down the sidewalk, coming closer to the gang of boys, holding the stick tightly. I was so full of fear that I could scarcely breathe. I was almost upon them now.

---

wrench (RENCH) twist

"There he is again!" the cry went up.

They surrounded me quickly and began to grab for my hand.

"I'll kill you!" I threatened.

They closed in. In blind fear I let the stick fly, feeling it crack against a boy's skull. I swung again, lamming another skull, then another. Realizing that they would retaliate if I let up for but a second, I fought to lay them low, to knock them cold, to kill them so that they could not strike back at me. I flayed with tears in my eyes, teeth clenched, stark fear making me throw every ounce of my strength behind each blow. I hit again and again, dropping the money and the grocery list. The boys scattered, yelling, nursing their heads, staring at me in utter disbelief. They had never seen such frenzy. I stood panting, egging them on, taunting them to come on and fight. When they refused, I ran after them and they tore out for their homes, screaming. The parents of the boys rushed into the streets and threatened me, and for the first time in my life I shouted at grownups, telling them that I would give them the same if they bothered me. I finally found my grocery list and the money and went to the store. On my way back I kept my stick poised for instant use, but there was not a single boy in sight. That night I won the right to the streets of Memphis.

---

lamming (LAM ing) striking
retaliate (rih TAL ee ayt) strike back
stark (STAHRK) complete; downright
utter (UT ur) complete
frenzy (FREN zee) madness; rage
egging (EG ing) urging
taunting (TAWNT ing) daring; teasing
poised (POIZD) set and ready

Richard Wright (1908–1960)

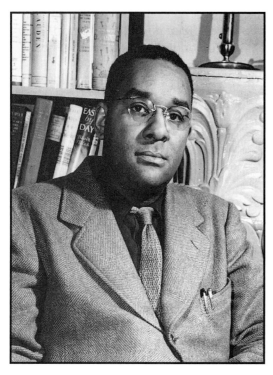

If the previous selection appeals to you, you might try looking for the book in a library. It is from *Black Boy*, the first volume of Richard Wright's autobiography, published in 1945. The book is powerful. The life Wright led as a child was a tough one, indeed.

Wright was born on a farm near Natchez, Mississippi, in 1908. His family moved here and there, at last settling in Memphis, Tennessee. When his parents separated, his mother had to work long hours to support the family. Wright hung out on the streets and in vacant lots. He learned to amuse the customers in bars by drinking liquor. "I was a drunkard in my sixth year," he tells us, "before I had begun school." Then his mother became very ill, and he spent some time in an orphanage. He quit school after the ninth grade and worked at several low-paying jobs. Always interested in books, he read more and more. He learned that life *could* be different. He began to believe that maybe he *did* have a chance at a happier life, after all. *Black Boy* ends as he leaves the South in 1927, to start a new life in Chicago.

But sadly, there was prejudice in the North, too. Wright still found that he was thought of as an African American first, a person second. After the success of *Black Boy* in 1945, he decided to move to Europe. He spent his last years in France and died in Paris in 1960. The second volume of his autobiography, *American Hunger*, written in the 1940s, was published in 1977.

Richard Wright had an interest that gave his life a turn for the better. What was this interest? How did it help him?

Review the Selection

UNDERSTAND THE SELECTION

Recall

1. In what way does hunger affect the boy physically?

2. What does his mother give him to defend himself with?

3. Where does the boy live?

Infer

4. What does the absence of the father mean for the family?

5. Why does the boy's mother keep sending him to the store?

6. What is the turning point in the story?

7. Why does the boy shout at the grownups, too?

Apply

8. Do you think the boy's mother did the right thing? Why do you think so?

9. Predict what might happen the next time the boy goes to the store.

10. Describe what kind of person the boy will be after his experience on the street.

Respond to Literature

Describe something that happened to you which you considered to be a turning point in your life.

WRITE ABOUT THE SELECTION

If you were asked to tell what happened in *Black Boy* in a few sentences, how would you do it? You could paraphrase the story, or retell it in a condensed, or shorter, form. This would include the most important events, characters, and their reactions. A lot happens in *Black Boy* that you will want to include, but remember to focus on the crisis, which is the most important part. Ask yourself what specific things lead up to the crisis. Write a paragraph that paraphrases the story.

Prewriting   Make a list of the events in the story as they happen, from beginning to end. Choose the ones you think are most important to include in your paragraph.

Writing   Using your list of events, write a paragraph that paraphrases the story in your own words. Write it as if you were telling a friend what happened in the story.

Revising   Reread your paraphrase to see if the events you wrote about follow each other logically. Does one event lead naturally to the next? If necessary, insert an event which helps your audience to make sense of the story.

Proofreading   Read over your paragraph to check for errors. Remember that proper nouns are capitalized. Make sure you have capitalized proper nouns such as the characters' names and the name of the city where the story takes place.

THINK ABOUT PURPOSE

People are innately curious about other people's lives. When these lives have impacted history, autobiographies may reveal new insights into events. The author may interpret facts and demonstrate his or her character or habit of mind.

1. What is Wright's purpose(s) in telling this incident—to inform, describe, entertain, or persuade?

2. What do you think the incident relayed in this excerpt represented to Wright?

3. What did Wright want to accomplish by telling this incident?

4. Why do you think Wright did not try to use the incident to "teach" readers how to raise children?

5. The incident is from Wright's autobiography. Why do you think he chose to write his life story?

READING FOCUS

Understand Meaning Through Context
As you read the excerpt from *Black Boy*, you guessed the meaning of unfamiliar words by looking for clues in the text. Choose four words that can be understood by looking at context. Then write the phrase or sentence that helped you understand each word.

DEVELOP YOUR VOCABULARY

At one point in the autobiographical incident, Wright admits that the gang of boys sent him "running home in panic." The word *panic* has an interesting history. It comes from Pan, Greek god of the fields, forests, flocks, and shepherds, who frightened people as they were traveling through the woods. An unreasonable fear is still called a *panic*.

The English language contains a number of words whose roots can be traced back to characters from Greek and Roman mythology. Look up the following words in a dictionary that has word histories. Give the meaning and origin of each word.

1. narcissus
2. martial
3. titan
4. jovial
5. atlas
6. Saturday
7. volcano
8. museum
9. tantalize
10. cereal

Focus ON NONFICTION

*T*o understand what an autobiography is, look at the word itself. It breaks down into three parts: *auto-*, *bio-* and *-graphy*. The dictionary will tell you that *auto-* means "self," *bio-* means "life," and *-graphy* means "a process, a manner or a method of writing."

When the three parts are combined, you can see that *autobiography* means "a self-written life story," or the story of a person's life written by himself or herself.

An autobiography can take one of several forms. There is the autobiography itself, a written story. There is also the journal, the diary, letters, and memoirs. These are all autobiographical works.

The first three, journals, diaries, and letters, are not usually intended for publication by the writer. They may serve the writer as a basis or as sources for the autobiography. Memoirs focus on the writer's involvement in public events and relationships with notable people.

Four elements are important in an autobiography. They are narrative style, point of view, purpose, and introspection. It is important to remember that autobiography, like all nonfiction, is based on fact. It consists of real events that happened to real people.

Narrative Style An autobiography is written in narrative style, that is, it tells a story. The narrative consists of events in the writer's life. A writer will organize the narrative in one of several ways. The most obvious—and the most common—is chronological. **Chronological** means "in time order." A chronological narrative is one that describes the events in the order in which they occurred.

Another method is to begin the autobiography with an event that the writer sees as most important in his or her life. The rest of the autobiography is then organized around this primary event.

Point of View In literature, point of view means the position from which the work is presented. In autobiography, since the writer is also the main character, the point of view is always first-person. The clues that tell the reader that the story is written from a first-person point of view are the words *I*, *me*, *my*, and *mine*.

The first-person point of view allows the reader to see the world through the eyes of the author. The reader gains a new perspective on events and other people. It seems as if the reader is inside the writer's mind, listening to his or her internal dialogue—the debate with self.

Purpose   When you read an autobiography, consider the purpose of the writer. Was it to inform, describe, entertain, or persuade? More specifically, was it to glorify the writer? Was the purpose to make a point or proclaim a message? Was it to moralize about aspects of life? Was the purpose to satisfy the reader's curiosity about a personality?

An autobiography may be written for one of these purposes or a combination of them. There is always a reason why a writer decides to write his or her autobiography.

Introspection   Introspection is an important element of autobiography. Introspection is the observation and analysis of oneself. An introspective person is one who closely and thoughtfully examines his or her own feelings, thoughts, and reactions.

Introspection can help the writer to analyze the role of self in a given situation. It thus adds another dimension to autobiography. It gives the reader a more complete portrait of the writer. It may also give the reader a chance to find something in common with his or her own life—something that every person shares. Reading an autobiography may tell the reader how different people are from each other, and in some ways, how much alike.

As you read "Little Things Are Big," examine the story to identify the elements of autobiography. Ask yourself these questions:

1. What form of autobiography is this story?
2. What is the point of view of the writer?
3. What do you think Colón's purpose was in writing this story?

Little Things Are BIG

ADAPTED

by Jesús Colón

FOCUS ON
NONFICTION
STUDY HINTS

The title gives you
a clue to the story's
theme, or message.

It was very late at night on the eve of Memorial Day. She came into the subway at the 34th Street station. I am still trying to remember how she managed to push herself in, with a baby on her right arm, a valise in her left hand, and two children, a boy and a girl about three and five years old, trailing after her. She was a nice-looking white lady in her early twenties.

At Nevins Street, Brooklyn, we saw her preparing to get off at the next station, Atlantic Avenue, which happened to be the place where I too had to get off. Just as it had been a problem for her to get on the subway, it was going to be a problem for her to get off. She had two small children to take care of, a baby on her right arm and a medium-sized valise in her left hand.

And there I was, also preparing to get off at Atlantic Avenue, with no bundles to take care of—not even the usual book under my arm, without which I feel that I am not completely dressed.

As the train was entering the Atlantic Avenue station, some white man stood up from his seat and helped her out of the car, placing the children on the long, deserted platform. There were only two adult persons on the long platform sometime after midnight on the eve of Memorial Day.

---

valise (vuh LEES) small suitcase

I could see the steep, long concrete stairs going down to the Long Island Railroad or into the street. Should I offer my help as the American white man had done at the subway door, placing the two children outside the subway car? Should I take care of the girl and the boy? Should I take them by their hands until they reached the end of the steep, long concrete stairs of the Atlantic Avenue station?

You begin to get an idea of what kind of person the narrator is.

Courtesy is a characteristic of the Puerto Rican. And here I was—a Puerto Rican. Hours past midnight, valise, two white children, and a white lady with a baby on her arm badly needing somebody to help her until she got down the long concrete stairs.

Introspection: The narrator describes his feelings, observations and an analysis of his reactions.

But how could I, a black and a Puerto Rican, approach this white lady? I knew she very likely might be prejudiced against blacks and everybody with foreign accents. And we were in a deserted subway station, very late at night.

What would she say? What would be the first reaction of this white American woman, perhaps coming from a small town, with a valise, two children and baby on her right arm? Would she say, "Yes, of course, you may help me?" Or would she think that I was just trying to get too familiar? Or would she think worse than that perhaps? What would I do if she let out a scream as I went toward her to offer my help?

Was I misjudging her? So many slanders are written every day in the newspapers against the blacks and Puerto Ricans. I hesitated for a long, long minute. The ancestral manners that the most illiterate Puerto Rican passes on from father to son were struggling inside me. Here was I, way past midnight, face to face with a situation that could very well explode into an outburst of prejudice.

It was a long minute. I passed on by her as if I saw nothing. As if I didn't care about her need. Like a rude animal walking on two legs, I just moved on. I half ran down the long subway platform, leaving the children and the valise and her with the baby on her arm. I took the steps of the long concrete stairs in twos until I reached the street. The cold air slapped my warm face.

---

characteristic (kar ak tuh RIS tik) special quality
slander (SLAN dur) lie; harmful statement
ancestral (an SES trul) coming from an ancestor
illiterate (ih LIT ur it) unable to read

This is what racism and prejudice and artificial divisions can do to people and to a nation!

Perhaps the lady was not prejudiced after all. Or not prejudiced enough to scream at the coming of a black man toward her in a lonely subway station a few hours past midnight.

If you were not prejudiced, I failed you, dear lady. I know that there is a chance in a million that you will read these lines. I am willing to take that millionth chance. If you were not that prejudiced, I failed you, lady, I failed you, children. I failed myself to myself.

I buried my courtesy early on Memorial Day morning. But here is a promise that I make to myself here and now: If I am ever faced with a situation like that again, I am going to offer my help regardless of how the offer is going to be received.

Then I will have my courtesy with me again.

---

racism (RAY siz um) racial prejudice

Review the Selection

UNDERSTAND THE SELECTION

Recall

1. When does the story take place?

2. Which is the narrator's subway stop?

3. How many children did the woman have with her?

Infer

4. Why do you think that the narrator feels he should help the woman?

5. Why might the woman be afraid of the narrator?

6. Why did the narrator decide not to help the woman?

7. Explain how the narrator felt after he passed the woman.

Apply

8. Predict what might have happened if the narrator had offered to help the woman.

9. Is the narrator prejudiced? Explain.

10. What is your opinion of the narrator's decision? If he had decided to help the woman, how could he have approached her?

Respond to Literature

How does the narrator's awareness of prejudice in the United States affect his actions? Is this a positive or negative effect?

WRITE ABOUT THE SELECTION

You have learned about elements of autobiography in this unit. One of those elements is point of view. Autobiography is written from the **first-person point of view**. This is because the person in the story, the "main character," is also the person telling the story.

There is another person in "Little Things Are Big" who is important—the woman with three young children. Suppose this story is part of *her* autobiography; suppose that she is telling you about the incident. She would likely see it in a different way. Retell this story in one paragraph from the woman's point of view.

Prewriting Make a chart that lists who you think the woman is; what you think she sees; and how you think she reacts. In each category, list key words or ideas which you can expand into a story.

Writing Using your chart, write a one-paragraph story that describes the events of "Little Things Are Big" from the woman's point of view.

Revising Read the story again to remind yourself of the sequence of events. Add details or explanations to your paragraph which make the reasons for her reactions understandable to the reader.

Proofreading Check your paragraph to make sure you have written consistently in the first person. Remember that the first-person point of view is indicated by the words *I*, *me*, *my*, and *mine*.

THINK ABOUT AUTOBIOGRAPHY

Autobiography is a true story in which the narrator/writer is the main character. Events in the life story of the writer are told from his or her point of view. The narrator also describes his or her emotions, reactions, and thoughts.

1. Describe Colón's instinctive reaction when he sees the woman and her children.

2. Colón says he usually has a book under his arm. What does this tell you about him?

3. List several ways the narrator describes himself.

4. What reactions does the incident cause in the narrator?

5. What lesson does Colón tell you he has learned?

DEVELOP YOUR VOCABULARY

Colón asks if he *misjudged* the woman in the subway. Perhaps, he mused, she was not *prejudiced* after all. Both *italicized* words in the preceding two sentences contain the Latin word part *jus* or *juris*, meaning "law." Some Latin and Greek word parts are at the core of whole families of English words. *Jus* and *juris* are the core part of a word family that includes all the words below.

Look up the meaning of each word in the list below. Do they all have something to do with law today? Think about their meanings. Then use each word in a sentence of your own.

1. just
2. injury
3. jurisdiction
4. jurisprudence
5. adjust
6. jury
7. justice
8. perjury
9. judge
10. jurist

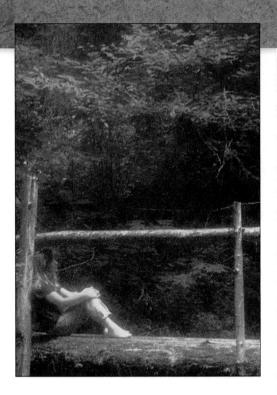

Poetry that does not depend on rhyme or a regular meter is known as **free verse**. For its effectiveness, free verse depends on a variety of natural rhythms and the repetition of images and phrases.

In conversation, people naturally emphasize or accent certain words. Their tone varies, their voices rise at the end of a question or fall at the end of a statement. Unlike other types of poetry, free verse is characterized by these natural rhythms. The rhythmical unit to note is the stanza, not the foot or line.

Certain words or whole lines of free verse are repeated for emphasis. A line may not be repeated word for word, but may be varied to enrich the emotion it expresses.

As you read "Where Have You Gone," ask yourself:

1. What does the poet repeat?
2. Does reading the poem aloud help you to understand it better?

READING FOCUS

Interpret Character All good writers give clues about the personalities of their characters. Active readers use these clues to form an impression of each character. As you read the next selection, think about the two characters: the speaker and the one being spoken of. What clues can you find to help you understand their personalities?

WRITING CONNECTION

Some verse can be read as if one person is talking to another. Write a short conversation with one person asking questions, and the other person answering. Then try casting the conversation in poetic units.

WHERE HAVE YOU GONE

by Mari Evans

Where have you gone

with your confident
walk with
your crooked smile

5   why did you leave
me
when you took your
laughter
and departed

10   are you aware that
with you
went the sun
all light
and what few stars
15   there were?

where have you gone
with your confident
walk your
crooked smile the
20   rent money
in one pocket and
my heart
in another. . .

Alta, Aaron Douglas. Collection of Fisk University Art Museum

Review the Selection

UNDERSTAND THE SELECTION

Recall

1. In the second stanza, what does the speaker say has been taken?

2. How is "you" described?

3. What was in the pockets of the "you" in the poem?

Infer

4. To whom is the speaker speaking?

5. What does "the sun," "all light," and "what few stars there were" imply?

6. How does the speaker feel about "you" in the poem?

7. What kind of person do you think "you" is?

Apply

8. Do you think that the speaker of the poem knew that "you" was going to leave? Why do you think so?

9. Do you think that the speaker is "blindly" in love with "you"? Why do you think so?

10. Predict how the speaker might feel if "you" returned.

Respond to Literature

What emotions does the speaker express in "Where Have You Gone"? What situations in your life have made you feel the same way?

WRITE ABOUT THE SELECTION

The speaker in "Where Have You Gone" uses a series of questions to carry her message and to express the way she feels about what has happened. Why do you think the "you" in the poem left? Do you think the speaker is more deeply affected than "you"? What is your opinion of the poem itself?

Prewriting Decide how you feel about the poem, and make a list of reasons to support your opinion. Arrange your list by putting the most important reasons first, the next most important second, and so forth. Use quotes from the poem to illustrate or back up your opinions. This will help lend weight to your viewpoint.

Writing Write a short paragraph to persuade your audience to share your opinion of the poem. Begin the paragraph by stating your opinion. Then build your case using the reasons in your list in the order that you listed them.

Revising Read your paragraph. Ask yourself if the statement of your opinion would be clear to someone reading it for the first time. Do all your reasons support your opinion? If you find one that doesn't, leave that sentence out.

Proofreading Read over your paragraph to check for errors. Remember that commas are used after introductory phrases and to separate adjectives that come before a noun.

THINK ABOUT FREE VERSE

Rhymes are not required in free verse. In this poem phrases are repeated in varying ways to create a poem. The poem is organized into stanzas and expresses an emotion, an opinion, or an idea. Because it is not bound by strict rules of rhyme or meter, free verse often reads like the natural rhythms of speech.

1. What is the main emotion expressed by the poem?

2. List the verbs in the poem that suggest that feeling.

3. The title of the poem is in the form of a question. Keeping that in mind, describe the content of the poem itself.

4. List all of the lines or phrases that literally, or with variations, are repetitions of the poem's title.

5. Why is "the/ rent money/ in one pocket and my heart/ in another" such a startling comparison?

READING FOCUS

Interpret Character As you read "Where Have You Gone" you looked for clues about the personalities of the speaker and the one being spoken to. What did you decide? Write a paragraph telling what you think each character is like, and tell what clues make you think so.

DEVELOP YOUR VOCABULARY

"I always *vote* in the election; I know my *vote* makes a difference."

The *italicized* words in the sentence look like the same word, but they are different from each other. How do they differ? The first time the word *vote* is used, it is used as a verb. The second time *vote* is used, it is used as a noun. **Nouns** are words that name a person, place, idea, or object. **Verbs** are words that express an action or a state of being.

Look at the italicized words in the following sentences and write down whether they are nouns or verbs.

1. Let's go for a *walk*.

2. Did you *label* the package?

3. The explorers hope to *land* safely in a friendly country.

4. We saw a *play* performed at the theater.

5. Shall I *paint* the ceiling white?

Learn About

THEME

The central idea of a literary work is called the **theme**. In nonfiction, the general topic of discussion is the theme. The writer takes a position on the topic and proves or supports that position.

The fiction writer, the poet and the dramatist have a variety of ways to express the theme of a work. It may be expressed through the character, through the action and events, or through the images the author uses. The theme is not the "moral of the story," however. It is a truth about life. It presents no rule to live by, but makes a statement about the way people behave. Sometimes the theme is not specified. Readers may have to draw their own conclusions about what it is.

As you read "Everyday Use" ask yourself:

1. What is the theme of "Everyday Use"?
2. Is the theme made clear in the story? If so, how?

WRITING CONNECTION

Write a five–sentence paragraph about a fictional person whose actions demonstrate or express some particular attitude toward patriotism.

READING FOCUS

Compare and Contrast When you compare two things, you look at how they are the same. When you contrast, you look at differences. One way to do this is to use a simple graphic organizer, with one column to note things that are the same and one column for differences. The next selection describes two sisters. Divide your paper in half. Write *Same* at the top of one half and *Different* at the top of the other. As you read about the two sisters, jot down your observations about how they are the same and how they are different.

Everyday Use

by Alice Walker

I will wait for her in the yard that Maggie and I made so clean and wavy yesterday afternoon. A yard like this is more comfortable than most people know. It is not just a yard. It is like an extended living room. When the hard clay is swept clean as a floor and the fine sand around the edges lined with tiny, irregular grooves, anyone can come and sit and look up into the elm tree and wait for the breezes that never come inside the house.

Maggie will be nervous until after her sister goes: she will stand hopelessly in corners, homely and ashamed of the burn scars down her arms and legs, eying her sister with a mixture of envy and awe. She thinks her sister has held life always in the palm of one hand, that "no" is a word the world never learned to say to her.

You've no doubt seen those TV shows where the child who has "made it" is confronted, as a surprise, by her own mother and father, tottering in weakly from backstage. (A pleasant surprise, of course: What would they do if parent and child came on the show only to curse out and insult each other?) On TV mother and child embrace and smile into each other's faces. Sometimes the mother and father weep, the child wraps them in her arms and leans across the table to tell how she would not have made it without their help. I have seen these programs.

Sometimes I dream a dream in which Dee and I are suddenly brought together on a TV program of this sort. Out of a dark and soft-seated limousine I am ushered into a bright room filled with many people. There I meet a smiling, gray, sporty man like Johnny Carson who shakes my hand and tells me what a fine girl I have. Then we are on the stage and Dee is embracing me with tears in her eyes. She pins on my dress a large orchid, even though she has told me once that she thinks orchids are tacky flowers.

---

awe (AW) wonderment; admiration
confronted (kun FRUNT id) set face to face
tacky (TAK ee) too showy; not fashionable

In real life I am a large, big-boned woman with rough, man-working hands. In the winter I wear flannel nightgowns to bed and overalls during the day. I can kill and clean a hog as mercilessly as a man. My fat keeps me hot in zero weather. I can work outside all day, breaking ice to get water for washing; I can eat pork liver cooked over the open fire minutes after it comes steaming from the hog. One winter I knocked a bull calf straight in the brain between the eyes with a sledge hammer and had the meat hung up to chill before nightfall. But of course all this does not show on television. I am the way my daughter would want me to be: a hundred pounds lighter, my skin like an uncooked barley pancake. My hair glistens in the hot bright lights. Johnny Carson has much to do to keep up with my quick and witty tongue.

But that is a mistake. I know even before I wake up. Who ever knew a Johnson with a quick tongue? Who can even imagine me looking a strange white man in the eye? It seems to me I have talked to them always with one foot raised in flight, with my head turned in whichever way is farthest from them. Dee, though. She would always look anyone in the eye. Hesitation was no part of her nature.

"How do I look, Mama?" Maggie says, showing just enough of her thin body enveloped in pink skirt and red blouse for me to know she's there, almost hidden by the door.

"Come out into the yard," I say.

Have you ever seen a lame animal, perhaps a dog run over by some careless person rich enough to own a car, sidle up to someone who is ignorant enough to be kind to him? That is the way my Maggie walks. She has been like this, chin on chest, eyes on ground, feet in shuffle, ever since the fire that burned the other house to the ground.

Dee is lighter than Maggie, with nicer hair and a fuller figure. She's a woman now, though sometimes I forget. How long ago was it that the other house burned? Ten, twelve years? Sometimes I can still hear the flames and feel Maggie's arms sticking to me, her hair smoking and her dress falling off her in little black papery flakes. Her eyes seemed stretched open, blazed open by the flames reflected in them. And Dee. I see her standing off under the sweet gum tree she used to dig gum out of; a look of concentration on her face as she watched the last dingy gray board of the house fall in toward the red-hot brick chimney. Why don't you do a dance around the ashes? I'd wanted to ask her. She had hated the house that much.

I used to think she hated Maggie, too. But that was before we raised the money, the church and me, to send her to Augusta to school. She used to read to us without pity; forcing words, lies, other folks' habits, whole lives upon us two, sitting trapped and ignorant underneath her voice. She washed us in a river of make-believe, burned us with a lot of knowledge we didn't necessarily need to know.

---

sidle (SYD ul) move sideways; edge along slyly

Family, Charles H. Alston. Whitney Museum of American Art

Pressed us to her with the serious way she read, to shove us away at just the moment, like dimwits, we seemed about to understand.

Dee wanted nice things. A yellow organdy dress to wear to her graduation from high school; black pumps to match a green suit she'd made from an old suit somebody gave me. She was determined to stare down any disaster in her efforts. Her eyelids would not flicker for minutes at a time. Often I fought off the temptation to shake her. At sixteen she had a style of her own: and knew what style was.

I never had an education myself. After second grade the school was closed down. Don't ask me why: in 1927 colored asked fewer questions than they do now. Sometimes Maggie reads to me. She stumbles along good-naturedly but can't see well. She knows she is not bright. Like good looks and money, quickness passed her by. She will marry John Thomas (who has mossy teeth in an earnest face) and then I'll be free to sit here and I guess just sing church songs to myself. Although I never was a good singer. Never could carry a tune. I was always better at a man's job. I used to love to milk till I was hooked in the side in '49. Cows are soothing and slow and don't bother you, unless you try to milk them the wrong way.

I have deliberately turned my back on the house. It is three rooms, just like the one that burned, except the roof is tin; they don't make shingle roofs anymore. There are no real windows, just some holes cut in the sides, like the portholes in a ship, but not round and not square, with rawhide holding the shutters up on the outside. This house is in a pasture, too, like the other one. No doubt when Dee sees it she will want to tear it down. She wrote me once that no matter where we "choose" to live, she will manage to come see us. But she will never bring her friends. Maggie and I thought about this and Maggie asked me, "Mama, when did Dee ever *have* any friends?"

She had a few. Furtive boys in pink shirts hanging about on washday after school. Nervous girls who never laughed. Impressed with her, they worshiped the well-turned phrase, the cute shape, the scalding humor that erupted like bubbles in lye. She read to them.

When she was courting Jimmy T she didn't have much time to pay to us, but turned all her faultfinding power on him. He *flew* to marry a cheap city girl from a family of ignorant flashy people. She hardly had time to recompose herself.

When she comes I will meet—but there they are!

Maggie attempts to make a dash for the house, in her shuffling way, but I stay her with my hand. "Come back here," I say. And she stops and tries to dig a well in the sand with her toe.

---

organdy (AWR gun dee) kind of thin crisp cotton cloth
pumps (PUMPS) kind of low cut shoes for women
furtive (FUR tiv) sly; shifty
recompose (ree kum POHZ) pulls oneself together; become calm again

It is hard to see them clearly through the strong sun. But even the first glimpse of leg out of the car tells me it is Dee. Her feet were always neat-looking, as if God himself had shaped them with a certain style. From the other side of the car comes a short, stocky man. Hair is all over his head a foot long and hanging from his chin like a kinky mule tail. I hear Maggie suck in her breath. "Uhnnnh," is what it sounds like. Like when you see the wriggling end of a snake just in front of your foot on the road. "Uhnnnh."

Dee next. A dress down to the ground, in this hot weather. A dress so loud it hurts my eyes. There are yellows and oranges enough to throw back the light of the sun. I feel my whole face warming from the heat waves it throws out. Earrings gold, too, and hanging down to her shoulders. Bracelets dangling and making noises when she moves her arm up to shake the folds of the dress out of her armpits. The dress is loose and flows, and as she walks closer, I like it. I hear Maggie go "Uhnnnh" again. It is her sister's hair. It stands straight up like the wool on a sheep. It is black as night and around the edges are two long pigtails that rope about like small lizards disappearing behind her ears.

"Wa-su-zo-Tean-o!" she says, coming on in that gliding way the dress makes her move. The short stocky fellow with the hair to his navel is all grinning and he follows up with "Asalamalakim, my mother and sister!" He moves to hug Maggie but she falls back, right up against the back of my chair. I feel her trembling there and when I look up I see the perspiration falling off her chin.

"Don't get up," says Dee. Since I am stout it takes something of a push. You can see me trying to move a second or two before I make it. She turns, showing white heels through her sandals, and goes back to the car. Out she peeks next with a Polaroid. She stoops down quickly and lines up picture after picture of me sitting there in front of the house with Maggie cowering behind me. She never takes a shot without making sure the house is included. When a cow comes nibbling around the edge of the yard she snaps it and me and Maggie *and* the house. Then she puts the Polaroid in the back seat of the car, and comes up and kisses me on the forehead.

Meanwhile Asalamalakim is going through motions with Maggie's hand. Maggie's hand is as limp as a fish, and probably as cold, despite the sweat, and she keeps trying to pull it back. It looks like Asalamalakim wants to shake hands but wants to do it fancy. Or maybe he don't know how people shake hands. Anyhow, he soon gives up on Maggie.

"Well," I say. "Dee."

"No, Mama," she says. "Not 'Dee,' Wangero Leewanika Kemanjo!"

"What happened to 'Dee'?" I wanted to know.

"She's dead," Wangero said. "I couldn't bear it any longer, being named after the people who oppress me."

---

cowering (KOU ur ing) *crouching in fear*

"You know as well as me you was named after your aunt Dicie," I said. Dicie is my sister. She named Dee. We called her "Big Dee" after Dee was born.

"But who was *she* named after?" asked Wangero.

"I guess after Grandma Dee," I said.

"And who was she named after?" asked Wangero.

"Her mother," I said, and saw Wangero was getting tired. "That's about as far back as I can trace it," I said. Though, in fact, I probably could have carried it back beyond the Civil War through the branches.

"Well," said Asalamalakim, "there you are."

"Uhnnnh," I heard Maggie say.

"There I was not," I said, "before 'Dicie' cropped up in our family, so why should I try to trace it that far back?"

He just stood there grinning, looking down on me like somebody inspecting a Model A car. Every once in a while he and Wangero sent eye signals over my head.

"How do you pronounce this name?" I asked.

"You don't have to call me by it if you don't want to," said Wangero.

"Why shouldn't I?" I asked. "If that's what you want us to call you, we'll call you."

"I know it might sound awkward at first," said Wangero.

"I'll get used to it," I said. "Ream it out again."

---

ream (REEM) enlarge; open up (here used figuratively)

Well, soon we got the name out of the way. Asalamalakim had a name twice as long and three times as hard. After I tripped over it two or three times he told me to just call him Hakim-a-barber. I wanted to ask him was he a barber, but I didn't really think he was, so I didn't ask.

"You must belong to those beef-cattle peoples down the road," I said. They said "Asalamalakim" when they met you, too, but they didn't shake hands. Always too busy: feeding the cattle, fixing the fences, putting up salt-lick shelters, throwing down hay. When the white folks poisoned some of the herd the men stayed up all night with rifles in their hands. I walked a mile and a half just to see the sight.

Hakim-a-barber said, "I accept some of their doctrines, but farming and raising cattle is not my style." (They didn't tell me, and I didn't ask, whether Wangero (Dee) had really gone and married him.)

We sat down to eat and right away he said he didn't eat collards and pork was unclean. Wangero, though, went on through the chitlins and corn bread, the greens and everything else. She talked a blue streak over the sweet potatoes. Everything delighted her. Even the fact that we still used the benches her daddy made for the table when we couldn't afford to buy chairs.

"Oh, Mama!" she cried. Then turned to Hakim-a-barber. "I never knew how lovely these benches are. You can feel the rump prints," she said, running her hands underneath her and along the bench. Then she gave a sigh and her hand closed over Grandma Dee's butter dish. "That's it!" she said. "I knew there was something I wanted to ask you if I could have." She jumped up from the table and went over in the corner where the churn stood, the milk in it clabber by now. She looked at the churn and looked at it.

"This churn top is what I need," she said. "Didn't Uncle Buddy whittle it out of a tree you all used to have?"

"Yes," I said.

"Uh huh," she said happily. "And I want the dasher, too."

"Uncle Buddy whittle that, too?" asked the barber.

Dee (Wangero) looked up at me.

"Aunt Dee's first husband whittled the dash," said Maggie so low you almost couldn't hear her. "His name was Henry, but they called him Stash."

"Maggie's brain is like an elephant's," Wangero said, laughing. "I can use the churn top as a centerpiece for the alcove table," she said, sliding a plate over the churn, "and I'll think of something artistic to do with the dasher."

When she finished wrapping the dasher the handle stuck out. I took it for a

---

doctrine (DOK trin) belief, theory
collards (KOL urdz) kind of green vegetable
chitlins (CHIT linz) hog intestines used as food
clabber (KLAB ur) sour, thick milk
dasher (DASH ur) plunger with paddles for stirring
alcove (AL kohv) opening off a room

moment in my hands. You didn't even have to look close to see where hands pushing the dasher up and down to make butter had left a kind of sink in the wood. In fact, there were a lot of small sinks; you could see where thumbs and fingers had sunk into the wood. It was beautiful light yellow wood, from a tree that grew in the yard where Big Dee and Stash had lived.

After dinner Dee (Wangero) went to the trunk at the foot of my bed and started rifling through it. Maggie hung back in the kitchen over the dishpan. Out came Wangero with two quilts. They had been pieced by Grandma Dee and then Big Dee and me had hung them on the quilt frames on the front porch and quilted them. One was in the Lone Star pattern. The other was Walk Around the Mountain. In both of them were scraps of dresses Grandma Dee had worn fifty and more years ago. Bits and pieces of Grandpa Jarrell's Paisley shirts. And one teeny faded blue piece, about the size of a penny matchbox, that was from Great Grandpa Ezra's uniform that he wore in the Civil War.

"Mama," Wangero said sweet as a bird. "Can I have these old quilts?"

I heard something fall in the kitchen, and a minute later the kitchen door slammed.

"Why don't you take one or two of the others?" I asked. "These old things was just done by me and Big Dee from some tops your grandma pieced before she died."

"No," said Wangero. "I don't want those. They are stitched around the borders by machine."

"That'll make them last better," I said.

"That's not the point," said Wangero. "These are all pieces of dresses Grandma used to wear. She did all this stitching by hand. Imagine!" She held the quilts securely in her arms, stroking them.

"Some of the pieces, like those lavender ones, come from old clothes her mother handed down to her," I said, moving up to touch the quilts. Dee (Wangero) moved back just enough so that I couldn't reach the quilts. They already belonged to her.

"Imagine!" she breathed again, clutching them closely to her bosom.

"The truth is," I said, "I promised to give them quilts to Maggie, for when she marries John Thomas."

She gasped like a bee had stung her.

"Maggie can't appreciate these quilts!" she said. "She'd probably be backward enough to put them to everyday use."

"I reckon she would," I said. "God knows I been saving 'em for long enough with nobody using 'em. I hope she will!" I didn't want to bring up how I had offered Dee (Wangero) a quilt when she went away to college. Then she had told me they were old-fashioned, out of style.

"But they're *priceless*!" she was saying now, furiously; for she has a temper. "Maggie would put them on the bed and in five years they'd be in rags. Less than that!"

"She can always make some more," I said. "Maggie knows how to quilt."

---

rifling (RY fling) searching; going through hurriedly

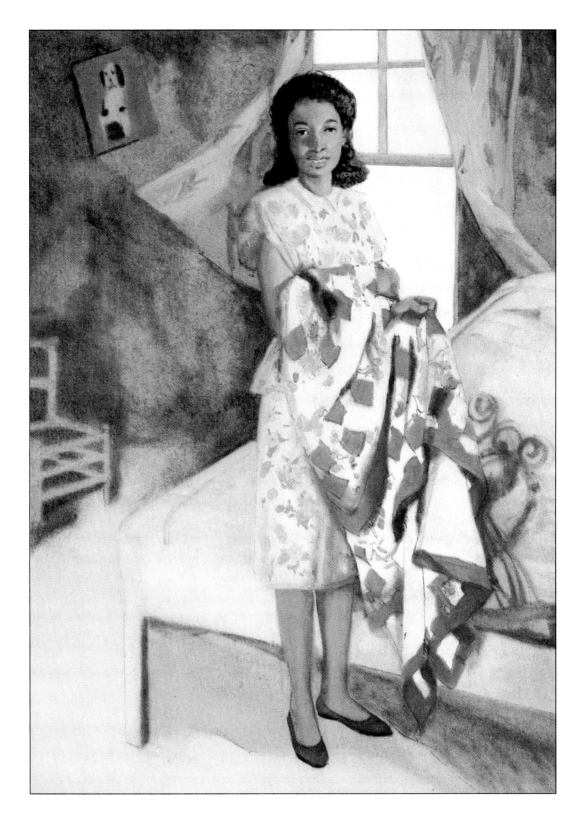

Dee (Wangero) looked at me with hatred. "You just will not understand. The point is these quilts, *these* quilts!"

"Well," I said, stumped. "What would *you* do with them?"

"Hang them," she said. As if that was the only thing you could do with quilts.

Maggie by now was standing in the door. I could almost hear the sound her feet made as they scraped over each other.

"She can have them, Mama," she said, like somebody used to never winning anything, or having anything reserved for her. "I can 'member Grandma Dee without the quilts."

I looked at her hard. She had filled her bottom lip with checkerberry snuff and it gave her face a kind of dopey, hangdog look. It was Grandma Dee and Big Dee who taught her how to quilt herself. She stood there with her scarred hands hidden in the folds of her skirt. She looked at her sister with something like fear but she wasn't mad at her. This was Maggie's portion. This was the way she knew God to work.

When I looked at her like that something hit me in the top of my head and ran down to the soles of my feet. Just like when I'm in church and the spirit of God touches me and I get happy and shout.

I did something I never had done before: hugged Maggie to me, then dragged her on into the room, snatched the quilts out of Miss Wangero's hands and dumped them into Maggie's lap. Maggie just sat there on my bed with her mouth open.

"Take one or two of the others," I said to Dee.

But she turned without a word and went out to Hakim-a-barber.

"You just don't understand," she said, as Maggie and I came out to the car.

"What don't I understand?" I wanted to know.

"Your heritage," she said. And then she turned to Maggie, kissed her, and said, "You ought to try to make something of yourself, too, Maggie. It's really a new day for us. But from the way you and Mama still live you'd never know it."

She put on some sunglasses that hid everything above the tip of her nose and her chin.

Maggie smiled; maybe at the sunglasses. But a real smile, not scared. After we watched the car dust settle I asked Maggie to bring me a dip of snuff. And then the two of us sat there just enjoying, until it was time to go in the house and go to bed.

---

checkerberry (CHEK ur ber ee) kind of small red berry (wintergreen)

Alice Walker (1944–   )

Alice Walker, winner of both the Pulitzer Prize and the National Book Award, became a writer at age eight. Her story is an interesting one.

One day in Georgia in 1952, an eight-year-old Alice was shot accidentally in the right eye with a BB gun by one of her brothers. The family had little money, and the best medical attention was not available. She went blind in that eye. The pain ceased after a few days, but the scar tissue remained.

Ironically, the loss of an eye enabled the girl to "see." She soon found herself writing down thoughts and impressions in a notebook, and she discovered that the writing made her feel better. She also started to read a great deal.

Writing and reading helped erase the mental scars, but the scarred eye remained until Alice was 14, when an operation removed the disfigurement. Other changes followed fast. By graduation time she was not only class valedictorian but also voted "Most Popular." Her partial blindness, as well as her ability, qualified her for a special scholarship for the handicapped to Spelman College. She later transferred to Sarah Lawrence College, graduating in 1965.

Walker continued to write in notebooks at Sarah Lawrence and soon found herself writing poetry at a furious pace. She showed the poems to one of her teachers, the poet Muriel Rukeyser. With Rukeyser's help and encouragement, the poems became Alice Walker's first book, *Once* (1968).

Author of poems, novels, short stories, and works of nonfiction, Alice Walker is recognized today as one of America's leading writers. Her most famous work is probably *The Color Purple*, which also became a well-known film. Of general interest are a book of essays, *In Search of Our Mothers' Gardens*, and a biography of her "spirit helper," *Langston Hughes: American Poet*.

Review the Selection

UNDERSTAND THE SELECTION

Recall

1. How are the three women in the story related to each other?

2. Where does the narrator live?

3. What is Dee's "new" name?

Infer

4. Why does the narrator describe her hands as "rough, man-working hands"?

5. Why did Dee change her name?

6. Name three other details that tell you that Dee has changed.

7. What do the quilts symbolize?

Apply

8. How does the story make you feel about Dee and why?

9. Name two qualities in the mother that you admire.

10. What do you think Dee represents as compared to her sister and her mother?

Respond to Literature

The women in the story share a heritage, but they value objects from that heritage for different reasons. Why does Dee value the objects? Why do Maggie and her mother value them?

WRITE ABOUT THE SELECTION

The setting of a story can affect your reaction to it. Visualize the mother and Maggie in "Everyday Use" living in a luxurious, ten-room apartment in New York City. Think about them living in an igloo in Alaska. Would the story seem real to you in either of those settings? Write a paragraph that describes the story's setting.

Prewriting   Find the details in the story which describe the setting. Then think up five more details which can help to illustrate the setting. List all ten.

Writing   In your own words, write a one-paragraph description of the story's setting which creates a vivid picture in the reader's mind. Start outside the house; describe the yard and the appearance of the house. End with a description of the rooms in the house.

Revising   To help your readers get a complete picture of the setting, use all five senses: sight, hearing, touch, taste, and smell. Add details which will make the reader feel the setting, as well as see it.

Proofreading   Read over your paragraph to check for errors. The possessive form of a noun is shown by using an apostrophe. An apostrophe and an s form the possessive of singular nouns. For plural nouns that end in s add only an apostrophe. Make sure you have spelled possessive forms correctly.

THINK ABOUT THEME

The **theme** of a work is its main, or central, idea. If you are stating the theme of a work, the wording should point out some general truth, or idea, about life. Some people confuse the theme of a literary work with a "lesson about life." Fables, like those of Aesop, always end with a **moral**, a lesson about how to conduct one's behavior. The theme statement observes a truth but makes no rules to imply it, leaving the reader to discover it by thought.

1. What is the theme of "Everyday Use"?

2. Why did Dee rename herself?

3. Why did the mother snatch the quilts away from Dee and give them to Maggie?

4. Do you think that Walker is making a moral statement about heritage? If so, what is it?

READING FOCUS

Compare and Contrast As you read "Everyday Use," you compared and contrasted aspects of the two sisters. Write one paragraph that describes their similarities and another paragraph that describes their differences.

DEVELOP YOUR VOCABULARY

Adverbs are words that modify verbs, adjectives, and other adverbs. To *modify* means "to limit or restrict in meaning." Many adverbs end in *-ly*; these adverbs usually tell *how*. **Adjectives** are words that modify nouns or pronouns. Descriptive adjectives tell *what kind*. Some of these adjectives also end in *-ly*.

Look at this sentence from "Everyday Use": "she will stand hopelessly in corners, homely and ashamed. . . ." *Hopelessly* modifies the verb *stand* and is an adverb. *Homely* modifies the pronoun *she* and is an adjective.

Tell whether the *italicized* word is an adjective or an adverb.

1. "She held the quilts *securely* in her arms. . . ."

2. "I can kill and clean a hog as *mercilessly* as a man."

3. "I never knew how *lovely* these benches are."

4. "She stumbles along *good-naturedly* but can't see well."

Learn About

CHARACTER

In literature, a character is simply a person in a story. In fiction, characters are imaginary people who spring from the mind of the writer. In nonfiction, the writer describes a real person.

There are three basic methods of revealing character in writing. In the first, the writer provides a clear and comprehensive description of the person. In the second, the writer shows the person in action. The personality is defined by what the individual does. In the third method, the writer tells the person's thoughts, emotions, and reactions to events. The third method, of course, is impossible for the nonfiction writer unless he or she learns about the inner life of the individual from interviews or close personal relationships. Even then, the writer must use his or her imagination.

As you read this personal recollection, ask yourself:

1. How does the writer show the personality of the main character?
2. Is the main character believable?

READING FOCUS

Understand Sequence of Events Story events are usually told in chronological, or time, order. The author describes the first happening, then the second, and so on. Sometimes, signal words such as *first*, *next*, or *finally* are used to indicate time order; sometimes there are no signal words, and you rely on story context. As you read the next selection, pay attention to the sequence of events. Jot down any signal words you notice.

WRITING CONNECTION

Write a short paragraph describing someone you know. Provide a clear and complete description of the person.

from
THE
WOMAN WARRIOR

by Maxine Hong Kingston

When she was about sixty-eight years old, Brave Orchid took a day off to wait at San Francisco International Airport for the plane that was bringing her sister to the United States. She had not seen Moon Orchid for thirty years. She had begun this waiting at home, getting up a half-hour before Moon Orchid's plane took off in Hong Kong. Brave Orchid would add her will power to the forces that keep an airplane up. Her head hurt with the concentration. The plane had to be light, so no matter how tired she felt, she dared not rest her spirit on a wing but continuously and gently pushed up on the plane's belly. She had already been waiting at the airport for nine hours. She was wakeful.

Next to Brave Orchid sat Moon Orchid's only daughter, who was helping her aunt wait. Brave Orchid had made two of her own children come too because they

could drive, but they had been lured away by the magazine racks and the gift shops and coffee shops. Her American children could not sit for very long. They did not understand sitting; they had wandering feet. She hoped they would get back from the pay t.v.'s or the pay toilets or wherever they were spending their money before the plane arrived. If they did not come back soon, she would go look for them. If her son thought he could hide in the men's room, he was wrong.

"Are you all right, Aunt?" asked her niece.

"No, this chair hurts me. Help me pull some chairs together so I can put my feet up."

She unbundled a blanket and spread it out to make a bed for herself. On the floor she had two shopping bags full of canned peaches, real peaches, beans wrapped in taro leaves, cookies, Thermos bottles, enough food for everybody, though only her niece would eat with her. Her bad boy and bad girl were probably sneaking hamburgers, wasting their money. She would scold them.

Many soldiers and sailors sat about, oddly calm, like little boys in cowboy uniforms. (She thought "cowboy" was what you would call a Boy Scout.) They should have been crying hysterically on their way to Vietnam. "If I see one that looks Chinese," she thought, "I'll go over and give him some advice." She sat up suddenly; she had forgotten about her own son, who was even now in Vietnam. Carefully she split her attention, beaming half of it to the ocean, into the water to keep him afloat. He was on a ship. He was in Vietnamese waters. She was sure of it. He and the other children were lying to her. They had said he was in Japan, and then they said he was in the Philippines. But when she sent him her help, she could feel that he was on a ship in Da Nang. Also she had seen the children hide the envelopes that his letters came in.

"Do you think my son is in Vietnam?" she asked her niece, who was dutifully eating.

"No. Didn't your children say he was in the Philippines?"

"Have you ever seen any of his letters with Philippine stamps on them?"

"Oh, yes. Your children showed me one."

"I wouldn't put it past them to send the letters to some Filipino they know. He puts Manila postmarks on them to fool me."

"Yes, I can imagine them doing that. But don't worry. Your son can take care of himself. All your children can take care of themselves."

"Not him. He's not like other people. Not normal at all. He sticks erasers in his ears, and the erasers are still attached to the pencil stubs. The captain will say, 'Abandon ship,' or, 'Watch out for bombs,' and he won't hear. He doesn't listen to orders. I told him to flee to Canada, but he wouldn't go."

She closed her eyes. After a short while, plane and ship under control, she looked again at the children in uniforms. Some of the blond ones looked like baby chicks, their crew cuts like the downy yellow on baby chicks. You had to feel sorry for them even though they were Army and Navy Ghosts.

Suddenly her son and daughter came running. "Come, Mother. The plane's landed early. She's here already." They hurried, folding up their mother's encampment. She was glad her children were not useless. They must have known what this trip to San Francisco was about then. "It's a good thing I made you come early," she said.

---

taro (TAHR oh) kind of tropical plant used for food
Filipino (fil uh PEE noh) native of the Philippines
downy (DOU nee) soft; fluffy
encampment (en KAMP munt) camp and equipment

Brave Orchid pushed to the front of the crowd. She had to be in front. The passengers were separated from the people waiting for them by glass doors and walls. Immigration Ghosts were stamping papers. The travellers crowded along some conveyor belts to have their luggage searched. Brave Orchid did not see her sister anywhere. She stood watching for four hours. Her children left and came back. "Why don't you sit down?" they asked.

"The chairs are too far away," she said.

"Why don't you sit on the floor then?"

No, she would stand, as her sister was probably standing in a line she could not see from here. Her American children had no feelings and no memory.

To while away time, she and her niece talked about the Chinese passengers. These new immigrants had it easy. On Ellis Island[1] the people were thin after forty days at sea and had no fancy luggage.

"That one looks like her," Brave Orchid would say.

"No, that's not her."

Ellis Island had been made out of wood and iron. Here everything was new plastic, a ghost trick to lure immigrants into feeling safe and spilling their secrets. Then the Alien Office could send them right back. Otherwise, why did they lock her out, not letting her help her sister answer questions and spell her name? At Ellis Island when the ghost asked Brave Orchid what year her husband had cut off his pigtail, a Chinese who was crouching on the floor motioned her not to talk. "I don't know," she had said. If it weren't for that Chinese man, she might not be here today, or her husband either. She hoped some Chinese, a janitor or a clerk, would look out for Moon Orchid. Luggage conveyors fooled immigrants into thinking the Gold Mountain was going to be easy.

Brave Orchid felt her heart jump—Moon Orchid. "There she is," she shouted. But her niece saw it was not her mother at all. And it shocked her to discover the woman her aunt was pointing out. This was a young woman, younger than herself, no older than Moon Orchid the day the sisters parted. "Moon Orchid will have changed a little, of course," Brave Orchid was saying. "She will have learned to wear western clothes." The woman wore a navy blue suit with a bunch of dark cherries at the shoulder.

"No, Aunt," said the niece. "That's not my mother."

"Perhaps not. It's been so many years. Yes, it is your mother. It must be. Let her come closer, and we can tell. Do you think she's too far away for me to tell, or is it my eyes getting bad?"

"It's too many years gone by," said the niece.

---

conveyor (belt) (kun VAY ur) endless moving belt or platform
  for carrying objects short distances
[1]Ellis Island: an island in New York harbor that served for years
  as an immigration examination center.
alien (AY lee un *or* AYL yun) non-citizen; foreigner

Brave Orchid turned suddenly—another Moon Orchid, this one a neat little woman with a bun. She was laughing at something the person ahead of her in line said. Moon Orchid was just like that, laughing at nothing. "I would be able to tell the difference if one of them would only come closer," Brave Orchid said with tears, which she did not wipe. Two children met the woman with the cherries, and she shook their hands. The other woman was met by a young man. They looked at each other gladly, then walked away side by side.

Up close neither one of those women looked like Moon Orchid at all. "Don't worry, Aunt," said the niece, "I'll know her."

"I'll know her too. I knew her before you did."

The niece said nothing, although she had seen her mother only five years ago. Her aunt liked having the last word.

Finally Brave Orchid's children quit wandering and drooped on a railing. Who knew what they were thinking? At last the niece called out, "I see her! I see her! Mother! Mother!" Whenever the doors parted, she shouted, probably embarrassing the American cousins, but she didn't care. She called out, "Mama! Mama!" until the crack in the sliding doors became too small to let in her voice. "Mama!" What a strange word in an adult voice. Many people turned to see what adult was calling, "Mama!" like a child. Brave Orchid saw an old, old woman jerk her head up, her little eyes blinking confusedly, a woman whose nerves leapt toward the sound anytime she heard "Mama!" Then she relaxed to her own business again. She was a tiny, tiny lady, very thin, with little fluttering hands, and her hair was in a gray knot. She was dressed in a gray wool suit; she wore pearls around her neck and in her earlobes. Moon Orchid *would* travel with her jewels showing. Brave Orchid momentarily saw, like a larger, younger outline around this old woman, the sister she had been waiting for. The familiar dim halo faded, leaving the woman so old, so gray. So old. Brave Orchid pressed against the glass. That old lady? Yes, that old lady facing the ghost who stamped her papers without questioning her was her sister. Then, without noticing her family, Moon Orchid walked smiling over to the Suitcase Inspector Ghost, who took her boxes apart, pulling out puffs of tissue. From where she was, Brave Orchid could not see what her sister had chosen to carry across the ocean. She wished her sister would look her way. Brave Orchid thought that if *she* were entering a new country, she would be at the windows. Instead Moon Orchid hovered over the unwrapping, surprised at each reappearance as if she were opening presents after a birthday party.

"Mama!" Moon Orchid's daughter kept calling. Brave Orchid said to her children, "Why don't you call your aunt too?

---

hover (HUV ur) stay nearby; linger about

Maybe she'll hear us if all of you call out together." But her children slunk away. Maybe that shame-face they so often wore was American politeness.

"Mama!" Moon Orchid's daughter called again, and this time her mother looked right at her. She left her bundles in a heap and came running. "Hey!" the Customs Ghost yelled at her. She went back to clear up her mess, talking inaudibly to her daughter all the while. Her daughter pointed toward Brave Orchid. And at last Moon Orchid looked at her— two old women with faces like mirrors.

Their hands reached out as if to touch the other's face, then returned to their own, the fingers checking the grooves in the forehead and along the sides of the mouth. Moon Orchid, who never understood the gravity of things, started smiling and laughing, pointing at Brave Orchid. Finally Moon Orchid gathered up her stuff, strings hanging and papers loose, and met her sister at the door, where they shook hands, oblivious to blocking the way.

"You're an old woman," said Brave Orchid.

"Aiaa. *You're* an old woman."

"But you are really old. Surely, you can't say that about me. I'm not old the way you're old."

"But *you* really are old. You're one year older than I am."

"Your hair is white and your face all wrinkled."

"You're so skinny."

"You're so fat."

"Fat women are more beautiful than skinny women."

The children pulled them out of the doorway. One of Brave Orchid's children brought the car from the parking lot, and the other heaved the luggage into the trunk. They put the two old ladies and the niece in the back seat. All the way home—across the Bay Bridge, over the Diablo hills, across the San Joaquin River to the valley, the valley moon so white at dusk—all the way home, the two sisters exclaimed every time they turned to look at each other, "Aiaa! How old!"

Brave Orchid forgot that she got sick in cars, that all vehicles but palanquins made her dizzy. "You're so old," she kept saying. "How did you get so old?"

Brave Orchid had tears in her eyes. But Moon Orchid said, "You look older than I. You *are* older than I," and again she'd laugh. "You're wearing an old mask to tease me." It surprised Brave Orchid that after thirty years she could still get annoyed at her sister's silliness.

---

slunk (SLUNK) moved in a fearful or embarrassed way
inaudibly (in AW duh blee) not being heard
gravity (GRAV ih tee) dignity; seriousness
oblivious (uh BLIV ee us) unaware; unmindful
palanquin (pal un KEEN) carriage on poles that is carried on people's shoulders

Review the Selection

UNDERSTAND THE SELECTION

Recall

1. How old is Brave Orchid?

2. When had she last seen her sister?

3. How many children does Moon Orchid have?

Infer

4. Why is Brave Orchid worried about her son?

5. Why does Brave Orchid bring food to the airport?

6. Who are the people Brave Orchid calls "ghosts"?

7. Explain how Brave Orchid feels when she first sees her sister.

Apply

8. Suppose you are meeting a family member you haven't seen for many years. What emotions might you feel?

9. Do you think the sisters are very similar or very different? Why do you think so?

10. How would you characterize Brave Orchid?

Respond to Literature

Does Brave Orchid feel more Chinese than American? What examples of her Chinese identity are found in the story?

WRITE ABOUT THE SELECTION

Characters in nonfiction are real people, but unless they are well known, the writer cannot assume that the reader knows them. The writer must supply details about the characters.

Suppose you are a newspaper reporter, and you have been assigned to interview the two sisters who have been reunited after thirty years. Write an interview with Brave Orchid and Moon Orchid.

Prewriting Write down two lists of five questions each. The first is a list of questions to ask Brave Orchid. The second is a list of questions to ask Moon Orchid.

Writing Write the interview using a question-and-answer format. Based on your list, write out the questions, addressing them to one or the other of the sisters. Then write the replies as you think the characters would answer.

Revising With a few adverbs, you can make this interview even more interesting. Insert adverbs to show the sisters' reactions to your questions. For example, does Brave Orchid reply calmly, seriously, excitedly, or angrily?

Proofreading Read over your interview to check for errors. Quotation marks are used to set off conversation. They are placed after the punctuation of a direct quotation, whether the punctuation is a comma, a question mark or an exclamation point. Be sure all of your quotation marks are in the right place.

THINK ABOUT CHARACTER

In fiction, the characters are imaginary, created in the writer's mind. In nonfiction the people described are real. Both fiction and nonfiction writers strive to present fully rounded depictions of personalities. They may include extensive physical description, a many-sided view of personality traits, and the individual's actions, opinions, beliefs, ideas, and thoughts.

1. Who is the most memorable character in the selection? Explain why.

2. What clues are you given about the character of Moon Orchid?

3. Are Brave Orchid's children well-rounded characters? Explain.

4. What does Brave Orchid's decision to arrive early at the airport tell you about her?

5. What does the emotion expressed in the final sentence tell you about Brave Orchid?

READING FOCUS
Understand Sequence of Events List the signal words and phrases that helped you understand the sequence of events. Use some of these words in a brief summary of the story's events.

DEVELOP YOUR VOCABULARY

Base words are English words that have no letters or syllables added to them. Prefixes are word parts that can be added to base words to change their meaning. For example, *un-* is a commonly used prefix. Add it to *smiling* or *wrap*, and you have formed *unsmiling* and *unwrap*, both of which mean the opposite of the original word. Here are some common prefixes and their meanings:

mis-: wrong, badly, incorrectly
un-: not, the opposite of
re-: back or again

Write the following words from the selection. Then add one or more prefixes from the list and tell the meaning of each new word.

1. spell
2. new
3. sure
4. faded
5. wrinkled
6. take
7. turned
8. known
9. easy
10. discover
11. understood
12. safe

Learn About

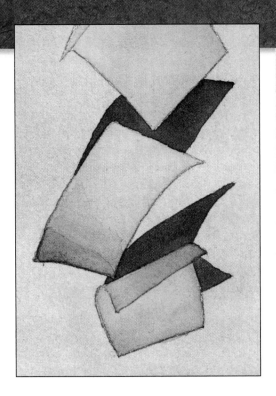

READING FOCUS

Compare and Contrast When you compare, you see how things are alike; when you contrast, you look at their differences. The two poems on the next page are by the same author, William Carlos Williams. After you have read both poems several times, look for ways in which the poems are alike and ways in which they are different. Think about their form, the main idea of each, the use of figurative language, and their tone.

OPEN FORM

Form is the structure of a poem. One frequently used form is open form. **Open form** means that the poem is written in one long, continuous structure with no stanzas.

Open form is often called **free verse** because it does not have meter, rhyme, or stanzas. It does, however, have some pattern of organization. Open form, or free verse, uses the length of the line and the way words and phrases are grouped to tie ideas together and emphasize them. The white spaces that are left between lines and words also add emphasis. Sometimes the white spaces are placed between lines at regular intervals, such as every four lines. These white spaces may make the poem look as if it has stanzas.

Open form makes it possible for a poet to express thoughts in new ways.

As you read "This Is Just to Say" and "The Term," ask yourself:

1. What is the form of "This Is Just to Say"?
2. What is the form of "The Term"?

WRITING CONNECTION

Open form allows a poet freedom. Use open form to write a four-line poem about something familiar, such as an apple.

This Is Just to Say

by William Carlos Williams

I have eaten
the plums
that were in
the icebox

5   and which
you were probably
saving
for breakfast

Forgive me
10   they were delicious
so sweet
and so cold

The Term

by William Carlos Williams

A rumpled sheet
of brown paper
about the length

and apparent bulk
5   of a man was
rolling with the

wind slowly over
and over in
the street as

10   a car drove down
upon it and
crushed it to

the ground. Unlike
a man it rose
15   again rolling

with the wind over
and over to be as
it was before.

---

rumpled (RUM puld) wrinkled

Review the Selection

UNDERSTAND THE SELECTION

Recall

1. In "This Is Just to Say," what did the speaker eat?

2. In "The Term," how big was the brown paper?

3. What happened to the paper when the car drove over it?

Infer

4. Why did the speaker eat the plums?

5. Why did the poet write the poem?

6. What are two ways that the paper is like a man?

7. How is the paper unlike a man?

Apply

8. Why do you think the poet chose plums rather than apples, bananas, or oranges?

9. Why do you think the poet compared the paper to a man?

10. What would you compare a piece of paper to? A man to?

Respond to Literature

Why do people, like the speaker in "This Is Just to Say," take things they should not take? How would you explain taking something that you should not have?

WRITE ABOUT THE SELECTION

Imagine that you have just received the poem "This is Just to Say." It is your plums that the poet has just eaten. How do you feel about the poet eating your fruit? Has the poem made you forgive the poet for eating them? Write a response to the poet, telling him how you feel. Your response should be in the form of a poem that is at least four lines in length.

Prewriting Write notes about what you will say to the poet. include details about what you had planned to use the plums for, how you felt when you found the plums missing, and what effect his poem had on you. Decide if the mood of your poem will be serious or amusing.

Writing Use your notes to write your poem, telling the poet how you felt about his taking your plums. Make sure your poem clearly indicates whether you forgive the poet or are unhappy with his actions. Choose words that will create the exact mood you want to convey.

Revising When you revise, add any details that will intensify the mood of your poem. Eliminate any boring phrases. Substitute interesting words for ordinary ones.

Proofreading Reread your poem to check for errors. You may not want to use any punctuation. However, be sure that you have capitalized the first word in each line.

THINK ABOUT POETIC FORM

Form refers to the shape, or pattern, of a poem. **Open form**, or free verse, does not have meter, rhyme, or stanzas. Using open form allows a poet greater freedom in presenting his or her ideas and emotions.

1. "This Is Just to Say" is written in open form. In what ways can this poem be called free verse?

2. Why are there spaces between every four lines?

3. What does the speaker tell about in the first four lines? In the next four? In the last four?

4. What is the form in "The Term"?

5. How many sentences are there in the poem?

6. Why are there open spaces every three lines?

READING FOCUS

Compare and Contrast As you read "This Is Just to Say" and "The Term," you compared and contrasted the poems. What is one way in which the poems are similar? What is one way in which they are different? Consider the form, the main idea, the use of figurative language, and the tone of each poem.

DEVELOP YOUR VOCABULARY

An **antonym** is a word that has the opposite or nearly the opposite meaning of another word. For example, *out* is an antonym for *in* because it has the opposite meaning.

1. Write antonyms for the following words.
a. sweet	e. slowly
b. cold	f. over
c. rumpled	g. down
d. man	h. to

2. Reread the two poems to find antonyms for the following words.
a. like	e. tasteless
b. blame	f. wasting
c. fell	g. unseen
d. after	h. without

3. Write an original sentence for each of the words that are antonyms for the words in question 2.

WRITING APPLICATIONS

Write About the Literary Period

"American" is often used as an umbrella term that applies to every citizen in this country. Yet many different kinds of people live under that umbrella. They represent different ethnic groups, different cultures, different heritages. The selections in this unit include works by American writers of various backgrounds.

Identify three distinct cultures described in the selections in this unit. What values are important to the characters within those selections?

Prewriting Make a chart with three headings across the top. Each heading should list the name of one selection you have chosen. Under each heading, list key words or phrases that identify the values you have discovered.

Writing Write a paragraph comparing and contrasting the differences and similarities in values found in the stories you have chosen.

Revising Illustrate your points by quoting from the selections. Choose sentences or descriptions that support your opinions.

Proofreading Capitalize all important words in the title of a book, poem, or short story. Underline the title of a book in your writing or italicize it if using a computer. Put quotation marks around the title of a poem or short story. Check your work to see if you have punctuated the titles correctly.

Write About Genre

In reading about autobiography, you have learned that it is a unique form of nonfiction. You have read about four important elements of autobiography—point of view, purpose, introspection and narrative.

Think of a memorable event in your life. How did it affect you? What did you learn from it? When and where did it happen? Write about this event as if it were a chapter in your autobiography.

Prewriting Make a chronological list—from beginning to end—of what happened during this event in your life. Make another list of words you would use to describe yourself. Make a third list of key words that describe how you felt and what you thought about the event.

Writing Based on your chronological list, write a narrative of the event. Use your other two lists to tell more about yourself and describe your thoughts and reactions during the event.

Revising Add vivid adjectives and adverbs to emphasize your reactions and to make your feelings clear.

Proofreading Make sure the verbs in your sentences agree with their subjects. Singular subjects take singular verbs; plural subjects take plural verbs. Check the verb in each sentence to make sure each verb agrees with the subject and not another word in the sentence.

BUILD LANGUAGE SKILLS

Vocabulary

Writers in this unit have represented various ethnic cultures. These same cultures —and many others—have contributed words to the English language.

English owes part of its richness to the thousands of words it has borrowed from other languages. The greatest number of borrowings are from Latin and French, but the German, Dutch, Scandinavian, and Greek languages are the sources of many others. The Near East, the Far East, Africa, Australia, Oceania, and our Native Americans have all contributed words to English. A common reason for borrowing is the use of a native name for an unfamiliar thing.

Look up each of the following words in a dictionary and write down the language or place from which the word originally came.

1. okra
2. shampoo
3. hurricane
4. coach
5. cockroach
6. chocolate
7. algebra
8. chipmunk
9. tea
10. boomerang
11. broccoli
12. geyser
13. bog
14. ceramic
15. morgue
16. kimono
17. yogurt
18. ukulele
19. amok
20. yacht
21. jaguar
22. pajamas
23. kindergarten
24. bayou
25. walrus
26. llama

Grammar, Usage, and Mechanics

The colon (:) is used before an extended quotation, explanation, or example.

Example: "Maggie will be nervous until after her sister goes: she will stand hopelessly in corners, homely and ashamed of the burn scars down her arms and legs, eying her sister with a mixture of envy and awe."

One use of the semicolon (;) is to separate related clauses of a sentence.

Example: "They did not understand sitting; they had wandering feet."

Read these sentences, which are taken from selections in this unit. Add a colon or semicolon in the blank space.

1. I was proud _____ I felt like a grownup.

2. "Then stay in the streets _____ don't come back here!"

3. I am the way my daughter would want me to be _____ a hundred pounds lighter, my skin like an uncooked barley pancake.

4. His words stopped _____ somehow, he couldn't get the right ones to come out.

5. Always too busy _____ feeding the cattle, fixing the fences, putting up salt lick shelters, throwing down hay.

SPEAKING AND LISTENING

Reader's debate is a chance for everyone in class to act as a critic and to discuss the pros and cons of a selection. There are several ways to organize a debate. One way is to have half the class defend and the other half criticize a selection. Another way is to select a panel to debate while other class members listen. A third way is to divide the class into groups and have group debates. Whichever method you choose, you will find that talking about literature, having the chance to listen to other opinions, and hearing different points of view will give you a better understanding of the selection.

Before you take part in a reader's debate, read the suggestions. They will give you ideas on how to prepare and conduct a reader's debate.

1. As a class, decide how you will organize your debate. Use one of the methods suggested, or come up with another that suits you.

2. Discuss the length of time for the debate. Both sides—the defending and the criticizing—should have equal time for their arguments. Decide if one side will present its entire argument first or if the discussion will go back and forth between sides.

3. Examine the selection you have chosen. Discuss the focus of the debate. There are endless possibilities here. You can concentrate on the plot of the story, the characters, the ending, the author's style, the use of literary devices, illustrations, or the title itself. Brainstorm for a minute or two and you'll come up with numerous options.

4. Give each side time to contemplate their argument. Whether you are defending or criticizing the selection, have definite arguments to make. Be sure to substantiate your views. Using facts, as well as opinions, is advisable.

5. Be courteous during the debate. Your purpose is to listen and learn from others' opinions. Comments should be made concerning the selection, not pointed toward other debators.

To begin your reader's debate choose a selection from this unit. It can be anything you have read, fiction or nonfiction. After you have made your choice, reread the steps above and begin to organize so that you can enjoy the successful experience of a reader's debate.

CRITICAL THINKING

Compare and Contrast To **compare** means "to show likenesses." To **contrast** means "to show differences." You will use these processes every time you make a choice. Suppose, for example, that you want to decide between two pairs of jeans. You would compare or contrast their style, price, workmanship, and so on. Noting the similarities and differences would give you a basis for deciding.

You can also compare and contrast people, actions, theories, and issues. The purpose is to find which is better, more useful, or more interesting.

Literature often invites readers to make comparisons or contrasts between types of selections or literary elements. Choose two stories, poems, autobiographical excerpts, or characters to compare and contrast. Then answer the following questions.

1. What common ground do the two items share? Are the items to be compared enough alike to make a comparison possible? Are they different enough to make a contrast useful?

2. Why is making a comparison or contrast helpful? What elements or aspects of the two items will it be useful to compare or contrast?

EFFECTIVE STUDYING

Outlining To study well or to write a paper well, you will need to organize your notes or ideas. One way to get your thoughts in order is to put them in an outline.

An **outline** is a summary of a topic; it lists the most important points and subpoints in the order in which you will present them in a paper or will want to recall them for study. The numbering and form of an outline follows fixed rules.

1. Write an outline this way:

   Title
   I. Main point
      A. Subpoint
      B. Subpoint
         1. Detail
         2. Detail
            a. Subdetail
            b. Subdetail
   II. Main point

2. Follow these rules:
   • If you subdivide a Main point, have at least two subpoints beneath it. You cannot subdivide any topic into fewer than two points.
   • Outlines may be written in sentences or in phrases. Do not mix types.

Test Preparation
When taking an essay test, you might first want to organize your thoughts by creating an outline. Although this takes some time, it will help you write a clearer essay more quickly.

GLOSSARY

PRONUNCIATION KEY

Accent is the force or stress given to some words or syllables in speech. In this book, accent is indicated by the use of uppercase letters. One syllable words are always shown as accented. Thus, the pronunciation of *hand* is (HAND). In words of more than one syllable, the accented syllable is printed in uppercase letters. The other syllable or syllables are printed in lowercase letters. Thus, the pronunciation of *handbag* is (HAND bag).

Letter(s) in text words	Letter(s) used in respelling	Sample words	Phonetic respelling	Letter(s) in text words	Letter(s) used in respelling	Sample words	Phonetic respelling
a	a	bandit	(BAN dit)	i	uh	possible	(POS uh bul)
a	ay	makeup	(MAYK up)	o	o	bottle	(BOT ul)
a	air	daring	(DAIR ing)	o	u	gallon	(GAL un)
a	ah	dart	(DAHRT)	o	oh	open	(OH pun)
a	uh	about	(uh BOUT)	o	aw	horn	(HAWRN)
a	aw	ball	(BAWL)	oo	oo	move	(MOOV)
e	e	denim	(DEN im)	oo	uu	football	(FUUT bawl)
e	eh	ingest	(in JEHST)	oo	oo	pool	(POOL)
e	ih	delight	(dih LYT)	oi	oi	point	(POINT)
e	u	darken	(DAHR kun)	ou	ou	output	(OUT put)
e	ee	he	(HEE)	u	u	upshot	(UP shot)
i	i	mitten	(MIT un)	u	uh	support	(suh PAWRT)
i	ih	gravity	(GRAV ih tee)	u	oo	ruler	(ROO lur)
i	y	idle	(YD ul)	y	i	rhythm	(RITH um)
i	eye	idea	(eye DEE uh)	y	ee	lazy	(LAY zee)
i	ee	medium	(MEE dee um)	y	y	thyme	(TYM)

A

abbot (AB but) a man who is head of a monastery *p. 49*

absently (AB sunt lee) with attention elsewhere *p. 400*

absurdity (ab SUR duh tee) something absurd or ridiculous *p. 291*

abyss (uh BIS) a thing too big for measurement *p. 144*

accountable (uh KOUNT uh bul) responsible for *p. 37*

accusations (AK yoo ZAY shunz) charges of wrongdoing *p. 468*

acute (uh KYOOT) sharp, sensitive *p. 123*

adjacent (uh JAY sunt) near or next to *p. 425*

admirably (AD mur uh blee) excellently *p. 331*

adversary (AD vur ser ee) opponent; enemy *p. 14*

agile (AJ ul) nimble; well-coordinated *p. 256*

ague (AY gyoo) violent fever *p. 28*

akin (uh KIN) related *p. 169*

alcove (AL kohv) opening off a room *p. 513*

alien (AY lee un or AYL yun) non-citizen; foreigner *p. 524*

ancestral (an SES trul) coming from an ancestor *p. 498*

anesthetic (an is THET ik) substance that lessens pain *p. 311*

annually (AN you ul ee) occurring each year *p. 176*

annuity (un NOO uh tee) regular payment *p. 102*

anonymous (uh NON uh mus) written by a person whose name is withheld *p. 35*

antisymphonic (an tih sim FON ik) against music *p. 401*

anxiety (ang ZY uh tee) worry *p. 126*

apathetically (ap uh THET ik lee) with little or no feeling *p. 309*

aphorism (AF uh riz um) a short, pointed sentence expressing a truth or precept *p. 42*

appeasingly (uh PEEZ ing lee) in a manner to please or obey *p. 311*

apprehension (ap rih HEN shun) worry; fear of a coming event; dread *pp. 132, 301, 478*

apprentice (uh PREN tis) a person under legal agreement to work for a specified time under a master craftsperson in return for instruction and, formerly, support *p. 36*

ardent (AHR dunt) very eager; passionate *p. 260*

arpeggios (ahr PEHJ ee ohz) notes in a chord played in quick succession *p. 465*

array (uh RAY) an orderly arrangement of troops *p. 14*

arrayed (uh RAYD) dressed *p. 331*

assuaged (uh SWAYJD) calmed *p. 37*

assumption (uh SUMP shun) idea accepted as true without proof *p. 423*

asterisk (AS tuh risk) star-shaped sign or symbol *p. 388*

audacity (aw DAS uh tee) boldness; daring *p. 127*

aureole (AWR ee ohl) a halo *p. 275*

awe (AW) wonderment; admiration *p. 507*

B

barter (BAHRT ur) trade; exchanging one thing for another *p. 323*

becalmed (bih KAHLMD) to make motionless from lack of wind *p. 33*

belfry (BEL free) bell tower *p. 165*

bellows (BEHL ohz) roars; loud noises *p. 462*

benediction (ben uh DIK shun) blessing *p. 170*

besieging (bih SEEJ ing) hemming in with armed forces; closing in; overwhelming *p. 285*

billet (BIL it) a brief letter *p. 29*

birthright (BURTH ryt) the rights that a person has because he/she was born in a certain family, nation, etc. *p. 75*

blackballed (BLAK bawld) to exclude from social life, work, etc. *p. 37*

bleating (BLEET ing) cry of sheep *p. 167*

blithe (BLYTH) happy; cheerful *p. 247*

boarded (BAWRD id) had rooms and meals provided regularly for pay *p. 33*

bobolink (BOB uh lingk) kind of song bird *p. 203*

bog (BOG) swamp; wet ground *p. 199*

Bornou land (BAWR noo) reference to homeland in Africa *p. 233*

bough (BOU) a large branch of a tree *p. 326*

brackish (BRAK ish) salty and marshy *p. 430*

brambles (BRAM bulz) prickly shrubs *p. 325*

brethren (BRETH run) brothers; fellow members of a group *p. 15*

bulk (BULK) object; shape *p. 166*

bulldozing (BUL dohz ing) bullying; threatening *p. 255*

burden (BURD uhn) heavy load *p. 469*

C

cambric (KAM brik) very fine, thin linen or cotton *p. 271*

capricious (kuh PRISH us) without apparent reason *p. 430*

carcass (KAHR kus) dead body, usually of an animal *p. 290*

Carrara (kuh RAHR uh) fine, white marble *p. 210*

cascade (kas KAYD) waterfall *p. 256*

cascaded (kas KAY dihd) flowed down like a small waterfall *p. 463*

censure (SEN shur) blame *p. 75*

chafed (CHAYFT) to have been worn away; eroded *p. 143*

chanticleer (CHAN tih klir) a rooster *pp. 177, 210*

characteristic (kar ak tuh RIS tik) special quality *p. 498*

chassis (CHAS ee) a car's frame *p. 478*

chastise (chas TYZ) punish *p. 134*

chastity (CHAS tuh tee) decency; modesty *p. 42*

chattel (CHAT ul) a moveable article of personal property; owned property *p. 71*

checkerberry (CHEK ur ber ee) kind of small red berry (wintergreen) *p. 516*

chided (CHYD id) scolded *p. 33*

chitlins (CHIT linz) hog intestines used as food *p. 513*

chorister (KAWR ih stur) singer in a choir *p. 203*

clabber (KLAB ur) sour, thick milk *p. 513*

clamor (KLAM ur) noise; excitement *p. 485*

cogwheel (KAHG hweel) a wheel with a rim notched into teeth, which mesh with those of another wheel to transmit or receive motion *p. 54*

coherently (koh HIR unt lee) clearly speaking *p. 134*

collards (KOL urdz) kind of green vegetable *p. 513*

commence (kuh MENS) begin *p. 346*

commodious (kuh MOH dee us) spacious; roomy *p. 268*

common (KOM un) piece of public land *p. 180*

commotion (kuh MOH shun) noisy confusion *p. 386*

compromised (KOM pruh myzd) to give up one's ideals for short-term convenient reasons *p. 74*

conceived (kun SEEVD) thought of; imagined *p. 123*

conflagration (kon fluh GRAY shun) huge fire *p. 307*

conformity (kun FAWR muh tee) behavior that is in agreement with current rules *p. 180*

confronted (kun FRUNT id) set face to face *p. 507*

congested (kun JEST id) clogged, overcrowded *p. 427*

conjecture (kun JEK chur) an opinion formed without facts but based on pertinent knowledge or experience; guess *p. 412*

consecrated (KON sih krayt id) dedicated *p. 424*

consolidation (kun sol uh DAY shun) strengthening *p. 22*

contracting (kun TRAKT ing) growing smaller *p. 255*

conveyor belt (kun VAY ur BEHLT) endless moving belt or platform for carrying objects short distances *p. 524*

convoluted (KON vuh loot id) twisting; indirect *p. 478*

cordon (KAWR dun) a line or circle of police stationed around an area to guard it *p. 418*

cot (KOT) cottage or small house *p. 27*

counsel (KOUN sul) advice *p. 20*

covet (KUV it) desire what belongs to another *p. 117*

covey (KUV ee) flock of birds *p. 344*

cowering (KOU ur ing) crouching in fear *p. 511*

cowlish (KOUL ish) hood shaped *p. 428*

cravat (kruh VAT) a necktie; scarf *p. 277*

crest (KREST) the top of anything; summit; ridge *p. 325*

crusty (KRUS tee) curt; rude *p. 176*

cultivated (KUL tuh vayt id) prepared and cared for the land on which plants grow *p. 175*

cumulus (KYOO myuh lus) a type of rounded, fluffy cloud *p. 457*

cunningly (KUN ing lee) slyly *p. 123*

curbstone (KURB stohn) stone or concrete edging of a sidewalk *p. 74*

D

dapper (DAP ur) neat, trim *p. 291*

dasher (DASH ur) plunger with paddles for stirring *p. 513*

dead reckoning (DED REK un ing) navigating without the assistance of stars *p. 179*

deferred (dih FURD) put off *p. 366*

defunct (dih FUNGKT) dead person *p. 294*

delusive (dih LOO siv) misleading; unreal *p. 14*

demeaning (dih MEEN ing) lowering in status or character; degrading *p. 36*

density (DEN suh tee) thickness *p. 426*

departed (dih PAHRT id) dead *p. 190*

deploying (dih PLOI ing) spreading out *p. 422*

descendant (dih SEN dunt) a person who is the offspring of a certain ancestor, family, group, etc. *p. 49*

deserts (dih ZURTS) reward or punishment; what is deserved *p. 101*

diadem (DY uh dem) crown (more like halo here) *p. 202*

diligent (DIL uh junt) hardworking; done with careful, steady effort *p. 43*

discreet (dih SKREET) wisely careful *p. 259*

discrepancy (dih SKREP un see) difference; variation *p. 293*

dispirited (dih SPIR it id) discouraged; low in spirits *p. 488*

disproved (dis PROOVD) shown to be incorrect or false *p. 469*

dissever (dih SEV ur) separate *p. 118*

diverge (dih VURJ) spread apart *p. 378*

divert (dih VURT) turn aside *p. 290*

doctrine (DOK trin) belief, theory *p. 513*

doggedly (DAWG id lee) persistently; stubbornly *p. 268*

dollops (DOL ups) mounds *p. 457*

Dourra (DUUR uh) (usually spelled durra) a kind of grain grown in Northern Africa *p. 233*

downcast (DOUN kast) sad *p. 75*

downy (DOU nee) soft; fluffy *p. 522*

draw (DRAW) to take air into the lungs; inhale *p. 150*

dreary (DRIR ee) dull; tiresome *p. 199*

drenched (DRENCHT) soaked; wet all over *p. 326*

E

ebb (EB) flow back or away *p. 306*

ecstasy (EK stuh see) a feeling of overpowering joy; great delight *p. 323*

edifice (ED uh fis) a large structure *p. 276*

egging (EG ing) urging *p. 490*

eject (ih JEKT) force out *p. 189*

elevation (el uh VAY shun) a high place *p. 477*

emaciated (ih MAY see ayt id) abnormally lean *p. 137*

emerge (ih MURJ) come out into view *p. 403*

emphatic (em FAT ik) very striking; definite *p. 357*

encampment (en KAMP munt) camp and equipment *p. 522*

encroach (en KROHCH) to intrude upon the rights of others *p. 22*

enlightened (en LYT und) to have given the lights of knowledge to *p. 73*

enthusiastically (en thoo zee AS tik lee) eagerly *p. 479*

enveloped (en VEL upd) wrapped up *p. 126*

ermine (UR min) a weasel whose fur turns to white in the winter *p. 210*

ethereal (ih THIR ee ul) of the upper regions of space *p. 409*

excerpt (ehk SURPT) a passage taken from a book; quotation *p. 33*

excessive (ik SES iv) going beyond what's right or usual *p. 477*

excruciating (ik SKROO shee ayt ing) very painful *p. 308*

extenuate (ik STEN yoo ayt) to lessen the seriousness of *p. 15*

extremities (ik STREM ih teez) hands and feet; parts farthest away *p. 306*

extricate (EK strih kayt) to set free; release; disentangle *p. 27*

exulting (ig ZULT ing) rejoicing; showing joy *p. 248*

eyewitness (EYE wit nis) person who actually saw something happen *p. 421*

F

fade in (FAYD IN) in radio, to become more distinct *p. 83*

fade out (FAYD OUT) in radio, to become less distinct *p. 84*

fallow (FAL oh) land that is plowed, but not seeded *p. 175*

fastidiously (fa STID ee us lee) very sensitive; dainty *p. 389*

favored (FAY vurd) featured *p. 331*

feat (FEET) accomplishment *p. 480*

feeble-minded (FEE buhl MIN dihd) an out-of-date expression for a person with a weak or slow mind *p. 385*

fetch (FECH) get and bring back *p. 377*

fiasco (fee AS koh) a humiliating failure *p. 468*

fieldpieces (FEELD pees iz) mobile artillery *p. 422*

Filipino (fil uh PEE noh) native of the Philippines *p. 522*

fine (FYN) summary; conclusion *p. 331*

firing (FYR ing) to light a fire in a boiler *p. 358*

flat (FLAT) an apartment with rooms on one floor *pp. 357, 488*

fleet (FLEET) very fast *p. 166*

flotilla (floh TIL uh) a fleet of boats or small ships *p. 57*

fluently (FLOO unt lee) easily (of talking) *p. 127*

flush (FLUSH) drive birds or animals from hiding place *p. 344*

Formica (for MY kuh) trade name for a heat-resistant plastic *p. 461*

fowler (FOUL ur) hunter of wildfowl *p. 143*

frenzy (FREN zee) madness; rage *p. 490*

friction (FRIK shun) resistance *p. 417*

frugality (froo GAL uh tee) careful economy; thrift *p. 42*

furtive (FUR tiv) sly; shifty; sneaky, secretive *pp. 429, 510*

futility (fyoo TIL uh tee) lack of success; uselessness *p. 439*

G

gait (GAYT) manner of walking or running *p. 303*

gauntly (GAWNT lee) in the manner of a thin bony person *p. 485*

Ghiblee (GIB lee) night wind that makes an eerie sound *p. 233*

girth (GURTH) strap that holds saddle on horse *p. 166*

gloaming (GLOHM ing) twilight *p. 210*

globular (GLOB yuh lur) rounded *p. 435*

grave (GRAYV) of a threatening nature; indicating great danger; serious *pp. 13, 132*

grave (GRAYV) burial plot *p. 138*

gravity (GRAV ih tee) dignity; seriousness *p. 526*

grenadier (gren uh DIR) foot soldier *p. 166*

grim (GRIM) very serious *p. 485*

guttural (GUT ur ul) harsh or growling sound *p. 385*

H

habitable (HAB it uh bul) fit to be lived in *p. 29*

hairline (HAIR lyn) very fine line *p. 299*

halloos (huh LOOZ) shouts; yells; calls *p. 275*

hashed (HASHT) jumbled; all mixed up *p. 257*

hasty pudding (HAY stee PUUD ing) cornmeal mush *p. 33*

hatter (HAT ur) hat maker *p. 247*

hearse (HURS) carriage for taking the dead to the grave *p. 294*

heartfelt (HAHRT felt) sincere; meaningful *p. 170*

heather (HETH ur) low evergreen plant that often grows on moors *p. 201*

heritage (HER ih tij) something handed down from one's ancestors, such as a characteristic, culture, or tradition *p. 49*

hideous (HID ee us) very ugly or frightening *p. 125*

highborn (HY bawrn) of noble birth *p. 117*

hillock (HIL uk) a small hill; mound *p. 269*

hover (HUV ur) stay nearby; linger about *p. 525*

Hula Hoops (HOO lah HOOPS) plastic hoops twirled around the body by rotating the hips *p. 466*

hulk (HULK) old ship *p. 165*

humiliating (hyoo MIL ee ayt ing) lowering of pride or dignity *p. 71*

humility (hyoo MIL uh tee) humbleness; the absence of pride *p. 42*

hypnotic (hip NOT ik) causing sleep *p. 478*

hypocritical (hip uh KRIT ih kul) false; not sincere *p. 127*

I

illimitable (ih LIM ih tuh bul) endless *p. 143*

illiterate (ih LIT ur it) unable to read *p. 498*

illuminate (ih LOO muh nayt) make clear *p. 259*

image (IM ij) mental picture *p. 486*

immortality (im awr TAL ih tee) unending life *p. 300*

impassioned (im PASH und) determined; filled with passionate feeling *p. 319*

imperative (im PER uh tiv) really necessary; essential *p. 305*

imperially (im PIR ee ul ee) supremely *p. 331*

imperturbably (im pur TUR buh blee) in a manner that cannot be excited; impassively *p. 282*

impetuous (im PECH oo us) eager; violent *p. 166*

impudent (IM pyoo dunt) rude; insulting *p. 105*

inanimate (in AN uh mit) not animated; dull; spiritless; without life *pp. 270, 435*

inaudibly (in AWD uh blee) not being heard *p. 526*

incidental (in suh DENT ul) casual; secondary *p. 75*

inclination (in kluh NAY shun) a particular disposition or bent of mind; tendency; a liking or preference *pp. 20, 34, 72, 480*

incoherently (in koh HIR unt lee) not logically; disjointedly *p. 277*

incompatible (in kum PAT uh bul) not in agreement *p. 73*

incongruity (in kon GROO ih tee) something not fitting or in harmony *p. 291*

indifference (in DIF ur uns) lack of interest *p. 189*

indifferent (in DIF ur unt) not caring *p. 290*

inevitable (in EV ih tuh bul) certain to happen *p. 15*

infest (in FEST) trouble; disturb *p. 170*

infinitesimal (in fin ih TES uh mul) too small to be measured *p. 268*

influenza (in floo EN zuh) disease usually called "flu" *p. 343*

ingenious (in JEEN yus) clever, resourceful *p. 477*

ingenuity (in juh NOO uh tee) cleverness; originality *p. 133*

innovators (IN uh vayt urz) makers of changes; introducers of new methods *p. 282*

instigate (IN stuh gayt) bring about; stir up *p. 255*

intensity (in TEN suh tee) strength; force *p. 412*

interlude (IN tur lood) musical performance between the acts of a play *p. 420*

interspersed (in tur SPURST) scattered among other things *p. 27*

intimacy (IN tuh muh see) very close friendship, even love *p. 305*

intolerable (in TOL ur uh bul) unbearable *p. 74*

intricacies (IN trih kuh seez) complexities; complications *p. 282*

J

jardiniere (jahr duh NIR) a decorative flower pot or stand *p. 357*

journeyman (JUR nee mun) a worker who had satisfied his apprenticeship and thus qualified himself to work at his trade *p. 43*

K

keel (KEEL) a piece of wood that runs along the center line from the front of the boat to the back; "backbone" of a ship *pp. 228, 248*

kilter (KIL tur) good condition; proper order *p. 79*

kin (KIN) relatives *p. 137*

kindling (KIND ling) small pieces of dry firewood *p. 388*

kith (KITH) archaic meaning for friends *p. 137*

L

laboriously (luh BAWR ee us lee) with much labor and care *p. 259*

lamming (LAM ing) striking *p. 490*

lash (LASH) whip *p. 79*

lax (LAKS) not strict or exact; careless; loose *p. 43*

lay (LAY) short song or story poem *p. 170*

leaden (LED un) dull, dark gray *p. 211*

levee (LEV ee) a morning reception held by a person of high rank *p. 29*

libel (LY bul) any written statement, not made in the public interest, tending to expose a person to public ridicule *p. 37*

lichen (LY kun) a mosslike plant which grows on rocks and trees *p. 478*

light-hearted (LYT hahrt id) free from care *p. 74*

luringly (LUUR ing lee) to tempt or attract *p. 390*

M

Magi (MAY jy) the three wise men who, according to the biblical story, made the journey to Bethlehem to present gifts to the Christ child *p. 255*

make-shift (MAYK shift) substitute; temporary *p. 439*

malice (MAL is) desire to see others harmed *p. 227*

manifold (MAN uh fohld) in many ways *p. 5*

man-of-war (man uv WAWR) warship *p. 165*

mantle (MAN tul) something that covers *p. 307*

marge (MAHRJ) edge or border *p. 143*

martial law (MAHR shul LAW) temporary rule by the military authorities *p. 420*

mason (MAY sun) stone worker *p. 247*

maxim (MAK sim) a statement of general truth *p. 277*

meditate (MED uh tayt) think deeply; ponder *p. 300*

meditatively (MED uh tayt iv lee) thinking quietly *p. 389*

mesmerizing (MEHZ muh ry zing) hypnotizing; casting a spell *p. 463*

metaphor (MET uh fur) figure of speech that makes a comparison *p. 257*

meteorite (MEET ee uh ryt) part of a heavenly body that passes through the atmosphere and falls to the earth's surface as a piece of matter *p. 412*

methodically (muh THOD ik lee) orderly; systematically *p. 307*

militia (muh LISH uh) an army of citizens rather than professional soldiers, called out in time of emergency *p. 420*

mockery (MOK uh ree) person or thing made fun of *p. 127*

moderate (MOD ur it) within reasonable limits; not excessive *p. 477*

moderation (mod uh RAY shun) avoidance of excess *p. 33*

molest (muh LEST) bother, annoy *pp. 108, 488*

monotony (muh NOT un ee) tiresome sameness *p. 477*

montage (mon TAHZH) picture made up of a number of separate pictures *p. 366*

moor (MUUR) open wasteland *p. 201*

Moor (MUUR) referring to the African slave traders *p. 233*

moorings (MUUR ingz) ropes to fasten a ship *p. 165*

moral philosophy (MAWR ul fuh LOS uh fee) ethics; standards of conduct and moral judgment *p. 73*

mortal (MAWR tul) fatal; causing death; subject to death *pp. 124, 409*

muster (MUS tur) roll call *p. 166*

mutely (MYOOT lee) silently *p. 388*

muzzle (MUZ ul) mouth and nose of an animal *p. 301*

mystical (MIS tih kul) mysterious; having a hidden meaning *p. 250*

N

navigating (NAV uh gayt ing) steering *p. 479*

night-tide (NYT tyd) nighttime *p. 118*

nimble (NIM bul) quick and accurate; agile *p. 259*

nonconductivity (non kun duk TIV uh tee) the ability to contain and not transmit heat *p. 421*

O

object (OB jekt) purpose; goal *p. 249*

oblivious (uh BLIV ee us) unaware; unmindful *p. 526*

oblong (OB lawng) rectangle shaped *p. 411*

obscure (ub SKYOOR) darken; dim; hide from sight *p. 480*

obstinate (OB stuh nut) stubborn *pp. 275, 357*

oilcloth (OIL klawth) waterproofed cloth *p. 457*

ominous (OM uh nus) dangerous; threatening; sinister *pp. 215, 433*

orb (AWRB) round object *p. 299*

organdy (AWR gun dee) kind of thin crisp cotton cloth *p. 510*

ought (AWT) anything (variation of *aught*) *p. 5*

outraged (OUT rayjd) insulted; made very angry *p. 106*

overshadowing (oh vur SHAD oh ing) hanging or looming over *p. 75*

P

palanquin (pal un KEEN) carriage on poles that is carried on people's shoulders *p. 526*

pangs (PANGZ) sharp pains *p. 486*

pantry (PAN tree) a small room or closet off the kitchen, where cooking ingredients and utensils, china, etc., are kept *p. 274*

parabolic (par uh BOL ik) bowl shaped *p. 421*

pathetic (puh THET ik) pitiful *p. 290*

pathos (PAY thos) an element in experience evoking pity *p. 275*

perceive (pur SEEV) become aware of *p. 190*

peril (PER ul) danger *p. 192*

persever (pur SEV ur) continue to uphold; keep on trying (Today the word is spelled *persevere* and pronounced *pur suh VEER*.) *p. 5*

petitioned (puh TISH und) made a formal request of someone in authority *p. 14*

petticoat (PET ee koht) type of woman's skirt *p. 388*

petticoats (PEHT ee kohts) lace or ruffles on the bottom of a skirt *p. 465*

phantom (FAN tum) something that seems real to the eye but does not exist; an unreal mental image *pp. 14, 229*

phenomenon (fih NOM uh non) a fact or event that can be described in a scientific way *p. 410*

pitch (PICH) a black sticky substance formed from distilling of tar *p. 124*

placid (PLAS id) quiet *p. 133*

plashy (PLASH ee) marshy; wet *p. 143*

plight (PLYT) bad condition or problem *p. 400*

plough (PLOU) plow; to make furrows in the earth *p. 79*

poignant (POIN yunt) sharp; keenly felt *p. 310*

poised (POIZD) set and ready *p. 490*

porcelain (PAWR suh lin) china *p. 275*

pore over (PAWR OH vur) study carefully *p. 400*

precipices (PRES uh pis iz) steep cliffs; vertical or overhanging rock faces *p. 280*

prejudice (PREJ uh dis) a judgment or opinion formed before the facts are known; intolerance or hatred of other races, creeds, etc. *p. 49*

presently (PREZ unt lee) in a little while *p. 359*

principle (PRIN suh pul) a fundamental rule of conduct *p. 34*

procure (proh KYUUR) to obtain or secure *p. 29*

prodigy (PRAHD uh jee) a child remarkably bright in some way *p. 461*

profound (pruh FOUND) wise; intellectually deep *p. 124*

prostrated (PROS trayt id) laid low; completely overcome *p. 281*

prudence (PROOD uns) the quality of being cautious or discreet in conduct *p. 73*

pulsate (PUL sayt) throb in a regular rhythm *p. 417*

pumps (PUMPS) kind of low cut shoes for women *p. 510*

purgative (PUR guh tiv) strong laxative *p. 343*

putrefactive (pyoo truh FAK tiv) rotting; decomposing *p. 434*

Q

quailed (KWAYLD) to lose courage; cower *p. 222*

quench (KWENCH) satisfy thirst or other need *p. 5*

quivering (KWIV ur ing) trembling; slight vibrating motion *p. 228*

R

racism (RAY siz um) racial prejudice *p. 499*

rack (RAK) hardship; torture *p. 248*

ranged (RAYNJD) set forth; arranged *p. 250*

ransacking (RAN sak ing) searching furiously *p. 257*

rash (RASH) reckless; foolhardy *p. 105*

ratified (RAT uh fyd) approved or confirmed *p. 23*

reality (ree AL uh tee) truth; fact *p. 389*

ream (REEM) enlarge; open up (here used figuratively) *p. 512*

recess (rih SES) interior place *p. 306*

recompense (REK um pens) repayment *p. 5*

recompose (ree kum POHZ) pull oneself together; become calm again *p. 510*

recourse (REE kawrs) a turning back for aid, safety, etc. *p. 29*

recurring (rih KUR ing) occurring again and again *p. 291*

reflect (rih FLEKT) think *p. 303*

reflection (rih FLEK shun) serious thought *p. 255*

reflexively (rih FLEK siv lee) an action done automatically *p. 138*

regalia (rih GAYL yuh) signs of royalty, such as special dress (here used ironically) *p. 401*

reiterate (ree IT uh rayt) repeat tiresomely *p. 302*

relate (rih LAYT) tell *p. 189*

renounce (rih NOUNS) reject; abandon with disgust *p. 290*

repose (rih POHZ) rest *p. 194*

reprieve (rih PREEV) postponement *p. 435*

reproachfully (rih PROHCH fuh lee) scolding; blaming *p. 388*

repulsed (rih PULST) drove back; repelled *p. 109*

resolution (rez uh LOO shun) decision as to future action *p. 34*

resolved (rih ZOLVD) determined; decided *p. 109*

resounding (rih ZOUND ing) loud, echoing, or prolonged sound *p. 15*

retaliate (rih TAL ee ayt) strike back *p. 490*

reverie (REHV uh ree) dreamy thoughts of pleasant things *p. 465*

rifling (RY fling) searching; going through hurriedly *p. 514*

riled (RYLD) irritated; angered *p. 416*

robust (roh BUST) strong; healthy *p. 247*

rogue (ROHG) rascal; villain *p. 193*

rumpled (RUM puld) wrinkled *p. 531*

rustic (RUS tik) of or living in the country, rural; simple, plain; rough, awkward *p. 278*

rut (RUT) a track made by a wheeled vehicle *p. 202*

S

saffron (SAF run) bright, orange-yellow color *p. 358*

salient (SAY lee unt) important; remarkable *p. 292*

satire (SA tyr) a literary work in which vices, stupidities, etc. are held up to ridicule and contempt *p. 37*

sauciness (SAH see nuhs) state of being bold or rude *p. 463*

savory (SAY vur ee) appetizing smell *p. 217*

scourge (SKURJ) to whip; to chastise, punish *p. 281*

seared (SIRD) scorched; burned *p. 480*

sedulous (SEJ uh lus) hard-working; diligent; persistent p. 271

seismograph (SYZ muyh graf) an instrument that records the intensity and duration of earthquakes *p. 412*

sepulcher (SEP ul kur) tomb; burial place *p. 117*

seraph (SER uf) kind of heavenly being; winged angel *p. 117*

sexton (SEKS tun) caretaker who rings the bells *p. 203*

sheath (SHEETH) protective covering or case *pp. 306, 414*

shied (SHYD) drew back *p. 303*

shroud (SHROWD) something that hides or protects *p. 229*

sidle (SYD ul) move sideways; edge along slyly *pp. 309, 508*

significant (sig NIF uh kunt) important; momentous *p. 13*

silhouettes (sil oo ETS) dark shapes, or outlines, seen against a light background *p. 416*

siren (SY run) in Greek and Roman mythology, a sea nymph represented as part bird and part woman who lured sailors to their death by singing *p. 13*

slander (SLAN dur) lie; harmful statement *p. 498*

slaughter (SLAWT ur) the killing of animals for food *p. 34*

slither SLITH ur) slip and slide *p. 344*

slunk (SLUNK) moved in a fearful or embarrassed way *p. 526*

slur (SLUR) make unclear; pass over carelessly *p. 290*

smites (SMYTS) inflicts a heavy blow; kills by striking *p. 233*

soaring (SAWR ing) rising or gliding high into the air *p. 323*

sociable (SOH shuh bul) enjoy the company of others *p. 39*

sombre (SOM bur) usually spelled somber; dark and gloomy *p. 166*

sonatas (suh NAH tuhs) compositions for one or two musical instruments *p. 464*

sounded (SOWND ed) dove deeply downward (by a whale or fish) *p. 225*

spar (SPAHR) pole attached to mast *p. 165*

spasmodically (spaz MOD ik lee) in sudden bursts *p. 308*

spectral (SPEK trul) ghostlike *p. 166*

spectroscope (SPEK truh skohp) a scientific instrument used to identify substances *p. 410*

speculatively (SPEK yuh luh tiv lee) thinking about possibilities *p. 300*

spinet (SPIHN it) small piano *p. 465*

spittle (SPIT ul) saliva; what one spits *p. 300*

spouse (SPOUS) husband or wife *p. 190*

staccato (stuh KAHT oh) short, distinct movement; music played with distinct breaks between notes *pp. 358, 465*

stanchions (STAN chunz) upright bars, beams or posts used as support *p. 280*

star (STAHR) to mark or set with stars, as a decoration *p. 323*

stark (STAHRK) complete, downright *p. 490*

stifled (STY fuld) muffled, smothered *p. 124*

still (STIL) make calm and quiet *p. 485*

stitch (STICH) slang for clothing *p. 388*

stock (STOK) farm animals *p. 104*

stolid (STOL id) expressing little motion *p. 273*

strife (STRYF) troublesome conflict; quarreling *p. 323*

subtle (SUT ul) faint and mysterious *p. 299*

sullen (SUL un) sulky and brooding; moody *p. 229*

superfluous (suu PUR floo us) beyond what is required *p. 179*

surplice (SUR plis) loose-fitting garment worn by members of the clergy and choirs *p. 203*

suspense (suh SPENS) uncertainty about what will happen *p. 223*

suspension (suh SPEN shun) temporary stoppage *p. 54*

sustained (suh STAYND) experienced; suffered *p. 290*

T

tablet (TAB lit) pad of writing paper *p. 387*

tacky (TAK ee) too showy; not fashionable *p. 507*

taro (TAHR oh) kind of tropical plant used for food *p. 522*

tart (TAHRT) small, filled pastry; small pie *p. 33*

taunting (TAWNT ing) daring; teasing *p. 490*

taut (TAWT) stretched tightly *p. 385*

tedious (TEE dee us) boring; tiresome *p. 291*

temperance (TEM pur uns) self-restraint in conduct, appetite, etc. *p. 133*

temperance (TEM pur uns) belief that no one should drink alcohol *p. 190*

tender-hearted (TEN dur hahrt id) easily moved to pity; sympathetic *p. 71*

thimbled (THIM buld) wearing a small, protective cap used in sewing *p. 385*

thoroughfare (THUR oh fair) passage; way through *p. 319*

thriving (THRYV ing) very successful *p. 193*

thunderbird (THUN dur burd) in the mythology of certain North American Indians, an enormous bird supposed to produce thunder, lightning, and rain *p. 9*

tinderbox (TIN dur BAHKS) formerly, a metal box for holding flint for starting a fire *p. 53*

Titans (TYT unz) giants *p. 434*

tranquil (TRANG kwul) peaceful; at rest *p. 194*

tranquility (tran KWIL uh tee) calmness, peacefulness *pp. 22, 42*

transient (TRAN shunt) not permanent; passing quickly *p. 409*

transistor (tran ZIS tur) here, it means a transistor radio *p. 456*

transverse (trans VURS) crossing from side to side *p. 411*

tread (TRED) step; walk *p. 249*

trifle (TRY ful) unimportant thing *p. 127*

trill (TRIL) play music with a quivering sound *p. 249*

trip (TRIP) run gracefully and lightly *p. 257*

tripod (TRY pod) three-legged support *p. 425*

tuft (TUFT) small bunch *p. 189*

tutus (TOO TOOZ) skirts worn by ballerinas *p. 466*

U

umbilical (um BIL ih kul) here, necessary for life; from "umbilical cord," which keeps an unborn baby alive *p. 456*

unaccountable (un uh KOUNT uh bul) for no apparent reason *p. 250*

unassuming (un uh SOOM ing) modest; quiet *p. 255*

uncolored (un KUL urd) not influenced by *p. 20*

underscored (UN dur skawrd) underlined *p. 385*

undulation (un juh LAY shun) wavy form or outline *p. 299*

unprovoked (un pruh VOHKT) not to stir up an action *p. 34*

utter (UT ur) complete *p. 490*

utterance (UT ur uns) expressing by voice *p. 138*

V

vain (VAYN) without success; useless *p. 125*

valise (vuh LEES) small suitcase *p. 497*

vanguard (VAN gahrd) the part of an army that goes ahead of the main body in an advance *p. 423*

variable (VAIR ee ih bul) likely to change *p. 71*

vengeance (VEN juns) causing harm to something in return for an injury or harm done *p. 221*

venomous (VEN uh mus) poisonous; spiteful *p. 189*

vexed (VEKST) disturbed; annoyed; irritated *p. 124*

W

wafted (WAHFT id) blown along smoothly *p. 169*

wanton (WAHN tun) mischievous, unruly *p. 138*

warm-hearted (WAWRM hahrt id) kind, sympathetic *p. 73*

weather (WETH ur) last through; endure *p. 248*

whetstone (HWET stohn) a stone used for sharpening tools *p. 221*

whither (HWITH ur) to what place, point, etc. *p. 143*

will (WIL) wishes; desires *p. 249*

wonder (WUN dur) feeling of surprise, admiration, awe, caused by something strange, unexpected, or incredible *p. 323*

wrench (RENCH) twist *p. 489*

INDEX OF TITLES AND AUTHORS

INDEX OF SKILLS

INDEX OF FINE ART

ACKNOWLEDGMENTS

Unit 1: "Godasiyo, the Woman Chief" from *Teepee Tales of the American Indian*. Retold by Dee Brown. **Unit 3:** All Dickinson poetry reprinted by permission of the publishers and the Trustees of Amherst College from *The Poems of Emily Dickinson*, Ralph W. Franklin, ed., Cambridge, Mass: The Belknap Press of Harvard University Press. Copyright © 1998 by the President and Fellows of Harvard College. Copyright © 1951, 1955, 1979 by the President and Fellows of Harvard College. "From Walden" from *The Writings of Henry David Thoreau, Walden*. Edited by: J. Lyndon Shanley. Copyright © 1971 renewed 1973 reprinted by permission of Princeton University Press. "from Nature" from *The Collected Works of Ralph Waldo Emerson*. Arranged by Alfred R. Ferguson. Harvard University Press. **Unit 4:** "I Shall Not Care." Reprinted with the permission of Scribner, a Division of Simon & Schuster from *The Collected Poems of Sara Teasdale*. Copyright © 1937 by Macmillan Publishing Company; copyright renewed © 1965 by Morgan Guaranty Trust Company of New York. "The Falling Star." Reprinted with the permission of Scribner, a Division of Simon & Schuster from *The Collected Poems of Sara Teasdale*. Copyright © 1937 by Macmillan Publishing Company; copyright renewed © 1965 by Morgan Guaranty Trust Company of New York. "The Long Hill." Reprinted with the permission of Scribner, a Division of Simon & Schuster from *The Collected Poems of Sara Teasdale*. Copyright © 1937 by Macmillan Publishing Company; copyright renewed © 1965 by Morgan Guaranty Trust Company of New York. "The Revolt of Mother" from *The Revolt of Mother & Other Stories* by Mary Wilkins. The Feminist Press. **Unit 5:** "Afternoon on a Hill" by Edna St. Vincent Millay. From *Collected Poems*, HarperCollins. Copyright © 1917, 1945 by Edna St. Vincent Millay. All rights reserved. Reprinted by permission of Elizabeth Barnett, literary executor. "Lament" by Edna St. Vincent Millay. From *Collected Poems*, HarperCollins. Copyright © 1921, 1948 by Edna St. Vincent Millay. All rights reserved. Reprinted by permission of Elizabeth Barnett, literary executor. "home" from *The World of Gwendolyn Brooks* by Gwendolyn Brooks. Copyright © 1971 by Gwendolyn Brooks Blakely. "Lily Daw & The Three Ladies" from *Selected Stories of Eudora Welty* by Eudora Welty. Copyright © 1936, 1937, 1938, 1939, 1941, 1943 by Eudora Welty. Harcourt, Inc. in the United States, Canada, and Open. Russell Volkening for British rights. "Fog" from *Carl Sandburg Selected Poems* Edited by: George Hendrick and Willene Hendricks. Copyright © 1996 by Maurice C. Greenbaum & Philip G. Carson as Trustees for the Carl Sandburg Farney Trust. "The Pasture" from *The Poetry of Robert Frost* edited by Edward Connery Lathem. Copyright © 1951 by Robert Frost, copyright 1923, 1939, 1967, 1969 by Henry Holt and Co. Reprinted by permission of Henry Holt and Company, LLC. "The Road Not Taken" from *The Poetry of Robert Frost* edited by Edward Connery Lathem. Copyright © 1951 by Robert Frost, copyright 1923, 1939, 1967, 1969 by Henry Holt and Co. Reprinted by permission of Henry Holt and Company, LLC. "Stopping by Woods on a Snowy Evening" from *The Poetry of Robert Frost* edited by Edward Connery Lathem. Copyright © 1951 by Robert Frost, copyright 1923, 1939 © 1967, 1969 by Henry, Holt and Co. Reprinted by permission of Henry Holt and Company, LLC. "Invasion From Mars" from *The Panic Broadcast* by Howard Koch. Copyright © 1940 by Hadley Cantril, © renewed 1967 by Howard Koch. "Theme for English B" from *Collected Poems* by Langston Hughes. Copyright © 1994 by the Estate of Langston Hughes. Reprinted by permission of Alfred A. Knopf, a Division of Random House Inc. "Harlem" from *Collected Poems* by Langston Hughes. Copyright © 1994 by the Estate of Langston Hughes. Reprinted by permission of Alfred A. Knopf, a Division of Random House Inc. "Dream Variations" from *Collected Poems* by Langston Hughes.

ART CREDITS

Illustrations

Unit 1: p. 32: Amanda Wilson; p. 45: Jeni Bassett; p. 49: Richard Martin; p. 56: Lonnie Knabel; **Unit 2:** p. 118: Ron De Felice; pp. 122, 125: Joe Ciardello; p. 151: Lisa Young; **Unit 3:** pp. 174, 176, 182: Den Schofield; p. 203: Donna Day; p. 204: Guy Porfirio; **Unit 4:** p. 246: John Labbe; pp. 254, 258, 260: Angelo Franco; pp. 266, 272, 279: Eva Auchincloss; p. 309: Bradford Brown; p. 330: Anthony Carnabuci; **Unit 5:** p. 372: Ruth Lozner/K. Hayes; p. 376: Laura Hartman-Maetro; pp. 414–415, 419, 434: Paul Casale/Melissa Turk and the Artist Network; **Unit 6:** p. 450: Edgar Blakeney; p. 454: Gary Underhill; pp. 461, 464, 466: Guy Porfirio; p. 472: Eva Auchincloss; p. 496: William Ramos; p. 506: Cindy Spencer; pp. 520, 523, 527: Kye Carbone; p. 530: Marlies Merk-Najaka.

Photographs

Unit 1: p. 8: Stone; p. 12: Archive Photos; p. 28: Vanessa Vick/Photo Researchers Inc.; p. 48: Dale Boyer/Photo Researchers Inc.; p. 52: Westlight; p. 59: Courtesy of Dee Brown; **Unit 2:** p. 97: The Granger Collection; p. 113: Corbis Bettmann; p. 119: The Granger Collection; **Unit 3:** p. 164: The Granger Collection; p. 171: Corbis Bettmann; p. 188: Gavriel Jecon/Stone; p. 191: John Chard/Stone; p. 195: The Granger Collection; p. 198: The Granger Collection; p. 201: Palmer Kane/The Stock Market; p. 205: J. Sommer Collection/Archive Photos; p. 232: The Stock Market; **Unit 4:** p. 251: The Granger Collection; p. 261: The Granger Collection; p. 272: Randy Masser/International Stock; p. 295: Library of Congress/The Bridgeman Art Library; p. 298: Chip Porter/Alaska Stock Images; p. 313: Corbis Bettmann; p. 316: Rafael Macia/Photo Researchers, Inc.; p. 322: Willard Clay; p. 327: Corbis Bettmann; **Unit 5:** p. 342: Corbis Bettmann; p. 347: Corbis Bettmann; p. 350: Corbis Bettmann; p. 352: Lowell Georgia/Photo Researchers Inc.; p. 353: The Granger Collection; p. 365: Courtesy of the Library of Congress; p. 369: The Granger Collection; p. 381: E.O. Hoppé/Corbis; p. 399: Corbis Bettmann; **Unit 6:** p. 460: Wayne Hoy/The Picture Cube, Inc.; p. 481: Bernard Gotfryd/Archive Photos; p. 491: Corbis Bettmann; p. 517: Renato Rotolo/Corbis.

Note: Every effort has been made to locate the copyright owner of material reprinted in this book. Omissions brought to our attention will be corrected in subsequent editions.